Saving the Seas

Saving the Seas

VALUES, SCIENTISTS, AND INTERNATIONAL GOVERNANCE

Edited by

L. Anathea Brooks and Stacy D. VanDeveer

A Maryland Sea Grant Book
College Park, Maryland

Printed in the United States of America.

Photograph on cover and on page xviii by Skip Brown. Book design by Sandy Rodgers.

Distributed by Maryland Sea Grant
University of Maryland
0112 Skinner Hall
College Park, MD 20742

Library of Congress Card Catalog Number: 96-078428
ISBN: 0-943676-62-2

To Donald C. Brooks
and to
Dorothy and George Taylor
and
Rita and Dale VanDeveer

Table of Contents

Tables and Figures

Tables

Figures

Abbreviations and Acronyms

ACME	Advisory Committee on the Marine Environment
AEC	Atomic Energy Commission
BAT	Best Available Technology
BCSD	Business Council on Sustainable Development
BEST	Biological Evaluation Standardized Technique
BWT	Boundary Waters Treaty
CPR	Common Property (or Pool) Resources
EC	European Community
ECS	Enclosed Coastal Seas
ECU	European Currency Unit
EEZ	Exclusive Economic Zone
EFTA	European Free Trade Agreement
EIS	Environmental Impact Statement ıl
EMECS	Environmental Management of Enclosed Coastal Seas
EPA	Environmental Protection Agency (U.S.)
EU	European Union
FAO	Food and Agriculture Organization (UN)
FHWA	Federal Highway Administration (U.S.)
GATT	General Agreement on Tariffs and Trade
GEF	Global Environment Facility
GLBDS	Great Lakes Biodiversity Data System
GLWQA	Great Lakes Water Quality Agreement
GLU	Great Lakes United
ICES	International Council for the Exploration of the Seas
IGO	Inter-governmental Organization
IIA	International Institute of Agriculture (precursor to the FAO)

IJC	International Joint Commission
IMF	International Monetary Fund
ISO	International Organization for Standardization
IUCN	World Conservation Union
JMG	Joint Monitoring Group
MAB	Man and the Biosphere Programme (UNESCO)
MITI	Ministry for International Trade (Japan)
MMP	Monitoring Master Plan
NAFTA	North American Free Trade Agreement
NCC	Nature Conservancy of Canada
NEPA	National Environmental Policy Act (U.S.)
NGO	Non-governmental Organization
NOAA	National Oceanic and Atmospheric Administration (U.S.)
NSTF	North Sea Task Force
OEEC	Organization of European Economic Co-operation
OECD	Organization for Economic Cooperation and Development
OPEC	Organization of Petroleum Exporting Countries
OSPARCOM	Oslo and Paris Commissions
QSR	Quality Status Report
RAP	Remedial Action Plan
TAC	Total Allowable Catch
TNC	The Nature Conservancy
U.K.	United Kingdom
UN	United Nations
UNCHE	United Nations Conference on the Human Environment
UNCED	United Nations Conference on Environment and Development
UNCTAD	United Nations Conference on Trade and Development

UNEP	United Nations Environment Programme
UNESCO	United Nations Educational, Scientific, and Cultural Organization
UNICEF	United Nations Children's Fund
UNIDO	United Nations Industrial Development Organization
U.S.	United States of America
USAID	United States Agency for International Development
USSR	Union of Soviet Socialist Republics
WET	Wetland Evaluation Technique
WHO	World Health Organization
WWF	World Wide Fund for Nature

Foreword

Saving the Seas: Values, Scientists, and International Governance provides a timely discussion of the interplay between science, policy and regulation, a discussion that is played out time and again in the effort to protect the environment and pursue the path of sustainable development. Striking the right balance to achieve harmony between conflicting values and interests, acting with sufficient foresight to address mounting scientific evidence of environmental degradation, and combining these in global, regional or bilateral agreements or national law can test the greatest intellects. The fact that the world community has achieved such success in so short a time since environmental problems came to the fore is a credit to the dedication of scientists, policy makers, and legislators world wide.

Two United Nations conferences on the environment, the first in Stockholm, Sweden in 1972 and more recently the United Nations Conference on Environment and Development (UNCED) held in Rio de Janeiro in July 1992, attracted world attention to the state of the environment. UNCED resulted in the adoption of Agenda 21 as the blueprint for future actions for safeguarding the environment and promoting development within the framework of sustainable development. Chapter 17 of Agenda 21 highlights activities for protection of the oceans, enclosed and semi-enclosed seas, and coastal areas. It also addresses the protection, rational use, and development of marine living resources. Activities to be pursued under this chapter include: integrated management and sustainable development of coastal and marine areas, sustainable use and conservation of marine living resources, addressing critical uncertainties for the management of the marine environment and climate change, strengthening global and regional cooperation and coordination, and the sustainable development of small islands.

Governments, international agencies such as the United Nations Environment Programme (UNEP), and nongovernmental organizations strive to create an international regime for the protection of the ocean and coastal marine environment. The regime is comprised of global, regional, and bilateral agreements as well as relevant national legislation to implement international obligations.

Global instruments include the United Nations Convention on the Law of the Sea (UNCLOS), which establishes an international framework regime to promote the conservation of the living resources of the seas and oceans and the study, protection, and preservation of the marine environment. Following the coming into force of UNCLOS, implementation of various elements of the Convention have gone ahead, including the development and adoption in November 1995 of the Global Programme of Action for Protection of the Marine Environment from Land Based Activities and the adoption in August 1995 of the Agreement for the Implementation of the United Nations Convention on the Law of the Sea of 10 December 1982 Relating to the Conservation and Management of Straddling Fish Stocks and Highly Migratory Fish Stocks. Other global agreements addressing specific issues such as the London Dumping Convention or the International Convention for the Prevention of Pollution from Ships help to support the aims of UNCLOS. Yet other international agreements, such as the United Nations Framework Convention on Climate Change and the Vienna Convention on Protection of the Ozone Layer and its Montreal Protocol on Substances that Deplete the Ozone Layer, though dealing with the atmosphere far above the ocean, are critical to the protection of the living resources of the seas, demonstrating the interconnectedness of all things and the need for a holistic approach to environmental protection.

In addition to these global instruments, UNEP has been involved in the development of Regional Seas Agreements, currently covering thirteen regions around the world. These instruments and related implementing protocols address pressing pollution and conservation issues, including dumping, oil pollution, pollution from land-based sources, and establishing protected areas. The most recent additions to this collection of agreements are the Convention on the Protection of the Black Sea Against Pollution and its related protocols and the Programme of Action for the Northwest Pacific. The success of the Regional Seas Programme can be attributed to the interdependence of the various components of the programs including the negotiation of legal agreements, management activities of states to address concerns raised within the context of the program, and scientific assessment to identify emerging problems and assess the effectiveness of the measures adopted.

International agreements for protection of the environment are only effective provided there is adequate implementation of and compliance with the agreements at the national level. Capacity building programs to encourage nations to be involved in the treaty-making process and to implement international obligations through the development of national legislation are critical to the success of the environmental agreements. Ultimately, however, observance of the commitments made in an international forum rests with the individuals that make up the community. It is only by educating ourselves about the value of environmental protection and practicing the art in our everyday lives that we can hope to achieve success.

Saving the Seas is about the international regime for protecting the ocean and coastal marine environment. I believe that this book will go a long way toward enlightening individuals about the state of the global seas and oceans and the important international measures adopted to address mounting environmental concerns. Furthermore, I am hopeful that it will inspire action to save our seas.

Elizabeth Dowdeswell
Executive Director
United Nations Environment Programme

Preface

Enclosed and coastal seas are integral parts of the world ocean that covers nearly three quarters of the earth. Their relationship to the world ocean is critical because they and their surrounding ecosystems are essential to marine life and because they are the waters most heavily impacted by human uses. These regional seas, as enclaves of the world ocean, contribute to the interplay of water and air that influences the climates of the world. Thus coastal seas are not only habitat for the most varied species of marine life, but also directly affect the climate and weather of the surrounding land. Since early times they have provided linkages between the various peoples of the world through long-established routes of trade, exploration, and migration.

All of these characteristics of coastal and enclosed seas are therefore highly relevant to human interests and activities. They are avenues of commerce (and conflict). They are accessible sources of food, medicinal compounds, minerals and energy. They are also important areas of scientific study and technological innovation. For all of these reasons, the greater part of human populations are found along or near their shores; and these numbers are growing. Although economic interest explains much of this pattern of settlement, humans have shown a deep fascination for the sea, expressed in painting, sculpture, music, literature, and myth. This tradition often includes depictions of gods and other deities of the sea, notably in the culture of seafaring peoples.

Prior to the twentieth century, cumulative human impact upon the seas was not great. But the formation of nation states, advances in navigational and maritime technology, and an explosive growth of manufacturing, agriculture, and human populations with demands for natural resources, enlarged and intensified the impact of human activities, initially in enclosed coastal and regional seas, but ultimately affecting the entire world ocean.

Coastal states became competitors for the resources of the sea and projected their artificial but legal jurisdiction into their adjacent waters. Thus the intensive use of enclosed and coastal seas developed without institutions appropriate to their governance. National state sovereignty and jurisdictions were exercised in the perceived interest of maritime countries, chiefly on behalf of their national economies, represented by fishing, shipping, energy and mineral development, naval strategy, waste disposal, and recreational tourist facilities.

As the maladaptive character of conventional international law for the management of human activities in multinational waters became evident, some governments negotiated joint institutional arrangements for protective purposes and the settlement of disputes. Early among these was the International Joint Commission (IJC), established by the Boundary Waters Treaty of 1909 between the United States and Great Britain (for Canada). The Canadian-American Great Lakes became a major focus for the IJC. But not until 1975 was a comprehensive multinational effort toward management of coastal seas initiated on a global scale. The United Nations Environment Programme (UNEP) launched the Regional Seas Programme, now the Oceans and Coastal Areas Programme. To date, UNEP has assisted in the establishment of thirteen regional and coastal seas arrangements, and separate transboundary agreements also have been made for the Baltic and North Seas. The relative effectiveness of these agreements is not easily measured. A new dimension to international policy for coastal and enclosed seas has been added by the UN Convention on the Law of the Sea, which came into effect in 1994.

The scope and volume of the many elements of the sea necessitate a comprehensive multidisciplinary approach to their description and understanding. The pressure of human uses on the seas and their littoral estuaries and tributaries requires coordinated management.

The chapters comprising this volume were originally prepared for the Second International Conference on the Environmental Management of Enclosed Coastal Seas (EMECS), held in Baltimore, Maryland, November 10-13, 1993. The first EMECS conference, meeting in Kobe, Japan in 1990 was sponsored by the Governors and Mayors' Conference on the Environmental Protection of the Seto Inland Sea and by Japan's Environmental Protection Agency. The Baltimore conference was initiated by the State of Maryland and the Coastal and Environmental Policy Program of the University of Maryland with assistance from federal agencies — especially the National Oceanic and Atmospheric Administration and the Environmental Protection Agency — and the Kobe government and others.

The fate of the seas and especially of enclosed coastal seas cannot safely be left to chance or to inappropriate legal regimes. This is why conferences such as EMECS are important and why the eighteen chapters comprising the volume are very diverse. If the full dimensions of the seas are to be comprehended, they must first be viewed through compound lenses. The various aspects must then be brought together in a synthesis that permits their sustainable management as complex integrated ecosystems. We are only now beginning to learn how to do this. These chapters represent a major step toward identifying the task in its multiple aspects while ignoring no significant value. This important volume is, in effect, a nautical chart showing us the course to be taken and the things to be done to save the seas from misguided human impact.

Lynton Caldwell
Professor Emeritus
Indiana University, Bloomington

Acknowledgments

Saving the Seas would not be possible without the EMECS '93 conference, and the generous support of the University of Maryland's Institute for Philosophy and Public Policy, Sea Grant College, and Center for Environmental and Estuarine Studies. We would also like to express our gratitude to the Japan Foundation for its support of EMECS '93. Many thanks are due to the members of these organizations. The papers and the research they represent were generously supported by a grant from the Ethics and Values Studies program of the National Science Foundation (NSF grant DIR-9109581), Maryland Sea Grant (R/PS-1), and by an EMECS internship awarded to L. Anathea Brooks.

Special thanks are due to William Donald Schaefer, former Governor of Maryland, for his generous support of EMECS and his eager cooperation with the Honorable Toshitami Kaihara, Governor of Japan's Hyogo Prefecture. Our acknowledgments would be incomplete without noting the important contributions of David A.C. Carroll, former Maryland Secretary of the Environment, who made everything (and everyone) work smoothly; Cecily Majerus, former Chesapeake Bay Coordinator, Governor's Office; Helene Tenner, Maryland Department of Natural Resources; and John Mitchell, Maryland Department of the Environment. We would also like to thank our many colleagues in Japan, including Governor Kaihara, Professor Nubuo Kumamato, Jiro Kondo, Takeshi Goda, Tomotashi Okaichi, Masataka Watanabe, Takeshi Kamiyama, Masahiko Inatsugi, and Akira Hasegawa.

Mark Sagoff, former Director of the Institute for Philosophy and Public Policy at the University of Maryland, College Park, ation. Arthur Evenchek, Carroll Linkins and Teresa Chandler, also of the Institute for Philosophy and Public Policy, contributed their advice, labor, and friendship and we want to thank them for all of these contributions. Jack Greer, Assistant Director of the Maryland Sea Grant College, was of incalculable assistance all along the way, and his support in publishing the book bears noting. We are also grateful for the hard work and eye for detail of Sandy Rodgers, Brighid Harpe and Ilse Grove, also at Sea Grant, who prepared the final manuscript. Wayne Bell and Martie Callahan, of the Center for Environmental and Estuarine Studies, must also be thanked for their support and energy.

Of course, *Saving the Seas* would be nothing without the interesting and innovative contributions of the chapter authors. We thank all of the authors for their ideas, dedication, and hard work. We are indebted to the contributors for their previous work and their consistent cooperation, supportive feedback, and patience from the conceptualization to the completion of this volume. We would also like to thank those individuals who attended the EMECS '93 conference in Baltimore, Maryland for their helpful and insightful comments.

Many thanks are due to the following individuals for their friendly advice regarding the manuscript and the relentless challenges of publication: Ken Conca, Virginia Haufler, Jean Thompson-Black, Peter Prescott, and three anonymous reviewers. Stacy would also like to thank a few individuals for their personal support, including Michael Harding, Cindy Burack, Jyl Josephson, Jonathan Olsen, Beata Rybczynski, Jennifer Yoder, and Diana Zoelle. Anathea would like to thank Don Melnick and Mary Pearl for their continued support. We would also like to remember our late colleague, Ellen Fraites, for her spirit, kindness, and dedicated work for EMECS. She cared deeply about the issues addressed in this book and she is sorely missed.

Saving the Seas

Seven Coastal Seas of the World

1. *Puget Sound*
2. *Great Lakes*
3. *Chesapeake Bay*
4. *North Sea*
5. *Baltic Sea*
6. *Mediterranean Sea*
7. *Seto Inland Sea*

Coastal seas are among the most productive ecosystems on earth. Shaped by the shores of continents, they provide seafood and safe harbor, history and heritage for many different cultures. Highlighted here are a number of coastal seas that have drawn the attention of scholars and researchers, who have focused on the strategic, economic and cultural significance of these very special boundary waters between land and open ocean.

Bearings: An Introduction

STACY D. VANDEVEER AND
L. ANATHEA BROOKS

Regional and coastal seas, like all large bodies of water, are strange and beautiful places, the setting and inspiration for a complex range of human activities. They have fed us, provided us with riches and fostered our dreams; they have brought us together and kept us apart. At the dawn of the twenty-first century, many of the earth's great seas are showing signs of wear. For their service to humanity they are now paying a considerable price. However, many among us are intent upon "saving the seas." The list of individuals and groups is long and varied: it includes research scientists, fishermen, tourists, environmentalists, private industries and property owners, elected officials from all levels of government, and public agencies, departments and ministries. All are engaged in innumerable political, social, economic, moral, and scientific debates concerning how the seventy or so seas of the world should be used and protected.

Saving the Seas is intended to afford students, scholars, and other interested citizens the opportunity to acquire a general understanding of the main processes of, and challenges to, environmentally inspired science, activism, and policy. Before we describe the volume in some detail and outline its themes and structure, let us first say what this book is not. *Saving the Seas* is neither a manifesto calling all good citizens to arms in the defense of the seas, nor a primer outlining why or how one should go about "saving" their local sea. In fact, given the lamentations (some almost eulogies) of many of the volumes's contributors regarding the state and utility

1

of knowledge in the respective disciplines, it is not at all clear that such a "how to" manual could even be written.

This volume examines the normative bases of environmental concern, science and governance through a focus on regional and enclosed coastal seas. The volume presumes that readers have only minimal knowledge of the range of scientific and philosophical issues relevant to the governance of coastal seas. While some issues addressed in the volume are unique to seas — or to a single body of water — many are not. How social actors attempt to deal with the tension between particularities of specific ecosystems and general characteristics of environmental management is a central theme of the contributed chapters. As such, the volume includes contributions from a number of individuals whose careers have been centrally concerned with seas-related values, science, or policy. In addition, chapters by distinguished scholars for whom this volume represents their first voyage into marine issue areas have also been included. We endeavored to combine this diverse group of scholars with the hope that their differing points of scholarly and professional origin would inform one another's work, and help to reveal the extent to which various aspects of contemporary environmental science, activism, and policy are grappling with similar issues related to the social and physical complexities of environmental management.

In recent years there has been a proliferation of single-author texts and articles on the plight of specific species and regional seas, international environmental cooperation, and the interface between science and policy (many of which were written by contributors to this volume). However, there have been few attempts to capture the spectrum of these issues and their relationships to one another.[1] In addition, little attention has been paid to the underlying motivations for environmental demands such as calls for "saving" seas. Yet scientists, policymakers, and citizens the world over are attempting to protect and restore their shared environments. The extensive scientific and political activity concerning the world's coastal seas affords numerous opportunities for innovative attempts at environmentally inspired cooperation.

Recently, a critical mass of general assessments of the state of the earth's marine environment has been completed. Although different in method and recommendation, these reviews agree that the oceans of the world, to which regional and enclosed coastal seas are connected, are in serious trouble. It has become clear that, despite their limitless appearance, the oceans' resources and capacity to absorb and disperse the by-products of human activity are not infinite.[2] Even the review of marine ecological quality and resource levels in *The True State of the Planet*, which is decidedly skeptical of environmentalist claims (billing itself as "a major challenge to the environmental movement"), states that "pollution, habitat destruction or modification, and over fishing" are serious problems, "particularly severe in estuarine and coastal areas."[3]

Seas differ from the open ocean not only in their proximity to land, their smaller size and relative shallowness, but also in their productivity and utility to human beings. Under the definition assumed here, the largest of lakes and estuarine bodies may be considered seas. The United Nations term "regional sea" applies to a landlocked sea or one with a very slow turnover rate with waters from the open ocean. Thus, the Baltic and the Black Sea are both regional seas. The term "coastal sea" describes that portion of a sea closest to shore and, for many reasons, of most concern to humanity. The Seto Inland Sea is an example of a coastal sea. For the purposes of this volume, regional and coastal seas serve as vehicles for an examination of the connectedness between science, moral, and aesthetic values, and regional and international governance.

ROUGH SEAS

There is no question that historic species extinctions and declines in abundance have occurred in many of the earth's coastal seas. In Europe, for example, one can look to Pliny the Elder for descriptions of the former abundance of fish in the Mediterranean.[4] In North America, accounts of settlers and explorers from a Europe already characterized by scarcity describe seas of plenty ripe for the centuries of commercial activity which ensued.[5] The effects of overfishing, pollution, exotic species introductions, and land use changes have been enormous, both on habitat and diversity of life, and the cumulative threat of global climate change portends still greater changes.[6] Anadromous and catadromous fish are rarer not only in coastal seas but in the brooks, streams, and oceans to and from which they migrate, and, consequently, the abundance and diversity of their prey and predator species have been altered as well.[7] Changes in nutrient loads carried in and out by tides or currents upset natural balances and processes, and may lead, in the absence of proper regulation, to frequent algal blooms and fish kills.[8] Top predators, be they sea lions, albatross or barracuda, are rarer now than in the past due to competition with humans for a limited catch and the effects of accumulated toxins in their bodies.

Some people were aware of these effects before the Earth Day generation appeared. Over a century ago George Perkins Marsh wrote cogently about the changes wrought in the seas by allowing new species to travel through canals from one sea to another, or by purposeful introductions for aquaculture. He wrote of the upstream erosion caused by logging and the subsequent turbidity and silting of coastal waters, and of overexploitation which led to the extinction of marine animals.[9] Marine pollutants, however, do not enter the seas exclusively by way of water transport in rivers and streams. It is estimated that approximately one-third of such pollutants find their way into marine environments through the air.[10] In addition, pollutants enter marine waters by way of ocean dumping and marine vessels.

Most biodiversity at higher taxa occurs in the sea; in fact, over half of all phyla are exclusively marine.[11] Coral reefs, located in shallow tropical seas, are ecosystems comparable to the neotropical rain forest in their diversity; they are especially at risk from changes in physical factors such as temperature, turbidity, salinity, and proportions of heavy metals. According to organizations such as the Fisheries Division of the FAO, overfishing, not pollution, is the single most significant cause of depletion of commercial fishing stocks.[12] In fact, FAO considers all seventeen of the world's major fishing areas to be exploited at or beyond their limits, with nine of these experiencing serious decline in stocks.[13]

When organisms of other trophic levels are considered, however, pollution accounts for a significant loss in species diversity. In the Baltic Sea, eutrophication is blamed for the decline in benthic invertebrates, while in the Great Lakes the levels of mercury, lead, and polychlorinated biphenyls are so high that consumption advisories have been issued for pregnant women.[14] Oysters in the Chesapeake Bay, already at the lowest numbers ever recorded, are infected with diseases quite likely brought on by the stresses of various contaminants and turbidity. The resilience of the oyster — and, by extension, the entire Bay — is being overtaxed.

WHAT SEAS, WHAT SHORES, WHAT GREY ROCKS AND WHAT ISLANDS[15]

Examining the roles of scientists and of the information they produce in social discourse and politics does not answer questions about the motivation for environmentally inspired advocacy, nor does it identify all of the values at the root of scientific research and political activity. The contributors to this volume are in general agreement that values lie at the foundation of environmental activism, and that a personal link to a location, a so-called "sense of place," is important in creating and maintaining community commitment to manage local resources. A sense of place is an attachment rooted in personal experience, history, religion, or culture, rather than economics alone.

Human relationships with their natural environment are enhanced by a sense of commitment to and identity with family, neighborhood and the local cultural heritage. It is in light of this commitment that the preservation of local ecosystems becomes a vital part of successful governance plans. Whenever communities revitalize harbor areas, designate historic coastal sites and national seashores, and control ocean dumping and pollution, they succeed in rekindling pride of place and a sense of partnership with the landscape. Cities from Boston to Trieste have demonstrated success in reviving the historical and cultural heritage of their waterfronts, and fostering a sense of community among neighborhood residents. A sense of community encompasses not only one's families and neighbors, but one's place in the local ecosystem as well.

Former Speaker of the U.S. House of Representatives Thomas P. "Tip" O'Neill was famous for his exhortation that "all politics is local." To a great extent, this is true of environmental protection as well. Ministerial meetings and national legislatures may sign conventions and make laws, but the effectiveness of these treaties and statutes depends largely on the political will of local communities to enforce them. Environmental scientists, activists, and policymakers may need to recognize that coastal seas have great value for people as *places*, not just as resources, and thereby come to understand environmental protection in cultural and political, not just scientific and economic terms. It may be that a sense of place must be actively fostered in order to mobilize the community commitment necessary for ecological protection.

But local "places" are not the only foci of community, nor the only type. There are communities based on experience and knowledge, as well. Members of such communities also share and promulgate certain values. They also have interests and preferences for environmental management. It has often been suggested that, if communities decide what kind of an environment they want and are willing to pay for based on their shared values and interests, science can help them get there.[16] Many of the chapters in this volume, however, remind us that scientists also have values and belong to communities.

SCIENCE, SCIENCE EVERYWHERE . . .

Scientific knowledge — its creation, dissemination and use — is central to environmental politics. One cannot hope to understand such politics without examining the sorts of informational "inputs" which scientific research provides to public debate and policymaking. This is especially true with respect to coastal and regional seas. Often there is as much debate among scientists about "what is really happening" in a body of water as there is on the floor of the most contentious of parliaments.

Whether one conceives of science as research, based on the scientific method of hypothesis testing and the accumulation of data over time, or as a more consensual praxis, it is usually funded by governmental agencies, private interests, universities, or organizations involved in political advocacy. These bodies are likely to have values, goals, interests and timetables different from those of research scientists. In addition, scientists are frequently engaged in setting (and sometimes enforcing) regulatory rules and norms, either through direct employment by states or by involvement in professional associations and political advocacy groups. Such organizations, if they are to speak with authority, must attain some measure of consensus on what they consider to be relevant norms, rules, values, and objectives. Participation in collective or societal decisions requires that scientists "leave the lab" and face the uses to which the information they produce is put. A number of contributors consider whether the necessities of funding and consensus conflict with or affect scientific research methods and agendas and if the products of such research are helpful in the formulation of ecologically sound policy.

Due to the magnitude of anthropogenic change to the environment, the management and planning focus of environmental policy must be broadened to consider larger ecosystems. However, much ecological information is specific to one scale, and is meaningless at another. If, for example, a small part of an ecosystem is destroyed — a marsh filled for development, say — the larger overall ecosystem remains viable. Yet the marsh, which can also be seen as a coherent, if much smaller, ecosystem, is gone. Eventually, if every marsh in an estuary is filled, the larger system will no longer be a fertile link between the land and the sea, and no longer serve as a source of nutrients, a breeding ground, or a sink for the wastes of human activities.

What is it that policymakers and citizens want from the authoritative voice of scientists in this situation? Do we want to know the exact number of marshes that can be filled, while leaving the larger ecosystem functioning for breeding or for waste recycling? Even if questions were put to scientists in this specific form (which they almost never are), could scientists answer them? Would they? Are the answers to such questions verifiable through scientific theory and testing? Are they political? Can the two spheres really be separated?

THE OLD IDEAS WON'T DO

Citizens, scientists, policymakers, and environmental managers call for "saving" coastal seas. What does this mean? How does one determine when an ecosystem needs to be saved or has been saved? Many who make such demands take liberties with scientific evidence, yet even when criteria for success exist parties often disagree about how to apply them. Vague and highly aspirational management goals land in the laps of regulatory bureaucracies and judicial systems which must then make the compromises that define them.

Must the governance of coastal seas respond to international democratic processes? Populist political movements and attitudes have strongly affected, for example, goals and policies governing environmental management in the Baltic and North Seas. However, professional and populist groups conceive of what is to be managed differently. From an economic perspective, a sea is a *resource*; this approach seeks to maximize benefits a sea offers to mankind, while, as mentioned earlier, a sea is a *place* to many ordinary citizens. At present, the two approaches propose very different goals for very different objectives.

If specific management goals prove elusive, should we then choose an ideology? The precautionary principle, for example, would shift the burden of proof, requiring industry to demonstrate it will not harm the environment, rather than forcing regulators to prove that an economic activity creates harmful externalities. The problem is obvious: press the precautionary principle hard enough and no human activity could pass its test. Concepts and principles such as contingent valuation, sustainable yield, biological integrity, ecological health, or the protection of biodiversity are also suggested as sources for reasonable management objectives. Like the precautionary principle, however, they do not preclude the necessity of drawing arbitrary lines and defending and legitimizing them.

Uncertainty exists as to what a "clean" marine environment actually is or would be. Management policies can be based on goals such as water quality standards or rules like effluent limits. At present coastal seas regulation generally relies on both standards and limits, that is, on goals and rules. Yet the relationship between them remains unclear. Some commentators suggest "restoring" marine environments to a previous condition — say, to the state of the ecosystem in 1955. The year is arbitrary, of course, except for the publication of Rachel Carson's *The Edge of the Sea*, and it may be economically unfeasible. However, restoration to an earlier condition might satisfy populist concerns while giving managers a realistic agenda.

Coastal and regional seas often lie within multiple national jurisdictions. The environmental issues such as those associated with these seas demonstrate the complexity of the relationships between international pressures, conceptions of a "national interest," and domestic political constituencies. National boundaries and economies are so porous to outside capital, pollution, ideas, constituencies, and norms that one may question their conceptual relevance. The traditional concept of sovereignty envisions "hard shell" borders around territorial units. Traditional international relations theory assigns nation-states domestic autonomy and has them act as relatively unitary, rational agents in the anarchical international arena. How relevant are the traditional approach and its conceptual foundations in designing solutions to environmental problems? Democratic publics may want the sea to be "clean" and the sea lions to be "saved," but citizens seldom rally in support of cod stocks.

CHARTING THE COURSE

Saving the Seas is organized into four sections. Consistent with our conviction that value orientations — some explicit, some implicit — are crucial to any understanding of environmental concern, governance, and the selection or identification of the types of environmental problems and the aspects of scientific information "most relevant" to such issues, the volume begins with five chapters which explore the moral, cultural and aesthetic bases of environmental concern, activism and scholarly inquiry. In Part I, "Values, Places, and Nature," six authors discuss various ways in which nature is defined and valued and why it is that we care deeply about natural places and environments. Fundamental issues such as the nature of the relationship of humans to their natural environment and the emotional and ideological content of environmental activism and politics are at stake in these debates. The authors in Part I agree that one can not ignore the strength of the normative concerns underlying public and elite attitudes and environmental policy and law. Nowhere is this more clear than with regard to the coastal and regional seas, on which so many of us live and to which so much history and culture is connected.

In chapter one, Mark Sagoff argues that the relationship of humans to environments such as enclosed seas is undergoing a fundamental transformation with important political and social ramifications. Seas, according to Sagoff, are not viewed in utilitarian terms by those who want to "save" them. Rather, many seas have achieved a kind of moral status. They are seen, by many who live around them, as "places" of glorious cultural heritage and aesthetic beauty. As with other morally-based restrictions on self-interested, profitable practices, cleaning up and protecting regional and enclosed seas has come to be viewed by many as "the right thing to do" even when it is not cost effective. However, human connections to environments or "places" vary dramatically across cultures and between individuals. Stephen Kellert's contribution (chapter two) enumerates and describes a set of values which define people's connections to coastal environments. Although individuals and collectives may prioritize the values differently, he asserts that the set of values remains important in its entirety — none can be ignored and tensions between different values are inevitable.

Given the degraded state of many natural environments, many must be restored before they can be protected. In the midst of debates over the "values" associated with pristine, degraded, and restored marine environments, Richard Ambrose (chapter three) addresses the difficult question of how to measure the ecological value of "restored" environments. In chapter four, Robert Nelson examines the culturally overdetermined motivations behind such "restoration," exploring the concept's ethical and religious foundations in order to explain the zeal with which ecological restoration has been pursued.

Michael Thompson and Alex Trisoglio (chapter five) close Part I with their illustration of the many complexities and ironies inherent in environmental management. Thompson and Trisoglio unpack the values embedded in our understanding of management. They discuss the so-called "Newtonian approach" to ecosystem management, outlining the concept's reliance on an understanding of a system as a series of linear relationships characterized by predictability. Given the extreme complexity of ecosystems such as regional seas and what Thompson and Trisoglio call their "intrinsic unpredictability," the authors call for a less control-oriented approach to environmental management which gets away from the need to order and direct the whole ecosystem. While the authors in Part I differ somewhat in the emphasis they place on specific values, they agree that it is this realm which shapes and links environmental science, public policy and activism.

Part II, entitled "Scientists, Certainty, and Knowledge," contains chapters by research scientists, social scientists, and policy scientists. These five chapters contain a similar proviso; science cannot provide the single correct answer, and it cannot, in fact, automatically inject objectivity into policy processes, thereby eliminating or reducing the influence of "politics." In addition, the authors in Part II are generally dismissive of ideas of linear science in favor of more holistic viewpoints. This view is especially important regarding ecology and conservation biology, sciences still quite weak in predictive ability. The practice of science entails precise, methodic work within the constraints of experimental design and various types and levels of uncertainty. Such uncertainty arises from sources such as variability within known confidence intervals, normal ranges of fluctuation over time within known parameters, and even from debate about whether the right model for a specific phenomenon has been selected. Scientists generally know that they are working to find "the right answer until they find a better answer." However, this is often difficult for layman to accept. Thus, scientific communities struggle to maintain their authoritative or "expert" status even when they cannot make promises to political actors.

The first two chapters of Part II, both written by ecologists, examine the nature of scientific research and the utility of its findings for the formulation of regulatory policy for the protection of regional and enclosed seas. Picking up themes from Thompson and Trisoglio's contribution, Frieda Taub (chapter six) discusses the predictability of ecosystem function and the difficulties of speaking to policy makers in the vocabulary of uncertainty. Daniel Simberloff (chapter seven) reviews the science and role of conservation biology in coastal preservation, assessing its substantial limitations as well as its current and potential contributions. As an illustration of the international science-policy cooperation necessary for a comprehensive assessment of a large marine ecosystem and the scientific knowledge associated with it, Jean-Paul Ducrotoy (chapter eight) presents a brief case study of the "scientific approach" to environmental management used by the North Sea Task Force (NSTF). Ducrotoy outlines the NSTF's contributions to North Sea science and discusses the role played by the so-called "scientific approach" in the successes, limitations, and eventual demise of the organization.

In chapter nine Peter Haas focuses on the role of scientific or "epistemic" communities in the international policy arena, comparing their influence on regional environmental cooperation and policy making in the Mediterranean and North Seas. Haas argues that institutionalized international environmental cooperation which is informed by an active epistemic community is more durable and superior to that which does not include such a community. Continuing themes from preceding chapters, Part II concludes with a chapter (ten) by Sheila Jasanoff which examines the relationship between science and policy. Jasanoff considers why it is that policy makers and publics turn to scientists, especially those associated with scientific communities, for authoritative information and policy recommendations. In addition, she explores the incentives for scientists to create and participate in professional "communities," thereby casting considerable doubt on the accuracy of simplistic understandings of the science-policy relationship.

As previously noted, most of the world's major regional and enclosed seas lie within multiple national jurisdictions. As such, the four chapters which constitute Part III, "International Governance, Actors and Institutions," examine changes in both the theory and practice of international relations, the neglect these changes have received in the field's literature, and the detrimental effects such neglect may have on the theory and practice of international environmental politics. In order to further the development of effective international governance, it is important to understand the processes of contemporary international policy making and their relationship to the theoretical and conceptual underpinnings of the international system. Thus, one must examine the motivations and institutional structures of some of the "new" actors in international politics such as international corporations, environmental NGOs, and "ordinary" citizens.

To begin Part III, Craig Murphy (chapter eleven) discusses the history and current role of diplomatic leadership in international governance. Murphy examines three types of leadership characterizing past successful international agreements in civil matters and assesses the availability of such forms of leadership vis-a-vis contemporary international environmental issues. He argues that effective international environmental agreements are unlikely to materialize in the absence of agreement on other conflicts associated with industrialism. Stacy VanDeveer (chapter twelve) addresses the role played by transnational norms in the changing nature and content of the concept of state sovereignty. VanDeveer argues that environmental politics at the international level, and the transnational norms contained therein, are already contributing to a reconceptualization of state sovereignty. Rather than viewing the international system as immobile and unchangeable, he suggests, those interested in environmental protection must push harder for institutionalization, at the state and international levels, of norms associated with ecological protection.

In chapter thirteen, Virginia Haufler explores the often neglected role of the private sector in international environmental protection regimes. Given the enormous resources of multinational corporations, Haufler argues, neither scholars nor environmental activists can afford to ignore the tremendous potential which exists for even a modest "greening" of the private sector. The final chapter in Part III, by James Rosenau (chapter fourteen), examines the changing capacities of citizens to participate in international relations. Rosenau identifies four types of citizens and four types of environmental issues. He argues that certain types of citizens are more likely to affect different types of environmental issues — and vice-versa.

In Part IV, "Approaching Ecosystem Governance," contributors discuss ongoing and potential regional and global arrangements for sound international environmental governance. These four chapters bring together the overlapping realms of values, science, and international relations through their reflections on various environmental governance experiences. In chapter fifteen, Ron Shimizu and his colleagues examine the evolution of the role of governmental organizations in ecosystem protection and rehabilitation in the Great Lakes Basin. In order to accommodate an "ecosystem approach," the authors suggest, environmental managers must balance the complex and often variable needs of an ecosystem with those of human stakeholders. They believe that such an approach can be informed by concepts from theoretical ecology which contribute to our understanding of dynamic and hierarchical systems. In a companion piece to this chapter, George Francis and Sally Lerner (chapter sixteen) discuss the influence of local citizens' groups and influential NGOs on science policy and governance in the Great Lakes Basin. Francis and Lerner outline a number of ways in which NGOs and governmental organizations can collaborate to produce more successful biodiversity conservation and the transformation of environmental politics.

The last two chapters represent much greater departures from traditional approaches to international relations and international environmental governance. In chapter seventeen Rafal Serafin and Jerzy Zaleski analyze the prospects for effective ecological governance around the Baltic Sea through the formulation of a "Baltic Charter" which would reflect, and help to enhance, shared regional interests, community and transnational identity. More than a set of vague environmental goals for the region, Serafin and Zaleski's

Charter would attempt to place regional environmental cooperation within the contexts of increased regional economic, political
and cultural integration. Finally, Ronnie Lipschutz (chapter eighteen) discusses emergent "global" cooperation through "networks
of knowledge and practice." These networks, Lipschutz argues,
may lay the groundwork for an "emerging global civil society"
which could facilitate greater environmental protection and preservation in a more decentralized, less state-centered fashion based on
grassroots communication and the transnational sharing of relevant knowledge.

NOTES

1. One noteworthy new book in this direction, which deals only
    with the Canadian context is Cynthia Lamson (ed.). 1994. The
    Sea Has Many Voices: Oceans Policy for a Complex World.
    McGill-Queen's University Press, Montreal.

2. See, for example, James M. Broadus and Raphael V. Vartanov
    (eds.). 1994. The Oceans and Environmental Security: Shared
    U.S. and Russian Perspectives. Island Press, Washington D.C. and
    Covelo, California; Sylvia Alice Earle. 1995. Sea Change: A Mes-
    sage of the Oceans. New York, G.P. Putnam's; Boyce Thorne-
    Miller and John Catena. 1990. The Living Ocean: Understanding
    and Protecting Marine Biodiversity. Island Press, Washington,
    D.C. and Covelo, California; Jon M. Van Dyke, Durwood Zaelke,
    and Grant Hewison, (eds.). 1993. Freedom for the Seas in the 21st
    Century: Ocean Governance and Environmental Harmony. Island
    Press, Washington, D.C. and Covelo, California; Michael Weber
    and Judith Gradwohl. 1995. The Wealth of Oceans. W.W. Norton
    & Company, New York; and Peter Weber. 1993. Abandoned
    Oceans: Reversing the Decline of the Oceans. Worldwatch Paper
    #116. Worldwatch Institute, Washington D.C.

3. Kent Jeffreys. 1995. Rescuing the oceans. In Ronald Bailey (ed.).
    The True State of the Planet. Free Press, New York, pp. 295-338,
    quotes from p. 300. See also, Thorne-Miller and Catena, op. cit.;
    and William G. Gordon. 1990. Fisheries. In R. Neil Sampson and
    Dwight Hair (eds.). Natural Resources for the 21st Century. Is-

land Press, Washington, D.C. and Covelo, California, pp. 222-230.

4. Caius Plinius Secundus. 1947 edition. Natural History. XXXII, l. 142. Loeb Classical Library. Harvard University Press, Cambridge, Massachusetts. See IX, l. 170 for an early mention of aquaculture practiced by the Romans.

5. Carl Ortwin Sauer. 1971. Sixteenth Century North America: the Land and the People as Seen by the Europeans. University of California Press, Berkeley, California.

6. The major types marine pollution include nutrients, sediments, pathogens, alien (or "exotic") species, persistent toxins, oil, plastics, radioactive isotopes, thermal and noise pollution. This list was compiled from numerous sources by the Worldwatch Institute. See, Peter Weber, op. cit., p. 18.

7. Anadromous fish, such as salmon, spawn upstream in fresh water and migrate to the seas to spend their adult lives, while catadromous fish, such as eels, spawn in the sea and migrate to spend their adult lives in fresh water.

8. See Mark Sagoff in this volume for an explanation of potential beneficial effects of such changes on commercial fish catches.

9. George Perkins Marsh. 1864 (reprint 1965). Man and Nature, Or, Physical Geography as Modified by Human Action. Harvard University Press, Cambridge, Massachusetts. See especially pp. 102-105 and 437-454.

10. Peter Weber, op. cit., p. 20.

11. M. Tundi Agardy. 7 July 1994. Advances in marine conservation: the role of marine protected areas. Trends in Ecology and Evolution 9: 267-270; and Elliott A. Norse. 1993. Global Marine Biological Diversity: A Strategy for Building Conservation Into Decision Making. Island Press, Washington D.C. and Covelo, California.

12. See, for example, Giulio Pontecorvo and William E. Schrank. 1995. Commercial fisheries: the results of stochastic supply and economic uncertainty. Paper presented at the Columbia Seminar on Sustainable Development and a Managed Resource: The Current Crisis in Fisheries Management. May 5-6. Harriman, New

York; and FAO. 1995. The Rome Consensus on World Fisheries. Paper Presented at the Ministerial Meeting on Fisheries, March 14-15, 1995. Food and Agriculture Organization of the United Nations, Rome, Italy.

13. FAO. 1993. Marine Fisheries and the Law of the Sea. Fisheries Circular # 853. Food and Agriculture Organization of the United Nations, Rome, Italy.

14. Anonymous. February 1992. Is our fish fit to eat? Consumer Reports, pp. 103-114.

15. Adapted from T. S. Eliot. 1970. Marina. In Collected Poems 1909-1962. Harcourt Brace Jovanovich, San Diego.

16. See, for example, William C. Clark. 1989. Managing planet earth. Scientific American, special issue. 261(3)(September): 47-54. Weber and Gradwohl, op. cit. quote Clark in their concluding discussion of the importance of values and community in determining the future course of seas protection. They do not, however, explore these subjects in depth. See pp. 225-227.

Part I

Values, Places, and Nature

1

Why Save the Seas?

Mark Sagoff

Environmental protection and economic exploitation cannot be justified using the same vocabulary. Protection is inspired by objective moral reasons and cultural attitudes, while exploitation is motivated by the self-interest of the individual, the corporation or the state. In fact, economic exploitation is often insensitive to the qualities of the seas that we cherish and wish to protect. As we analyze why is it that nations should agree to save the seas, morally and culturally contingent views often take precedence over purely economic considerations. Thus, for example, the precautionary principle became more important than cost-benefit analysis in regimes protecting the North Sea and other areas. In this chapter I explain that our moral imperatives make us wish to keep nature, an object of contemplation, from turning into environment, a basket of functional uses. Likewise, we wish to keep places, our sacred connections to the earth, from becoming simply resources.

Who Cares?

On January 16, 1990, six protesters swarmed aboard the British National Power ship *MVA* as it prepared to discharge 500 tons of coal ash in the North Sea. Greenpeace in its flamboyant way acted as a vigilante to enforce an agreement European Environmental

Ministers signed in London in 1987 and strengthened at another Ministerial meeting held at The Hague in 1990. The British ship — clinker and all — returned to port. Afterwards, National Power said it would suspend dumping "for the time being."[1] In this informal way, Greenpeace protesters forced the British government to comply with an international agreement it had signed prohibiting ocean dumping. Members of environmental organizations have tried to make international rules stick by disrupting and videotaping illegal whaling operations and occasionally by sinking illegal ships in port.[2] Why do they do this? What inspires environmental groups to oppose those whose economic interests depend on activities detrimental to the ecological character and integrity of enclosed and coastal seas?

These protesters themselves have no apparent economic interests of their own at stake. They act from ethical commitment rather than economic investment. Their members and supporters are moved by ideological, moral, or political beliefs rather than by self-interest. Those of us in the general public who support the aims of Greenpeace, if not its methods, likewise have no financial stake, as a rule, in the fate of walruses, sea horses, or whales. Members of the general public may root for or against Greenpeace as they would for a soccer team, wholly as a matter of principle or partisanship, not because they have a monetary interest in the result.

The ideological, ethical, or political — as opposed to economic — basis of support for Greenpeace and other environmental organizations raises an amusing question. Why is it that those who seek to protect the environment generally are motivated by non-economic concerns, while their opponents nearly always have economic interests at heart? Those who have no financial stake in an enclosed coastal sea are the most likely to argue for regulations to protect its ecological integrity and aesthetic quality. It seems that anyone who has an economic interest or stake in the condition of enclosed and coastal seas, in contrast, opposes the policies environmentalists promote. Commercial fishermen in the Chesapeake Bay, the Baltic, and the North Sea, for example, have an economic stake in the quality of the seas, particularly in the integrity of fisheries now decimated by overharvesting. Nevertheless, fishermen lobby furiously against total allowable catch (TAC) limits and other restraints intended to limit the overharvesting responsible for the collapse of coastal fisheries. Why is it that those who use the seas seem hellbent on destroying them, while those intent on saving the seas have no financial interest at stake?

ECONOMIC EXPLOITATION OF COASTAL SEAS

When The Netherland's royal consort Prince Claus opened a conference of Environmental Ministers at The Hague in 1990, he said that the North Sea was becoming a "cesspool."[3] No one replied that this might be a good thing from an economic point of view. A rigorous weighing of costs and benefits, however, might come to that conclusion and call for looser rather than more restrictive controls on dumping into coastal and inland seas.[4] Perhaps economic efficiency — the allocation of resources to their most highly valued economic uses — is consistent with the ecological destruction rather than protection of coastal and enclosed seas. This would explain why user groups oppose while ideological groups favor stricter rules for environmental protection.

At first impression, it might seem that a perfectly competitive market — one that allocates resources to their most profitable uses — would not protect the seas. This is because the major economic uses of coastal seas are largely insensitive to water quality. Three such uses come to mind. First, many of these seas drain highly populated industrial areas. From this point of view, indeed, one might characterize the North Sea, the Baltic Sea, the Chesapeake Bay, and other seas as God's Own Cesspools, created so that industrialized nations may cheaply and safely discharge their wastes. Second, regional seas are used as liquid highways. The North Sea, for example, may have the most intensive traffic: over 420,000 major commercial shipping trips occur there each year. Third, coastal seas are often sites for mining, particularly, for the production of gas and oil. In 1990, there were 160 gas and petroleum drilling platforms in the North Sea, and proven reserves of oil, in just the area of the North Sea controlled by Norway, exceeded 12 billion barrels and proven reserves of natural gas exceeded 82 trillion cubic feet.[5] Figures such as these suggest asking whether the efficient and economically rational thing to do is to make the North Sea an environmental sacrifice zone. What economic argument could possibly provide a justification for efforts to restore the Sea to its preindustrial ambience?

These three basic economic functions of enclosed and regional seas — to dispose of wastes, to carry ships, and to mine gas and oil — are basically insensitive to water quality. A sea will float boats equally well whether or not it is in pristine ecological condition. The use of the seas as liquid highways — and for recreational boating, for that matter — is consistent with a great deal of pollution. And the legendary abundance of gas and oil is a cause of — not a reason to prevent — ecological deterioration in the North Sea. When we consider the enormous amounts of money involved in disposing of industrial and municipal wastes, shipping, and the mining of gas and oil, we may wonder whether an honest cost-benefit analysis would call for more, not less, pollution and ecological deterioration of coastal and inland seas. Why not regard the North Sea, the Baltic Sea, the Seto Inland Sea, and so on, as intended by Nature to be consecrated as sewers, as liquid highways, and as mining fields for valuable minerals? Plainly, this is not a conclusion any of us wishes to reach. Why not? What reasons have we for saving the seas?

One might look to fisheries for a reason to protect coastal and enclosed seas. The protection of fisheries, however, would not clearly provide grounds to regulate pollution, for example, to roll back nutrient loadings by 50 percent or 40 percent, as called for by conventions covering the North Sea, the Baltic Sea, and the Chesapeake Bay. This is true for several reasons. First, commercial fishing in these areas and worldwide is unprofitable and, in that sense, lacks economic value. According to the Food and Agriculture Organization, "A comparison of estimated gross revenues of marine catch with the estimated costs of the global fishing fleet produces a remarkable conclusion. These calculations indicate that the annual operating cots of the global marine fishing fleet in 1989 were in the order of US$22,000 million greater than the total revenues, with no account being taken of capital costs."[6]

Second, it is far from clear that all pollutants affect fisheries only in negative ways. Dumping that occurs far out at sea — in open water — may have no affect on shallow areas where nutrients exist to support fish populations. Sewage loadings, by adding to nutrient levels, can feed pelagic fishes as well as filter-feeding shellfish. The United Kingdom has contended for years — offering an enormous amount of scientific evidence — that its marine disposal of sludge has no deleterious effect on fisheries.[7] Exhausted stocks such as herring, the subject of a moratorium in the 1970s, bounced back when harvesting abated even though pollution increased. In the Baltic, reportedly, total "fish catches, dominated by herring, sprat, and cod increased tenfold in the past fifty years and doubled in the last twenty-five years." This increase is attributed in part to added nutrients since these feed young fish.[8] Certain pollutants, notably heavy metals, plainly can be harmful in significant concentrations, which may occur in the immediate vicinity of a polluting source, but this would not justify a 50 percent reduction in nutrient loadings or an end to dumping ash, sewage, and many other wastes in open waters.

The principal problem for fisheries in the North Sea, the Baltic Sea, and the Chesapeake Bay has not been pollution but overexploitation.[9] The same situation obtains worldwide: overfishing is the preeminent cause of fisheries declines. One would think, then, that the maritime nations would do something to halt overfishing and then turn to the comparatively insignificant problem of controlling pollution. Yet as of this writing, the members of the European Community have not been able to agree on effective TAC limitations. The fishing industry, though it is doomed to harvest itself out of business without TACs, zealously opposes them.

Many observers might think that it is insane for commercial fishermen to oppose controls on their free access to the commons, knowing, as they must, that without limits of some sort they will surely destroy the resource on which they all depend. Commercial fishermen may have little choice in this matter, however, in view of the technology they have acquired to hunt fish. The imposition of a two-day fishing season for halibut on the Pacific coast of the United States, for example, led only to a violent high-tech fishing frenzy, involving fatalities, copious spoiled fish, and lost boats, while consumers almost never see fresh halibut in shops.

To counter depletion of oysters in the Chesapeake Bay, authorities have imposed tight harvesting restrictions, requiring that only sailing craft (skipjacks) and other eighteenth century technologies be employed. The Bay may succeed as a museum under these restrictions; aquaculture produces 90 percent of all oysters sold on the market today.[10] Short of requiring a technologically advanced and highly industrialized capture fishing fleet to return to seventeenth or eighteenth-century methods, there seems to be no good way to regulate it. Industrial exploitation is fundamentally inconsistent with a hunting-and-gathering economy.

According to Elizabeth Mann Borgese, chair of the International Ocean Institute in Halifax, it makes no sense to apply industrial-strength technologies to harvest wild species, whether turkeys, cranberries, or fish. "The industrialization of hunting and gathering is a contradiction in terms. It is simply untenable."[11] Trying to maintain a capture or wild fishery in the next twenty years or so might be compared with the attempt to continue to hunt turkeys and chickens in the wild. When technology is applied to capturing natural populations of animals — rather than in cultivating domestic stocks — it has to destroy the limited resource it exploits.

The supply of some of the most desirable species — salmon, for example — suffers from another problem: glut. Norway's immense salmon farming industry produced about 150,000 tons in 1989 and earned US$1.35 billion. Similarly rising production in Scotland, Canada, the U.S. and elsewhere has caused prices to fall. In the resulting trade war, the U. S. government slapped a 26 percent duty on Norwegian salmon.[12]

Many experts expect capture fisheries to succumb not to overfishing nor to pollution but to competition from aquaculture, much of which will be based in computer-controlled tanks inland.[13] Aquaculture, in turn, seems doomed eventually to follow agriculture in Europe in a march toward rising surpluses, subsidies, and an unholy competition for swamped markets. Norway already produces in the North Sea more salmon than it can sell, having developed a productive capacity — despite strict governmental controls on development — of 600 million pounds annually. "But the growth to new records in production in Norway and other salmon farming countries, has resulted in falling prices [and] charges of dumping...Norwegian production of salmon over the next few years could skyrocket if nothing is done to curb it."[14]

Over the next several years, according to most estimates, "the commercial availability of major fresh water fish such as striped bass, walleye, and yellow perch, as well as shellfish species will have shifted almost entirely to aquaculture production."[15] Farm raised salmon and shrimp, which now account for about 30 percent of global consumption of these species, are expected to increase to much higher levels, while "basically 100 percent of the catfish, trout, and hybrid striped bass consumed domestically are farm raised here in the United States."[16] Nations such as China and India each vastly outproduce the United States in aquaculture. China now produces more fish on farms than it catches in the wild.

Aquaculturalists do not aim simply to replace capture fisheries as the main source of the more desirable fish species, for this is inevitable. The industry goal is to bring the price of these fish down to become competitive with poultry. "Aquaculture has an advantage over its competitors — the pork, chicken, and beef industries — because fish farming is more efficient." The ratio of feed to meat in weight is 7 to 1 for beef, 4 to 1 for pork, and 2.2 to 1 for chicken. "Fish, in contrast, need 2 kilograms or less of feed per kilogram of live-weight gain. Suspended in the water, fish do not have to expend many calories to move about, and since they are cold-blooded, they do not burn calories trying to heat their bodies."[17]

Aquaculture has in common with waste disposal, shipping, and mining a negative effect on the environment. Waste products from aquaculture can cause eutrophication downstream. Shrimp farming and other kinds of aquaculture, moreover, often require the clearing of mangrove and other natural areas that support wildlife not used for human consumption. To be sure, aquaculture will require fairly clean conditions in those specific areas — Norwegian fjords, for example — where it is practiced, but its overall effect on the natural environment could be devastating. Industrial fish farming leads, with respect to coastal seas, to the same kind of world that ordinary farming has produced on land — a world, according to John Stuart Mill:

> with nothing left to the spontaneous activity of nature; with every rood of land brought into cultivation, which is capable of growing food for human beings; every flowery waste or natural pasture ploughed up; all quadrupeds or birds which are not domesticated for man's use exterminated as his rivals for food, every hedgerow or superfluous tree rooted out, and scarcely a place left where a wild shrub or flower could grow without being eradicated as a weed in the name of improved agriculture.[18]

Whether the reason is industrial aquaculture, silviculture, or agriculture, the result is the same: nothing is to be left to the spontaneity of nature. The use of coastal seas for the economically dominant purposes of waste disposal, shipping, and mining exacerbate this trend. To be sure, as high-rise resorts and tourist meccas operate along coastal seas, developers will have an incentive to maintain decent water conditions for swimming, but this is easily done, with proper planning. Great Britain among other North Sea nations has been able to "blue flag" an increasing number of its beaches (in other words, declare them "clean") by keeping its dump sites 200 miles from them.

The planned cleanup of the Baltic and the North Sea will cost billions. To justify this investment in economic terms, one would have to point to enormous benefits, especially if one applies a normal discount rate. These factors create at first impression the suggestion that economic arguments do not necessarily favor the protection of coastal and marine ecosystems. Indeed, economic exploitation and environmental protection, one might argue, cannot be justified in the same terms.

GREENER THAN THOU

Those who wish to save the Chesapeake Bay, the Baltic, the Mediterranean, or the Great Lakes are not generally motivated by economic concerns. These environmentalists are concerned about the state of the environment for the same kinds of reasons that people are concerned about the state of education, the poor, racial equity, religious toleration, and so on — not necessarily because of anything they expect to gain personally but because they regard these various ideals as good and worth supporting in themselves.

It is quite possible for people to support causes they believe are right but from which they do not expect personally to benefit. It is a matter of moral persuasion rather than self-interest. And politicians know that if they want to get good grades with the large and growing environmental constituency, they must appeal to principled ethical commitments not just to what people want for themselves. Welfare or well-being, as economists understand these terms, do not lie at the basis of the concerns of many environmentalists. Rather, they value environmental protection for objective moral reasons or for the sake of its intrinsic properties, rather than for any benefit they expect as a result.

More than a century ago, public opinion turned against treating people merely as chattels or resources; hence slavery was abolished. Similarly, child labor strikes us as abhorrent; laws against it do not have to pass a cost-benefit test. Regional and coastal seas seem to have achieved a similar sort of moral status. They are to be protected, treasured, revered, and respected for their natural qualities and for their own sakes. Legislative efforts to protect regional seas represent attempts to treat them not simply as means to productivity or profit but also as ends-in-themselves. These efforts may appear morally appropriate even if they cannot pass a cost-benefit test.

Lester Milbrath, comparing environmental beliefs in the United States, Britain, and West Germany, ascribed to the New Environmental Paradigm: "(1) love and respect for nature; (2) concern for public goods in contrast to an emphasis on private goods; (3) conservation of resources for future generations....(7) environmental protection over economic growth" and other attitudes that would resist a cost-benefit or "efficiency" approach to resource allocation.[19]

Students of the governance of the North and Baltic Seas have observed that since 1987, public opinion at home rather than any conception of national or economic interest accounts for the pace and stringency with which public officials have adopted environmental regulations. Peter Haas, for example, notes that ministers attending the Third International Conference at The Hague "felt that they had to do better than the previous ministerial conference to prove their green credentials."[20] He adds that governments and environmental ministries "have been accountable to their domestic electorate."[21] Countries with strong prior environmental standards sought to encourage other countries to adopt similar standards, to reduce any competitive disadvantages to their own industries. The spectacle of officials vying with each other to appear "green," has become as familiar in European as in American politics. According to a 1989 survey, "the environment is becoming hot politics, across the world.... Never have so many politicians seized so quickly on one idea."[22]

Public opinion surveys and research amply confirm the trends to which these politicians respond — trends which might reasonably be characterized as a populist juggernaut. Social scientists generally consider symbolic, ideological, and cultural factors far more influential than perceptions of personal welfare or self-interest in determining attitudes toward the environment.[23] The literature ascribes the rise of environmentalism in Western Europe to a number of cultural factors, including "post materialism" and a "New Environmental Paradigm."[24] In Europe and America environmentalism reflects ethical more than economic concerns. Environmentalists do not seek, as a rule, to benefit themselves but to protect nature for its own sake, to preserve it for future generations, or simply to punish polluters as if they were criminals.

POLLUTION: MORE LIKE A CRIME THAN A COST

It is hard not to draw an analogy with international agreements to ban the slave trade.[25] Slavery was extremely profitable. It was big business.[26] Throughout the nineteenth century, leading nations, especially Britain, badgered, shamed, and cajoled laggard countries, like the United States and Brazil, to prohibit slavery and the slave trade, which for centuries had been accepted social and commercial institutions. Shall we say that abolitionists were led by moral outrage or by economic calculation to dedicate their lives to protect the natural rights of human beings?

No one can deny the enormous ethical importance — one would have to say sanctity — of ending the slave trade. The cause of environmental protection likewise responds to moral commitments more than to economic interests. The technical literature concerning the North and Baltic Seas ignores the cost-benefit question, as perhaps it should. The goals the Ministers adopted — to reduce and then eliminate the ocean disposal of wastes and pollutants — were motivated by moral not primarily by economic concerns.

The United Kingdom acted as a "laggard" by mentioning economic factors and by arguing that it might be appropriate to consider costs in determining what counts as the "best available technology" (BAT). Its regulators continue to speak of the "Best Practicable Environmental Option" and "Best Available Technology Not Entailing Excessive Costs." Finland has likewise called for the "Best Available Economically Feasible Technology." On any interpretation of "best," however, the North Sea Ministerials adopted a technology-based and technology-forcing approach similar to the U.S. Clean Water Act of 1972. This approach refuses to consider the capacity of the receiving waters to absorb pollution. It bypasses the question whether pollution controls represent an efficient allocation of resources, i.e., whether they would pass a cost-benefit test. The Ministerials, in other words, took it as a premise that their job was to do the "right" thing, in other words, to protect the environment. The Ministers from more environmentally committed nations then went about shaming and cajoling the others to get on the bandwagon.[27]

The Ministers, like politicians in their own countries, played directly to overwhelming popular sentiment that something dramatic had to be done about pollution. The principles adopted by the North Sea and Baltic Ministerials make political and moral if not economic sense. These include BAT requirements, the 50 percent reduction in nitrogen and phosphorus loadings, the cut in toxic pollutants, the ban on industrial waste dumping and marine incineration, and severe restrictions on the disposal of sewage sludge.

Peter Haas notes that the 50 percent cut in nutrient and other loadings "was a triumph of politics over economics or ecology. Such cuts are inefficient and introduce real distributional costs between countries." He adds:

> It is not clear that all substances in the region require such extensive cuts, and the declaration does not take into account to any differential efforts already taken by governments. Thus, states that had not yet undertaken domestic measures would find it easier and cheaper to cut emissions by 50 percent than states that had already started to cut their emissions.[28]

The triumph of politics over economics is the characteristic of environmental legislation not only at the international but also at the national and state levels. Section 112 of the U.S. Clean Air Act of 1970, for example, requires the Administrator of the U.S. Environmental Protection Agency to promulgate air quality standards that provide "an ample margin of safety to protect the public health."[29] Areas that would have to make huge changes — Los Angeles, for example — were given a few extra years (until 1975, in the original Act) to bring themselves into compliance. Many of these areas, of course, have yet to and may never meet this goal, but urban centers from Detroit to San Francisco have succeeded.[30]

The ban on ocean dumping after 1989 adopted for the North Sea resembles prohibitions found in various statutes in the United States, where ocean dumping has been illegal (although frequent) since 1934.[31] Here is a representative stipulation from the Ocean Dumping Act:

> The Administrator of the Environmental Protection Agency...shall end the dumping of sewage sludge and industrial waste

into ocean water…as soon as possible after November 4, 1977, but…in no case may the Administrator issue any permit…which authorizes any such dumping after December 31, 1981.[32]

The same year European Environmental Ministers convened upon a 50 percent reduction in nutrient loadings entering the North Sea, representatives of five littoral states signed the 1987 Chesapeake Bay Agreement, pledging to reduce by 40 percent nitrogen and phosphorus loads entering that body of water. Although some experts speculated that it could cost US$15 billion to achieve this goal, there was no attempt at cost-benefit analysis. Rather, in the Chesapeake Bay area, as in the Baltic and North Sea region, the 40 percent and 50 percent goals echoed what the public wanted to hear. Maryland State Senator Bernard Fowler summarizes the thinking that set the goal for the Chesapeake and may apply to other regional seas as well:

> The Executive Council, which was working with the Governor's Cabinet…came up with this magic 40 percent. I don't know whether there is any solid justification for 40; why not 50 or 60? I think 40 percent just happened to be the one that triggered them and they thought it would make a difference.[33]

The goals of environmental legislation, whether at the international, national, or state level, reflect popular moral and cultural attitudes rather than national, state, or regional interests. Theories that analyze international conventions on the model of rational bargaining between self-interested players need to be reexamined in this light.

THE PRECAUTIONARY PRINCIPLE

Prince Charles introduced the 1987 Ministerial Conference in London with a call for dramatic efforts to clean up the North Sea. He argued against delay because "while we wait for the doctor's diagnosis, the patient may die."[34] In fact, the doctor had already presented a diagnosis. A group of scientists had prepared a *Quality Status Report of the North Sea* for a Ministerial meeting three years earlier — the First North Sea Conference held in Bremen in 1984.

The 1984 Report presents a consensus among scientists that the effects of wastes, effluents, and pollutants on fisheries were insignificant in comparison with the impact of fishing itself. The evidence did "not in general allow clear cause-effect relationships between contaminant inputs and effects on marine organisms to be identified." Similarly, "there appears to be no evidence that anthropogenic nutrients have caused any significant change in productivity in the North Sea, or even in the Southern Bight."[35]

A second *Status Report* prepared for the 1987 Conference reached essentially the same conclusion. It said:

> There is no evidence that man's activities other than fishing are having any significant deleterious effects on the fish stocks of the North Sea as a whole....deleterious effects, at present, can only be seen in certain regions, in the coastal margins, or near identifiable pollution sources. There is as yet no evidence of pollution away from these areas.[36]

In spite of this hopeful diagnosis, the Environmental Ministers meeting in London in 1987 held that the patient could die, so they explicitly accepted "a precautionary approach...which may require action to control inputs of such substances even before a causal link has been established by absolutely clear scientific evidence."[37] In 1990, the Third North Sea Ministerial Conference meeting at The Hague undertook to "apply the precautionary principle, that is to take action to avoid potentially damaging impacts of substances that are persistent, toxic, and liable to bioaccumulate even where there is no scientific evidence to prove a causal link between emissions and effects."[38]

The precautionary principle functioned in this context, as it generally does, to provide a utilitarian, instrumental, or economic rationale for what are plainly ethically or politically motivated actions. One could argue that prudence suggests not that we protect nature but that we domesticate it — that we replace its spontaneity with our industry. This might seem to be the path caution recommends because it is precisely the one humanity has followed in building civilization. Not the protection of nature but rather its conquest has been the path to historical progress — and a conservative or cautious attitude may urge us to do what has worked in the past.

In fact, the precautionary principle is so vague that it can be used to justify virtually any policy that might not have a clear economic rationale. According to ecologist Robert Costanza, the way the precautionary principle is to be applied is itself uncertain. Costanza concedes that it "offers no guidance as to what precautionary measures should be taken."[39] The principle instructs us in general to save resources we might need and to avoid decisions with potentially harmful ecological effects. But it "does not tell us how many resources or which adverse future outcomes are most important."[40]

The precautionary principle, perhaps because it is so vague, found a great deal of support among environmental ministers from Germany, Denmark, and Sweden, where green parties had done well. By advocating a precautionary approach, these ministers succeeded in using the glare of publicity to shame recalcitrants like Great Britain and France into joining the consensus behind the precautionary principle. One observer describes the mood of the Ministerials as follows:

> Environmental ministers are under pressure to provide a public demonstration of their green credentials. The greenest Minister will, by definition, be he or she who demands the earliest phase-out dates or the largest percentage reductions applicable to the longest possible list of chemicals or waste disposal practices. It is this political competition which has become a driving force for North Sea policy which was never in evidence when the matter was left to the Paris and Oslo Commissions.[41]

The effect of this approach was to shift the burden of proof from those seeking to prohibit pollution to those seeking to pollute. As scholars often point out, shifting the burden of proof can be crucial in environmental law. Having adopted the precautionary approach, the Ministers meeting in London set ambitious environmental rules, including a ban on toxic, persistent, and bioaccumulative substances reaching the North Sea from rivers and estuaries, and an end to incineration at sea by 1994. They called for a 50 percent reduction by 1995 in nitrogen and phosphorus.[42] The parties agreed to apply BAT controls to point sources and "best environmental practices" for nonpoint sources in waters feeding the North Sea.

The regulation of the Baltic has lagged just behind that of the North Sea. In 1980 the Helsinki Convention took force, establishing the Helsinki Commission, which by 1987 had regulated the most dangerous pollutants. The Baltic is not in immediate ecological danger, though there are many "hot spots." The pace and stringency of regulatory activity for the Baltic picked up dramatically in 1988, when Sweden, looking over its shoulder at the success of the North Sea Ministerials, convened the Baltic Environmental Ministers. This meeting, the 1990 Baltic Sea Declaration, and resulting Commission actions called for BAT controls, 50 percent reductions in discharges of nutrients, metals, and organic toxins, and so on, to ensure a chance for self-restoration of the marine environment and its ecological balance.

The similarity of rules and principles governing the North and Baltic Seas is not coincidental; many of the same governments and ministers are involved. As Peter Haas notes, the efforts to protect the Baltic and the North Sea are effectively combined in "a single international institution which is responsible for developing a single policy system and a set of legally binding rules for both the Baltic and North seas."[43] How can we understand these events? So far, we have seen that economic motives will not do the job. But economic motives — *pace* the Marxist account of history — will not account for many social and political movements. Moral commitments are often more influential. The rest of this essay explores some of these commitments.

THE DISTINCTION BETWEEN NATURE AND ENVIRONMENT

Nature and the environment are best understood as distinct concepts. *Nature* is the object of religious, aesthetic, and cultural contemplation and appreciation; in the nineteenth century, it was also the province of natural history, which attended to natural facts without inquiring into their practical usefulness to human beings. The *environment*, in contrast, is a concept of more recent origin. It is the object of the economic and biological sciences that attempt to predict, control, and "price" flows of materials and resources (from genetic materials to biospheric systems) in order to maximize benefits from their use.

John McPhee, Edward Abbey, and many other Nature writers — who eulogize the earth's vanishing natural heritage — tend to define Nature and technology as opposites. As essayist Noel Perrin remarks, Nature comprises "everything on this planet that is at least partially under the control of some other will than ours."[44] Moreover, many of us believe that human beings, by "conquering" Nature and imposing our will upon it, contaminate it. This sense of "contamination" is of religious origin; as we use technology to control and manipulate Nature, we reenact the crime that expelled us from paradise.[45]

The environment, in contrast, is what Nature becomes when we see it as a source of raw materials and as a sink for wastes. The environment is, in fact, a kind of "found" technology. It is the "plumbing" and "infrastructure" we discover, as distinct from that which we build ourselves. Its value is instrumental — not religious, moral, cultural, or aesthetic. The environment is what Nature becomes when we view it as a life-support system and as a collection of resources. It is "natural capital" as distinct from "human capital"; it is a collection of "services" that often come "free" in the sense that because nobody owns them, nobody can charge a fee for their use.

Thus, when Greenpeacers and hard-nosed economic analysts clash over how much dolphins are "worth," they may be seeing different things. The environmentalist may identify dolphins as belonging to the great scheme of Nature over which God has made us stewards. An economic analyst, in contrast, would have to consider whether dolphins or whales or whatever have any value as resources or as cogs in the wheels that keep "life support" systems running. So, you get quite a different picture of these animals whether you think of them as belonging to Nature or to the environment.

To a large extent, human beings have prospered by pushing Nature back and putting a largely man-made environment in its place — cities where there were forests, farms where there were praries. Today, a widely shared moral and aesthetic commitment to retain the last vestiges of creation has led us to try to stop this process — to protect rain forests, for example, from the economic forces that would replace them with ranches and farms. But this commitment to preserving Nature stems primarily from a belief in its intrinsic value, rather than from a desire to preserve natural resources for our future use. In "saving the seas" then, we are saving Nature from becoming environment; we are keeping places natural although it may be in our economic interest to manipulate them for our own use.

PLACE VS. RESOURCE

Michael Thompson has shown that objects, both natural and man-made, exist in one of three normative states.[46] First, they may be transient; a conference center and its furnishings belong to that category. They are useful for a time, wear out, and then decay into the second category, rubbish. A conference program becomes rubbish when tossed out. Third, they may become permanent objects of which art works are the best examples. Antiques also fit this description; even conference programs, once they are a century old, may attain the status of "ephemera" and become collector's items. They would then have lost all their initial utility — having been purged of any usefulness by resting in the junk heap for a hundred years — to emerge as antiquities that serve an expressive rather than an instrumental function.

Michael Thompson carries out his analysis using a number of examples, notably, the way buildings that appeared for all the world to be rat-infested slums, no longer suitable housing, may be eventually discovered as examples of a glorious architectural heritage. A change of perception that bestows iconic significance on the buildings can convert "many square miles of inner London from rat-infested slums into glorious heritage — the phenomenon known as 'gentrification.'"[47] The same phenomenon occurred in Baltimore's Inner Harbor on the Chesapeake Bay and is occurring in many "old" city centers of East Central Europe.

What happened to the houses near the Bay has now happened to the Bay itself. At first, we conceived the Bay as something useful — a collection of resources to be used, to be exploited. Like any transient object, the Bay after a while became "used up" — it became literally a rubbish heap as sewage and trash poured into it. Over the past few decades the Bay and, indeed, Nature as a whole has been rediscovered as something that has historical, ancestral, and permanent value: "sustainable" is the word most in use. We are to protect it as much for its sake as for our own.

Thompson argues that those with wealth and power are the most concerned with possessing "permanent" objects. "No great or revolutionary insights are involved in the realization that those who own and control durable objects enjoy more power and prestige than those who live entirely in a world of transience or, worse still, a world of rubbish."[48] It makes perfect sense to suppose, then, that as nations become wealthier and take more pride in themselves, they also take pride in the waters that surround them. Just as an excellent museum and preserved relics and monuments express the greatness of a people, so, too, the condition of its magnificent ecosystems speak to the permanence of its culture and therefore its durability as a nation.

The contrast between economic and ethical goals in environmental policy becomes most apparent in the efforts Americans make to "save" environments, such as old growth forests, historic urban landmarks, and the Chesapeake Bay. These efforts are typically thought to inhibit economic development — and this is often true in the short run. In the longer run, however, historical and environmental preservation often produces the kinds of amenities that anchor the economic well-being of communities. Seas we once viewed as economic resources we perceive differently: we recognize them as *rei publicae* — public places to be valued for their character, identity, and history, not just for the uses they may serve.

Attitudes have changed similarly toward children. At various times and places, people have treated children as resources: a hundred years ago, more than a million American children tended bobbins in sweat shops and "hurried" coal in mines. Today, we regard children as objects of moral love and respect and not of economic exploitation. It is the same with other species, such as wolves, bald eagles, and whales. As their economic utility decreases, they gain value as objects of moral respect and aesthetic appreciation.

Whales present a relevant example. No one seeks to protect magnificent species of these animals because of their economic importance, for example, as sources of oil and blubber. Similarly, it is hard to justify the protection of whales on ecological grounds — the fear, perhaps, that in the absence of whales the seas will fill up with krill. No; it is plainly the intrinsic value of these creatures and the moral repugnance of killing them that motivates the crusade — largely successful — to prohibit whaling. Many people believe hunting whales is morally wrong even if it is sustainable in strictly economic or scientific terms.

Those who are eager to save treasured landscapes have introduced a concept that is helpful in understanding the non-instrumental — the ethical, cultural, and aesthetic — values that attach to the environment. This is the concept of place, of a landscape as it is understood in relation to local culture and history, of the environment as it constitutes a community that includes both nature and humanity. The concept of place joins natural and human history: it connects us in maintaining a *res publica* — a public good or object we historically hold and enjoy in common.

What may worry us most is the prospect of becoming strangers in our own land, of never quite settling it, of losing touch with places that constitute the identity of our community, of being no more at home here than anywhere. For the sake of our own identities, we may need to protect the identifying characteristics of the places that surround us. The motive for saving coastal ecosystems like the Chesapeake Bay may fundamentally lie in our need to feel at home — to attach ourselves to what becomes safe and secure because it retains its aesthetic and cultural characteristics in the midst of change.

ACKNOWLEDGMENT

Research for this chapter was partially funded by the National Science Foundation (grant DIR-9109581) and the Maryland Sea Grant College (grant R/PS-1). L. Anathea Brooks, Teresa Chandler, Arthur Evenchek, and Stacy D. VanDeveer assisted in the research for this chapter and in their useful comments and suggestions on its previous drafts.

NOTES

1. Reuters Library Report. January 18, 1990. Greenpeace prevents dumping of power station ash in the North Sea.

2. For the Greenpeace view, see David Day. 1987. The Whale War. Sierra Club Books, San Francisco; and Robert McNally. 1981. So Remorseless a Havoc. Little Brown, Boston. For an account of the effectiveness of privateers in enforcing environmental conventions, see Robert Mandel. 1980. Transnational resource conflict: the politics of whaling. International Studies Quarterly 24 (March 1980): 99-127.

3. United Press International Newswire. March 8, 1990. North Sea nations bitterly protest to Britain.

4. As Oppenheim has said, "we must avoid interpreting 'welfare' in an all-inclusive sense; thus, it should not be applied to the psychological satisfaction someone may derive from foregoing material well-being for the sake of doing what he happens to think is morally right." Felix E. Oppenheim. 1975. Self interest and public interest. Political Theory 3(1975):262.

5. See Peter H. A. Hooweg et. al. 1990. North Sea strategies. Proceedings of the EMECS '90 Conference, pp. 57-61.

6. FAO. 1992. Marine Fisheries and the Law of the Sea: A Decade of Change. Food and Agriculture Organization of the United Nations, Rome.

7. J.M. Heap, M. Elliott and T. ap Rheinallt. 1991. The marine dis-

posal of sewage sludge. Ocean & Shoreline Management 16 (1991):291-312. This article finds that "sea disposal of this waste is an environmentally sound option," p. 311.

8. Sture Hansson and Lars Rudstam. 1990. Eutrophication and Baltic Fish Communities. Ambio 19:123-125. Quotation p. 123.

9. See Jørgen Wettestad. 1989. Uncertain science and matching policies: science, politics and the organization of North Sea environmental cooperation. in Steinar Andresen and Willy Østreng (eds.). International Resource Management: The Role of Science and Politics. Belhaven Press, London, pp. 168-197.

10. Hal Kane. 1994. Aquaculture output up. in Lester Brown, Hal Kane and David Roodman. Vital Signs 1994. Worldwatch Institute and W. W. Norton, New York, p. 34.

11. Swardson, op. cit., p. A28.

12. See Caroline E. Mayer. April 14, 1991. Caught up in a salmon rivalry: Norway's imports stalled by Maine's fish farmers. Washington Post, p. E1.

13. See Jack Egan. 1990. The fish story of the decade. U.S. News and World Report. 109(21): 52; and Harold H. Webber. 1984. Aquabusiness. In Rita Colwell, A. Sinskey and E. Pariser (eds.). Biotechnology in the Marine Sciences: Proceedings of the First Annual MIT Sea Grant Lecture and Seminar. John Wiley & Sons, New York, pp. 115-121. Webber argues that large-scale industrial mariculture based on biotechnology, which can push fish populations far beyond the carrying capacity of "natural" ecosystems, will render capture fisheries obsolete. He notes that we depend on tradition fisheries only because the "results of recent research and development in the biological sciences have not yet been integrated into the broader context of large-scale, vertically integrated, high technology, centrally-controlled, aquabusiness food production systems." Quotation pp. 115-116.

14. Anon. July 1994. Norway's salmon capacity is now nearly 300,000 tonnes. Fish Farming International, p. 22.

15. David J. Harvey. 1994. Outlook for U.S. Aquaculture. Aquaculture Magazine, January/February: 40-51. Quotation p. 40.

16. Ibid., p. 44.

17. Kane, op. cit., p. 34.

18. John Stuart Mill. 1987 [1848]. Principles of Political Economy With Some of their Applications to Social Philosophy, Book IV, Chapter VI, § 2. Augustus M. Kelley Publishers, Farifield, New Jersey, p. 750.

19. Lester Milbrath. 1981. Environmental values and beliefs of the general public and leaders in the United States, England, and Germany. In Dean E. Mann (ed.). Environmental Policy Formation: the Impact of Values, Ideology and Standards. Lexington Books, Lexington, Massachusetts, pp. 43-61. Quotation pp. 59-60.

20. Peter M. Haas. 1993. Protecting the Baltic and North Seas. In Peter M. Haas, Robert O. Keohane and Marc A. Levy (eds.). Institutions for the Earth: Sources of Effective International Environmental Protection. MIT Press, Cambridge, Massachusetts, p. 158.

21. Ibid., pp. 177-178.

22. Anon. 1989. Editorial. The Economist, September 2:1.

23. See, for example, Robert Rohrschneider. 1990. The roots of public opinion toward new social movements. American Journal of Political Science 34(1990):1-30; and Debra Holzhauer. 1991. The development of pro-environmental attitudes in Western Europe: a cross-national test of four psychological models. Paper prepared for the 1991 annual meeting of the American Political Science Association, Washington, D.C., August 29-September 1, 1991; David O. Sears and Richard R. Lau. 1983. Inducing apparently self-interested political preferences. American Journal of Political Science 27(1983):223-252.

24. Ronald Inglehart. 1990. Culture Shift. Princeton University Press, Princeton; Milbrath, op. cit.; Lester Milbrath. 1984. Environmentalists. State University of New York Press, Buffalo.

25. The criminalization of the slave trade, under leadership provided principally by Great Britain, was accomplished at the Congress of Vienna in 1815, the Congress of Verona in 1822, the Treaty of London of 1841 and the Treaty of Washington of 1862. The regime was finally codified in the 1890 Brussels Convention.

26. For a view of the enormous economic losses the end of the slave trade implied for Britain, which led the world to criminalize it, see Seymour Drescher. 1977. Econocide: British Slavery in the Era of Abolition. Pittsburgh University Press, Pittsburgh.

27. Haas argues this point persuasively in Haas, op. cit.

28. Ibid., p. 157.

29. 42 U.S.C. Section 7409(b)(1) (Supp. 1977).

30. Anon. April 25, 1995. San Francisco meets U.S. smog standard. The New York Times, p. A15.

31. Lori Gilmore states that "Ocean dumping of sewage sludge, however, is still a persistent problem facing the United States." See Lori Gilmore. 1989. Comment: the export of nonhazardous waste. Environmental Law 19(Summer 1989):884.

32. 33 U.S.C.A. Section 1412a.

33. Personal interview by William Clark with Senator Fowler on October 17, 1991, reported in William Clark. November 12, 1991. Can we justify the Chesapeake Bay cleanup program or should we just pave the Bay? Unpublished manuscript.

34. Wettestad, op. cit., p. 184.

35. Ibid., p. 180.

36. Ibid., p. 182.

37. Paragraph VII, Ministerial Declaration of the Second International Conference on the Protection of the North Sea. The Hague, March 8, 1990.

38. Op. cit., Preamble.

39. Robert Costanza. 1994. Three general policies to achieve sustainability. In Ann Marie Jansson, Monica Hammer, Carl Folke and Robert Costanza. Investing in Natural Capital. Island Press, Washington, D.C. and Covelo, California, p. 39.

40. Ibid., p. 399.

41. Anon. February 1990. The ever-widening agenda for the North Sea environment. ENDS Report 181; p. 13.

42. Second International Conference on the Protection of the North Sea, Ministerial Declaration, London, 24-25 November, 1987.

43. Haas, op. cit., p. 133.

44. Noel Perrin. 1987. Forever Virgin: The American View of America. Book excerpt included in Daniel Halpern (ed.). On Nature: Nature, Landscape, and Natural History. North Point Press, San Francisco, pp. 13-22. Quotation p. 15.

45. For examples of the paradise metaphor, see the chapter by Robert Nelson in this volume.

46. Michael Thompson. 1979. Rubbish Theory: The Creation and Destruction of Value. Oxford University Press, Oxford.

47. Ibid., p. 45.

48. Ibid.

2

Environmental Values, the Coastal Context, and a Sense of Place

STEPHEN R. KELLERT

The coastal values which derive from the biophilia hypothesis have inspired all the contributors to this volume. Sagoff particularly deals with aesthetic and humanistic values, while he shares with Nelson a concern for moralistic values. Ambrose and Taub are most concerned with ecologistic values, Thompson and Trisoglio with negativistic ones, and Haufler with utilitarian values. None of the contributing scientists or governance scholars writes in a value-free world. And we must clearly understand that all these value dimensions need to be considered as motivations, that they are all essential to our coastal policy decisions. The coast, ever a magnet to humankind, has experienced both ecological and economic deterioration in our lifetime, and this has resulted in its impoverishment as a meaningful place to us all. This is why coastal restoration, a topic further explored in the next two chapters, is an essential and growing component of contemporary environmental science, activism, and policy.

The majority of the American population resides near large bodies of water, whether along rivers, lakes, bays, estuaries, enclosed seas, or the open coast. This, in itself, suggests the extraordinary value people place on what is collectively called the coastal context. If pressed to provide an explanation for this distribution pattern of the American population, many would suggest it simply reflects the influence of economic history, the prevailing transportation and industrial patterns prior to the age of the internal combustion engine, the availability of rich agricultural land and fresh water resources. Without question, these and other material factors have greatly influenced human behavior in relation to the coastal environment but, I contend, these materialistic explanations provide only a partial and incomplete understanding of why so many people have been drawn to this natural context.

The American coasts have also provided people with physical areas historically rich in intellectual, emotional, aesthetic, and even spiritual opportunities for growth and development. It is these latter attributes, as much as the more obvious materialist values, that have resulted in a deeply compelling attraction to the coastal environment. In other words, the coastal context has been a place redolent with promise for seeking meaningful and satisfying individual and community lives. This combination of commodity and non-commodity values has rendered the coasts a profoundly attractive site for nourishing human identity and for seeking a sustainable and secure sense of place.

This notion of place is similar to Mark Sagoff's argument that the "concept of place combines the meaning we associate with nature and the utility we associate with environment. [It is a notion of] surroundings that arises from harmony, partnership, and intimacy."[1] What has made the coastal context a remarkably attractive site for human habitation is its special blend of opportunities for intimate human relationship with nature across a wide spectrum of utilitarian, ecological, aesthetic, psychological, intellectual, and ethical dimensions. In short, the coastal environment is viewed as a peculiarly capable carrier of human values toward the natural world. It is the contemporary erosion and degradation of these environmental values which threatens the continuing capacity of the coastal context to function as a satisfying place for human growth and development.

The writer Simone Weil remarked that a sense of place may be among "the most important and least recognized needs of the human soul."[2] Weil suggested, in effect, that healthy and attractive places provide humans with a basis for cultural meaning, a sense of community, and opportunities for achieving familiarity and protection in close association with one another. A meaningful sense of place also reflects the human need for an intimate connection with their natural surroundings, particularly its variety of life and the lifelike processes which support ecologically healthy and productive natural systems.

Humans are, of course, not apart from nature but an integral component of it, having evolved in close and continuous association with varying ecological forces, and most especially with other forms of life. Our species' ability to achieve feelings of well-being and meaning depends on a highly varied, intricate, and subtle matrix of interactions with the natural world. Few environmental settings provide a more diverse, textured, and multilayered opportunity for this degree of connection between people and nature than the coastal context. This attribute has been among the major attractions of the coast as a site for people to sink deep roots, build viable communities, and find an enduring and secure sense of place.

The erosion and degradation of these connections between people and nature lies at the heart of the environmental crisis along America's coasts, as much as the impact of pollution and habitat destruction does on various economic and health related processes. Alan Grussow powerfully captured this profound and elusive consequence of environmental deterioration when he remarked: "It is not simply nostalgia for a romantic and rural past that causes us to grieve over the loss of natural open spaces, it is a concern over the loss of human values. For we are not distinct from nature; we are part of it, and so far as our places are degraded, we too will be degraded."[3] Henry Beston, following a year of reflection on coastal Cape Cod, similarly noted that: "Whatever attitude to human existence [we] fashion for [ourselves], [we] know that it is valid only if it be the shadow of an attitude to nature…The ancient values of dignity, beauty, and poetry which sustain [us] are of nature's inspiration…Do not dishonor the earth lest you dishonor the spirit of man."[4]

The lepidopterist Robert Pyle referred to the "extinction of experience" to express this serious and often little recognized aspect of the environmental crisis, particularly the loss of biological diversity.[5] Pyle, a leading conservation biologist and one of the authors of the IUCN red data book on endangered invertebrates,[6] was certainly cognizant of current projections of an estimated 27,000 global extinctions annually,[7] particularly of invertebrates in the moist tropical forests. Yet Pyle recognized that, from an anthropocentric view, this erosion of life meant, first and foremost, a profound loss of human psychological bearings, the phenomenological degradation of experience, as much as the diminution of future material options and the lessening of various ecological life support systems. He remarked: "The extinction of experience is not just about losing personal benefits…It also implies a cycle of disaffection…The extinction of experience sucks the life from the land, the intimacy from the connections."[8]

Grussow, Beston, Pyle and others all recognized that important habitats for human settlement, such as the coasts, represent for people the opportunity for achieving meaningful lives, a deeply felt sense of intimate relationship with their natural surroundings, and a chance for attractive and rewarding communities and places. They appreciated that far more appeared to be at stake in the ecological degradation and impoverishment of places like the coast than simply the erosion of pretty neighborhoods or the risks to human health from pollution.

The concept of biophilia has been suggested as an apt expression for describing the full valuational measure of the human craving for deep and intimate association with life and lifelike processes, which are at the core of the concept of place asserted here.[9] This hypothesis purports that the human need for varied interaction with the diversity of life is an evolutionary expression of our dependence on nature not just for material sustenance and survival but, also, for a wider range of emotional, intellectual, aesthetic, and ethical needs as well. The biophilia concept is employed here to describe various ways the coastal environment has provided humans with an unusually rich and varied habitat for securing a meaningful sense of place.

BIOPHILIA AND THE COASTAL CONTEXT

A range of values associated with the biophilia hypothesis are identified which delineate various human benefits derived from the coastal context.[10] Brief definitions of these coastal values are indicated in Table 2.1.

Table 2.1. Coastal values.

AESTHETIC: The importance of the coastal context as a source of beauty and physical attraction.

DOMIONISTIC: The opportunities provided by the coastal context for achieving mastery, prowess and control.

ECOLOGISTIC: The opportunities offered by the coastal context for understanding the systematic functioning, and the structure of living resources and their habitats.

HUMANISTIC: The importance of the coastal context for expressing strong emotional attachments and bonds with nature.

MORALISTIC: The opportunities provided by the coastal context for attaining a strong sense of affinity, ethical concern, and spiritual reverence for nature.

NATURALISTIC: The opportunities provided by the coastal context for direct exploration and contact with nature.

UTILITARIAN: The practical material and commodity benefits derived from the coastal context.

NEGATIVISTIC: The coastal context as a source of fear, risk, and awe of nature.

Utilitarian

This value of the coastal environment is the easiest to recognize, as it reflects the bias of our market economy and materialistic culture. The utilitarian value refers to the many ways coastal habitats have provided humans with a steady stream of practical and commodity benefits derived from exploiting the land/water interface and the associated natural resources. The coast has historically yielded an enormous range of transportation, agricultural, industrial, and other material products derived from its estuaries, rivers, lakes, bays, enclosed seas, and shores.

The rich organic soils frequently associated with coastal plains and wetlands, and a readily accessible topography, have led to intensive agriculture, perhaps to a degree greater than in any other land type. In Japan, for example, despite intensive competition from various industrial and other development uses, the coastal plain remains that nation's primary site for growing its staple rice crop. Coastlines have many attractive attributes for industry, including relative ease of transportation, access, available water for cooling and other uses, proximity to human population centers and other features. The biological and ecological characteristics of coastal habitats have also yielded a wide range of commercial benefits from fisheries production to flood control and water recharge to a variety of product developments as human knowledge expands to exploit the natural processes and abundant genetic variation found in this environment. If for no other reason, these utilitarian values suggest a certain profligacy in allowing such benefits to be degraded by short-sighted overexploitation and environmental degradation.

Ecologistic

The species richness, physical complexity and ecosystem dynamics of the coastal environment have resulted in an enormous range of ecological benefits, perhaps to a greater degree than in any other habitat. Tidal and fresh water wetlands have generated significant understandings from studying their biotic and abiotic elements in a systemic context. The biological productivity of these ecosystems is often considered to be among the greatest known. Collectively, coastal environments are important areas for water catchment and groundwater recharge, prevention of soil erosion and sediment control, maintenance of soil fertility, storage and recycling of organic materials, decomposition of human wastes, the expression of various biological control mechanisms, provision of migration and nursery habitats, conservation of biological diversity, transfer of energy and nutrients from one trophic level to another, and the provision of habitats for many organisms.[11] Various practical benefits are derived from these ecological processes including, for example, the production of most of our nation's commercial fish species, and the decomposition of more than 90 percent of human generated organic wastes.[12]

In a broader scientific sense, coastal environments have been extremely important for the study of biological and physical processes, systematics, evolutionary biology, organismal structure and function, hydrology, and aquatic chemistry. While such subjects are typically the concern of only a small number of scientists, one is struck by the rapidly growing interest among nonspecialists in studying coastal habitats compared to other natural areas.

Aesthetic

The coastal context has long been a source of beauty and physical inspiration. A well established tradition in Western civilization has been that of travelling to coastal environments to experience their aesthetic charm and attraction. People are drawn to such features as the brilliance of a setting sun casting colors across the rolling surface of a coastal sea, or the beauty of a sandy beach stretching off into the distance, or the vitality of a flock of waterfowl landing in raucous synchrony onto a tidal estuary.

The physical basis for the aesthetic appeal of the coast is difficult to define with precision, yet one can assume important elements of vista, prospect, diversity, contrast, light, color, texture, and movement are all involved. More psychologically, few would dispute the important emotional benefits derived from this aesthetic experience including feelings of harmony, order, grace, a measure of tranquility and relaxation, and even an overwhelming sense of well-being and security. It may not be an exaggeration to suggest that an unspoiled and attractive coast is among the most significant sources of physical beauty and inspiration found in all of nature.

Naturalistic

A closely related value of the coast is the satisfaction derived from direct contact and physical immersion in it. Vast numbers of Americans engage in walking and exploring shores, beaches, and wetlands. The mental and physical benefits associated with heightened awareness and contact with the coast may be among the most ancient outdoor recreational activities known.

The naturalistic appeal of the coast is probably due to the abundant opportunities this environment provides for exploration and discovery. Celebrated expressions of this naturalistic attraction are found in such books as Thoreau's *Cape Cod*, Lindbergh's *Gift from the Sea*, Carson's *The Edge of the Sea* and Beston's *The Outermost House* to mention only a few.[13] Each author powerfully articulated the naturalistic wonder, mystery, discovery, and exploration of the coastal context, well reflecting Edward O. Wilson's insight:

> The [natural] world is the...domain of the more restless and paradoxical part of the human spirit. Our sense of wonder grows exponentially: the greater the knowledge, the deeper the mystery and the more we seek [experience] to create new mystery...Our intrinsic emotions drive us to search for new habitats, to cross unexplored terrain, but we still crave this sense of a mysterious world stretching infinitely beyond.[14]

The coastal environment is an unrivaled habitat for exploring, discovering, and engaging feelings of wonder and mystery, in an almost childlike manner independent of one's age. Despite the strenuous physical exertions often involved, many derive significant feelings of relaxation, peace of mind, and an enhanced sense of creativity and imagination from this naturalistic experience of the coast.

Humanistic

The humanistic value is indicative of strong feelings of emotional attachment to individual elements of the coastal environment. This affective response is typically directed at particularly salient aspects of the coast including large animals such as waterfowl and wading birds, or striking geological forms such as certain beaches, cliffs, or tidal marshes. People often express pronounced attachment to these elements of the coast, often invoking terms of endearment not unlike those they use toward other humans when describing the depth and quality of their emotions. The therapeutic value of the humanistic perspective of the coast can sometimes be quite significant, most dramatically illustrated by the Western tradition of seeking the shore for solace and rehabilitation at times of acute mental and physical stress. Conversely, it is not unusual to encounter extreme feelings of loss when particular elements of the coast are despoiled or degraded.

Dominionistic

The coast can also offer significant physical and mental challenges testing the capacity of people to persevere in the face of formidable opposition. Both by choice and necessity, people have long contested elements of the coastal environment and, in the process, demonstrated their ability to subdue, control, dominate, and master difficult and sometimes threatening elements of the natural world.

While this dominionistic relationship may foster, particularly in the modern era, tendencies toward excessive mastery and manipulation, this recent capacity should not dissuade us from recognizing this value's more ancient and functional roots. Perhaps this intuitive understanding accounts for the continuing interest in sports like sailing or sculling, where vessels of anachronistic utility remain popular because of the challenge and skill embedded in their contest with nature. The evolutionary struggle has always necessitated some degree of mastery and control over nature, and the prowess involved rarely results in the victim's complete destruction: in fact, much the opposite can result. As Holmes Rolston III suggests: "One reason we lament the passing of wilderness is that we do not want entirely to tame this aboriginal element... Half the beauty of life comes out of it... The cougar's fang sharpens the deer's sight, the deer's fleet-footedness shapes a more supple lioness... None of life's heroic quality is possible without this dialectical stress."[15]

The coastal environment has long been a worthy and defiant adversary for humans. Even in the modern era, waterfowl hunters continue to seek the competition of their crafty prey, while homeowners struggle to withstand the vagaries of the most unstable of all terrestrial environments. While any exercise of dominionistic tendencies can be brought to self-defeating excess, it may be a false arrogance to deny the legitimacy of this human urge to master and control nature. The management challenge is not to deny this dominionistic value but to render its expression safely within the ecological carrying capacity of the coastal environment.

Moralistic

The coastal context frequently evokes strong ethical and moralistic affinities for nature. These sentiments can be so powerfully manifest that they sometimes lead to an attitude of reverence and even spiritual awe for the natural world. The basis for this powerful bonding with the coastal environment remains elusive and, to a degree, inexplicable. Yet, one supposes the intense expression of life in the seemingly integrated coastal context may be associated with this moralistic wonder and reverence. This nearly religious response to the coast is powerfully articulated by John Steinbeck when musing upon life in the tidal pool:

> It seems apparent that species are only commas in a sentence, that each species is at once the point and the base of a pyramid, that all life is related.... And then not only the meaning but the feeling about species grows misty. One merges into another, groups melt into ecological groups until the time when what we know as life meets and enters what we think of as non-life: barnacle and rock, rock and earth, earth and tree, tree and rain and

air. And the units nestle into the whole and are inseparable from it.... And it is a strange thing that most of the feeling we call religious, most of the mystical outcrying which is one of the most prized and used and desired reactions of our species, is really the understanding and the attempt to say that man is related to the whole thing, related inextricably to all reality, known and unknowable.... That all things are one thing and that one thing is all things — a plankton, a shimmering phosphorescence on the sea and the spinning planets and an expanding universe.[16]

Negativistic

This attempt to delineate various coastal values has largely emphasized positive attributes derived from intimate contact with this natural environment. Like any habitat, the coast can also connote negative values including fear, aversion, and disdain. Even from this negativistic perspective, one is struck by the capacity of the coast to provoke unusually strong human responses to a degree not often encountered in other environments. Most people, for example, express considerable fright in the face of a furiously raging coastal storm, or toward the danger posed by predators such as crocodiles or sharks, or when confronted with the seemingly malarial, disease-ridden sight of a stagnant marsh or the detritus of a decomposing swamp. These and other features of the coastal environment can provoke avoidance and even alienation from this habitat.

While such sentiments of fear, aversion, and antipathy can foster unwarranted harm and destruction, they can also result in a healthy distancing and even respect for this natural environment. Negativistic sentiments reflect a functional evolutionary process when manifest at a reasonable level of occurrence. Avoidance of injury and harm in nature is one of the most ancient biological tendencies of any species, and a realistic tension between humans and the threat posed by the coastal environment is to be expected and sometimes welcomed. This fear may even, at times, nourish a healthy deference and avoidance of certain habitats and admiration for the powerful and menacing in nature.

A SENSE OF PLACE IN THE COASTAL CONTEXT

These diverse coastal values reflect a deep human need to associate with nature and they collectively reflect the material, intellectual, emotional, and even spiritual bases for the human attraction to the coast. These relationships, in other words, express a matrix of subtle and complex human interdependencies with nature, which allow people to develop intimate and abiding attachments to their coastal communities as secure, familiar and meaningful places.

For this level of relationship to occur, however, at least two conditions seem necessary. First, coastal environments must be ecologically healthy, aesthetically appealing, and materially productive. Second, the human presence in the coastal landscape must be intimate, functionally meaningful, and economically sustainable. The coastal context must, in other words, meet the conditions for viable communities where people are neither outsiders nor a destructive or debilitating force. Unfortunately, both conditions have been seriously eroded in contemporary America, the result being a significantly degraded capacity of the coastal context to provide a secure and meaningful sense of place for many people.

The foremost problem has been the physical degradation of the coastal environment, a situation described in great detail elsewhere. Yet, if briefly examined in light of the biophilia values described above, one can obtain another perspective on the harm that has been incurred. Ecologically, extensive pollution, chemical contamination, habitat destruction, resource overexploitation, and the widespread invasion of exotic organisms are among the more serious causes for declining biological carrying capacity and productivity in many coastal environments. From a more practical perspective, these environmental insults have resulted in serious health hazards, declines in commercial fisheries and other resource production, and the deterioration of such critical ecological services as decomposition, flood control, storm protection, water purification and recharge, and the control of soil erosion and sediments.

Aesthetically, the almost mythic beauty and physical attraction of the coast has been replaced in many areas by congestion, litter, waste, depletion, and human and biotic communities which are characterized more by haphazardness than grace, charm, and loveliness. More intangible losses include an eroded capacity of the coast to evoke strong emotional bonds, spiritual inspiration, naturalistic wonder, and a sense of challenge and awe. The therapeutic value of the shore as a source of recuperation and recovery from mental and physical stress has become for many an exercise in nostalgia.

In many coastal areas still replete with various positive environmental values, the opportunities for experiencing these benefits have often given way to denied access and limitations on human habitation and deep personal involvement. This latter phenomenon brings us to the other condition for a satisfying and meaningful sense of place in the coastal context: intimate human interaction with the coastal landscape. This condition is subtle, yet it strikes at the heart of how people must be a part of nature, not separate or alien from it, to obtain the deepest measure of the human relationship to nature, and a meaningful experience of a sense of place. Sagoff alludes to this need for familiar relationships when he remarks:

> Much of what we deplore about the human subversion of nature — and fear about the destruction of the environment — has to do with the loss of places we keep in shared memory and cherish with instinctive and collective loyalty. It has to do with [the] loss of…security one has when one relies upon the characteristic aspects of places and communities one knows well. What may worry us most is the prospect of becoming strangers in our own land.[17]

Various elements of coastal environmental degradation — congestion, aesthetic deterioration, habitat destruction and fragmentation — are also associated with increasing alienation and separation from the coastal context. Human estrangement from the coastal landscape is further exacerbated by declines of regional economies, the increase in what could be termed the "suburbanization and commuterization" of the coast, even the expanding number of isolated and restricted protected areas. Collectively, these factors all contribute to the separation and distancing of people from the coast as a secure and meaningful place of human habitation.

Ironically, more people reside in coastal communities than ever before, although the great majority seem disconnected from this environment as a source of food, energy, or experience. This disassociation from the basic processes of life seriously limits the capacity of the coast to be a meaningful place, no matter how aesthetically attractive it may be. Communities elicit loyalty and attachment, David Orr suggests, when they "reweave the local ecology into the fabric of economy and life patterns."[18] Sustainable and vital coastal communities require more than just protection and restoration of natural landscapes or the preservation of aesthetic attractions. These areas must also be places where people can, to quote Orr, "find...sources of food, livelihood, energy, healing, recreation and celebration."[19]

We have too often assumed the only means for arresting the deterioration of the coast is to establish more protected and restricted areas. While this option may at times be ecologically necessary, its fundamental flaw is the relegation of humans to the role of outsider and transient. Preservation efforts are often unavoidable in the face of continuing coastal degradation, but they represent a biocentric approach to landscape protection, failing to address the anthropocentric heart of the malaise caused by the decline of the coastal environment as a site for human experience and community. They fail to recognize the human need for intimate, spontaneous, and ongoing interaction with nature. Without this level of familiar, unrehearsed involvement, the coastal environment becomes merely pretty, a place to admire from afar, with typical aloofness. As Pyle suggests:

> Intimate association is necessary...A face-to-face encounter with a banana slug means much more than a komodo dragon seen on television...Nature reserves...are not enough to ensure connection. Such places, important as they are, invite a measured, restricted kind of contact...There need to be places...where we

can wander off a trail, lift a rock, poke about, and merely wonder.[20]

This deeper level of connection means integrated access with an aesthetically appealing, ecologically productive, and economically viable coastal environment. Modern economies necessarily preclude returning to the bucolic fantasy of a self-sufficient coastal landscape. For the foreseeable future most energy, food, and material resources will continue to be obtained from elsewhere and transported over long distances. Still, the restoration of meaning, community, and place in the coastal context will necessitate some revitalization of regional economies, the assurance that some substantial element of primary production remains available for sight, smell, touch, and participation. As Jaquetta Hawkes remarked, this means "relearning…a patient and increasingly skillful love-making that [persuades] the land to flourish."[21]

The preservation and restoration of bioregional economies necessitates, as Orr suggests, some degree of willingness, "to rediscover and reinhabit our…family farms, rural villages, towns, communities and urban neighborhoods."[22] This process of sinking deep roots into a place entails nurturing our interdependence with nature, allowing the coastal environment to become an integral aspect of our personal and community lives, and a source of material sustenance and well-being. As Sagoff suggests, "A natural landscape becomes a place…when it is cultivated, when it constrains human activity and is constrained by it, when it functions as a center of felt value, because human needs, cultural and social as well as biological, are satisfied in it."[23]

The utilitarian value must never be achieved at the expense of the other ecological, aesthetic, intellectual, emotional, and spiritual values previously associated with a rich and rewarding coastal environment. Antagonism between economic and noneconomic environmental values, however, is almost always avoidable and rarely an intrinsic conflict. More often than not, discords between nature and economy are a consequence of an unnecessary economic narrowness. As the economist Malcolm Gillis suggests, "Good economics not only is good ecology but indeed is required for good ecology. The dichotomy that many perceive to have arisen between economics and ecology is false and has persisted primarily because of bad economics."[24]

Moreover, it is not unusual to encounter economic decision-making that seeks to maximize the experience of noneconomic environmental values, even where monetary incentives suggest otherwise. Businesses often relocate in environmentally attractive and healthy places, despite the presence of alternative locations overflowing with industrial advantages, a myriad of tax incentives and elaborate infrastructural and logistical support. Many environmentally degraded communities, for example, have unsuccessfully marketed themselves on the basis of monetary incentives alone, only to find corporations relocating in areas lacking equivalent tax and infrastructural benefits but brimming with an array of positive environmental attributes. In other words, economics often follows ecologically healthy and attractive communities, and many municipalities would be well-advised to improve their environmental amenities for economic reasons alone.

Advocacy of a meaningful sense of place in the coastal context emphasizes the importance of protecting a range of environmental values, as well as the sustainable connection between coastal habitats and local economic and social structures. One potentially misleading possibility is that it may suggest to some an idealization of the rural landscape, and the related insinuation of urban life as intrinsically harmful to human emotional, intellectual, and aesthetic links with the coastal environment. The view presented here might be regarded as romantic, elitist, and denigrating toward those mired in poverty and residing in the inner city. This interpretation would be erroneous. The environmental values and socioeconomic structures advocated here, while perhaps less obvious and readily accessible in the urban context, represent more a problem of design and opportunity than a matter of irrelevance for an entire class of people.

The coastal environment can enrich the human experience just as much in the urban context as it can on the rural shore. Society's challenge is not to lament the degraded state of the coast in many of our urban settings but to render its positive experience more readily accessible, ecologically healthful, and socioeconomically meaningful. This means integrating environmentally sound coastal areas into the design of urban neighborhoods and built structures, rehabilitating degraded coastal wetlands and parks, restoring coastal regional economies and livelihoods. Many cities have begun to marshall this capacity through the creation of community gardens, urban forestry programs, wetlands and harbor restoration, enhanced watershed protection, and coastal greenways.[25] These are only a few examples of creative pursuits designed to improve the modern coastal city.

It will not be easy to arrest many of the current forces of ecological decline or achieve the restoration of degraded environments in coastal cities, towns, and villages. A necessary beginning is the recognition that a secure and meaningful sense of place in the coastal context must be addressed across all the value dimensions described. Living diversity and the ecological process that support it are not just a matter of material well-being, but also the foundation for our emotional, intellectual, aesthetic, and ethical existence. The human species evolved in a rich, diverse, and productive natural environment and this condition remains necessary for our personal identities, community structures, and sense of meaningful places. The restoration and enhancement of this potential means not just restoring the health of the coastal environment, but also its capacity to animate humans aesthetically, to nurture them ecologically, to awe and frighten them with its grandeur and magnificence, and to inspire their varied capacities for exploration and wonder, affection and bonding, challenge and physical fitness, and spiritual inspiration and solace. These represent the basic goals of environmental enhancement and remediation in the coastal context and should guide management efforts whether they be in the areas of pollution compliance, ecological restoration, land and species protection, integrated conservation and development, human population control, or public education and awareness.

The greatest challenge is to expand and enrich the understanding of how the human personality depends on the natural environment for emotional and spiritual, as much as physical, well-being. We need to cultivate awareness of how humans depend on an intimate connection with their natural context in order to achieve the goals of community and security. The challenge is as much one of changing values as of expanding scientific knowledge or engineering capacities. The restoration and enhancement of the coastal environment as a meaningful place of human habitation depends on how much we recognize that nature and biological diversity are a critical basis for what it means to be fully human.

NOTES

1. Mark Sagoff. 1992. Settling America or the concept of place in environmental ethics. Journal of Energy, Natural Resource & Environmental Law 12(2):351-418. Quotation p. 389.

2. Simone Weil. 1971 [1952]. The Need for Roots. Harper Colophon, New York, p. 43.

3. Alan Grussow. 1972. A Sense of Place: The Artist and the American Land. Friends of the Earth, San Francisco, p. 27.

4. Henry Beston. 1971. The Outermost House. Ballantine Books, New York, p. 394.

5. Robert M. Pyle. 1993. The Thunder Tree. Houghton-Mifflin, Boston, p. 145.

6. Susan M. Wells, Robert M. Pyle and N. Mark Collins. 1983. The IUCN Invertebrate Red Data Book. IUCN, Gland, Switzerland.

7. Stephen R. Kellert and Edward O. Wilson. 1993. The Biophilia Hypothesis. Island Press, Washington, D.C.

8. Pyle, op. cit., p. 147.

9. Kellert and Wilson, op. cit., and Wilson. 1984. Biophilia: the Human Bond with Other Species. Harvard University Press, Cambridge.

10. Stephen R. Kellert. 1993. The biological basis for human values of nature. In Kellert and Wilson, op. cit., pp. 42-69.

11. Robert DeGroot. 1992. Functions of Nature. Wolters-Noordhoof, Amsterdam.

12. Stephen R. Kellert. 1993. Values and perceptions of invertebrates. Conservation Biology 7(4):845-55.

13. Henry David Thoreau. 1987 [1865]. Cape Cod. Penguin Books, New York; Anne Morrow Lindbergh. 1955. Gift From the Sea. Random House, New York; Rachel L. Carson. 1955. The Edge of the Sea. Oxford University Press, New York; Henry Beston. 1971. The Outermost House. Ballantine Books, New York.

14. Wilson, op. cit., p. 76.

15. Holmes Rolston III. 1986. Philosophy Gone Wild. Prometheus Books, Buffalo, p. 88.

16. John Steinbeck. 1941. Log From the Sea of Cortez. P. P. Appel, Mamaroneck, New York, p. 93.

17. Sagoff, op. cit., Quotation pp. 352-3, 358.

18. David Orr. 1993. Love it or lose it: the coming biophilia revolution. In Kellert and Wilson, op. cit., pp. 415-440. Quotation p. 432-33.

19. Ibid.

20. Pyle, op. cit., pp. 146-47.

21. Jaquetta Hawkes. 1951. A Land. Random House, New York, p. 202.

22. Orr, op. cit., p. 433.

23. Sagoff, op. cit., p. 358.

24. Malcolm Gillis. 1991. Economics, ecology and ethics: mending the broken circle for tropical forests. In F. Herbert Bormann and Stephen R. Kellert (eds.). Ecology, Economics, Ethics: The Broken Circle. Yale University Press, New Haven, pp. 153-179. Quotation p. 159.

25. Two examples of such cities are New York and Baltimore. For New York's coastal parks, see, for example, Michael A. Matthews, Robert P. Cook, John T. Tanacredi and Joseph J. Pane. 1991. Inter-agency cooperation in restoring freshwater wetlands in an urban national recreation area. National Institute for Urban Wildlife, Columbia, Maryland. In Baltimore, river courses emptying into the Harbor are part of an urban greenway system and the city's Critical Area regulations provide for restoration of wildlife habitat

where possible, and for public access to the entire perimeter of the Inner Harbor. The Harbor-city interface is once again a focus for citizens and visitors alike. See, for example, Department of Planning, Baltimore, Maryland. 1992. Baltimore City's Critical Area Management Plan.

3

Ecological Value in Restored Coastal Ecosystems

Richard F. Ambrose

It is perhaps only natural that, as more and more habitats become degraded as a result of increasing development in the United States and elsewhere, there is increasing interest in restoring degraded habitats.[1] Some of the psychic and spiritual bases for the public's current fascination with habitat restoration are discussed in this volume by Mark Sagoff, Stephen Kellert and Robert Nelson. Whatever the reasons, and there are undoubtedly many, for the public's concern with restoring damaged ecosystems, there has been a concomitant interest in the scientific community, as evidenced by the number of recent books on restoration science and the recent founding of the Society for Ecological Restoration, which has launched a journal, *Restoration Ecology*, devoted exclusively to restoration research.[2] Although restoration practice has perhaps favored inland habitats in the past, the obvious need for the restoration of coastal habitats has recently been recognized.[3]

We recognize that restoration is of the utmost importance, but the question arises, how can we measure the success of restoration? In order to answer this question we need to understand and measure what the ecological value of habitats, whether pristine, degraded or restored, may be so that before and after comparisons can be made. How are we to measure ecological value? Sagoff eloquently chides us for comparing apples and oranges when we talk of economic exploration and environmental protection, yet, pragmatically, we must find a common vocabulary in order to proceed with any meaningful evaluation. In order to measure ecological value, we must first define what the term means. This chapter reviews several terminologies and widely used valuation techniques. Since the ecological value of ecosystems should be based on critical ecosystem functions, I review the meaning of habitat functions and attributes, or indicators, of such functions, and how they can be related to an ecosystem valuation framework.

Currently, most habitat restoration projects are required as mitigation. The National Environmental Policy Act (NEPA) of 1969 and other legislation has focused attention on mitigating environmental impacts by rehabilitating or restoring damaged habitats, and habitat restoration is becoming increasingly common. One could ask whether this is a good thing. The answer is clear, at least from the perspective of the environment, for habitats that are so severely degraded that restoration efforts provide an obvious environmental benefit. For example, when strip mines are revegetated, there is little doubt that the rehabilitated habitat has greater value than would be the case without rehabilitation. Similarly, there are clear environmental benefits when a polluted river is restored by controlling discharges. However, there are other cases where it is less clear whether restoration has a positive effect. Is it beneficial to allow an environmentally damaging project to proceed because of the promise that restoration can replace the lost functions of the damaged habitat?

There is also the question of whether the benefits of restoration, which can be quite expensive, are worth the cost. Such issues are traditionally addressed by economic cost benefit analyses. Some economists have recognized that natural resources are undervalued when judged by market value alone. The field of ecological economics has developed to address these issues.[4] However, ecological economics remains anthropocentric in that its assessments concern the value of natural resources to humans. Perhaps a more fundamental issue is the value of the natural resources *to the ecosystem*. NEPA, for example, promulgates the policy of "no net loss" of resource values — but how can we know if there is a net loss unless we can measure the *ecological* value of the resources lost and the *ecological* value of the resources gained through restoration?

There are other reasons to measure ecological value for a given habitat. A major issue in wetland restoration concerns the success of restoration. An early study indicated that few wetland restoration projects in San Francisco Bay were completely successful, and many were outright failures.[5] More recent studies have also raised questions about the success of wetland restorations.[6] Much of the concern about the restoration of coastal wetlands revolves around the issue of whether a restored wetland can duplicate the functions of natural wetlands.[7] If restored wetlands do not duplicate natural wetland functions, then destroying such areas will result in a net loss of wetland values and functions, even if the destruction is mitigated by requiring wetland restoration. One approach for determining success of wetland restoration and ensuring that there is no net loss of wetland values and functions is to define success as occurring when the ecological value of the restored wetland equals the value of natural reference wetlands. To use this approach, we must know how to measure ecological value.

Before proceeding to a consideration of how to determine value, it is worth considering whether we should even try to measure it and what we mean by it. One might ask, "Isn't it enough just to say everything has intrinsic value?" In many ways, this is true. In fact, from an ecological perspective it is hard to get past the intrinsic value of, for example, species. Each species plays a unique role in an ecosystem, and no species can truly replace another. From an ecological perspective, how can we say that one species is more valuable than another, or even that two species are of equal value? The driving force for measuring the value of habitats is a pragmatic one. Development will occur, and its unavoidable impacts should be mitigated. In many cases, this will mean compensatory mitigation, where, for example, x acres of a particular habitat must be restored as mitigation for damage to y acres of that same habitat type elsewhere. Decision-makers need to know what mitigation ratio (tradeoff ratio) is needed to achieve no net loss of resource value. The ratio will be determined with or without the input of scientists. Thus, the challenge to scientists is to provide a scientifically defensible basis for these ratios. Furthermore, there are legal and policy imperatives for considering ecological value. A Memorandum of Agreement (MOA) between the U.S. Army Corps of Engineers and the Environmental Protection Agency (dated February 7, 1990) addresses mitigation obligations under § 404 of the Clean Water Act. The MOA specifies that the unit of measure for determining "no net loss" should be ecological value rather than acreage.

DEFINING AND MEASURING VALUE

The first step to measuring the value of a habitat, whether restored or not, is to define what is meant by value. In a general sense, anything that is worthwhile or desirable has value. Utility can also contribute to value; for example, the American Heritage Dictionary defines value as "worth in usefulness or importance to the possessor; utility or merit."[8] For the purposes of habitat valuation, a useful working definition of value is: the capacity to satisfy a need.

For the purposes of this chapter, I consider *ecological* value, that is, value from the perspective of a system of organisms, rather than anthropocentric values. Clearly, a habitat has other values, including the commodity and non-commodity values that provide "a sense of place."[9] Nonetheless, the efforts to assign a value to non-consumptive uses or to the intrinsic value of a natural resource relate back to the value of that resource to humans. This value will vary with the evaluator: the value of a wetland to a developer is likely to be very different from the value to a birdwatcher. In addition, circumstances will affect economic values; for example, the value of an acre of coastal mangrove swamp may be judged very high by the general public when the public perceives that the mangrove swamp can provide valuable seafood, but the value may decline if this same seafood can be produced as easily in aquaculture tanks. Although determination of these economic values can be important, I have not considered them here because I am concerned with ecological value. This is an important distinction, because the characteristics that make a habitat valuable from an economic point of view do not necessarily correspond to the characteristics that make the habitat valuable to a bird or a fish. To use the mangrove swamp example, the *ecological* value of the mangrove swamp is not diminished by the capability of producing seafood by aquaculture, even though the economic value may be.

In habitat valuation, there are two main valuation issues. First, we need to assess the value of something to the system. How well does this something (for example, nutrient cycling) satisfy the needs of the system? This is an issue of determining relative values of different components within one system. Second, we need to assess the relative values of different states of a system, or different systems. For example, we might be interested in comparing the value of a restored wetland to a natural wetland. We might also want to compare the relative values of different habitats, such as a coastal harbor compared to a coastal wetland. An interesting and important issue in assigning value concerns the equivalence of different objects or services. In assigning value using a common currency, there is an assumption that items and services are, to some extent, interchangeable. This idea is implied in the American Heritage Dictionary definition of value as "an amount considered to be a *suitable equivalent* for something else; a fair price or return for goods or services" (emphasis added).[10] This presents a fundamental dilemma for an ecologist trying to place a value on a habitat because it is clear that, from an ecological perspective, species are *not* equivalent to each other: each species is different, and each plays a unique role in an ecosystem. The practical need for habitat valuation forces a broader view of ecosystems, one that focuses on fundamental functions and processes that are common to different systems.

With our working definition of value as the capacity to satisfy a need, how do we go about measuring it? A first step would be to identify the needs — in this case, the "needs" of the ecosystem. Having identified the needs, one must then determine how well a particular habitat satisfies them. Habitat valuation techniques have been developed for a variety of reasons, and some of the existing techniques adopt an approach based on "needs," although it is not stated explicitly. The Habitat Evaluation Procedures (HEP), developed by the U.S. Fish and Wildlife Service, uses models to relate physical features of a habitat to the suitability of the habitat for a particular target species.[11] Critical features of the habitat are identified based on the needs of the target species, functions are constructed to relate these features to habitat suitability dependent upon how well a particular area satisfies those needs, and these suitabilities are combined to yield a single number.

Because the habitat suitability models can be applied in different habitat types, HEP can be used to determine the acreage of one habitat type necessary to compensate for an impact to another type of habitat. Detailed information about the natural history of the target species is required for HEP, and relatively few models have been developed so far for coastal species. To circumvent the limitation imposed by the need for detailed models, a modified HEP analysis is sometimes performed based on the subjective "best professional judgment" of experts. In any case, HEP is not comprehensive, since there will be many species in a habitat that are not targeted but which nonetheless add value to the habitat. In addition, HEP focuses on individual species rather than communities or ecosystem processes.

Another commonly-used habitat valuation technique is the Wetland Evaluation Technique (WET), developed by the Federal Highway Administration and used by the U.S. Army Corps of Engineers.[12] As the name implies, WET is restricted to use in wetlands, but within this habitat type WET takes a more comprehensive approach to habitat evaluation than HEP. WET is based on a number of physical, hydrological, and biological functions performed by wetlands, including things such as groundwater discharge, nutrient removal/transformation, and aquatic diversity/abundance (see Table 3.1). WET does not produce a single number to represent the value of a habitat (in fact, it does not really assign a value to a habitat at all), instead it uses a series of predictors to judge the probability that a particular wetland has the opportunity and effectiveness to perform wetland functions; the probabilities are determined on a scale of low, moderate or high. There is a procedure for comparing wetlands, but it is not quantitative. In addi-

Table 3.1. Example wetland functions and values.

Wetland Evaluation Technique	Zedler
Groundwater recharge	Provision of habitat for wetland dependent species
Groundwater discharge	Support food chains
Flood flow alteration	Transformation of nutrients
Sediment stabilization	Maintenance of plant populations
Sediment/toxicant retention	Resilience (ability to recover from disturbances)
Nutrient removal/transformation	Resistance to invasive species (plant or animal)
Production export	Pollination
Aquatic diversity/abundance	Maintenance of local gene pools
Wildlife diversity/abundance for breeding	Access to refuges during high water
Wildlife diversity/abundance for migration and wintering	Accommodation of rising sea level
Recreation and uniqueness/heritage	

tion, only a few of the functions included in WET relate to ecological functions.

Other habitat valuation techniques have also been developed.
For example, the Biological Evaluation Standardized Technique
(BEST), developed by MEC Analytical Systems, Inc. for the Port
of Los Angeles, was developed specifically to avoid some of the
problems associated with HEP and WET.[13] Like HEP, BEST requires the identification of target species upon which the evaluation will be based; this introduces a subjective and/or anthropocentric factor into the analysis, and also results in an evaluation
based on only a subset of the important elements of a habitat. A
BEST analysis typically includes about ten target species and perhaps a few additional factors, such as fish productivity and habitat
scarcity. BEST does not attempt to include all important features of
a habitat. More importantly, BEST does not attempt to determine
how well a particular habitat satisfies critical ecosystem needs.

Davis argues that the assessment of ecological value should emphasize the ecosystem as a total functional unit rather than as individual species. She identifies the critical functions of an ecosystem
as the ability to accomplish the following:

- the ability to produce food and transfer energy
- the ability to supply habitat that supports a
  diversity of species
- the ability to interact with other ecosystems
- the ability to maintain itself
- the ability to develop and evolve[14]

Davis notes that the performance of these functions is often intimately related to the geographic setting of the ecosystem. Finally,
Davis suggests that ecological value, like value in other areas, can
be defined by the relationship between scarcity of supply and the
level of demand. Thus, a rare habitat type would have higher value
than a widespread one because of its scarcity. We can use critical
ecosystem functions as the "needs" of an ecosystem, so basing

habitat value on these functions is appropriate. Ecosystem functions allow a comprehensive assessment of a habitat's value. In addition, most functions are not restricted to a particular habitat type, so focusing on functions allows the values of somewhat different habitats to be compared — a necessary condition for out-of-kind mitigation, but an elusive one.

IDENTIFYING FUNCTIONS AND ATTRIBUTES

A function is an action performed for a purpose. A habitat function is an action performed by the habitat for a specific ecological purpose, such as nutrient cycling or support of fish. Wetland ecologists have been concerned about wetland functions for some time, and a great many functions have been identified. Some of these have already been mentioned, but there are many more representing a diversity of perspectives (see Table 3.1).[15]

It probably is not possible to generate a short list of critical ecosystem functions that would be universally accepted. Instead, a working list (Table 3.2) is presented that is a reasonably comprehensive compilation of functions from a variety of sources. This list is likely to change, but it provides a basis for future discussions. It is also purposefully general, but specific valuations may need to incorporate additional locally-important functions.[16] Note that many functions also include subfunctions, some of which are noted in Table 3.2. The form of the subfunctions for functions that involve support of a taxon is similar. For example, the "Support of Fish" function is very general, and there are many aspects of "fish" that would influence the value of a habitat (see Table 3.3). Certainly, the abundances of different lifestages would be important, since habitats could be important breeding grounds (support for egg and larval stages) or nursery grounds (support of juveniles) as well as supporting adult populations. In addition, the diversity of fish that a habitat supported would contribute to its value.

An attribute is an inherent characteristic. We are concerned with an attribute of a function, that is, a measurable characteristic of the function that can be used to assess the degree to which the function is performed. In this sense, attributes are synonymous with the "indicators" discussed by Kentula and her colleagues.[17] They describe indicators as "variables so closely associated with particular wetland functions that their presence or value is symptomatic of the existence or level of function."[18] While functions are the basis for an ecosystem valuation, the attributes of functions tell us what actually must be measured. For example, the function "support of fish" has a number of subfunctions relating to the support of different lifestages and the support of diversity (Table 3.3). What should be measured to determine how well the habitat ful-

Table 3.2. Potential ecosystem functions.

Population Level

Support of fish
Support of plants
Support of insects
Support of aquatic invertebrates
Support of birds
Support of other vertebrates

Community Level

Support of Community Structure
    Species diversity
    Genetic diversity
    Resilience

Ecosystem Level

Ecological integrity
Nutrient cycling
Productivity
    Primary production
    Secondary production
    Tertiary production
    Production export
Strategic Linkage to Other Ecosystems
    Connectivity to other systems
    Rarity
    Migration

fills each of these functions? A measure of abundance is the most obvious attribute — as abundance increases in a habitat, the value of the habitat with respect to that function increases.

It would be possible to use total abundance of, for example, adults, if species composition did not matter. Typically, this will not be the case, and it will be desirable to measure the abundances of different taxa separately. The most obvious taxonomic unit is the species, and this is typically what has been used in previous habitat valuation methodologies. However, as discussed below, species are frequently habitat-specific, and other classifications may be better. Identifying appropriate attributes for some functions can be problematic. For example, resilience is an important subfunction of Support of Community Structure (see Table 3.2), but what is the appropriate attribute? In this and other cases, there is also the problem of how the attribute can actually be measured. For example, we would want to measure resilience based on how the community responded to perturbations. We cannot simply visit a wetland and measure this. Ideally, resilience would be judged based on manipulative field experiments, which generally will not be practical in the course of a habitat valuation.

Ecosystem functions and attributes can be used to identify the "needs" of an ecosystem, but how do we measure the capacity of a

Table 3.3. Example of a function (support of fish) with its subfunctions and attributes.

Support of Fish	
Support of Egg/Larval Abundance:	egg/larval abundance for Guild 1
	egg/larval abundance for Guild 2
Support of Juvenile Abundance:	juvenile abundance for Guild 1
	juvenile abundance for Guild 2
Support of Adult Abundance:	adult abundance for Guild 1
	adult abundance for Guild 2
Support of Diversity:	diversity for Guild 1
	diversity for Guild 2

particular habitat to satisfy those needs? The attributes tell us what to measure, and in some cases it may be obvious from attribute measurements whether one habitat is more or less valuable than another. For example, if the attribute is "abundance of adult fish," the habitat with more fish may be more valuable than a habitat with fewer fish. There are several shortcomings to this simplistic measure of relative value. In some cases, more may not be better. This would be the case for exotic species, for example. More importantly, relative value tells us nothing about absolute value. In the example above, both habitats may support few fish compared to other habitats; although one habitat may be more valuable than the other, what we really want to know is that both have a low capacity to support fish, and thus have little value *for fish*. Measurements must be compared to a *standard* that is the optimal or best condition known for the attribute.

This is an area with clear differences in the approaches taken by different techniques. HEP, through detailed understanding and models of habitat suitability, compares the value of a particular habitat to the optimal situation for that habitat characteristic. Thus, HEP uses an absolute standard. WET also uses an absolute standard, but very loosely. In contrast, BEST uses a relative standard, comparing the abundance of a species in one particular habitat to its abundances in the other habitats included in the assessment. Thus, with BEST one can determine which site is relatively good for a species, or relatively poor, compared to the other habitats in that particular assessment, but there is no absolute standard of comparison.

HABITAT INDEPENDENCE

If one habitat were being compared to another identical habitat, it would be possible to base a valuation on specific details about the particular habitat type. But this is often not the case. Even when restoring a coastal wetland, the restored wetland will have a mix of habitat types that is different from the original degraded wetland. For example, the restored wetland may have lower marsh, tidal creeks, subtidal unvegetated areas and so on, while the degraded wetland may have been mostly seasonal wetland and high marsh. Each of these areas will have different species. How can the value of the two areas be compared when there are, for example, 100 individuals/m² of species x in the restored wetland and 50 individuals/m² of species y in the degraded wetland? In other words, how can disparate sets of attributes be compared?

Thus, comparative valuation of different things must be done by using a criterion that is common to all. If the values of different habitats are to be compared, the criteria that are habitat-dependent cannot be used. The need for habitat-independence is particularly important for three aspects of habitat valuation:

- *Functions* should be general ecological functions.
- *Standards* must apply over the general region.
- *Taxa* included should generally not be restricted to one habitat or the other.

The difficulty of comparing across habitat types has been a major shortcoming of previous habitat valuation techniques. The issue of appropriate taxonomic categories has been particularly troublesome. Ecologists tend to think in terms of species, and both HEP and BEST utilize target species. Yet species tend to have rather specific habitat requirements. One solution to this problem is to use *guilds* instead of species in habitat valuations. Guilds are groups of species that are ecologically similar. Guilds can be defined in a number of different ways, but as an example, guilds could be defined according to primary habitat, feeding habitat, and prey type (see Table 3.4). Different habitats are likely to have representatives of the same guilds even though the species may differ.

AN ECOSYSTEM VALUATION FRAMEWORK

Having identified the roles of functions and standards in valuing ecosystems, a framework for an ecosystem valuation methodology must be developed. There is also a need to be practical. An ecosystem valuation methodology must provide a reasonable representation of value, but it must also be usable. For example, the logic and procedures should be easily comprehended and used. Table 3.5 presents some desirable characteristics of a habitat value methodology.

The details of how all the issues identified here can be combined into a valuation methodology are beyond the scope of this chapter, but the basic steps that are required can be outlined. First, attributes would be measured in the habitat(s) to be valued. Next, the measured attribute values would be standardized by comparing them against a standard for the region. One approach to standardization would be to divide the measured value by the standard, yielding a value between 0 and 1, with 1 indicating an optimal habitat for that particular function. Finally, the standardized values would be combined to generate an overall value. Many different approaches could be taken, but the simplest way to combine the standardized values would be to add them. This process would be repeated for each of the subfunctions and functions, ultimately yielding a single number for the value of the habitat.

It is likely that no wetland, natural or restored, would be optimum in every function. In judging whether a restoration is successful, the value of the restored wetland would need to be compared to the values of reference natural wetlands. Kentula and col-

Table 3.4. Possible guild classification for fishes.

Primary Habitat	Feeding Habitat	Prey Type
Water Column	*Water Column*	Plankton
Benthic	Water Column/Benthic	Invertebrates
	Benthic	*Fish*
		Plants

NOTE: Guilds would be defined according to primary habitat, feeding habitat and prey type. For example, California halibut, which lives on the bottom and feeds primarily on fish in the water column, would belong to the *benthic, water column, fish* guild.

Table 3.5. Desirable characteristics of a Habitat Valuation Methodology.

Characteristic	Comments
Objective	Conclusions should not be unduly influenced by subjective judgements
Flexible	Should be able to adjust the level of detail without changing the logic or structure; should allow both quantitative and qualitative information to be used
Systematic	Method steps should be logical and results should be replicable
Robust: data species	Conclusions should not be greatly affected by slight differences in data or the species included
Scientifically defensible	Should be based on ecologically sound principles
Quantitative	Should utilize quantitative information as much as possible to minimize subjective influences and provide appropriate output
Simple data requirements	Should not have impossible data requirements, and should be reasonably fast to produce results
Output: single number value/unit area	To facilitate comparisons of different habitats, output should provide (1) single quantitative measure of value, and (2) value/unit area
Comprehensive	Should include all of the relevant aspects of ecosystem value
Comparable across habitat types	Should be relatively habitat-independent so that different habitat types can be compared

leagues discuss a number of aspects of such a comparative study, including how to select reference wetlands.[19] They propose that the success of wetland restoration be based on performance curves for indicators (functions), which are generated by sampling a number of restored and natural wetlands. Each performance curve is related to a different ecosystem function. Determination of wetland value as outlined here complements the approach proposed by Kentula et al., allowing their separate performance curves to be integrated and facilitating a judgment about the overall success of the restoration.

I have proposed that the ecological value of ecosystems should be based on critical ecosystem functions. Most of the concern about the success of habitat restoration also revolves around ecosystem functions, particularly the question of whether a restored habitat can replace or duplicate natural ecosystem functions. Thus, the valuation method provides a useful framework for determining the success of restoration. The most successful restorations, those that achieve the highest levels of ecosystem functions, will have high ecological value. For assessing both restoration success and ecological value, it is crucial that an appropriate standard be defined. Kentula et al. emphasize this point when discussing the selection of reference natural wetlands to be used in an evaluation of restored wetlands.

There is clearly much work to be done to develop a habitat or ecosystem valuation methodology. I have discussed a number of features that should form the basis of an ecological valuation method, starting from a consideration of what comprises value. It must be recognized that a habitat or ecosystem is more than simply a collection of things (species); the value of the ecosystem emanates from how well it performs its functions. Any ecological valuation methodology needs to recognize the existence of a wide range of ecosystem functions. In some cases, a narrow view of the value of a habitat may be all that is necessary, especially for an agency with a restricted mandate such as the National Marine Fisheries Service, which is concerned primarily with fish. But a valuation methodology that bases the value of a habitat on a relatively few target species will not provide a complete evaluation, and for many purposes this will not be adequate.

Ecological valuation is an important and difficult problem for applied ecologists and decision-makers. It exemplifies problems at the interface between science and policy, because scientists working on habitat valuation are motivated by policy needs. However, the direct application of ecological valuation is relatively narrow, involving mainly mitigation decisions and restoration evaluations and focused mainly on science. How does ecological value relate to the broader concept of value from a human perspective?

Ecological valuation gives a measure of the quality or integrity of the ecosystem, of how well the ecosystem is working. There are economic dimensions to ecological value, since ecosystems with high value may be more likely to support productive fisheries, have a high level of groundwater recharge or flood control, provide a more enjoyable recreational experience, and so forth. There are also less obvious, but equally important, nonuse dimensions to ecological value. For example, Stephen Kellert recognizes the link between ecological value and nonuse values when he argues that "[l]iving diversity and the ecological processes that support it are not just a matter of material well-being, but also the foundation for our emotional, intellectual, aesthetic and ethical existence."[20] Habitats with high ecological value have high existence value, since the public has repeatedly indicated a willingness to pay for the preservation of natural areas they are never likely to visit. Thus, ecological value is the basis for many of the aspects of habitats that humans value.

ACKNOWLEDGMENT

Eric Stein, Cindy Lin and Tim Downs assisted with the development of the valuation framework. This research was funded by the California Coastal Commission; I am especially grateful to Peter Douglas, the Executive Director of the Commission, and Susan Hansch, Manager of the Energy and Ocean Resources Unit, for guidance and helpful comments.

NOTES

1. See, for example, John J. Berger. 1987. Restoring the Earth. Doubleday, New York and John J. Berger. 1990. Environmental Restoration: Science and Strategies for Restoring the Earth. Island Press, Washington, D.C.

2. For example, John Cairns, Jr. (ed.). 1988. Rehabilitating Damaged Ecosystems. Volumes I and II. CRC Press, Boca Raton, Florida; William R. Jordan, Michael E. Gilpin and John D. Aber (eds.). 1987. Restoration Ecology: A Synthetic Approach to Ecological Research. Cambridge University Press, Cambridge, UK; and National Research Council. 1992. Restoration of Aquatic Ecosystems: Science, Technology and Public Policy. Committee on Restoration of Aquatic Ecosystems - Science, Technology and Public Policy, Water Science and Technology Board, Commission on Geosciences, Environment, and Resources. National Academy Press, Washington D.C.

3. Gordon W. Thayer (ed.). 1992. Restoring the Nation's Marine Environment. Maryland Sea Grant College, College Park, Maryland.

4. Robert Costanza. 1984. Natural resource valuation and management: Toward an ecological economics. In Ann-Marie Jansson (ed.). Integration of Economy and Ecology: An Outlook for the Eighties. University of Stockholm Press, Stockholm, pp. 7-18.

5. Margaret S. Race. 1985. Critique of present wetlands mitigation policies in the United States based on an analysis of past restoration projects in San Francisco Bay. Environmental Management 9: 71-82.

6. See, for example, Kevin L. Erwin. 1991. An evaluation of mitigation in the South Florida Water Management District. Volume I. South Florida Water Management District, West Palm Beach, Florida; Stephanie E. Gwin and Mary E. Kentula. 1990. Evaluating design and verifying compliance of wetlands created under Section 404 of the Clean Water Act in Oregon. EPA/600/3-90/061. U.S. Environmental Protection Agency, Environmental Research Laboratory, Corvalis, Oregon; Michael Josselyn, Joy Zedler and Theodore Griswold. 1990. Wetland mitigation along the Pacific Coast of the United States. In John A. Kusler and Mary E. Kentula (eds.). Wetland Creation and Restoration: The Status of

the Science. Island Press, Washington, D.C.; Stephanie E. Gwin, Mary E. Kentula and D. L. Frostholm, in conjunction with R. L. Tighe. 1991. Evaluating design and verifying compliance of created wetlands in the vicinity of Tampa, Florida. EPA/600/3-91/068. U.S. Environmental Protection Agency, Environmental Research Laboratory, Corvalis, Oregon; and Cindy C. Holland and Mary E. Kentula. 1994. Impacts of Section 404 permits requiring compensatory mitigation on wetlands in California. Wetlands Ecology and Management.

7. See Joy B. Zedler, René Langis, John Cantilli, Margaret Zalejko, Kendra Swift and Sue Rutherford. 1988. Assessing the functions of mitigation marshes in southern California. In Jon A. Kusler, Sally Dalky and Gail Brooks (eds.). Proceedings of the National Wetland Symposium: Urban Wetlands. Association of State Wetland Managers. Byrne, New York; René Langis, Malgorzata Zalejko and Joy B. Zedler. 1991. Nitrogen assessments in a constructed and a natural salt marsh of San Diego Bay, California. Ecological Applications 1:40-51; Joy B. Zedler and René Langis. 1991. Comparisons of constructed and natural salt marshes of San Diego Bay. Restoration and Management Notes 9:21-25; Anne D. Marble. 1992. A Guide to Wetland Functional Design. Lewis Publishers, Boca Raton, Florida; and Joy B. Zedler. 1992. Restoring cordgrass marshes in Southern California. In G. W. Thayer (ed.). Restoring the Nation's Marine Environment. Maryland Sea Grant College, College Park, Maryland, pp. 7-78.

8. American Heritage Dictionary. 1987. Houghton Mifflin Co., New York.

9. See chapters by Stephen Kellert and Mark Sagoff in this volume.

10. American Heritage Dictionary, op. cit.

11. Melvin L. Schamberger, Cathleen Short and Adrian Farmer. 1978. Evaluation of wetlands as wildlife habitat. In P. E. Greeson, J. R. Clark and J. E. Clark (eds.). Wetland Functions and Values: The State of Our Understanding. American Water Resources Association, Minneapolis, pp. 74-83.

12. Paul R. Adamus, Ellis J. Clairain, R. Daniel Smith and Richard E. Young. 1987. Wetland Evaluation Technique (WET) Volume II: Methodology. Operational Draft, Report from the Department of

the Army to the Federal Highway Administration. Govt. Accession No. PB89-143028.2

13. MEC Analytical Systems, Inc. 1988. Biological baseline and an ecological evaluation of existing habitats in Los Angeles Harbor and adjacent waters. Final Report to the Port of Los Angeles, San Pedro, California.

14. Noel Davis. 1991. Comparison of the ecological values of the restored Ballona salt marsh with lost ecological values from implementation of the Ports of Los Angeles/Long Beach 2020 Plan. Report prepared by Chambers Group for Maguire Thomas Partners. Chambers Group, Inc., Santa Ana, California.

15. Ibid.

16. Pacific Estuarine Research Laboratory. 1990. A Manual for Assessing Restored and Natural Coastal Wetlands with Examples from Southern California. California Sea Grant Report No. T- CSGCP-021. La Jolla, California.

17. Mary Kentula, Robert P. Brooks, Stephanie E. Gwin, Cindy C. Holland, Arthur D. Sherman and Jean C. Sifneas. 1993. An Approach to Improving Decision Making in Wetland Restoration and Creation. Smoley/CRC Press, Boca Raton, Florida.

18. Ibid.

19. Ibid.

20. See Stephen Kellert in this volume.

4

Calvinism Minus God: Environmental Restoration as a Theological Concept

ROBERT H. NELSON

On the twenty-fifth anniversary of Earth Day, "Archdruid" David Brower spoke before a rapt congregation in Washington's National Cathedral. He preached a special message, "CPR for the earth." Conservation, preservation and restoration would save the earth and all of us along with it. The first two terms, conservation and preservation, connote the biblical injunction to be stewards of the earth, but this chapter is limited to a consideration of the last term, to "restore." It has a good sound. It is simply better than "clean up," "improve," "mitigate," "protect," or a host of other terms commonly applied to the environment. As I shall explain, it is not a scientific concept; rather it is a strong metaphor, powerful precisely because it has a strong ethical and even religious flavor. It offers the possibility of sensing a divine presence behind nature and it relates to redemption of the individual following the fall of mankind. After all, the basic goal of the Christian religion is to restore humanity to the harmony with nature that once existed in the Garden of Eden. In the current environmental lexicon, to restore versus to degrade an element of nature is the moral equivalent of good versus evil.

As a matter of public policy, the restoration of degraded habitat has become an increasingly important environmental objective. In September 1990 the United States National Oceanic and Atmospheric Administration (NOAA) held a Symposium on Habitat Restoration in Washington, D.C. Speaking at the symposium, the Chair of the President's Council on Environmental Quality, Michael Deland, said that not only must we "preserve existing ecosystems to the fullest extent," but we must "add significantly to the restoration column of the ledger."[1] For example, given that some degree of wetland loss would be unavoidable, Deland commented that President Bush's policy of "no net loss of wetlands" required the restoration (or creation) of equal amounts of wetlands.

Most of the symposium papers concerned the scientific problems of seeking to improve and perhaps to reestablish an earlier condition of currently degraded fish and wildlife habitat, as well as other environmental features. There is much to say about these problems, both as a matter of theory and as a matter of digesting the lessons of past restoration experiences. That is not my purpose in this chapter, however. Here, I want to examine the philosophical — or theological, as I will argue — foundations for the very goal of restoring the environment.

NOT A SCIENTIFIC CONCEPT

To begin, it may be helpful to recognize that the goal of "restoration" in fact has little meaning in a strict scientific sense. No one can say precisely the state of affairs that, if it could be attained, would constitute true restoration. Even if a definition could be agreed upon, true restoration in many cases would be technically impossible. Indeed, the term "restore" is not typically meant in a scientifically precise sense. Jimmy Bates, Chief of the Policy and Planning Division at the United States Army Corps of Engineers, says that "we would not set, nor pursue, unrealistic and unpractical goals such as restoring the fish and wildlife habitat of Chesapeake Bay to the conditions that Captain John Smith found and recorded." Rather, in the real world of government policy making, the goal is much more modest: "to return the existing but degraded productivity of fish and wildlife habitats to their modern historic levels — this means the natural, normal levels of fish and wildlife productivity of recent times."[2] But what are "recent times"? It could be 1980 — or 1970. Perhaps others would find an appropriate benchmark in the conditions of the Chesapeake Bay prior to World War II. Another common reference point in contemplating the past is the turn of a century. Recent times thus might mean around the end of the nineteenth century.

For various practical reasons, even if we could agree on a date, there are many other arbitrary elements in setting a standard for "restore." How can the state of an environment at any given time be characterized? Some would like to use words or pictures in their mind. But this enters the realm of poetry; it will inevitably be subjective. Any operational characterization of the environment for policy purposes is likely to rely on quantitative measures. Such measures, however, will only capture a limited part of the overall picture, that which is both measurable in concept and for which there is available data. What would it mean, for example, to restore the Chesapeake to the environment of the Bay as it existed prior to World War II? Is this goal to be defined in terms of the harvest of rockfish, bluefish, crabs, oysters, and other commercial species? They capture the most attention and are likely to be the only data readily available from much earlier periods. But how can the neglect of other species be justified?

The cleanliness of the waters might be an appropriate criterion for a restoration project. But water quality can be measured by sediment levels, phosphates, concentrations of mercury, presence of algae, and in many other ways. Few if any such measures are likely to be available from a century ago. Many will not be available even for much more recent periods. Thus, compounding the arbitrary elements, it could well be that the availability of data ends up driving the definition of the point in time taken to represent the achievement of a state of "restoration."

Even then, it is unlikely that true restoration can be accomplished. Some would argue that, like an art work by an old master, no restored place — however exactly it replicates the original —

can ever be the same. Leaving this metaphysical question aside for the moment, the current state of scientific knowledge and the technical skills simply will not be adequate in most cases to achieving a genuine restoration. A United States EPA official said that "artificial wetlands don't have the same capacity and same environmental effect as natural wetlands," and the best that can be hoped for at present is that "improved efforts may make them closer in the future."[3]

Why, then, has so much government and public attention been focussed on the idea of restoration? Metaphysically, it is not a well grounded concept; it embodies a sense that there is some "true" state, when in fact nature is subject to constant flux. Practically speaking, even if some past environmental state could be established as the correct goal — however arbitrarily — the technical means of restoration are not available. To "restore" in actual practice is likely to mean simply taking some useful and incremental steps to clean up and otherwise improve the environment. It is no more profound, no deeper than that.

RESTORATION AS METAPHOR

Why, then, the attachment to describing such pragmatic environmental efforts as "restoration?" Here we must leave the realm of the environment as a physical and scientific entity and enter the realm of the environment as the object of powerful imagery and symbolism. As a matter of poetry, a "restored" environment is much better than a "cleaner" environment. So appeals to restore the environment, among other advantages, are effective in attracting further financial and other resources to the environmental cause.

But this begs the question of why the image of restoration works as poetry, when many other metaphors do not. I propose to address this issue by examining some efforts by philosophers to explain why the preservation of species should be a matter of great ethical concern. This is similar to the question of why we should seek to restore environmental conditions as they existed in the past. Species preservation seeks, among other objectives, to ensure that for future generations the meaning of "restore" is not to recover the conditions of the world as they exist right now.

According to philosopher Claudia Mills one possible reason for preserving species is that around the world "the biota contains ten million species, [that may]…represent ten million successful solutions to a series of biological problems, any one of which could be immensely valuable to us in a number of ways." However, after examining this argument, Mills concludes that it "cannot bear a great deal of weight. It sounds too much like the reasoning of our old Aunt Tillie, who saves every bit of string or bottle cap on the off chance that it may someday come in useful. Clutter mounts up exponentially, and someday never comes." Philosophically, it simply will not do to "appeal to the possible future usefulness of species" to justify the preservation of all current species.[4] Utilitarian arguments will not work.[5]

It may be possible to argue instead that species have an "intrinsic value" that requires their preservation — that they should be preserved "not merely in virtue of what else they are good *for*, but because they are good in *themselves*."[6] Or, as we might now ask, assuming there were such a thing as a true "natural" condition of the past, and assuming also that we could somehow specify this condition, would there be an intrinsic value in restoring this condition? Again Mills is skeptical: "while these claims have considerable rhetorical force…they raise more questions than they answer. *Why* do we think species have intrinsic value? In what is it grounded? What is it about species [or restored environments] that makes them valuable [in themselves]?"[7] To these questions, there are no philosophically well grounded answers.

Western tradition says that human life is intrinsically valuable because human beings alone among species are self-conscious and have rationality. This is also what many theologians have interpreted the Old Testament to mean when it says that man is made "in the image of God."[8] However, most animal species, to say nothing of a mere body of water, rock or other physical object, cannot qualify for preservation — or restoration — under this criterion.[9]

If preserving a species or restoring a portion of nature cannot be defended for what it does for us in practical terms, and does not have an intrinsic value in itself, does this mean that no philosophical defense is possible? Such a conclusion, for Mills and many other people, would be unacceptable.[10] It might even cause one to wonder about the meaning and validity of the entire enterprise of philosophy. So it is not surprising that Mills proposes an alternative. Indeed, she develops an argument based on a concept called "transformative value." It is important to preserve species, Mills argues, because "there is a deeper element of value in nature" that reflects the fact that nature can not only "fulfill human desires but also transform them."[11] The popular rhetoric of the environmental movement poses a false dichotomy between preservation as justified for utilitarian reasons and preservation as justified for its own sake. Both must fail. However, a valid argument is that "experiences of...and study of the natural world lead us to question our values, to criticize and reform them, to alter them altogether."[12]

Applying this philosophical test, and disagreeing with many environmentalists, Mills in fact questions whether it is necessary to preserve "each individual scrap of creation." Rather, what has "transformative value" for Mills is "the magnificence and vulnerability of the whole. It is nature itself, in all its diversity, that uplifts and sustains us. That is what we are bound to preserve."[13] Mark Sagoff also explores what is uplifting about the experience of nature. It is the "natural history" of the Chesapeake Bay, not the assembly of "raw materials, biotic and abiotic, of various sorts" that is important.[14] It is the existence of "the bay as natural resources whose form is somehow 'given' by events in the past" that gives it transformative value.[15] Indeed, rather than numbers of fish caught, levels of oyster harvests, days of sailing, or other practical benefits, "we owe more to the history and beauty of nature."[16] In an awareness of the wonder of nature, it becomes possible to move beyond "nature simply as a material basis for economic exploitation."[17]

To be sure, the appeal of Mills to the grandeur of nature in our lives, and of Sagoff to the sense of a place in history, raises a further question: Why do nature and history have this transformative power? Why do they "uplift and sustain us," and show us the way to higher and better values, as Mills writes? Such questions are, historically, the domain of theology. Indeed, understanding the term broadly, they are still today theological in character.

A THEOLOGY OF RESTORATION

History and nature are hardly new subjects for western theology. Indeed to explore these areas is to take up what some have regarded as the central questions of western theology. In the Judeo-Christian tradition, "history is not meaningless but meaningful. Though we are not always able to discern the meaning of each historical event, we know what the ultimate outcome of history will be. We eagerly look forward to the new earth as part of a renewed universe in which God's good creation will realize finally and totally the purpose for which he called it into existence."[18]

The protection of nature, and even the preservation of species, also is hardly a novel subject in Judeo-Christian theology. There is, of course, the biblical story of Noah and his ark, saving all the species of the world. Calvin in the sixteenth century would argue that God intends "for the preservation of each species until the Last Day."[19] But all of Nature has a power to instruct us in proper values. Calvin further speaks of "the knowledge of God [that is] sown in their minds out of the wonderful workmanship of nature" and of Nature as offering "burning lamps" that "shine for us...the glory of its Author" above.[20] Where many people today argue that materialism promotes false values in American life, Calvin finds essential values in Nature that must supersede the "superfluous wealth" that yields a mere array of "prodigious trifles."[21] Indeed, for Calvin the experience and study of the diverse species found in Nature makes it possible to be "instructed by this bare and simple testimony which the [animal] creatures render splendidly to the glory of God."[22]

Such ideas would be secularized in the transcendental movement of mid-nineteenth century New England, the original center of Puritan (and Calvinist) theology in the United States. Arthur

Ekirch, writes that for transcendentalists such as Emerson and Thoreau "nature was the connecting link between God and man;" thus, "God spoke to man through nature."[23] Christopher Lasch explains how Emerson secularizes "his Calvinist forebears...Our fallen nature, 'our lapsed estate,' discloses itself precisely in our blindness to the 'deep remedial force' in nature."[24] Emerson, Thoreau and other transcendentalists are the American intellectual precursors of the twentieth century environmental movement. John Muir, for example, regarded himself as a devoted disciple of Emerson.

If nature, as Calvin preached, is the messenger of God, Calvin would no doubt find that all too many modern men and women have turned away from God to all manner of false beliefs. Above all, they have been blinded by the temptations of "progress," a particularly insidious heresy. This false gospel preaches that human beings can replace God; that they can control their fate; that economic necessity can be abolished; and that through scientific and economic progress it will be possible to reach heaven on earth.[25]

Many environmentalists do not speak directly of God but they often say much the same thing. They argue that true values are not to be found in technology and material progress but in Nature. The experience of Nature makes it possible to find spiritual renewal, to be uplifted and to rejoice in the wonder of the Creation. If Nature is degraded or destroyed, as in the extinction of a species or the pollution of a regional sea, it is to commit the very essence of an evil act. Calvin said all these things as well. He simply added that the significance of Nature was in offering a visible sign of God's presence in the world. By making contact with Nature, it was possible to make direct contact with God's own Creation and thus indirectly with God himself. Matters of vocabulary aside, environmentalists often seem to be saying something very similar.

Where does the deep moral passion of current environmentalism originate? It is not to be found in the clinical detachment (the "value neutrality") of scientific analysis. It is not to be found in a Darwinian view, which regards species extinction, for example, as part of the normal and natural flux of the world. Perhaps implicitly, hesitantly and with some confusion, environmentalism is actually preaching to a secular world that there must truly be some type of God somewhere. Indeed, without some such message, there may be no well-founded philosophical or theological basis to justify the environmental outlook on the world. "Restoration" of Nature, then, may have such appeal because it offers the possibility of reexperiencing a divine presence in the world. For those who wish to be spiritually renewed, it is important to be able to encounter in Nature — and if necessary, many believe, even a "restored" nature will do — an outward manifestation of the power of the Creator.

RESTORING THE GARDEN OF EDEN

There is a second source of powerful religious appeal found in the image of restoration. Indeed, there is no more important idea in the Christian tradition. The essential message of the New Testament is the intervention of God to save mankind — and thereby to restore human beings to an innocent existence in true harmony with Nature that existed before the fall of man into sinfulness and so many evils. Thus far, I have spoken of "Nature" mostly in a physical sense — the actual world of animals, plants, mountains, streams, etc. The message of the Bible speaks of Nature in this sense but also in another sense as well, as in the term "human nature." In Genesis, following the creation of the world, Adam and Eve lived in perfect joy and happiness in the Garden of Eden. They were in true harmony with their essential natures, never even knowing, for example, the existence of hatred, anger, jealousy, or other base thoughts. Even the animals, according to some accounts, lived in harmony with one another, not having to prey upon one another but provided with all their needs according to the design of God.

The fall of man meant the end of all this. Henceforth, the world would be filled with fighting, stealing, lying, and many other evils. Animals often had to eat other animals to survive. These terrible developments reflected the wrath of God resulting from Eve's transgression. It meant that the original and truer nature was lost to mankind, corrupted by the stain of human sinfulness. Only in heaven in the hereafter — or on earth following an apocalyptic final intervention by God — as related in the Book of Revelation among other places in the Bible — would the original existence of human beings in true harmony with their essential natures be restored.

Colleen McDannell and Bernard Land speak of "the collapsing together of the medieval images of paradise restored and the abode of God."[26] In the Renaissance many people dreamed of the time to come in heaven when all would enter a new realm "of loving company in a pastoral setting."[27] In one part of heaven we can know that "the realm of the saints is paradise restored... Trees, birds, flowers, and meadows flourish. It is not wild nature which survives, but nature suited for human interests and needs."[28] In short, the message of Christianity is fundamentally nothing less than a story of "restoration." It is the restoration of nature — human and physical alike — that was long ago lost due to the fall of man in the Garden of Eden. As poetry and rhetoric, if not literally, the current movement to restore Nature evokes once again the hope of finding paradise, of being saved from sin. To make a contribution to environmental restoration is to declare oneself for the side of the good in the world — as Calvin would have put it, to put one's faith in God.

AN ENVIRONMENTAL RENDITION OF THE FALL

Environmental morality is usually not derived from any full fledged theological position. Many leading environmentalists are part of secular culture and are uncomfortable with traditional theological arguments or explicit references to God as a justification for environmental policies. However, some environmentalists have developed a full "secular theology" of the fall of man and the necessity to restore the world to the conditions of an earlier time.

Environmental theologies, moreover, are not the first in the modern era to follow in this path. In Rousseau, it is the progress of knowledge and industry in "civilization" that has corrupted our truer and far better nature — a nature which we must now seek somehow to restore, the secular equivalent of returning to the Garden of Eden.[29] For Marx, alienation is the product of the separation of human beings from their true natures brought about by the economic forces of the class struggle. In prophesying the cataclysmic triumph of the proletariat, Marxism continues in the apocalyptic tradition of western theology. The ideas of Rousseau and Marx concerning man's original nature by now have largely faded into history. Their messages, however, have found new secular outlets within the contemporary environmental movement.

Consider the secular theology of Dave Foreman, a founder of the radical environmental organization Earth First!, who offers a precise exploration of the origins of sin and of the way of possible salvation.[30] As he sees matters, the world was a blissful place until about 10,000 years ago. It was then that the beginnings of organized agriculture commenced the corruption of the human condition, leading to the current evils of "city, bureaucracy, patriarchy, war" and many others.[31] Foreman describes the growing separation of human beings and nature, the environmental version of the Biblical rift between God and humanity following the expulsion from the Garden of Eden:

> Before agriculture was midwifed in the Middle East [the same place, of course, where Judeo-Christian religion was born], humans were in the wilderness. We had no concept of "wilderness" because everything was wilderness and we were a part of it. But with irrigation ditches, crop surpluses, and permanent villages, we became apart from the natural world and substituted our fields, habitations, temples and storehouses. Between the wilderness that created us and the civilization created by us, grew an ever-widening rift.[32]

As in Christianity, for Foreman the environmental path of salvation means the recovery of natural conditions found long ago, before the arrival of organized society plunged mankind into a state of deep alienation. The whole world — or at least as much as is at all practically possible — should be returned to the original wilderness, the secular equivalent of restoring the biblical paradise.

Foreman suggests that as a beginning step perhaps twenty-five percent of the land area of the United States should be entered into the wilderness system.[33]

Other prominent environmental writers such as Bill McKibben explain that "it is not utter silliness to talk about ending — or, at least, transforming — industrial civilization."[34] McKibben is prepared at least to hope for "a different world, where roads are torn out to create vast new wildernesses, where most development ceases, and where much of man's imprint on the earth is slowly erased."[35] This would bring humanity back to the "blooming, humming, fertile paradise" that existed before the earth was corrupted by the spread of civilization — a paradise that could be found as recently as a few centuries ago in the Americas, until then spared the evil consequences of European civilization.[36]

To recover the original earthly paradise of 10,000 years ago, a massive atonement for the sins of the past will be necessary. The impact of mankind has resulted in the widespread degradation of the environment of the earth. If there is to be hope for the future, a comprehensive project of restoration will be necessary. Admittedly, each little restoration effort can only play a small part in this great task. The prospects of complete success are, to say the least, daunting. But the supreme worthiness of the goal calls upon all human beings to make sacrifices in its cause.

Environmental writings are in fact filled with metaphorical allusions to the return to Eden. A book on the history of the global environmental movement is titled *Reclaiming Paradise*.[37] In *Time* magazine, an article on "the last unexplored rain forest on earth" is titled "the last Eden."[38] The 500th anniversary of Columbus' arrival in the new world has precipitated a great debate, some claiming that he introduced the sinful ways of fallen Europeans into an innocent American paradise, others that "the America encountered by the first European settlers was no primeval Eden."[39]

ENVIRONMENTAL CREATIONISM

A 1991 Gallop poll found that 47 percent of Americans believe that "God created man pretty much in his present form at one time within the last 10,000 years."[40] Politically and socially, Christian creationists and environmental activists live in different worlds. Yet, there is a surprising similarity; a similarity that may, in fact, be disconcerting to each side. Indeed, the focus on the past 10,000 years is only one of a number of significant elements linking fundamentalist Christian creationism with environmental theologies of "the Creation."

To begin with, both are fundamentally at odds with Darwin. Limited to scientific analysis alone, the goal of preserving every individual species cannot have much importance. As Claudia Mills writes: "Of course, almost every species that has ever lived has gone extinct, so extinction itself is natural, normal, routine. Even extinctions caused by human practices such as hunting and habitat fragmentation cannot be called unnatural: Humans are part of nature, too, as much as any other predators."[41] Yet, Mills does find strong reasons to "preserve biological diversity generally, to protect the integrity of the natural world."[42] Although this case can plausibly be grounded in a Darwinian framework — biological diversity will help to enhance the overall prospects for survival of the human species — even then there is no particular reason to worry about the preservation of every single species. Indeed, as Mills writes, "each species is only one tiny unit of the world's overall diversity, so perhaps [in utilitarian terms] no one species matters very much."[43]

Why, then, do we have the Endangered Species Act, which says that every single species must be saved almost without regard to costs? Although hardly justifiable in the "value-neutral" terms of ordinary science, it is nevertheless justifiable in theological terms. Morally, both Christian and environmental theologies are saying that the Creation, as a manifestation of the divine in the world, must be preserved. This is necessary to uphold essential values and religious truths. In both cases, the argument involves rejecting the very framework of Darwinian analysis.

Environmental creationists like Christian creationists reason from a beginning assumption of an original or true state of nature. In both cases, this state existed until only a few thousand years ago. Each animal and plant in that original state is intended with a specific purpose in mind. Both theologies agree that for human beings to destroy a species is to tamper with the Creation; it is to put utilitarian and material needs of human beings in the place of higher moral values. In Christianity the offense is committed directly against God; human beings are seeking to usurp the place of God. If environmental theology admittedly does not speak directly of God, the difference seems to be more a matter of vocabulary than of the essence of belief.

Contemporary environmentalism seems to be responding to the needs of a secular age when traditional religion has lost its force in the lives of many people. Indeed, to speak in traditional Judeo-Christian terms of the sacredness of Creation, of God's plan for the world, of the importance in God's plan of every individual species, is to be excluded from mainstream political and policy discussion. What is possible in the mainstream is to devise a whole new language — necessarily grounded in a secular vocabulary — to express much the same substance. Contemporary environmentalism may in fact be attracting such a large following because it is serving that linguistic purpose, because it provides a sense of meaning to people who otherwise would lack religion in their lives.

The borrowing of old religious themes has been a pervasive feature of the modern age.[44] The great Protestant theologian, Paul Tillich, once rated Marx "the most successful of all theologians since the Reformation."[45] It was said of French socialism in the nineteenth century that it was "Catholicism, minus God."[46] It might similarly be said today of important segments of contemporary environmentalism that they offer Calvinism, minus God.[47] It is a faith with a particular appeal in an American society that has its deepest roots not in Catholicism, but in a Calvinist and Puritan outlook on the world first brought by the early settlers of New England.

More broadly, these elements of environmentalism are making a call for a revival of religious faith in the face of the corrosive influence of modernity on traditional religion. The "post-modern" age, if it is truly upon us, may in fact prove to be a time of great religious ferment. New religions — or old faiths in new forms — may emerge to replace the modern gospel of progress. Who can believe any longer in the transcendent powers of progress, when the twentieth century has been marked by world wars, genocide, and so many other horrors of scientifically and economically "advanced" nations and peoples?

SCIENCE VERSUS ENVIRONMENTALISM?

By and large, institutional science in America has not seen itself as in opposition to environmental religion. Indeed, many current scientists are active participants in the environmental movement. However, a new sense that a conflict may exist has emerged among some scientists in recent years. Environmental creationism may in reality be no more congenial to scientific orthodoxy than Christian creationism has been. In 1992 more than 200 scientists, including 27 American Nobel prize winners, presented an appeal to the heads of state attending the Earth Summit in Rio de Janeiro. Addressing the rise of religious environmentalism, their statement declared that "we are worried, at the dawn of the twenty-first century, at the emergence of an irrational ideology which is opposed to scientific and industrial progress and impedes economic and social development."[48]

For their part, a number of leading environmental thinkers have acknowledged that a deep tension exists between their convictions and the basic outlook of modern science. For example, Bill Devall and George Sessions explain that "deep ecology goes beyond the so-called factual scientific level to the level of self and Earth Wisdom."[49] They quote approvingly the observation of biologist Neil Everndon that "ecology undermines not only the growth addict and the chronic developer but science itself."[50] They find that the use of science to master and to control nature — at the heart of the western vision of "progress" — must be rejected in no uncertain terms.

A remarkable development seems to be occurring in American life at the end of the twentieth century. Religion, which in a secular age has been banished from the center of public life, is returning, so to speak, through the back door. It is, surprisingly enough, among leading segments of "avant-garde" opinion that the rediscovery of old religion is most influential. Our new environmental prophets are telling us, if in a brand new vocabulary designed for a secular age, that God exists and that his message — encountered most directly in Nature — must be heeded at the peril of future human existence. For the many sophisticates of the twentieth century, who have believed that modernity and scientific progress must gradually mean the end of religion, events today must fill them with a great sense of surprise, a deep sense of irony and perhaps considerable unease as well. Yet today's events can be seen historically as simply another instance of that particularly American phenomenon — religious revivalism. As each wave of pioneers moved further westward to tame the wilderness and wave the banner of progress, they were followed by a generation which sought spiritual redemption, but in a form different from their brethren back East or back in Europe.

The emotional power of "to restore" is derived from its ability to summon perhaps the core message of the religious heritage of the west — that human beings have fallen into deep sinfulness, and must be restored to their original natural condition of innocence and harmony. This task requires good works and men and women of true faith. As more and more people see the light, we can at least hope that paradise on earth will be restored. Even for those who do not believe this to be literally true, the image is powerful, the poetry immensely appealing. Perhaps some of the skeptics actually believe it more than they readily admit.

NOTES

1. Gordon W. Thayer (ed.). 1992. Restoring the Nation's Marine Environment. Maryland Sea Grant, College Park, Maryland, p. 638.

2. Ibid., p. 653.

3. Ibid., p. 662.

4. Claudia Mills. 1992. Preserving Endangered Species: Why Should We Care? in Mills (ed.). Values and Public Policy. Harcourt Brace Jovanovich, New York, p. 37.

5. See Roderick Frazier Nash. 1989. The Rights of Nature: A History of Environmental Ethics. University of Wisconsin Press, Madi-

son; also Bryan G. Norton. Fall 1991. Thoreau's insect analogies: or why environmentalists hate mainstream economists. Environmental Ethics 13(3):235-251.

6. Mills, p. 39.

7. Ibid., p. 39.

8. Genesis 1:27.

9. See Bryan G. Norton (ed.). 1986. The Preservation of Species. Princeton University Press, Princeton, N.J. and Bryan G. Norton. 1987. Why Preserve Natural Variety? Princeton University Press, Princeton, New Jersey.

10. Steven Fox. 1985. The American Conservation Movement: John Muir and His Legacy. University of Wisconsin Press, Madison.

11. Mills, p. 41.

12. Ibid., pp. 40-41.

13. Ibid., p. 42.

14. Mark Sagoff. 1992. The biotechnology controversy. In Mills, op. cit., p. 46.

15. Ibid., p. 46.

16. Ibid., p. 47.

17. Ibid., p. 47.

18. Anthony A. Hoekema. 1977. Amillennialism in Robert G. Clouse (ed.). The Meaning of the Millennium: Four Views. InterVarsity Press, Downers Grove, Illinois, p. 187.

19. John Calvin. Institutes of the Christian Religion. All materials quoted from the Institutes below are from a recent compendium. See Hugh T. Kerr (ed.). 1989. Calvin's Institutes: A New Compendium. Westminster/John Knox Press, Louisville, Kentucky, p. 41.

20. Ibid., p. 26.

21. Ibid., pp. 26, 99.

22. Ibid., p. 27.

23. Arthur A. Ekirch. 1963. Man and Nature in America. Columbia University Press, New York, pp. 51-52.

24. Christopher Lasch. 1991. The True and Only Heaven: Progress and its Critics. Norton, New York, pp. 269-70.

25. See Robert H. Nelson. 1991. Reaching for Heaven on Earth: The Theological Meaning of Economics. Rowman and Littlefield, Lanham, Maryland.

26. Colleen McDannell and Bernhard Lang. 1988. Heaven: A History. Yale University Press, New Haven, p. 118.

27. Ibid., p. 142.

28. Ibid.

29. Jean Starobinski. 1988. Jean-Jacques Rousseau: Transparency and Obstruction. University of Chicago Press, Chicago.

30. Dave Foreman. 1989. The destruction of wilderness. Earth First! - The Radical Environmental Journal. Decmber 21.

31. Ibid., p. 20.

32. Ibid.

33. Dave Foreman. 1991. Confessions of an Eco-Warrior. Harmony Books, New York, Chapter 17.

34. Bill McKibben. 1989. The End of Nature. Random House, New York, p. 186.

35. Ibid., p. 180.

36. Ibid., p. 50.

37. John McCormick. 1989. Reclaiming Paradise: The Global Environmental Movement. University of Indiana Press, Bloomington.

38. The Last Eden. 1992. Time. July 13: 45.

39. William K. Stevens. 10 August 1993. The heavy hand of European settlement. New York Times, p. C1.

40. Ronald L. Numbers. 1992. The Creationists: The Evolution of Scientific Creationism. University of California Press, Berkeley, p. ix.

41. Mills, op. cit., pp. 37-38.

42. Ibid., p. 39.

43. Ibid., pp. 38-39.

44. See Nelson, op. cit.

45. Paul Tillich. 1967. A History of Christian Thought: From its Judaic and Hellenistic Origins to Existentialism. Simon and Schuster, New York, p. 221.

46. F. A. Hayek. 1979. The Counter-Revolution of Science: Studies on the Abuse of Reason. Liberty Press, Indianapolis, p. 221.

47. See also Robert H. Nelson. 1991. Environmental Calvinism: the Judeo-Christian roots of eco-theology in Roger E. Meiners and Bruce Yandle (eds.). Taking the Environment Seriously. Rowman and Littlefield, Lanham, Maryland; and Robert H. Nelson. Summer 1990. Unoriginal sin: the Judeo-Christian roots of eco-theology. Policy Review.

48. Reprinted in the Wall Street Journal. 1992. June 1: op. ed. page.

49. Bill Devall and George Sessions. 1985. Deep Ecology. Peregrine Smith Books, Salt Lake City, p. 65.

50. Neil Everndon. 1978. Beyond Ecology. In Bill Devall and George Sessions, op. cit., p. 48.

5

Managing the Unmanageable

MICHAEL THOMPSON AND ALEX TRISOGLIO

The science that supplies us with the facts that enable us to define the problems — such as those that we perceive as afflicting our enclosed coastal seas — is in considerable disarray. The argument, recently summarized in a number of readable books on chaos and complexity, is that the science on which we have depended has missed out all the squiggly bits and, unfortunately, it is the squiggly bits that matter.[1] Esoteric though this may sound, it has some far-reaching implications for policy.

    The intrinsic complexity of ecosystems and social systems renders them fundamentally different from non-complex systems, that is, from systems in which the linear cause-and-effect relationships between components render them predictable and manageable. Traditional policy making is appropriate only to non-complex systems. It involves establishing the facts, weighing up the probable costs and benefits of various possible interventions, and moving from there to the right answer. But, in setting out to manage things like enclosed coastal seas, we have put ourselves far beyond the reach of this "Newtonian" approach: the approach in which we find the right answer by the single-minded pursuit of a single rationality. In our attempt to comprehend not just ecological and social systems, but their interactions, we have placed ourselves, whether we like it or not, in a world of complexity, multiple rationalities, chaos, sensitivity to initial conditions, non-linearities and intrinsic unpredictability. Reaching, uncritically, for our familiar Newtonian tools — neo-classical economics, in particular, but also things like risk assessment and the "realist" approach to international relations — we are committing ourselves to a most unwise path. We are aspiring to *manage the unmanageable*.

What, then, is the wise path? The first essential is a thorough-going rejection of Newtonian policy making, the tools on which it relies and simplistic and insufficiently variegated understandings of social institutions. Then, with that cleared out of the way, we can set about constructing a new, post-Newtonian approach, and identifying the sorts of tools that would be appropriate to it. These tools, of course, are all around us: in notions such as decision making under contradictory certitudes, myths of nature, visions of the future, the theory of surprise, clumsy institutions, and indicators of technological inflexibility. This chapter is concerned with only a few of these. The change in approach that is entailed in this embracing of plurality and complexity is profound and more than a little confusing given our Newtonian understandings and expectations of the world. Before explaining this requisite variety of institutional forms and the various constructions of nature that accompany it, and to show that such discussions are not entirely esoteric, we relate a little story to illustrate the complexity involved in recent attempts to manage the Baltic environment.

A SHORT STORY

The Swedes already have very clean power stations, but they want to make them even cleaner. The money they propose to spend will certainly produce a slight reduction in Sweden's polluting emissions, but the same money spent on improving the filthy power stations of its neighbor across the Baltic — Poland — would make an enormous difference to Sweden's environment. Indeed, if the Swedes were to spend the money in Egypt they would do better than if they spent it on themselves.[2] This little story suggests that the policy path towards a healthy Baltic Sea is far from smooth, and, in the context of international relations, it raises a host of awkward and confusing questions. After posing and discussing a number of questions to illustrate this analytical mess, we will suggest a way out.

Should we see Egypt as a Baltic nation? If Egypt is a Baltic nation do we, perhaps, need to see Poland as a Mediterranean nation? Should Swedish money which is spent in Poland in pusuit of greater environmental quality for Swedes be considered domestic spending?

The Swedish voters, during uncertain and recessionary times, are unlikely to warm to the proposal that their taxes be spent in Poland. But the pill could be sweetened by insisting that all the contracts for the work in Poland be placed with Swedish companies.

Assuming that in these days of "late capitalism" you can tell whether a company is Swedish, would that be fair to companies in other countries — companies that could probably do the work much cheaper? Would such a disregard for fair competition be fair to the Swedish voters and taxpayers? In view of these confusions over fairness and competition, should all these Swedish-Polish-Egyptian transactions be seen as trade or as aid? What about "moral hazards"?

There are no incentives here for Poland, or Egypt, to clean up their acts. Quite the opposite: the dirtier they make themselves the more aid they can expect.

Might the whole tangled web make more sense if we looked at it, not from the perspectives of the individual nation states, but from the points of view of the different enclosed coastal seas: the Baltic, the Mediterranean and, presumably, many others?

Of course, seas don't have points of view. But we can pretend that they have one, and that they prefer to be free from substances like mercury, and that they are happiest when there are lots of fishes swimming around inside them. In other words, we could agree to treat these common property resources as the "primary actors," and then decide where the money should be spent, Sweden, Poland, Egypt or wherever, so that the seas themselves get the greatest improvement per currency unit. Such "joint implementation" requires a remarkable level of agreement and mutual trust between the large number of nations involved.

What about national sovereignty?

Countries that have grave doubts about surrendering a few powers to the European Community are hardly likely to jump at the suggestion that they should hand the whole lot over to a watery waste that can not even articulate what it wants.

All of the above questions assume, as does most policy analysis, that environmental improvement costs money but, as John Adams is always pointing out, it need not. He notes: "There are expensive ways by which a fat person can lose weight — health farms, exercise machines, liposuction — but walking or cycling to work and eating less are likely to be more effective and actually save money."[3] This is the neglected consumption-reducing option, in which all those expensive and fattening cream buns that one goes without are translated directly into money in the pocket. Much the same is true of the environment. All those bilateral transfers of funds, and all those ingenious retrofittings of power stations, may just be a way of perpetuating grossly inappropriate lines of technological development. Perhaps governments and firms are the problem, not the solution.

Could it be that the biggest improvement in environmental quality could come from the grassroots: from major shifts in consumer preferences as citizens come to trust activist groups, like Greenpeace, more than government ministers and advertising agencies?

The implication here is that activist groups are opposed to cozy alliances between government and business. However one must be careful not to assume that this is always the case. Businesses, especially those that are responding to the consumption-reduction demands of their customers, can fall out of love with government and start cuddling-up to the critics of the established government-business alliance.[4] The CFC-free refrigerator that Greenpeace has recently helped develop is an example of this "new alliance." There may emerge more of this kind of institutional pairing and less of the type generally assumed.[5]

THERE'S MORE TO LIFE THAN HIERARCHIES AND MARKETS

One plausible answer to the "trade or aid" question — an answer that also copes with the moral hazard business — is that the transfers to Poland begin as aid but, over time, change into trade. The argument here is that Poland, thanks to its years of communist central planning, now has such an outmoded technological base that it really is in no position to compete with Western market economies. The aid transfers, therefore, should continue until that disadvantage has disappeared. At that moment the playing field will be level and trade — fair trade between roughly equal partners — should begin.

This argument draws on the familiar institutional distinction between *markets* (the competing players merrily bidding and bargaining with one another) and *hierarchies* (the benign authorities who ensure that the conditions needed for the playing of this trading game are in place).[6] There is much good sense in this distinction. The trouble, however, is that since neither markets nor hierarchies are in the business of reducing our intake of cream buns, this cannot be the whole story. The hierarchies-and-markets framework is deficient on two important counts. First, it is an incomplete typology. Second, it does not take account of the very different convictions about the world and its people that each of these arrangements for conducting social transactions induces in the individuals who constitute those arrangements. In other words, it is *insufficiently variegated* and it ignores the social construction of human and physical nature. Once these two deficiencies have been remedied, we will have a framework capable of sorting out messes like those that currently engulf Swedes, Poles, Egyptians, and the Baltic and Mediterranean Seas.

THE REQUISITE VARIETY OF INSTITUTIONAL FORMS

Since markets promote competition and institute equality whilst hierarchies set limits on competition and institute inequality, there are two discriminators at work in this classic distinction. Thus, the full typology includes two other permutations: equality without competition, or "egalitarianism" and inequality with competition, or "fatalism" (see Figure 5.1).[7] It is the egalitarians — the Greenpeaces and Earth First!s of this world — who are the cream bun rejectors. As their dumping of tons of non-returnable bottles on the steps of the headquarters of multinational companies suggests, they are not entirely convinced that market forces will solve all our environmental ills. Their T-shirt, with the rhetorical question, "Who Saved the Whales: Greenpeace or the Royal Society?" similarly confirms their less-than-total trust in the hierarchical institutions of the modern state. Egalitarianism is a distinct and undoubtedly influential institutional category that is uncompromisingly opposed to both markets and hierarchies: the only institutional forms that conventional analysis recognizes.

Fatalists, for their part, are a sort of black hole, into which disappears everything that is produced by the other three quadrants

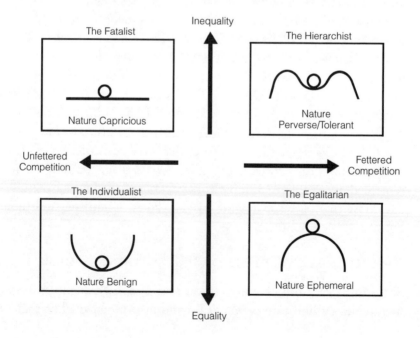

Figure 5.1. The full typology.

but not wanted by them. John Carman, an archaeologist, has called fatalists "dumpees": a neologism that nicely captures the way in which those who find themselves on the outside of all three organized ways of life — markets, hierarchies and egalitarian groups — cope with that situation: cheerfully guzzling whatever good things happen to come their way and stoically enduring the bad.[8] Fatalists lose little sleep over things like ozone holes that may or may not be opening up above them. After all, if the holes are there what can they do about them? "Why Bother?" is the fatalist's not unreasonable response to the policy issues that so incite those who are not fatalists.

It would be a mistake, however, to conclude from this that fatalists are irrelevant to the policy debate. Fatalists are the great "risk absorbers" (acceptance and rejection are not issues) without whom none of the actors who *are* engaged in the debate could get their policies to work. Just as rubbish — that which has no value — is vital to the viability of that from which it is excluded (the dynamic process by which value is formed and transformed), so fatalists are indispensable to deciding policy. They are indispensable to the policy process precisely because they take no part in it.[9]

Increasing the number of institutional varieties from two (markets and hierarchies) to four takes us well out of the reach of predictable change, or well beyond the sort of situation in which we can say, "if we make this intervention, that will happen." For instance, if there are only two places to be and you set out, as Margaret Thatcher did, to knock people out of hierarchy then they will all end up in the other one: markets. The evidence suggests that this did not happen.[10] While some made this transition and embraced the "enterprise culture," others ended up in fatalism (the "underclass") and still others entered into an unstratified solidarity (egalitarianism) whose members were bitterly critical both of that which Mrs. Thatcher was against (hierarchy) and that which she was for (individualism). Mrs. Thatcher's downfall, therefore, can be explained in part by this mismatch between what she expected would happen and what actually transpired. That is where the theory of surprise comes in, because Newtonian policies are being applied to a non-Newtonian system.

THE SOCIAL CONSTRUCTIONS OF NATURE

Surprises result from discrepancies between expectation and outcome, or between how we believe the world to be (our myth of nature) and how it actually is. For instance, if we believe, like individualists, that nature is so robust as to be able to bounce back from any insult we happen to inflict then we will be surprised when it collapses catastrophically (when suddenly every last oyster snuffs it, or the earth's atmosphere flips across into a new system-state that happens to contain no oxygen). Similarly, if we are convinced, like hierarchists, that we can manage natural systems then we will be surprised when they turn out to be unmanageable. Conversely, if we believe, like egalitarians, that nature is precarious — that the word "ecosystem" should always be preceded by the word "fragile," and that we must all tread lightly on the earth — then we will be surprised when those who have disregarded those injunctions, and who have persisted in stamping wildly about (the individualists and, in a rather more disciplined way, the hierarchists), do not get the come-uppances predicted for them. Finally, if we are convinced, like fatalists, that nature operates without rhyme or reason then we will be surprised if the cosmic fruit machine keeps on coughing up in our direction. In other words, no event is absolutely surprising. Surprise is relative: relative to the largely unquestioned assumptions as to how the world is — the myth of nature — of the person who suffers the surprise.

These myths of nature can be condensed (see Figure 5.1) into little pictures of a ball in a landscape, each of which captures, in elegant and simple form, some essence of experience and wisdom. Newtonian policy makers tend to get uneasy at this stage of the argument. The world, they insist, *must* be just one of these four ways, and science will tell us which one it is. Our reply is twofold.

Part I: Much recent work in fields such as ecology, evolutionary theory and artificial life suggests that the world, at times and in places, can be any of these four ways.[11] Indeed, so the strong argument goes, it *has* to be. After all, if the world was not sometimes benign (ball in a basin) the omnivorous, fast-breeding and opportunistic species would never be able to prosper. Conversely, if the world was never perverse/tolerant (ball in a depression on top of a mesa) then the climax community, with its specialized, slow-breeding and cautious constituents would never come into existence. If the region of stability — the depression on the mesa — did not implode from time to time there would be no compost — no generalized resource on which all the different strategists could draw in the process of renewal that the climax community's collapse makes possible.[12]

Part II: Science can and often does reduce uncertainty about the world, and there are those (the Newtonians) who believe that one day it may succeed in getting rid of it all. Nevertheless, in any policy debate relevant to coastal seas, that day, if ever it dawns (and the non-Newtonians believe that it won't), is a long way off. The shape of the dose/response curve at low levels of radiation is a nice example. If it is *linear*, as those who advise government on safety standards insist it is, then the risks of nuclear technology are "neutral," in the sense that they are neither all reducing themselves nor all increasing themselves. But they are manageable: all that is needed are certified experts to establish just where the dividing line between increasing and decreasing risks lies, and legally enforced regulations to ensure that the technology remains on the right side of that line. This is the myth of nature *perverse/tolerant*, and it can be discerned as a major (indeed, often the dominant) input to any debate over environmental policy. Whenever we hear such phrases as "assimilatory capacities," "safe limits," "permissible loads," "carrying capacities," or "tolerable risks" we are in the presence of this — the hierarchist's — myth.

But if the dose/response curve is not linear but *quadratic* (as many pro-nuclear types are convinced it is) then there will be a threshold below which no harm will befall anyone. Provided the technology is engineered below this threshold (the logics of legal liability and insurance premiums will ensure that it is) then statutory regulation is unnecessary. This, of course, is the myth of nature benign. Since there is no region of instability as in the perverse/tolerant case, individual firms that get it wrong will harm only themselves (again through liability and insurance premiums).

There is no risk of triggering catastrophe for the totality, and therefore no justification for placing restrictions on individual experimentation. On the contrary, trial-and-error is something to be actively encouraged: that is how we interrogate nature and discover new ways of transforming raw materials into valuable resources. Stop this process, these myth-holders maintain, and you really will provoke disaster.

However, if the dose/response curve is neither linear, nor quadratic but *parabolic* (that is, it bends away from the linear in the opposite direction to the quadratic curve) then the risks are neither neutral nor decreasing. They are irrevocably increasing. This means that the more of the technology we have the more we will be harmed by it. The myth of nature ephemeral is the set of convictions that is held by those who are the nuclear industry's most persistent and intransigent critics. Trial-and-error, if this is how the world is, must not be permitted, because the first mistake likely will be the last. Even statutory regulation is unacceptable, because it assumes there are limits within which catastrophe is not possible. The egalitarian's myth, however, allows no safe limits. Trial-without-error, or the precautionary principle, is the only way.[13]

This dose/response curve story can be seen as a parable for all environmental decision making. With so much hanging in the balance — the future of an entire technology, not to mention "life as we know it" — it would be nice to know what the shape the dose/response curve really is. In other words, if science is going to sort this one out, it must tell us which of these contradictory certitudes is the right one. Unfortunately, in order to make this determination, in the present state of science, you would have to attempt to give tumors to more mice than there are atoms in the universe. Even so, the builders of the different certitudes would still be able to take up different positions on the vexed question of how to extrapolate the findings from rodents to humans.

Pending the arrival of this Scientific Millennium when all uncertainty will finally vanish (a millennium, moreover, that the non-Newtonians argue has been cancelled), what can be done? The answer lies in the rejection of single answers. If each myth of nature captures some essence of experience and wisdom, then the Newtonian insistence that we latch onto just one and discard the other three has to be wrong because it deliberately discards three-quarters of what little with which we have to work. This is clearly a stupid way of making decisions under contradictory certitudes.

So the answer, whatever it is, must have to do with keeping all the certitudes "in the game" while, at the same time, reducing all those uncertainties that (a) can be reduced (given the present state of the scientist's art) and (b) would make a difference if they were reduced. Once policy making has been re-defined in this way, the answer is all around us: in all those institutional arrangements that, for one reason or another, have addressed themselves to the task of living with, and making the most of, that which they cannot get rid. The jurist, Michael Schapiro has dubbed these arrangements "clumsy institutions," and clumsy they are when compared with the elegant and beautifully optimized structures that are produced by those who insist on just a single truth: just one out of the four repositories of available wisdom and experience.[14] But clumsiness is to be welcomed if, like the flight of the bumblebee, it works. Elegance is of dubious worth if it can only be secured by the denial of ignorance.

OUT WITH THE ELEGANT, IN WITH THE CLUMSY

The implications of this argument are more easily grasped if we distinguish between two very different meanings of the word "manage." One, the meaning we have been using up to now, is synonymous with control. This idea refers to systems such as a factory production line, but not an enclosed coastal sea or an economy, that can be fully understood and taken command of in their entirety. While this meaning conjures up images of gung-ho, can-do characters in smart suits and tearing hurries, the second meaning is best represented by our colleague Steve Rayner's Auntie Flo. Auntie Flo's husband passed away, and she herself was getting on in years. Living by herself, with little in the way of savings, she became a cause of concern to her relatives. "Don't worry about me," she told them brightly, "I'll manage!"

Auntie Flo did not take complete control of anything. Rather, she coped successfully and effectively with a system that she well knew was, to a large and not entirely knowable extent, beyond her control. We have no quarrel with this meaning of the word "manage." What is more, we suspect that those chief executive officers who are successful in keeping their vast multinationals afloat on the boundless and turbulent ocean of life, also tend to see themselves as Auntie Flos. Somewhere between their dizzy heights and Auntie Flo's humble achievements, the first meaning of the word "manage," that involving control, insinuates itself. It insinuates itself in government, in "middle management" and, most of all, in policy advice and in the harnessing of science to public policy. We argue that it should not. In a complex world, when it comes to managing things like economies and ecosystems, only Auntie Flo's meaning is valid.[15] In practical terms this means we must depose of the invalid meaning and replace it with the valid one. Neither of these tasks is going to be easy. However, as the history of physics demonstrates, they are not impossible.

THE RISE OF NEWTONIAN DECISION MAKING

For centuries the great challenge for physicists was astronomical: to predict the movements of the celestial bodies. Success, when it came, was so great that it transcended the bounds of astronomy: Newton's laws of motion made *everything* predictable. Or did they? They certainly made a lot of things predictable — nowadays even cheap wristwatches can predict solar eclipses — but a lot is not everything. This little quibble over the difference between *a* lot and *the* lot, however, was brushed aside by those who embraced what might be called "Newtonian thinking."

Newtonian thinking is based on deterministic laws. Problems are dealt with by measuring the values of the relevant variables, inserting them into the appropriate analytical equations and then solving those equations to find the solutions. Newtonian description, therefore, is mechanistic, deterministic and equilibrium-assuming. It has been spectacularly successful, not just for objects like planets and billiard balls, but in the much less discrete realm of thermodynamics as well. Indeed, the Newtonian paradigm —

Newtonian thinking institutionalized into widely shared habits of thought — soon came to dominate the fields of motion and heat which, together, formed the basis for the Industrial Revolution. This paradigm remained in force, and not just in physics, through the end of the nineteenth century. Other, initially less confident, fields of intellectual inquiry — most notably economics — modelled themselves on the physical sciences with the resultant "physics envy." The irony, however, is that these disciplines modelled themselves on what they thought physics was just as physics itself was painfully discovering that that was not how it was.

At the beginning of the twentieth century, the physical sciences underwent a profound revolution: a revolution spearheaded by the ideas of relativity and quantum physics. Now, at the end of the century, these once-revolutionary ideas have been augmented with notions like complexity and chaos, and supercomputers and the software of artificial life have been added to the array of laboratory instruments and techniques. Physicists, in consequence, have almost gotten used to a life of permanent revolution, and they have travelled a long way.

At the end of the nineteenth century, physics (and engineering, which physicists like to see as applied physics) presided over a world of predictability, mechanistic behavior, and manageability (in the controlling sense of the word). Machines could be designed, steamships, bridges, and railways could be built, and the world could be "civilized." Today, physics looks at a world of unpredictability: a world in which much behavior is far from equilibrium and in which there is very little that is manageable in the way the Victorians took control of things. Where once we thought we had conquered the world, we now realize that we cannot even forecast next week's weather. We have moved into the complex world, and physicists are entering a new period of humility about what can be predicted, managed, and controlled. What is more, they realize that it will always be this way: we have come up against the fundamental limits of uncertainty, ignorance, and uncontrollability. So where does this leave the physics-envying economists? The short answer is: "A long way behind, and in a deplorable state." The longer answer, however, will be more constructive: to close this yawning gap and banish from the complex world the invalid meaning of the word "manage."

The economist's array of tools, each of which fits neatly into the tool-bag known as "neoclassical economics," has been developed entirely within the Newtonian paradigm. These tools are routinely relied upon in the design and evaluation of government policy in every industrialized nation of the world. Industrialized…Newtonian…neoclassical: the combination is no accident. Economic policy, for instance, is still a matter of determining the right model, inserting the relevant variables, and finding the answer. Of course, there are too many variables to manually determine the solution in the way the Victorians did; now powerful computers to do that. The principle, therefore, has remained the same. General equilibrium models can be used to reproduce the "momentum" of economic trends, and hence predict outcomes in, say, twelve months' time. Naturally, this sort of advance information is essential for effective policy making. Decisions on interest rates, money supply, taxation, employment and so on — decisions that are vital for our economic development — can only be taken with a clear understanding of the consequences. That, at any rate, is the conviction of all those who share the Newtonian habit of thought. There would be nothing wrong with this if they were dealing with a simple system, and steering the economy was no more of an undertaking than putting a man on the moon.

Most policy making is a variant on this basic and profoundly flawed theme. Thus, transportation ministries carry out elaborate cost-benefit analyses of proposed new roads, and ministries of the environment hire economists to ask people how much they would be willing to pay to preserve some landscape they have never seen or to prevent the extinction of some animal they have never heard of (contingent valuation, as it is called). Whatever the policy area, the shared conviction is that the consequences of actions have to be modelled, costs and benefits have to be assigned to the outcomes, and good decision making becomes a matter of choosing the path that maximizes benefits and minimizes costs.[16] Economists, and those whom they advise, are still in a world of predictability and equilibrium. They believe in a world that is manageable in a way that those on whom the economists have modelled themselves — the physicists — know is no longer valid.

According to this argument, those who are trying to manage in this invalid manner should be running into all sorts of surprises. They certainly are. Economic predictions are often spectacularly wrong, nor are they getting any better. Indeed, economic forecasters consistently do worse than weather forecasters, which is why they have to wear sober business suits and carry confidence-inspiring briefcases, while weather forecasters can (and do) wear anything they want.

THE FALL OF NEWTONIAN DECISION MAKING

Despite their increasingly farcical predicament, there is little evidence that physics-envying economists are prepared to admit the error of their ways. However, this does not mean that things are not changing. As with the paradigm shift in physics at the start of the twentieth century, or the more recent collapse of the Soviet Union, the replacement is accepted only when the evidence of the failure of that which is in place becomes overwhelming. If it was hard for physics, where resistance came only from physicists, imagine how much harder it is going to be in economics, where the defenders of the established ways march shoulder-to-shoulder, down the corridors of power, with politicians and the policy makers. Of course, one does not look for the first signs of paradigm change in the heart of the established paradigm. Rather, one looks in places such as business and industry where pragmatism, not dogmatism, prevails. One looks for the Auntie Flos.

These pragmatists, it turns out, have themselves been looking across at those who form the core of the established paradigm, and they do not like what they see. For example Pierre Wack, former head of strategic planning at Shell, stated, "in the summer of 1981 the median one-year-ahead forecast of five prominent forecasters had predicted 2.1 percent growth in the U.S. economy for 1982. Instead, the economy plunged into deep recession, with a GNP decline of 1.8 percent. This is like forecasting partly cloudy and getting a ten-inch snowstorm instead."[17] Both Peter Drucker, the doyen of management science, and Simon Jenkins, former editor of *The Times*, point out that economic ministries are actually powerless in a complex global economy, and that the role of future Chancellors of the Exchequer will be little more than that of today's weathermen.[18]

Pragmatists are interested in what works and what does not work. They quickly pick up on the distinction between simple and complex systems. If Newtonian decision making only works well for simple systems, then we must become sensitive to signs that tell us when we have strayed into the complex. In fact, the signs are not so little: the predictive success of Newtonian models plummets, and solutions based on just one definition of the problem at hand are bitterly resisted by those who cling to different certitudes. However, the dogmatists refuse to read the signs.

The European Commission, in discussing environment and development policy, correctly observed that different "policy actors" place very different values, and very different kinds of values, on animal species.[19] They note that "the pharmaceutical industry would probably put a higher value on an indicator of diverse genetic resources than would the public — who might not even want to value them (sic) at all [in monetary terms, that is], on ethical grounds."[20] In other words, these actors do not, and could not, agree. But the Commission insists on a single (monetary) value, because "we have to reach an agreed figure if our information is to guide policy."[21] Put plainly, they are saying that the economic model on which they rely assumes that the world is not the way they know it actually is.

WHAT CAN BE DONE?

The first lesson is to recognize that what is good for the simple is not automatically good for the complex; and seas, like all large ecosystems, certainly lie in the realm of the complex. If neoclassical economics requires highly educated (and highly paid) bureaucrats to spout nonsense, then neoclassical economics (regardless of the light it may shed on how markets function) is useless for management. Since neoclassical economics assumes agreement where there is disagreement, singularity where there is plurality, simplicity where there is complexity, certainty where there is uncertainty, and predictability where there is unpredictability, it is, quite simply, a non-starter in the complex world. If it is no use — and it is no use — *don't use it.*

If neoclassical economics is not to be used, then what is? There are already a number of well developed ideas about how to work, Auntie Flo-like, with complex systems. The disagreements over values that the European Commission cannot handle, for instance, are nicely captured by the typology of myths of nature that we have set out. Much of modern management science is about how to respect, and make the most of, this sort of ineradicable plurality. Scenario planning, for instance, is based fairly and squarely on disagreements about what the future holds. Different "visions of the future" are laid out, in colorful and often alarming terms, and different business strategies are tried out against them to see how they would fare. Strategies that are marvelously successful in one future, but disastrous in the others, can then be assessed against those strategies that turn out to be resilient across all the futures. It turns out that good scenarios by and large capture the plurality that is predicted by the fourfold typology that underlies the theory of surprise. Thus, successful management techniques can now be strengthened and developed further by bringing practice and theory together.

Theorists of complex systems, armed with increasingly powerful computers, have also found new tools for modelling evolutionary (that is, profoundly under-determined) behavior. Plurality is a pre-requisite for these new tools — artificial life, as they are collectively called. Programs that represent different behavioral strategies are developed and then put into a computer and left to evolve. Modelers of artificial life are non-Newtonian. They do not need to be able to find equations that describe the system, nor do they have to try to solve for equilibrium conditions. All they do is describe some strategies, let them evolve and then, after a few thousand "generations," look to see which ones are doing well and how the interacting "individuals" (automata with strategies) combine to form the whole.

These tools have now been used to model ecosystems, financial markets and many other complex systems, and they have subsumed all the "single certitude," prediction-based models into an exploratory approach that grants some credence to all myths of nature. Of course, the prediction-based modelers do not know this yet, but they are about to be swept away in what non-Newtonian economists call a Schumpeterian gale of destruction.[22] We can not model seas with certitude; we can not control them. Instead, we must put these ideas, the theory of surprise, scenario planning, artificial life and clumsy institutions together, add some intellectual spice and get Auntie Flo to stir the whole lot vigorously — and a much more productive way of managing ourselves in the midst of the unmanageable may emerge.

NOTES

1. See for example, James Gleick. 1987. Chaos: Making a New Science. Penguin, London and Viking-Penguin, New York; M. Mitchell Waldrop. 1992. Complexity and the Emerging Science at the Edge of Order and Chaos. Simon and Schuster, New York; and E. Christopher Zeeman. 1977. Catastrophe Theory: Selected Papers, 1972-77. Addison-Wesley, Reading, Massachusetts.

2. The money needed to reduce CO^2 emissions in Sweden by 10 percent could achieve greater reductions if spent in Egypt (Swedish Energy Administration, 1989). Similarly, 90 percent of the acid rain damage in Sweden is caused by SO^2 and NO_x that are emitted from sources that are outside Sweden — in Eastern Europe and Britain, mostly. In addition, most of the pollutants in the seawater that laps Sweden's Baltic shores come from sewage that is not Swedish in origin.

3. John Adams. 1993. The Emperor's old clothes: the curious comeback of cost-benefit analysis. Environmental Values. 2(3):247-260

4. Michiel Schwarz and Michael Thompson. 1990. Divided We Stand: Redefining Politics, Technology and Social Choice. Har-

vester-Wheatsheaf, London and University of Pennsylvania Press, Philadelphia.

5. Ibid., especially Chapter 6.

6. Charles Lindblom. 1977. Politics and Markets: The World's Political-Economic Systems. Basic Books, New York and Oliver Williamson. 1975. Markets and Hierarchies, Analysis and Antitrust Implications: A Study in the Economics of Internal Organization. Free Press, New York.

7. For a complete description of this so-called cultural theory, including the centrally important role played by the fifth type (the "hermit"), see Michael Thompson, Richard Ellis and Aaron Wildavsky. 1990. Cultural Theory. West View, Oxford and Boulder, Colorado.

8. John Carman. 1992. Inverted World: Cultural Theory and Valuing Things From the Past. Unpublished paper presented at a graduate seminar, Department of Archaeology, University of Cambridge. April 30.

9. This is not just an analogy. Rubbish and fatalism (as Mark Sagoff argues in his contribution to this volume) are functionally related components in the complex dynamic processes that are entailed in the interaction of natural and social systems. For an explanation of the social processes by which value is conferred and withdrawn, see Michael Thompson. 1979. Rubbish Theory: The Creation and Destruction of Value. Oxford University Press, Oxford.

10. Michael Thompson. 1992. The dynamics of cultural theory and their implications for the enterprise culture. In Sean Hargreaves Heap and Angus Ross (eds.). Understanding the Enterprise Culture. Edinburgh University Press, Edinburgh, pp. 182-202.

11. Holling is the leading ecological theorist, both in terms of this essential plurality (which enables him to posit a fourfold "ecocycle") and in terms of the various sorts of surprises that are likely to befall those who aspire to control such systems. See C. S. Holling. 1986. The resilience of terrestrial ecosystems: local surprise and global change. In William C. Clark and R. E. Munn (eds.). Sustainable Development of the Biosphere. Cambridge University Press, Cambridge, pp. 292-320. Developments in evolutionary theory and artificial life are covered, in a non-technical way, in

Gleick, op. cit. and Waldrop, op. cit. An important precursor of this work is John Maynard Smith. 1982. Evolution and Theory of Games. Cambridge University Press, Cambridge.

12. This "strong argument," and its validity for both socio-cultural systems and ecosystems, is explained at length in Thompson et al. 1990, op. cit., Chapters 4 and 6.

13. For instance, M. MacGarvin. 1994. The implications of the precautionary principle for biological monitoring. Helgoländer Meeresunter, p. 49, which argues in favor of the precautionary principle by showing that "assumptions about the assimilative capacity of the environment...lack scientific rigor."

14. Michael H. Schapiro. 1988. Judicial selection and the design of clumsy institutions. Southern California Law Review 61(6):1555-69.

15. There are, of course, many situations — production lines, moon landings and so on — where this gung-ho meaning is valid because the simple systems involved permit a high level of predictability. However many systems — the weather, the economy, the global ecosystem, the evolution of technology and so on — are not like this. It is for these low-predictability systems that we should stop using Newtonian thinking and start using non-Newtonian thinking.

16. See, for example, Department of the Environment. 1991. Policy Appraisal and the Environment: a Guide for Government Departments. H.M. Stationery Office, London; Department of Transport. 1981. COBA 9. Assessments, Policy and Methods Division. Department of Transport, 2 Marsham Street, London SW1; H.M. Treasury. 1991. Economic Appraisal in Central Government: a Technical Guide for Government Departments. H. M. Stationery Office, London.

17. Pierre Wack. 1988. Scenarios: uncharted waters ahead. Harvard Business Review. September-October: 73-89.

18. Peter Drucker. 1989. The New Realities. Heinemann Professional Publishing, London; Simon Jenkins. 1990. The Sunday Times. February 11.

19. Commission of the European Communities. 9 November 1993. Environment and development: towards a European model of sus-

tainable development. Paper presented at a seminar on Environment and Development, Brussels.

20. Ibid., p. 8.

21. Ibid.

22. For examples of non-Newtonian economics see, for example, Joseph A. Schumpeter. 1911. Theory of Capitalist Development [English transl. 1934]; and 1939. Business Cycles. He was grappling with sudden discontinuous changes in technological evolution long before the mathematics for describing such non-linear behavior had been developed; Another "hero" is F. T. Moore, who dared to suggest that the long-run cost curve (the U-shape of which is an article of faith among neoclassical economists) might, in fact, be "scalloped." That is, it might allow for more than one optimal size for a production unit and hence for discontinuous jumps from one "best solution" to another. F. T. Moore. 1959. Economies of scale: some statistical evidence. Quarterly Journal of Economics. 73:232-245. Even Alfred Marshall refused to express his ideas in the form of equations, because he did not feel that "the forces that cause movement" could be adequately described by the sort of mathematics that gave rise to the general equilibrium models. Alfred Marshall. 1890. Principles of Economics [quote is from the 8th ed. 1922]. Macmillan, London; and W. Brian Arthur on "increasing returns to scale": phenomena whose existence has to be denied by the neoclassicists, because they would introduce "nonergodicity" into economic reasoning. That is, economists would have to concede that, often enough, small historical events, far from cancelling themselves out, actually determine the outcome. It is, of course, this "sensitivity to initial conditions" that puts economic systems into the realm of the complex and, in so doing, renders them inaccessible to Newtonian thinking. W. Brian Arthur. 1989. Competing technologies, increasing returns and lock-in by historical events: the dynamics of allocation under increasing returns. Economic Journal 99:116-31.

Part II

Scientists, Certainty, and Knowledge

6

When Ecology Doesn't Play Straight

Frieda B. Taub

Coastal seas are complex ecological systems upon which society often imposes an array of political jurisdictions. The science of ecology has not reached the stage of being reliably predictive, and ecologists acutely realize that it is imperative to select a proper scale of investigation for a given subject. Ecosystems are too complex and hierarchical for causes and effects to be linear for all but the most circumscribed sub-systems. As one variable changes, for example as tree density on a steep slope a hundred miles upstream is reduced by clearcutting, another may be affected, such as shrimp numbers in the receiving estuary. There is a relationship between the trees and the shrimp, but it may not be clear or linear: the trees and their roots bound the soil to the slope, but now that soil makes its way to the river emptying into the estuary, blanketing it in silt which covers the grasses where the shrimp lived, ultimately reducing the income of the shrimpers. Policy makers look for straightforward solutions to problems; they wish to pinpoint the cause and correct it with the least possible disruption of the status quo. When ecologists assist them in identifying such causes and solutions, they use the vocabulary of uncertainty, a concept which prickles generally risk averse policy makers.

131

In this chapter I review a case study of a successful — because the system is relatively simple — example of science demonstrating a predictable cause and effect relationship in a polluted lake system, and suggesting a solution. Lake ecosystems may seem less complex than those of enclosed seas, and some problems may be more intractable than eutrophication, but the necessary skills and principles at work at the science-policy interface are the same.

For many coastal environments, the increasing nutrient and toxicant inputs to receiving waters are current problems. Eutrophication is thought to contribute to the increasing frequency of red tide events, many of which are toxic, and to oxygen depletion of benthic communities. Although the catchment basin may be a clear ecosystem unit, it rarely corresponds to one specific governmental unit. Thus, the management of many enclosed coastal seas is complicated by the fact that they encompass numerous political entities.

To the naive individual, it would be seem logical to measure the inputs of each political unit, determine their proportion of the total inputs, and assign them their share of responsibility. If costly measures have to be invoked to reduce nutrient inputs, it would seem fair to assign costs according to the proportion of nutrients to be diverted by each governmental unit. If costs per unit of diverted nutrient were a constant, then it would be tempting to believe that costs, nutrient diversion, and ecological responses would be proportional to one another. It would be convenient if the ecology of enclosed seas responded so simply to nutrient inputs: more nutrients, proportionally more phytoplankton; less nutrients, proportionally less phytoplankton. Unfortunately, there are valid scientific reasons why the responses of lakes and enclosed coastal seas are often not so straightforward. In highly eutrophic areas with a long history of nutrient inputs, the first 50-90 percent of nutrient diversion may yield meager results, and no government is inclined to undertake expensive treatment and stringent regulation with only a meager response to show its constituency. Additional nutrient diversions may yield more impressive responses, albeit at ever higher costs, but each government wants its expenditures to be the most cost effective possible.

In many cases, observed ecological responses do not appear to be proportional to stress in any obvious manner. In many realistic cases, especially those involving enclosed coastal seas, continuing and increasing stresses appear to be absorbed by the system's assimilatory capacity without obvious effects that impel costly modifications. This may be an artifact of complex water movements and seasonal variability of biota. Measurements in estuaries are so variable that virtually any measurement is within "normal range." Often, existing sources of nutrients and toxicants increase their inputs, and new input sources arise. Each unit believes it has the right to contribute as much new pollution as every other unit, as a condition of fairness. This is often exacerbated by the existence of several entities which feel entitled, as a matter of historical practice, to use the resource for disposal, while new entities feel that their development depends on being allowed the same privileges as the historical polluters.

Early warnings of harm are often ignored because troublesome events are episodic, unpredictable and possibly caused by factors such as the weather. Subsequently, demonstrations of large scale harm are dismissed as being only vaguely related to controllable stresses or too expensive to correct given the uncertainties of improvements in the face of large scale expenditures. In the absence of strong proof of cause and effect, skeptics can undermine preventive or corrective actions, since these involve costs and restrictions. When troublesome events such as red tides, fish kills and anaerobic incidents are judged intolerable, the magnitude and cost of corrective action appears unreasonable. The frustrated ecologist is asked, "Why didn't you warn us and prevent the problems from occurring?"

Observed ecological responses often appear to be disproportionate to stress intensity because the stress is a necessary but not sufficient condition to cause observable damage. For example, for added nutrients to cause a demonstrated algal bloom, loss factors such as grazing, settling and horizontal dispersion must not mask the increase in algal cell production. Because observations are the net result of several processes, knowledge of isolated processes can fail to explain the observations. If any of these other factors change, in addition to changes in nutrients, then we don't expect nutrient information alone to predict ecosystem responses. Given the many processes involved, it is not surprising that ecosystem responses are often not proportional to the intensity of a stress. These ecological uncertainties create problems in the political sector. The inability to relate damages as proportional to a single factor makes it difficult for political entities to allocate responsibility and costs among themselves. This results in time and effort lost as each entity tries to interpret the data to minimize its own costs. It is tempting to consider the adverse effect as being caused by the addition of the "last straw" rather than to admit that all loads must be reduced.

A Success Story: Lake Washington

In those cases where ecological responses are proportional to stress it is likely that scientists will be able to (1) convincingly demonstrate cause and effect relationships, (2) substantiate predictions of responses to increased stress, (3) substantiate predictions of improvements via remediation efforts, and (4) convince people that the present cost (sacrifice of current benefits) will result in future benefits. For an example of a relatively straightforward case of this scenario, the diversion of sewage from Lake Washington, in Washington State, is often quoted as a success story.[1]

The problem in Lake Washington was the excess biomass of algae caused by sewage inputs to the lake. As the public became aware of the worsening "muddy" condition of the lake, various theories were offered. "Lake Washington Brown — That's Algae, Not Mud and It'll Be There For the Next 10 Years" was the headline in the Seattle Post-Intelligencer on 3 July 1962. Limnologist Thomas Edmondson had earlier predicted that the lake would continue to deteriorate unless the sewage, specifically the phosphorus (P) loading, was reduced. The worsening condition of the lake confirmed his predictions.

It was generally, although not universally, accepted that P was the limiting nutrient in most lakes, and specifically the nutrient most limiting algal biomass in Lake Washington. The plot did not lack for characters who argued that the available information did not warrant action, that the costs of sewage diversion were excessive, that P recycling from the lake sediment would negate any corrective action, and that the diversion of sewage from Lake Washington to Puget Sound was a totally unjustified plot to waste taxpayers' money. Because multiple political entities had to be involved in corrective action, a new political structure needed to be developed, known as "METRO" (Municipality of Metropolitan Seattle). Edmondson summarized the various rationales put forth to discredit the scientific information and throw suspicion on the political motives of those involved. He also documented the nutrient diversion and improvement in lake condition.

The relationship between P loading and lake condition is shown in Figure 6.1. A more straightforward, simplistic relationship would be hard to find; lake condition becomes worse as P loading increases, until another factor becomes limiting, at which point, the lake is insensitive to additional P loading. The caption makes clear that a decrease within the non-limiting range (from 100% to 50% of the loading in this example) will not affect the condition of the lake, but a decrease of P within the range where P is limiting

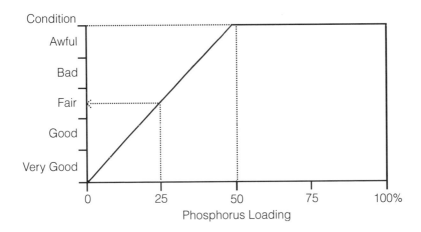

Figure 6.1. The relationship between phosphorus loading and lake condition.

(from 50% to 25%) will make a great improvement.

Edmondson claimed that the increased algal biomass (expressed as Secchi disc transparency) was the result of P input in sewage, and he predicted that sewage diversion would result in greater lake clarity, approaching the level of the 1950s. With the staged diversion of sewage, the dissolved P concentration decreased and the lake transparency increased, as predicted by Edmondson, and shown in Figure 6.2. Not only did the lake meet the performance criteria by returning to earlier transparency levels by the mid 1970s, but subsequently the clarity increased to an even greater degree than initially predicted after *Daphnia* reappeared in the lake. Had the lake failed to respond in the direction, and on the schedule predicted, Dr. Edmondson and other limnologists would have been discredited. To have the lake become clearer than predicted was regarded as a bonus.

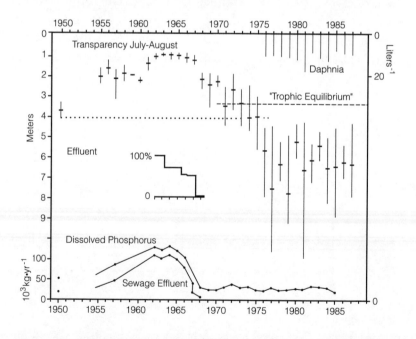

Figure 6.2. Responses of Lake Washington transparency to changes in sewage effluent loading and dissolved phosphorus loading.

The Lake Washington story, in which scientists convincingly demonstrated a cause and effect relationship, substantiated a prediction of response to increased stress, verified predicted improvements via remediation efforts, and convinced people that the funds were a good investment, has been widely used as a justification for sewage diversion or treatment.

POLITICAL RESPONSES TO ECOLOGICAL UNCERTAINTIES

When causal relationships and effects are not clearly understandable, the way is open for parties to interpret the complexities to serve their own interests. There are several methods of steering the information to alternative conclusions. It is analogous to playing the children's game of connect the dots with various special interest groups drawing different pictures from the same dots, or facts.

One method of discrediting the scientific opposition is to discredit scientists as a special interest group motivated by its own greed for research funds and public adoration. Non-professional supporters are depicted as followers who seek to give purpose to their lives, and to bask in the glory of the scientists they admire; it is claimed that even if the theory is found to be invalid, the organization has too much to lose by such an admission, and will continue to carry the cause even if it is known to be false.[2] Scientists are depicted as people who use predictions of catastrophe to siphon funds from more important societal needs in order to feed their own projects, and who make predictions not supported by critical analyses. Another method of discrediting the opposing side is to call for quantification and reduction of uncertainty. This appears to support the application of scientific methodology, but may be motivated by the wish to delay and confuse. Funtowicz and Ravetz distinguish between the quality and uncertainty associated with information, and show that requests for greater certainty may merely serve to delay a decision:

> Procrastination is as real a policy option as any other, and indeed one that is traditionally favoured by bureaucracies; and 'inadequate information' is the best excuse for delay. More generally,

those who operate in a political context may attempt to influence the ways in which their statements and actions are perceived and evaluated. This involves affecting public attitudes, controlling the flows of information and misinformation, and setting the agenda and terms for debate on major issues. Now that uncertainty has been politicized, as an accepted element of public concern, it too will be manipulated. Parties in a policy debate will invoke uncertainty in their arguments selectively, for their own advantage."[3]

People will accept, uncritically, any scrap of information that supports their side, but will require infinitely greater measures of certainty for information that appears to refute their preference. This is related to cognitive dissonance, the response to the discomfort of holding contradictory beliefs "...wherein once a belief is formed thru [sic] cognitive dissonance, the person will not discard it even though he may receive contradictory information, and not only will he reject this information, he will seek sources of information that confirm his belief."[4] Thus, those who must bear the costs of pollution abatement will demand high levels of certainty that their inputs caused the problem and that their costs will result in obvious improvements which will justify the expense.

Measures of uncertainty and much of the vocabulary of risk use mathematical symbols and concepts that make it difficult to communicate these ideas to the public. Policy makers, who must bridge the gap between scientific inputs and recommendations for public expenditures, have no easy task. Many intelligent people will reject an abstract argument that they cannot understand, especially if the conclusions appear counter-intuitive. Scientists lose credibility when the arguments appear to be convoluted to the point of fogging an issue. Yet many ecologically important relationships are complex, and results can be presented to appear counter-intuitive.

Management problems with enclosed seas are very complex, and therefore very troublesome. Complex mixing patterns, resulting from tidal and river flows as waters of different salinity and temperature mix, make measuring changes difficult because each time one samples, one is examining a different water mass. The shore is complex, and one therefore can't depend on "mid-channel" simplifications. There is a multitude of point and nonpoint inputs. Given that different political entities are likely to be involved, the information may be incomplete, in different units, or otherwise difficult to compare or use. Since information exchange may involve potential liabilities, there may be some question of bias; for example entities may underestimate their pollutant releases and overestimate their cleanup effectiveness.

It is rare that only one factor is the controlling one. Controlling factors are likely to change seasonally and vary from location to location, and from year to year. For example, the anoxic conditions in the Chesapeake Bay are thought by some to be caused by excess nitrogen (N) and associated algal biomass decaying in the hypolimnion, the lower stagnant water layer. Others think they are caused by low rainfall and low river flow. It may be that each of these conditions, or combinations of them, may be the cause in some places at some times.

THE SUBSYSTEM WITHIN A COMPLEX, HIERARCHICAL SYSTEM

As scientists come to understand and describe individual processes, each process is likely to become a component or subsystem in a more complex model. As argued here, a relationship may be valid but may lose its predictive power within a more complex, hierarchical system. Let us return to the concept that nutrients such as P or N control algal biomass. Since each algal cell requires a certain minimum amount of each required element to survive, and an additional amount to reproduce, more nutrient supply generally translates into more algal production. The rate of algal growth is often described by the Michaelis-Menton curve, shown in Figure 6.3. Although this relationship is not linear, it is a straightforward one. As nutrient concentration is increased, growth rate increases until the cells are growing at their maximal rate (μ_{max}); a nutrient

concentration that supports 1/2 the maximum growth rate is referred to as K_S. The entire curve is defined by specifying μ_{max} and
K_S. It seems irrefutable that increased nutrient input rates should
lead to faster growth rates and increased abundance of algae, especially in simplified cases where grazers are not present and the algae can't sink out of the zone where photosynthesis is possible.

Now let us consider algal biomass-nutrient relations in the slightly more complex case of a chemostat, in which a limiting concentration of an algal nutrient enters a growth chamber, the input is
mixed within the growth chamber, and the overflow (yield) is
washed-out of the growth chamber. This is analogous to a river or
enclosed sea if the volume of water entering the system has constant nutrient concentration, but the flow rate is subject to change.
If the chemostat is run at a very low dilution rate (relative to the
maximum growth rate of the cells, as in position A in Figure 6.4),
virtually all of the nutrient will have been taken up by the phytoplankton, and cell biomass will be maximal. If the dilution rate is
increased (position B), the cell biomass will decrease so slightly
that the change will probably not be obvious. It will appear as if
the increased nutrient input (more per unit time) has not resulted
in increased biomass; the increased rate of nutrient input appears
to have been absorbed by the assimilatory capacity of the culture.

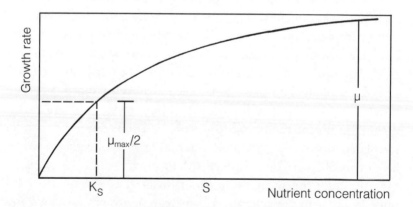

Figure 6.3. Michaelis-Menton relationship between nutrient concentration and algal growth.

However, if one is monitoring output, it will be obvious that the increased rate of input has been matched by an increased rate of output (yield biomass/ml x ml/day). Chemostats tend to exhibit very high degrees of stability because of the Michaelis-Menton relationship. If uptake or growth is reduced temporarily (by temperature or light intensity being reduced temporarily) nutrient concentration will increase, and growth rate will increase, thus bringing the culture back to the predicted biomass.

If the dilution rate is increased from position A to position B in Figure 6.4, the biomass of the culture will appear to be very stable, and one might be tempted to state that biomass is a very robust property, and that dilution rate can be increased without danger. However, as the dilution rate approaches the maximal growth rate of the cells (position C), the biomass will be very sensitive to dilution rate; slight reductions and the biomass will increase, slight increases and the biomass will approach zero as the cells wash out. If the dilution rate is increased to equal the maximal growth rate (position D), the cell biomass will approach zero, and the nutrient concentration will come to equal the input concentration. In the case of ecosystems, there are currently no ways to assess the limits

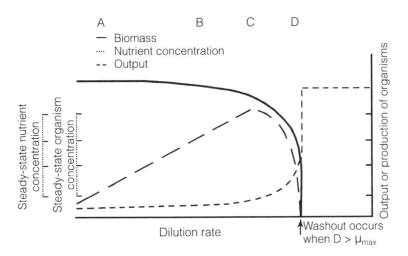

Figure 6.4. Biomass and output (yield, production) as a function of dilution rate in a chemostat.

to this compensatory range within which the system can adjust one property to control another, and outside of which the system collapses.

CASCADING TROPHIC LEVELS: EFFECTS OF TROPHIC COMPLEXITY

In real bodies of water, algal biomass is not just a function of nutrient inputs and dilution rates. Losses from death, sinking, and grazing are important in determining algal biomass. In many situations, the algal biomass is controlled by grazing, in a situation analogous to the dilution phenomenon shown in continuous culture. In the presence of large populations of grazers, increased algal nutrients may result in greater algal production, but it is removed as fast as it grows. Therefore, with heavy grazing, algal abundance may not appear to be related to nutrient availability. If planktivores (fish or invertebrates that feed on zooplanktonic grazers) are abundant, they may so reduce the populations of grazers, that algal biomass may again reflect nutrient supply. If top carnivores are abundant, they can reduce the population of planktivores, thus increasing the abundance of grazers, and again prevent the accumulation of algal biomass in response to nutrients. Thus each added trophic level reverses the outcome. This phenomenon has been called "cascading trophic relationships" and it provides an example of the importance, in some situations, of "top down" or predator control of ecosystem function.[5]

Thus, it is not safe to predict that increased nutrients will always result in increased algal biomass, or that the reduction of nutrient inputs will always result in reduced algal biomass if, in addition to changes in nutrient input, there are changes in trophic level structure. Does another factor (such as grazing) disprove the nutrient-algal relationships described above? No, the nutrient-algal relationships remain valid, but that relationship, by itself, is inadequate to predict total system behavior.

In this regard, Swartzman and Rose undertook mathematical simulations of cascading trophic relationships in a model microcosm populated by eight algal groups and five species of zooplankton.[6] Although the model was based on freshwater organisms, the relationships would be the same in the estuarine or marine environment. This model has been extensively tested, but we shall limit our observations to a large-grazer controlled community and a predator controlled community.[7]

Let us first consider a large-grazer controlled community, as in Figures 6.5 and 6.6. If the initial "standard nutrient" concentration is increased tenfold, the phytoplankton is only slightly increased (36.9 as compared to 32.5 µg dry weight per ml) during the spring bloom and at other times is barely distinguishable from the standard level. The reason for the relatively minor response to the increased nutrient is that light becomes limiting, because at high phytoplankton standing crops, transparency is reduced and light penetration in the water column decreases. As time progresses (after day 15), the phytoplankton abundance is constrained by grazers and appears unresponsive to the nutrient increase. Thus given a tenfold increase in nutrients, the response of phytoplankton is modest because light penetration and grazing constrain its abundance. Because the phytoplankton response was modest, the increase in abundance of large grazers was also modest (see Figure 6.5).

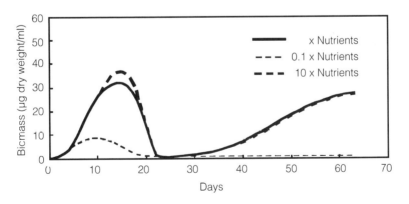

Figure 6.5. Effects of three nutrient conditions (0.1, 1 and 10 ×) in a large grazer controlled community on phytoplankton abundance (µg dry weight/ml).

If the nutrient is reduced from the standard initial concentration by 90 percent, the reduction in phytoplankton abundance is notable, but it is only 24 percent less, not 90 percent less. The large-grazer abundance decreases in proportion to the decrease in phytoplankton available to be eaten (see Figure 6.6). If one is considering increasing nutrients from the lowest level, it appears that the phytoplankton increase is less than proportional to nutrient inputs, and as one gets to high concentrations, the system appears to be relatively insensitive to additional increases. This can be considered the assimilatory capacity of the system to process added nutrients. This information is very discouraging if one has an extremely enriched water body, and wishes to reduce phytoplankton abundance. If the current concentration were ten times the standard, a 90 percent decrease in nutrients would show little effect. A 99 percent decrease might be necessary to obtain the desired outcome. This psychological asymmetry contributes to the tendency to tolerate eutrophication.

Now let us consider a community in which the large grazers have been reduced to very low abundance (in this case by a 25 percent daily chronic mortality) such as might occur in a predator controlled community. The loss of large grazers could also have been caused by toxicants, seasonal flushing of the estuary, or any other cause. With the rarity of large grazers (see Figure 6.7) the

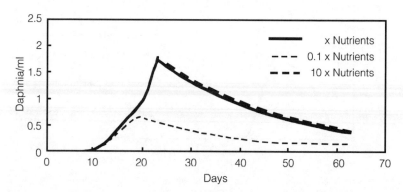

Figure 6.6. Effects of three nutirent conditions (0.1, 1 and 10 ×) in a large grazer controlled community on large grazer abundance (Individual *Daphnia* per ml).

phytoplankton abundances are much greater and persist all summer, at initial nutrient concentrations of both standard and ten times standard (see Figure 6.7). Note that at times the phytoplankton abundances are greater in the standard concentration and other times greater in the ten times standard. However, they are so similar to each other that they would rarely be distinguishable in sampling natural areas. If the initial nutrients are 10 percent of standard concentration the phytoplankton is less abundant, but persists throughout the growing season. Again, when nutrient inputs are increasing, the system seems to absorb much of the increase, but when they are decreasing, the system requires more than proportional nutrient reduction to obtain reduced phytoplankton abundance.

One more example of loss of predictive capability when the restraints that previously controlled a subsystem are eliminated may be useful. Budworms periodically defoliate trees; the outbreaks are seen as intermittent events occurring approximately every thirty-five years. By observation, the budworms increase modestly as foliage increases as long as birds are constraining the budworm population. When the budworms become so abundant that the birds are no longer a constraint, the budworms increase until they deplete their food base by defoliating the trees. The poor biologist who has developed a predictive equation for budworms, based

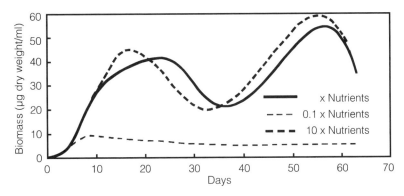

Figure 6.7. Effects of three nutrient conditions (0.1, 1 and 10 ×) in a predator controlled community on phytoplankton abundance (µg dry weight/ml).

only on foliage, will not be able to predict the budworm response when the bird constraint changes due to disease, limited nesting sites, insecticides, or any other factor that was external to the budworm-foliage subsystem process model.[8]

Our ability to predict how ecosystems will respond is hampered by the scale and degree of complexity on which researchers tend to operate. Most researchers study a particular process and are confident that the resultant information is necessary for intelligent management. However, as shown here, relationships based on subsystems may lose their ability to predict how a total system will behave if the subsystem is constrained by other processes. The potential always exists for constraints such as grazing to be imposed or removed, for example by predation of the grazers. To improve prediction larger scale monitoring and greater awareness of the interactions among the subsystems is needed.

Even with the greatest confidence in ecological understanding and predictions, there are still problems to be encountered with management. If the first 50-90 percent of nutrient reduction is unlikely to provide dramatic improvements in water quality, each government will want the other units to do the initial cleanup. It will want to do the last, and most obviously effective cleanup. In cases of moderate enrichment, where the initial nutrient reductions are likely to have the most obvious effects, each government will want to take the first step, but not make future efforts.

The consideration of trophic cascading also brings additional insights. If predation has eliminated grazers, the system may not be very responsive to insecticides that reduce grazer abundance. In contrast, a grazer controlled system may be very sensitive to insecticides, and may respond by reductions in grazer abundances and dramatic increases in phytoplankton standing crops. Thus trophic complexity becomes an important issue in understanding and predicting ecosystem responses and in communicating with political entities.

Given the complexity of real systems — and enclosed seas are as complex as they come — individual subsystem processes are likely to lose their predictive value when they are imbedded within a more complex system. This allows the potential for scientifically predicted results (if you increase nutrient inputs, more algae will occur) that may fail to occur. Predictions based only on subsystems may be opposite to the response of the total system. This is especially troublesome in real cases where several inputs or losses are occurring simultaneously, such as changes in fishing pressure due to conservation or pollution, invading competing species and increases in marine mammal populations. It is critical that the total ecosystem and all of the subsystem interactions be considered in predicting system behavior.

ACKNOWLEDGMENT

Figures 6.1 and 6.2 are adapted from Edmonson op. cit. with permission from the University of Washington Press, while figures 6.3 and 6.4 are adapted from Eugene B. Welch and T. Lindell. 1992. Ecological Effects of Wastewater. Chapman and Hall, London. I would like to thank Jack H. Taub for assistance using the model and generating the graphics in figures 6.5, 6.6 and 6.7; Gordon Swartzman and Kenneth Rose for developing the model, and Kenneth Rose for adapting the model to my computer system. Funding for the development of the model was provided by EPA, while the FDA funded microcosm studies that led to the model's development and testing.

NOTES

1. W. Thomas Edmondson. 1991. The Uses of Ecology — Lake Washington and Beyond. University of Washington Press, Seattle, p. 329.

2. This is very much the approach of such books as Walter J. Karplus. 1992. The Heavens Are Falling: The Scientific Prediction of Catastrophes in Our Time. Plenum Press, New York; and Rogelio A. Maduro and Ralf. Schauerhammer. 1992. The Holes in the Ozone Scare. 21st Science Associates, Washington, D.C.

3. Silvio O. Funtowicz and Jerome R. Ravetz. 1990. Uncertainty and Quality in Science for Policy. Kluwer Academic Publishers, Dordrecht, p. 15.

4. Miles Raizin and G. Michael Meaburn. 1989. The economic costs of informing the public on seafood safety matters. NOAA Technical Memorandum NMFS-SEFC-225, citing George A. Akerlof and William T. Dickens. 1982. The economic consequences of cognitive dissonance. American Economic Review 72:307-319.

5. This has been summarized by Stephen R. Carpenter, James F. Kitchell and James R. Hodgson. 1985. Cascading trophic interactions and productivity. BioScience 35:634-639 and expanded upon by Stephen R. Carpenter (ed.). 1987. Complex Interactions in Lake Communities. Springer-Verlag, New York, p. 283.

6. Gordon L. Swartzman and Kenneth A. Rose. 1983/84. Simulating the biological effects of toxicants in aquatic microcosms. Ecological Modelling 22:123-134.

7. Kenneth A. Rose, Gordon L. Swartzman, Andrew C. Kindig and Frieda B. Taub. 1988. Stepwise iterative calibration of a multispecies phytoplankton-zooplankton simulation model using laboratory data. Ecological Modelling 42:1-32; and Gordon L. Swartzman, Kenneth A. Rose, Andrew C. Kindig and Frieda B. Taub. 1989. Modeling the direct and indirect effects of streptomycin in aquatic microcosms. Aquatic Toxicology 14: 109-130; Gordon L. Swartzman, Frieda B. Taub, James P. Meador, Chisheng Huang and Andrew C. Kindig. 1990. Modeling the effect of algal biomass on multispecies aquatic microcosms response to copper sulfate. Aquatic Toxicology 17:93-118.

8. C. S. Holling. 1986. The resilience of terrestrial ecosystems: local surprise and global change. In William C. Clark and R. E. Munn (eds.). Sustainable Development of the Biosphere. Cambridge University Press, Cambridge. Cited in Timothy F. H. Allen and Thomas W. Hoekstra. 1992. Toward a Unified Ecology. Columbia University Press, New York.

7

Conservation Biology and Nearshore Biodiversity

DANIEL SIMBERLOFF

As marine policy practitioners look to science for guidance, they often turn to the multi-disciplinary science of conservation biology, which aims to identify the best strategies for preventing species extinctions. Yet, exactly what comprises conservation biology, and what its role in managing marine biodiversity may be, are subjects in need of careful analysis and greater understanding. This, then, is the objective of this chapter. Using marine examples, it reviews the historical underpinning of the discipline, and the specific research concerns of conservation biologists. These interests include understanding the dynamics of small populations, of populations of populations (metapopulations) and of known extinctions, and considerations for the design and management of reserves to protect remaining biodiversity. Next, the chapter reviews a major specific threat to endangered species — the introduction of exotic species — from a marine conservation perspective. I conclude by questioning the assumption that achieving some level of coastal development compatible with the preservation of ecosystem health can be extended by analogy to state that sustainable development and multiple use is always compatible with the continued persistence of all native species. Conservation biology may provide guidelines for specific species in particular locations, but it is not yet a predictive science; ecosystems are idiosyncratic and predictions about them are necessarily general. What the field may provide are new considerations for policy makers which may prove crucial to the continued existence of marine biodiversity.

Conservation biology has two threads, one quite old and the other very new.[1] By the early part of this century, autecological studies focussed on habitat requirements of species of interest and many refuges in the United States were established based on intensive habitat study. Such research continues, but it tends to be the province of wildlife biologists and is not at the heart of the "new" conservation biology.[2] The latter arose in biology and ecology departments in the mid-1970s and has grown enormously during the last decade. The thrust of the new conservation biology was originally the application of equilibrium island biogeographic theory to the design of refuges and formal study of habitat suitability played a minuscule role. Island biogeographic theory predicts that the number of species increases as islands are larger and closer together and that the number of species on an island is due to equilibrium between the rates of colonization and extinction.[3] Later, as it was recognized that island biogeography provided at best a metaphor for refuges and not specific rules or guidance, the chief focus of the new conservation biology came to be the application of population genetics and population ecology to maintenance of small populations.[4] This remains the main focus, although a second area of interest has developed, loosely arranged around the notions of landscape ecology (itself a new field) and ecosystem management. Landscape ecology is concerned with the patterns formed by the distribution of different habitat types at a regional scale, and how these patterns affect ecosystem processes and species distribution.[5] The two foci intersect in such problems as the effects of habitat fragmentation.[6]

METAPOPULATIONS AND THREATS TO SMALL POPULATIONS

The new conservation biology has forced conservation planners and managers to address several important factors that, even twenty years ago, were either unconsidered or at best implicit in management decisions. Many of these considerations concern the reasons small populations are at great risk and how one determines a minimum viable population size.[7] The most obvious of the new considerations are genetic and evolutionary factors. Until the 1980s, animal breeders worried about inbreeding depression, or the reduction in fitness caused by matings between closely related individuals, but almost no conservation planners did. However, it is apparent that a small population in a completely isolated reserve will become very inbred very quickly. Is this process likely to threaten the very existence of the population and, if so, can management avoid this deterioration? There seems general agreement that, at least in the short term, inbreeding depression is less likely to weigh on very small populations than are ecological factors.[8] A variety of breeding schemes can potentially ameliorate the threat.[9]

If inbreeding depression were a serious concern, one way to prevent it might be the introduction of individuals from other populations. However, a new concern arises, the occasional phenomenon of outbreeding depression — a decline in fitness sometimes seen in crosses of genetically distinct stock.[10] Although outbreeding depression has not been observed as frequently as inbreeding depression, entire populations have foundered from it. It is more often observed in rare plants which may hybridize with a related, common species, but examples do occur among animals. For example, the locally adapted Iberian waterfrog (*Rana perezi*) is threatened due to inadvertent translocations of several other species and races of *Rana* into Spain.[11] Further, even when outbreeding depression cannot be documented, there is both practical and ethical concern over the prospect of destroying or diluting locally adapted (or at least distinctive) genotypes when one introduces individuals from other populations.[12]

Another area of genetic and evolutionary concern is longer term. Whereas inbreeding depression consists of the phenotypic manifestations of homozygous genes, that is, the existence of individuals with a double complement of a possibly deleterious gene, genetic drift — the chance loss of the different varieties of a particular gene, or alleles, in finite populations — has another effect. As alleles are lost to drift, there is less genetic variation upon which natural selection can operate. Unless the variation is replenished by mutation or gene flow, evolution will slow down. Drift, like inbreeding, increases in smaller populations. At present we do not know how quickly this effect will occur, how small a population has to be before loss of variation is a problem, and how important a decrease in evolutionary rate would be relative to other threats to population persistence.[13]

The role of stochastic demography in maintenance of small populations is another new concern injected into conservation decisions.[14] Given enough time, random variation in birth and death rates will drive any population to extinction. For large populations this process would take so long that we can view it as purely hypothetical. But how small does a population have to be before the hypothetical becomes possible or even probable? And how can managers guard against species loss from demographic stochasticity? Again, general answers are unavailable, although sufficient data for individual species can permit estimates of danger points.[15]

Metapopulation dynamics are one of the chief foci of conservation biologists today; they seem largely to have replaced equilibrium island biogeography as a framework for conceiving of refuge design and species persistence.[16] Although the formal mathematics of population crashes from demographic stochasticity are largely a product of the new conservation biology, the process was clearly in the minds of earlier workers.[17] They recognized the risk to any single small population and thus concluded that, in nature, species must be organized into metapopulations, that is, collections of local populations. Populations would wink in and out, but they would never disappear all at once. The site vacated by any extinct population would be recolonized eventually by immigrants from other populations. As these latter populations disappear, they in turn would be recolonized. Even though each component population might be destined to rather swift extinction, the entire metapopulation would be nearly immortal.

The various forces acting on natural populations might act concurrently and their effects need not be additive.[18] In fact, natural populations must constantly be buffeted by several forces, so it might not be easy to determine what actually caused the extinction of a population or species even if there were extensive data available. Worse, there are rarely substantial data on the disappearance of populations. However, if one seeks information on the extinction spasm that convulses the earth today, one finds a very different picture. Numerous authors list causes of extinction and virtually all those listed are induced by human activity.[19] For example, of animal extinctions known since 1600, Groombridge lists 173 caused at least partially by species introduced by humans, 103 caused by habitat alteration by humans and 15 deliberately destroyed as pests. In fact, none of these extinctions are attributed to causes other than human activities (a point also made by Soulé), although for many species the causes are unknown.[20] There is no mention in these lists of inbreeding, genetic drift, demographic stochasticity, or the failure of metapopulation dynamics.

Part of the problem is that proximate and ultimate causes of extinction must be distinguished.[21] Human activities may well reduce a species to a point that extinction from the various genetic and demographic forces discussed above is inevitable; the final disappearance could be caused by demographic stochasticity, for example, but this outcome may have been determined by habitat change that left few individuals, making the outcome inevitable. Extinction can occur even if we set aside a refuge network specifically to maintain a species.

A particularly well-studied extinction, that of the heath hen (*Tympanuchus cupido cupido*), shows that most or all of the forces discussed above came into play after human activity greatly reduced the range and numbers of the species.[22] This bird was numerous from Maine to Virginia in sandy scrub-oak habitat, but populations were destroyed by hunting and habitat destruction until the last individuals were restricted to Martha's Vineyard by 1870. This population declined to 200 by 1890, 100 by 1896 and only 50 by 1908. A refuge of 650 hectares was established then and by 1915 the population had increased to 2,000. However, a fire during a gale devastated the breeding grounds in 1916, followed by an unusually harsh winter punctuated by an exceptional flight of goshawks. The population fell below 150, mostly males. Extensive inbreeding was accompanied by declining sexual vigor and, in 1920, a poultry disease killed many individuals. By 1927 only 13 birds remained (11 males) and the last individual was last seen in 1932. In sum, even though hunting and deliberate habitat destruction were halted by the establishment of the refuge, the population apparently had become so precarious that it was destined to disappear owing to one or more of the forces setting minimum viable population size.

If small, refuge-bound populations are doomed, one may ask if it is worth studying the causes of their extinctions closely. It behooves conservationists to do so because, until humankind comes to its senses and stops activities that ultimately produce extinctions, the only hope is a holding pattern, emergency maintenance of small, isolated populations in refuges which are often suboptimal ones. These natural factors that can lead to extinction in small populations have to be identified and combatted. Such emergency care cannot go on forever; the only hope is that the overall situation changes before too many "patients" have been lost. For this emergency care to be effective, the symptoms and causes of the threat have to be understood in detail. This will, of course, be a difficult undertaking. So long as the average reproductive rate is only slightly less than the average mortality rate over many generations, a population will decline to extinction. Thus, while the last individuals of a remnant population might be apparently healthy, the population nonetheless may be doomed.[23] Obviously, very intensive study will be required to determine which among several plausible potential problems are the real culprits.

Such intensive study is really in its infancy. It is a relatively straightforward matter to predict analytically certain genetic consequences of small population size. This tidiness may have led to an overemphasis on evolutionary as opposed to environmental factors weighing on small populations. Lande has argued that inbreeding depression, even though worth considering in any evaluation, is not as likely as demographic and other ecological forces to terminate small populations.[24] Templeton and Read have even argued for deliberately breeding near relatives to remove genes causing inbreeding depression in captive propagation programs.[25] As for the failure of natural selection to occur due to genetic impoverishment, this seems to be a rather abstract and probably distant threat in the face of more immediate and concrete dangers.[26] In the short term — and extinction is occurring in the short term — there is, as yet, no compelling example of a species extinguished because it seemed unable to evolve as rapidly as other species do to changing environmental conditions.

The failure of metapopulations may be of more immediate concern, but numerous questions remain unanswered. Whatever the dynamic interactions of populations of the same species, the very existence of several small populations rather than a single large one confers insurance against some catastrophes. Several bird subspecies restricted to small islands have recently been eliminated by hurricanes and similar reports of extinction or near-extinction of species by hurricanes, volcanic eruptions and other catastrophes abound in the older literature.[27] When Hurricane Hugo hit Puerto Rico in 1989, it struck a major blow against recovery efforts for the Puerto Rican parrot (*Amazona vittata*), largely because the bird had been restricted to a single wild population.

Whether metapopulation dynamics is a normal force maintaining populations in nature and the loss of constant recolonization is a major threat or not, is less evident and demands a major research effort to study who moves where and mates with whom. Despite numerous statements that most species are distributed as metapopulations and that metapopulation dynamics are thus key to their survival, it is still an open question whether the model of continued extinction and re-immigration originally proposed by Levins is commonly applicable.[28] Harrison has reviewed the literature and suggests it is not.[29] She found many more instances in which species appear to constitute one large, loosely knit population, or a metapopulation in the sense of Boorman and Levitt: a large central population that is virtually immortal and numerous ephemeral peripheral populations whose origin and extinction are irrelevant to the fate of the species.[30] A recent incarnation of this model posits a large, persistent "source" population, or a group of them and numerous, possibly ephemeral, "sinks."[31]

Another problem in evaluating the importance of metapopulation dynamics is that the spatial arrangement of individuals of a species undergoing a geographic retreat, for whatever reason, is very likely to produce intermediate stages that approximate a metapopulation of more or less distinct populations.[32] If the retreat ultimately leads to extinction, one can hypothesize that the extinction was caused by the breakdown of metapopulation dynamics when the metapopulation was, in fact, a result of some other process.[33]

Nevertheless, numerous models point to the potential importance of metapopulation dynamics in maintaining species. The general result is that, given the right demographic and dispersal parameters, species that could not exist as single populations, or pairs of species that could not coexist in a single site, might do so in a metapopulation.[34] Further, a metapopulation might have a threshold number of populations such that, if enough component populations disappeared, the remainder might collapse even if, individually, they appeared healthy.[35] It is interesting and of potential importance in coastal marine systems, that field studies in which populations are dispersed among small, isolated fragments often are more highly preyed upon, a force not frequently adduced in the minimum viable population and metapopulation literature but one that could easily lead to local extinction.[36]

INTRODUCED SPECIES

Elton's classic work, *The Ecology of Invasions by Animals and Plants*, de-emphasized the marine environment. He went so far as to say, "In contrast to land and fresh waters the sea seems still almost inviolate."[37] The last decade has shown an explosion of interest in introduced species, partly driven by the recognition that they have greatly affected "pristine" terrestrial environments, not only human-dominated ones and new research has cast doubt on Elton's statement.[38] The apparent relative invulnerability of marine habitats is likely a consequence of their being studied less and the fact that most of them are covered with water and thus invisible to the casual observer.[39] Millions of people have seen kudzu while driving at 60 mph; even casual observers can detect the effects of the gypsy moth. Marine environments, especially the sea floor, are more recondite. However, a catalog of the means by which exotic marine organisms invade new regions and the effects they wreak upon arrival demonstrate that introductions are one of the main threats to marine biodiversity, perhaps rivalling chemical pollution.[40]

The greatest changes wrought by introduced species are those that modify an entire ecosystem by changing its physical structure.[41] Nearshore marine habitats are not immune. Soft intertidal substrates in the sheltered bays and estuaries of Hawaii, unlike those in most other tropical regions, had no mangroves and were sparsely vegetated. In 1902, the American Sugar Company planted red mangrove seedlings from Florida, while a second planting of Philippine mangroves occurred in 1922. Mangroves, dispersed naturally and perhaps assisted by humans, spread to many parts of the archipelago, replacing native vegetation and forming new forests 20 m high in some areas. There has been only preliminary study of the marine food web housed in mangrove roots and virtually none on the arboreal community.[42] However, because the roots of mangrove swamps form critical habitat for fishes, shrimp and other marine animals and accumulate sediment and build land, while the trees drop 4.5 tons of leaves per acre annually, this introduction must dominate energy flow, nutrient cycling and the entire composition of the community.[43]

Another example of an enclosed coastal area completely changed by an invader that provides new physical structure is from the United Kingdom.[44] Seeds of cordgrass (*Spartina alterniflora*) from eastern North America were accidentally introduced in shipping ballast along the southern coast of England. These seeds produced plants that subsequently hybridized with the native *S. maritima*. This hybrid, first noted in 1872, was sterile, but later underwent a doubling of chromosome number to produce a fertile form, *S. anglica*, in a process known as allopolyploidy. *S. alterniflora* itself has never been particularly invasive in the United Kingdom.

The hybrids initially spread slowly, but the invasion accelerated greatly beginning approximately in 1890. It is possible that the allopolyploidy arose at that time, allowing spread by seed as well as by rhizomes. In any event, by 1914 *S. anglica* had "spread all so much indeed, that it altered completely the aspect of the foreshore and the estuarine reaches of the rivers from Chichester Harbour in the East to Poole Harbour in the West."[45] Leaves and culms of *S. anglica* trap sediment, while its roots aid accretion. Thus it was deliberately used in marsh reclamation and spread widely around the British coast. Its long-term impact on salt marsh succession is uncertain, but it is difficult to believe that extensive, dense swards of cordgrass where none had previously existed have not wrought myriad ecological changes. There has been concern that this species will damage holiday beaches and change and/or decrease invertebrate communities and there have been claims that it has contributed to a decline of wading birds. More research is needed to clarify these threats.

Keystone species, by definition, change an entire ecosystem by massively modifying its community. Introduced species can also play a keystone role not by constituting a structural element of the community but by modifying the structure. Again, such effects are known in coastal marine habitats. For example, through the eighteenth and much of the nineteenth centuries, most of the northeastern North American coast was dominated by mud flats and salt marshes. The European periwinkle snail (*Littorina littorea*) was introduced to Nova Scotia for food around 1840 and slowly worked its way south, grazing algae off rocks and rhizomes of marsh grasses, thus destabilizing sediments.[46] By the twentieth century, it transformed much of the New England coast to its present well-known rocky shore. In the process it must have generated enormous ecological change.[47]

Introduced species can have innumerable effects short of such cataclysms.[48] These have been studied far more intensively in terrestrial and freshwater systems than in marine ones, but numerous examples of nearshore ecological impact are known. A large Japanese brown kelp, *Undaria pinnatifida*, was introduced in ballast water to the east coast of Tasmania where its habitat is similar to that of the native kelp, *Macrocystis pyrifera*, the normal substrate for the abalone and sea urchin fisheries.[49] It already covers four km of previously bare rocky coastline with tens of thousands of plants 50-180 cm high, from near low water mark to depths of eight meters, a total biomass of some 400 tons. Because it produces millions of spores per plant per day, it seems currently ineradicable and it appears capable of invading most of the temperate Australian coastline. It was also introduced to France in 1971, probably associated with spat of the Japanese oyster, *Crassostrea gigas*, and to New Zealand in 1987, most likely on hulls of Japanese fishing boats. Although research is underway to determine its ecological impact, it is too soon to do more than guess at the outcome of this invasion.

Numerous freshwater introduced plants plague native species and entire ecosystems; in Florida alone, water hyacinth, hydrilla, Eurasian watermilfoil and others have received extensive scientific and popular attention.[50] Fewer marine examples are known, but this lacuna may simply result from less research and the greater difficulty in observing submarine phenomena. Certainly there are several horror stories.[51] For instance, the European alga *Codium fragile* was of sufficient concern as a detriment to shellfisheries that NOAA attempted unsuccessfully to remove it from the waters off Long Island. It now also threatens to foul Florida coral reefs.[52]

It is often claimed that introduced terrestrial species displace native ones by competing for some limiting resource, but the critical research to establish such an interaction is almost always lacking.[53] The same is true of marine introductions. For instance, several mollusks and a species of *Sargassum* introduced to British coastal habitats are suggested as outcompeting native species, but the evidence is ambiguous.[54] For example, the decline of the native oysterdrill was contemporaneous with the arrival of the American one, but the cause may have been the greater susceptibility to cold by the native species, combined with a series of unusually cold winters.[55]

The effect of introduced diseases is more easily established.[56] For instance, the nematode *Anguillicola crassus* has spread rapidly in Europe, where it infects the native eel, *Anguilla anguilla*, since its introduction in 1980 when a shipment of Japanese eels, *Anguilla japonicus*, was released. Similarly, worldwide movement of shrimp for aquaculture has disseminated numerous disease organisms, some of which have infected native species.[57]

Numerous examples are known in which hybridization between introduced and native terrestrial and freshwater species essentially destroys the native species through genetic introgression.[58] Lester found no example of interspecific hybridization in the marine literature, though the research effort on marine organisms is probably far lower than that for terrestrial species.[59] Many instances of intraspecific hybridization between hatchery stock and wild strains of fishes and other organisms occur, often to the detriment of the species.[60] Of course, hybridization also can lead to other problems that do not entail the loss or even decline of the original native species, as in the earlier cordgrass example.

Elton argued that oyster culture is the greatest agency of marine introductions and he may be correct.[61] If one considers only transport associated with the Japanese oyster, *Crassostrea gigas*, the basis for his claim is clear. This species is worth exploring in detail bause of continuing controversy over its potential introduction to the Chesapeake Bay. A shipment of only 3,000 hatchery-reared individuals of *C. gigas* contained six other invertebrate species and an alga.[62] Shipments to the Pacific Northwest brought two species of oyster drill (one of which, *Ceratostoma inornagtum* is a major pest), *Sargassum muticum* (which is replacing eel grass in some habitats), a harmful flatworm (*Pseudostylochus ostreophagus*), a nest-building mussel that is viewed as a nuisance and a parasitic copepod that attacks a native oyster.[63] New disease organisms also probably arrived with *C. gigas*. *C. gigas* certainly carried the Manila clam (*Tapes japonica*) along with it; this clam is now so numerous in some areas that it constitutes a new fishery of some 4 million pounds.[64] In Australia, competition for food and space by the introduced *C. gigas* has led to the decline of a native oyster; a related New Zealand native was similarly outcompeted by *C. gigas*.[65] In sum, "Maryland feels that the worldwide record of *Crassostrea gigas* is so tainted with unpleasant phenomena that the use of this species in oyster culture without adequate controls is not worth its potential risk to the environment and health of shellfish in the Chesapeake Bay," while the State of Virginia seems ready to embark on the project.[66]

ECOSYSTEM MANAGEMENT AND MULTIPLE USE

Under the aegis of the Sustainable Biosphere Initiative of the Ecological Society of America and the New Perspectives of the U.S. Forest Service, the ideas of ecosystem management and multiple use have attracted increasing attention from conservation biologists.[67] Other new currents, such as the Bioreserve initiative of The Nature Conservancy, are very much in this spirit. The Conservancy's Virginia Coast Reserve is specifically designed to allow economic development and social progress that are compatible with environmental protection of an entire ecosystem.[68] It is, in turn, a designated Biosphere Reserve, thus part of a United Nations program to establish multi-use protected areas that conserve natural communities while developing compatible human uses of the environment. The "New Forestry" advocated in the Pacific Northwest similarly aims to allow harvest of resources while maintaining native biodiversity.[69]

The human population in U.S. coastal regions increased 69 percent, to 75.2 million, between 1950 and 1980; about 75 percent of the population lives within 50 miles of a coast.[70] Such tremendous population growth has produced massive habitat alteration and pollution. Because the popularity of coastal regions for human habitation and activity is not likely to decrease, the pressure to use them for various purposes while not destroying habitats or organisms that live in them is particularly acute. Certain communities in enclosed coastal seas are threatened primarily by direct human activity. For example, even though introduced species threaten to smother some coral reefs (as noted above), the key threats to reef communities are sedimentation and chemical pollution, especially chronic, low-level hydrocarbon pollution, and

sewage.[71] It is difficult to see how human activity could *not* generate a fair amount of sedimentation, pollution, and sewage on a regional basis and it seems obvious that these problems will have to
be solved on an ecosystem level. Further, in many enclosed coastal
areas, sediment, pollution, and sewage are the sums of many small
sources and thus are not easily regulated except on a comprehensive, regional basis.[72]

Though the goals of all these initiatives are laudable, they do
not yet provide much guidance to managers. Some, like the New
Forestry, are little more than collections of ideas with little synthetic underpinning or empirical base. Others, like the New Perspectives, are vaguely defined; thus they seem comforting without actually saying what is to be done. Those that reflect management
experience on the ground, such as the Nature Conservancy's
Bioreserves, are highly idiosyncratic and explicitly tailored to local
conditions. Thus they can, if suitably described, provide hints on
how to approach a similar project in another ecosystem and what
things to worry about, but cannot provide a list of rules or a cook-
book of management procedures. The Sustainable Biosphere Initiative is hortatory but not directly applicable to specific problems;
it basically says that almost all types of research ecologists do are
necessary to conserve biodiversity and ecological processes, but
that we need much more of this work and more central direction.

Another problem with all these approaches except, perhaps, the
Sustainable Biosphere Initiative, is that they seem to take for granted that sustainable development *is* compatible with ecosystem
health and the persistence of existing species. For some enclosed
marine communities, this proposition is highly suspect. For example, long-term stability of corals and therefore the reef communities based on them, is threatened by remarkably small amounts of
sediment and/or pollution.[73] In some instances bioassays of the effects on organisms are better indicators of the presence of a pollutant than any chemical reaction.

Little attention is paid to testing the hypothesis of compatibility or to estimating just how much development of what kinds can
be permitted without ecological damage. The certainty that we

can have owls and a big timber industry in the Northwest is reminiscent of the "guns and butter" claims during the Vietnam War. What testing of the compatibility hypothesis exists seems explicitly or implicitly to be by adaptive management.[74] This boils down to using a natural resource at some level, seeing if it is able to withstand that amount of use and if it is, trying to use even more of it. In some settings this procedure may be useful; in others it can be inappropriate. With introduced species, for example, the record of attempted eradications is extremely poor; almost all introductions are currently irreversible.[75] Fisheries may have thresholds such that a decline below a certain point leads to long-term collapse.[76]

THE ROLE OF CONSERVATION BIOLOGY

What role, then, can conservation biology play in managing biodiversity? It is fruitful to begin by saying what role it *cannot* play. A priori, conservation biology cannot give precise, prescriptive advice about specific problems, such as how to design a particular refuge, how to regulate a harvest, whether to introduce a species, or whether to mount an eradication campaign. This is not a shocking conclusion and fits with those of others who have considered similar matters.[77] Worse, adoption of a specific management plan based solely on theoretical conservation biology is irresponsible and could be ruinous. As noted earlier for small, isolated populations, a variety of forces are potential problems, the key forces need not be the same in each instance and there is no consensus about which are the most important most frequently.

Concerning *C. gigas* and other marine introductions, Druehl wrote that it would be many years before scientists could predict with much certainty the effects of an introduced species on the target ecosystem.[78] Although others feel confident that much progress has been made, I am unconvinced.[79] It is true now as then that the ecological effects of many introductions seem idiosyncratic and complex, that explanations are either absent or after the fact and that many effects of introductions, even important ones, are probably unrecognized. This is not to say that thoughtful research before an introduction cannot help to lower the probability of an unexpected event. But the probability remains very high nonetheless.

In fact, recently there has been a greatly increased catalog of well-documented introductions, but very little progress towards the goal of prediction, or of subsuming them under some overall theory of introductions.[80] The main synthetic theory today, which I have termed that of "biotic resistance," states that introductions are more likely to succeed where there are fewer species, such as on islands or in disturbed habitats.[81] In fact, this is the very notion propounded by Elton and is similar to the concept of "environmental resistance" defined by Chapman.[82] Certainly this concept, even if true, would not provide the precision needed for management decisions and it is questionable whether it is even true.[83] It is almost depressing that it is still cited as a principle that might give management guidance, including in the marine realm.[84]

In seeking an explanation for the apparent lesser invasibility of marine systems than terrestrial and freshwater ones, Lester has recourse to the hypothesis of biotic resistance, arguing that low species diversity (and genetic diversity) renders islands (among terrestrial habitats) and lakes (among aquatic ones) more prone than the oceans to serious disruption from introductions and their species less competitive with invaders.[85] In fact, it is not very clear that islands *are* more easily invaded and damaged by introduced species than are continents and the role of species richness in any differences in invasibility is murky.[86] In any event, even if the principle were true on average, there are so many exceptions that it would be folly to believe it could aid in risk analysis.

As for how to manage on an ecosystem basis, there is not even the catalog of well-studied special cases that exist for small, isolated populations and introduced species. A few studies of entire ecosystems have yielded much about nutrient cycling and energy flow, but the generalities deriving from these studies are at too high a level to give specific management guidelines for other ecosystems. The highly idiosyncratic nature of ecosystems and their biotic communities demands detailed individualized study for informed management.

Conservation biology and its allied sciences do have a role to play in managing biodiversity. They are both inspirational and instructive. For any particular ecosystem, they suggest a catalog of considerations of potential forces that must be taken into account for sound management. Further, much of this catalog is relatively new. As I noted in the introduction, refuges set aside in the first half of this century were largely established on the principle of finding the suitable habitats for target species or small groups of them, then designating chunks of that habitat to be used only for conservation of these species. Considerations of minimum viable population sizes, metapopulation dynamics, the interactions of the target species with others in the community, the nature and relevance of ecosystem processes, the vulnerability of the refuge to external forces (including introduced species) — all these foci of current research were secondary or completely absent. Yet each of these forces, in particular cases, is possibly crucial. This knowledge puts an onus on managers and planners to study the full gamut of phenomena that might bear on the success of a conservation effort.

In the marine environment in particular, this onus should lead to certain types of study that are difficult and not traditional. For instance, the particular spacing of individuals and populations of resident species and how that spacing relates to who mates with whom, are critical to understanding the importance of metapopulation dynamics and potential fragmentation. New molecular techniques can assist such studies. As another example, the vulnerability of a site to introduced species should always be a concern and the possibility of evolution of native species in response to invaders should be an aspect of that concern. At the ecosystem level, at the very least, keystone species, if any, should be defined and the nature of their interactions with the rest of the community should be clarified. For example, at the turn of the century, the eastern oyster, *Crassostrea virginica*, reportedly removed particles of 2-20nμ in the Chesapeake Bay by filtering the entire volume of water about once a week. The hundred-fold decline in this oyster means that, today, the bay volume is filtered only once a year.[87] Because suspended particles can be living organisms and themselves can transport nutrients, affect the penetration of light and determine sedimentation rates, this catastrophic alteration in cycling rates must have profoundly affected the entire ecosystem. Until we understand such effects and can begin to predict them with some accuracy, effective management of biodiversity will be hamstrung.

ACKNOWLEDGMENT

Michael Beck provided numerous useful suggestions to improve this chapter.

NOTES

1. Daniel Simberloff. 1988. The contribution of population and community biology to conservation science. Annual Review of Ecology and Systematics 19:473-511.

2. See, for example, Jared Verner, Michael L. Morrison and C. John Ralph. 1986. Wildlife 2000. University of Wisconsin Press, Madison.

3. The classic work in the field is Robert H. MacArthur and Edward O. Wilson. 1967. The Theory of Island Biogeography. Princeton University Press, Princeton, New Jersey. For examples of its application to reserve design see, for example, John Terborgh. 1974. Preservation of natural diversity: the problem of extinction-prone species. BioScience 24:715-722; Jared M. Diamond. 1975. The island dilemma: lessons of modern biogeographic studies for design of natural reserves. Biological Conservation 7:129-146; and Edward O. Wilson and Edwin O. Willis. 1975. Applied biogeography. In Martin L. Cody and Jared M. Diamond (eds.). Ecology and Evolution of Communities. Harvard University Press, Cambridge, pp. 523-534.

4. Michael E. Soulé and Daniel Simberloff. 1986. What do genetics and ecology tell us about the design of nature reserves? Biological Conservation 35:19-40.

5. Zeev Naveh and Arthur S. Lieberman. 1984. Landscape Ecology: Theory and Applications. Springer-Verlag, New York.

6. Daniel Simberloff. 1993. Fragmentation, corridors and the longleaf pine community. In Craig Moritz, Jiro Kikkawa and D. Doley (eds.). Conservation Biology in Australia and Oceania. Surrey Beatty, Chipping Norton, Australia, pp. 47-56.

7. For references, see Simberloff 1988, op. cit.

8. See Russell Lande. 1988a. Genetics and demography in biological conservation. Science 241:1455-1460; David S. Woodruff. 1989. The problems of conserving genes and species. In David Western and Mary Pearl (eds.). Conservation for the Twenty-first Century. Oxford University Press, New York; and Edward O. Guerrant, Jr. 1992, pp. 76-88; Genetic and demographic considerations in the sampling and reintroduction of rare plants. In Peggy L. Fiedler and Subodh K. Jain (eds.). Conservation Biology. The Theory and Practice of Nature Conservation, Preservation and Management. Chapman and Hall, New York, pp. 321-344.

9. For references, see Simberloff 1988, op. cit.

10. For references, see Simberloff 1988, op. cit.

11. Begoña Arano, Gustavo Llorente, Mario García-Paris, and Pilar Herrero. 1995. Species translocation menaces Iberian waterfrogs. Conservation Biology 9(1):196-98.

12. For example, see Alan R. Templeton. 1986. Coadaptation and outbreeding depression. In Michael E. Soulé (ed.). Conservation Biology: The Science of Scarcity and Diversity. Sinauer, Sunderland, Massachusetts, pp. 105-116.

13. Simberloff 1988, op. cit.

14. For references, see Simberloff 1988, op. cit.

15. For example, Robert Lande. 1988b. Demographic models of the northern spotted owl (*Strix occidentalis caurina*). Oecologia 75: 601-607.

16. Ilkka Hanski and Michael E. Gilpin. 1991. Metapopulation dynamics: brief history and conceptual domain. Biological Journal of the Linnean Society 42:3-16 and Gray Merriam. 1991. Corridors and connectivity: animal populations in heterogeneous environments. In Denis A. Saunders and Richard J. Hobbs (eds.). Nature Conservation 2: The Role of Corridors. Surey Beatty, Chipping Norton, Australia, pp. 133-142.

17. For example, Herbert George Andrewartha and L. Charles Birch. 1954. The Distribution and Abundance of Animals. University of Chicago Press, Chicago.

18. See, for example, Simberloff 1988, op. cit.; Michael E. Gilpin and Michael E. Soulé. 1986. Minimum viable populations: Processes

of species extinction. In Soulé op. cit.; Brian Groombridge (ed.). 1992. Global Biodiversity: Status of the Earth's Living Resources. Chapman and Hall, London, pp. 19-34.

19. Paul R. Ehrlich and Anne H. Ehrlich. 1981. Extinction: The Causes and Consequences of the Disappearance of Species. Random House, New York; T. H. Johnson and A. J. Stattersfield. 1990. A global review of island endemic birds. Ibis 132:167-180; and Groombridge, op. cit.

20. Michael E. Soulé. 1983. What do we really know about extinction? In Christine M. Schonewald-Cox, S. M. Chambers, B. MacBryde and L. Thomas (eds.). Genetics and Conservation. Benjamin/Cummings, Menlo Park, California, pp. 111-124.

21. Daniel Simberloff. 1986a. The proximate causes of extinction. In David M. Raup and David Jablonski (eds.). Patterns and Processes in the History of Life. Springer-Verlag, Berlin, pp. 259-276 and Simberloff. 1994a. The ecology of extinction. Acta Palaeontologica Polonica, 38:159-174.

22. Arthur C. Bent. 1932. Life Histories of North American Gallinaceous Birds. Smithsonian Institution. U.S. National Museum Bulletin 162. Washington, D.C. and Simberloff 1986a, op. cit.

23. Simberloff 1994a, op. cit.

24. Lande 1988a, op. cit.

25. Alan R. Templeton and B. Read. 1983. The elimination of inbreeding depression in a captive herd of Speke's gazelle. In Schonewald-Cox et al., op. cit., pp. 241-261.

26. Simberloff 1988, op. cit.

27. R. L. Pyle. 1993. Hawaiian Islands region. American Birds 47: 302-304; H. Raffaele. 1977. Comments on the extinction of *Loxigilla portoricensis grandis* in St. Kitts. Condor 79:389-390; and Simberloff 1986a, op. cit. and 1988, op. cit.

28. Edward O. Wilson. 1992. The Diversity of Life. Harvard University Press, Cambridge, Massachusetts; Reed F. Noss. 1993. Wildlife corridors. In Daniel S. Smith and Paul C. Hellmund (eds.). Ecology of Greenways. University of Minnesota Press, Minneapolis; William E. Odum. 1982. Environmental degradation and the tyranny of small decisions. BioScience 32:728-729; and Richard

Levins. 1968. Evolution in Changing Environments. Princeton University Press, Princeton.

29. S. Harrison. 1991. Local extinction in a metapopulation context: An empirical evaluation. Biological Journal of the Linnean Society 42:73-88.

30. S. A. Boorman and P. R. Levitt. 1973. Group selection of the boundary of a stable population. Theoretical Population Biology. 4:85-128.

31. Ronald H. Pulliam. 1988. Sources, sinks and population regulation. The American Naturalist 137:S50-S66.

32. Harrison, op. cit.; Simberloff 1994a, op. cit.

33. Simberloff 1994a, op. cit.

34. See references in Hanski and Gilpin, op. cit.

35. Lande 1988b, op. cit.

36. Simberloff 1993, op. cit.

37. Charles S. Elton. 1958. The Ecology of Invasions by Animals and Plants. Methuen, London.

38. Daniel Simberloff. 1995. Introduced species. Encyclopedia of Environmental Biology. Academic Press, San Diego, 2:323-336.

39. See G. Carleton Ray. 1988. Ecological diversity in coastal zones and oceans. In Edward O. Wilson (ed.). Biodiversity. National Academy Press, Washington, D.C, pp. 36-50.

40. James T. Carlton. 1992a. Dispersal of living organisms into aquatic ecosystems as mediated by aquaculture and fisheries activities. In Aaron Rosenfield and Roger Mann (eds.). Dispersal of Living Organisms into Aquatic Ecosystems. Maryland Sea Grant College, University of Maryland, College Park, pp. 13-46; James T. Carlton. 1992b. Marine species introductions by ships' ballast water: an overview. In M. Richard DeVoe (ed.). Introductions and Transfers of Marine Species: Achieving a Balance between Economic Development and Resource Protection. South Carolina Sea Grant Consortium, Columbia, pp. 23-26; L. James Lester. 1992. Marine species introductions and native species vitality: genetic consequences of marine introductions. In DeVoe, op. cit., 79-90; and Earnest H. Williams, Jr. and Carl J. Sindermann. 1992. Effects of

disease interactions with exotic organisms on the health of the marine environment. In Devoe, op. cit., pp. 71-77.

41. Simberloff. 1991. Keystone species and community effects of introduced species. In Lev R. Ginzburg (ed.). Assessing Ecological Risks of Biotechnology. Butterworth-Heinemann, Boston, pp. 1-19.

42. Gerald E. Walsh. 1967. An ecological study of a Hawaiian mangrove swamp. In George H. Lauff (ed.). Estuaries. American Association for the Advancement of Science, Washington, D.C., pp. 420-421.

43. William E. Odum, Carole C. McIvor and Thomas J. Smith, III. 1982. The Ecology of the Mangroves of South Florida: A Community Profile. U.S. Fish and Wildlife Service, Office of Biological Services, Washington, D.C.; Patricia A. Hutchings and Peter Saenger. 1987. Ecology of Mangroves. University of Queensland Press, St. Lucia; J. H. Davis, Jr. 1940. The ecology and geologic role of mangroves in Florida. Carnegie Institute, Washington, D.C., Publication 517. Tortugas Laboratory Paper 32:303-412; L. R. Holdridge. 1940. Some notes on the mangrove swamps of Puerto Rico. Caribbean Forester. 1:19-29; and James Carey. 1982. Mangroves — swamps nobody likes. International Wildlife 12(5): 19-28; Simberloff 1991, op. cit.

44. John D. Thompson. 1990. *Spartina anglica*, characteristic feature or invasive weed of coastal salt marshes? Biologist 37:9-12; John D. Thompson. 1991. The biology of an invasive plant. BioScience 41:393-401; Verner et al., op. cit.

45. O. Stapf. 1914. Quoted in Thompson 1991, op. cit., p. 394.

46. Mark D. Bertness. 1984. Habitat and community modification by an introduced herbivorous snail. Ecology 65:370-381 and C. Dean. 1988. Tiny snail is credited as a force shaping the coast. New York Times, Aug. 23, pp. B-15, 19.

47. Some documented examples are summarized by Simberloff 1991, op. cit.

48. James A. Drake, Harold A. Mooney, F. di Castri, R. H. Groves, F. J. Kruger, M. Rejmanek and M. Williamson (eds.). 1989. Biological Invasions: A Global Perspective. Wiley, Chichester and Simberloff 1994b, op. cit.

49. S. E. Humphries, R. H. Groves and D. S. Mitchell. 1991. Plant invasions of Australian ecosystems: A status review and management directions. In Richard Longmore (ed.). Plant Invasions: The Incidence of Environmental Weeds in Australia (Kowari 2). Australian National Parks and Wildlife Service, Canberra, pp. 1-127.

50. D. C. Schmitz, B. V. Nelson, L. E. Nall and J. D. Schardt. 1991. Exotic aquatic plants in Florida: A historical perspective and review of the present aquatic plant regulation program. In T. D. Center, R. F. Doren, R. L. Hofstetter, R. L. Myers and L. D. Whiteaker (eds.). Proceedings of the Symposium on Exotic Pest Plants. U.S. Department of the Interior/National Park Service. Washington, D.C., pp. 303-326.

51. Michael Neushul, C. D. Amsler, D. C. Reed and R. J. Lewis. 1992. Introduction of marine plants for aquacultural purposes. In Rosenfield and Mann, op. cit., pp. 103-135.

52. Ibid. and D. M. Wilkinson. 1992. Development of the program mandated under the Non-Indigenous Aquatic Nuisance Prevention and Control Act of 1990. In DeVoe, op. cit., pp. 127-129.

53. Simberloff 1994b, op. cit.

54. Thompson 1990, op. cit.

55. Elton 1958, op. cit.

56. Williams and Sindermann, op. cit.

57 James A. Brock. 1992. Selected issues concerning obligate pathogens of non-native species of marine shrimp. In DeVoe, op. cit., pp. 165-172 and Carl J. Sindermann. 1992. Principal issues associated with the use of non-native shrimp species in aquaculture. In DeVoe, op. cit., pp. 149-154.

58. Simberloff 1988, op. cit. and 1994b, op. cit.

59. Lester, op. cit.

60. Ibid. and Mart R. Gross. 1991. Salmon breeding behavior and life history evolution in changing environments. Ecology 72:1180-1186.

61. Elton, op. cit.

62. Carlton 1992a, op. cit.

63. Lester, op. cit. and Terry Y. Nosho. 1992. History of the Pacific

oyster industry in Washington State. In DeVoe, op. cit., pp. 97-102.

64. Nosho, op. cit.

65. Lester, op. cit.; Roger Mann, Eugene M. Burreson and Patrick K. Baker. 1992. The decline of the Virginia oyster fishery in Chesapeake Bay: Considerations for introduction of a non-endemic species, *Crassostrea gigas* (Thunberg). In DeVoe, op. cit., pp. 107-120 and George E. Krantz. 1992. Present management position on *Crassostrea virginica* in Maryland with comments on the possible introduction of an exotic oyster, *Crassostrea gigas*. In DeVoe, op. cit., pp. 121-126.

66. See Krantz, op. cit., p. 123 for Maryland and Mann et al., op. cit. for Virginia.

67. Jane Lubchenco, Annette M. Olson, Linda B. Brubaker, Stephen R. Carpenter, Marjorie M. Holland, Stephen P. Hubbell, Simon A. Levin, James A. MacMahon, Pamela A. Matson, Jerry M. Melillo, Harold A. Mooney, Charles H. Peterson, H. Ronald Pulliam, Leslie A. Real, Philip J. Regal and Paul G. Risser. 1991. The sustainable biosphere initiative: an ecological research agenda. Ecology 72:371-412.

68. C. J. Badger. 1990. Eastern shore gold. Nature Conservancy 40(4): 7-15.

69. Jerry F. Franklin. 1989. Toward a new forestry. American Foresters 95(11,12):37-44.

70. M. R. Dardeau, R. F. Modlin, W. W. Schroeder and J. P. Stout. 1992. Estuaries. In Courtney T. Hackney, S. Marshall Adams and William H. Martin (eds.). Biodiversity of the Southeastern United States. Aquatic Communities. Wiley, New York, pp. 615-744.

71. Robert E. Johannes and B. G. Hatcher. 1986. Shallow tropical marine environments. In Soulé, op. cit., pp. 371-382.

72. See William E. Odum. 1982. Environmental degradation and the tyranny of small decisions. BioScience 32:728-729.

73. R. H. Richmond. 1993. Personal communication.

74. W. B. Kessler, H. Salwasser, C. W. Cartwright, Jr. and J. A. Caplan. 1992. New perspectives for sustainable natural resources development. Ecological Applications 2:221-225.

75. Simberloff 1994b, op. cit.

76. National Research Council. 1986. Ecological Knowledge and Environmental Problem-Solving. Concepts and Case Studies. National Academy Press, Washington, D.C.

77. For example, Louis W. Botsford and Subodh K. Jain. 1992. Applying the principles of population biology: assessment and recommendations. In Subodh K. Jain and L. W. Botsford (eds.). Applied Population Biology. Kluwer Academic Publishers, Dordrecht, pp. 263-286.

78. L. D. Druehl. 1973. Marine transplantations. Science 179:12.

79. See, for example, Neushul op. cit. and Simberloff 1994b, op. cit.

80. See, for example, Drake, op. cit.

81. Simberloff. 1986b. Introduced insects: A biogeographic and systematic perspective. In Harold A. Mooney and James A. Drake (eds.). Ecology of Biological Invasions of North America and Hawaii. Springer-Verlag, New York, pp. 3-26.

82. Elton, op. cit. and R. Norton Chapman. 1931. Animal Ecology with Special Reference to Insects. McGraw-Hill, London & New York.

83. Simberloff 1986b, op. cit. and 1994b, op. cit.

84. See, for example, Neushel, op. cit.

85. Lester, op. cit.

86. Daniel Simberloff. 1995. Why do introduced species appear to devastate islands more than mainlands? Pacific Science 49(1):87-97.

87. Roger I. E. Newell. 1988. Ecological changes in Chesapeake Bay: Are they the result of overharvesting the American oyster, *Crassostrea virginica*? In Understanding the Estuary: Advances in Chesapeake Bay Research. Proceedings of a Conference, 29-31 March 1988. Chesapeake Research Consortium, Baltimore, pp. 536-546.

8

Scientific Management in Europe: The Case of the North Sea

Jean-Paul Ducrotoy

The North Sea has been fished and traveled for millennia. It comes as no surprise that it has been the subject of numerous, often concurrent, governance and management arrangements. Unweaving the web of acronyms to trace the history and function of perhaps the most successful international scientific advisory body to any North Sea regime, the North Sea Task Force (NSTF), is no easy task. Briefly, the London Declaration of 1987 deemed the Oslo and Paris Conventions to be insufficiently scientific and thus inadequate to provide the scientific advice needed to identify proper policy options and choices. The Declaration mandated the creation of the NSTF, which had as its mission the creation of a uniform data monitoring system throughout the North Sea, the compilation and dissemination of all scientific data via North Sea Quality Status Reports (QSRs), and the identification of any gaps in existing knowledge.

The NSTF accomplished its mission successfully from 1987 to 1993, at which time its functions were subsumed into a new body created out of the Oslo and Paris Commissions, known as the Convention for the Protection of the Marine Environment of the North-East Atlantic. From an international regimes standpoint, it is useful to look carefully at the NTSF as a case study of an epistemic community, to use Haas' term, and at how its function was differently conceptualized by different North Sea actors. The need for scientific expertise and guidance remains constant, yet the ways in which the epistemic community is admitted into the management process can vary and affect its usefulness. The precautionary principle was introduced into North Sea regional environmental management during NSTF's tenure, changing policy thinking not only in the North Sea, but worldwide. NSTF scientists raised suggestions to improve the utility of data and data sharing and to explain the nature of uncertainty and variability to policy makers, all subjects which arise repeatedly in other chapters of this volume.

Twenty years ago, the North Sea, an enclosed, relatively shallow body of water having limited exchange with the Atlantic Ocean, was declared "one of the most heavily polluted sea areas in the world."[1] Such shallow and enclosed seas are thought to be at risk from problems caused by pollution. Human activities around the North Sea have developed over centuries on a scale unsurpassed in most parts of the world. Thus, it should not be surprising that human environmental impacts have become a threat to the continued welfare of this important sea. Both localized and general pollution problems exist. Areas of persistent long-term pollution are found mainly near the sources of discharge, yet the open sea is not free of chemical contamination. Although not considered severe pollution, low concentrations of organic contaminants such polychlorobiphenyls (PCBs) are common. More worrying are the effects of activities such as commercial fishing and agriculture. North Sea fishing affects commercial and noncommercial species, including benthic organisms such as molluscs which are disrupted by trawling, and predators such as seabirds and marine mammals which may suffer from reduced food supply. As Simberloff notes in the preceding chapter, genetic drift in fish populations due to decades of heavy fishing is now a distinct possibility. Agriculture has an indirect impact through eutrophication on the biological structure and functions of marine ecosystems.

In response to such events as the *Torrey Canyon* grounding of 1967 and in an attempt to solve environmental problems in the

North Sea, politicians have installed several intergovernmental organizations aimed at regulating the use of the marine environment for waste disposal.[2] These agreements include the London Dumping Convention (1972), the MARPOL Convention (1973) and the relevant protocol of 1978, the Law of the Seas Convention (1983), and the recommendations of Part B in the Oceans Chapter of Agenda 21 of the United Nations Conference on Environmental and Development (1992). Agreements specific to the North Sea include the Convention for the Prevention of Marine Pollution by Dumping from Ships and Aircraft, or Oslo Convention (1972), and the Convention for the Prevention of Marine Pollution from Land-Based Sources, or Paris Convention (1974), jointly known as OSPAR.

Recently, efforts have been underway to improve the decision making procedures in the North Sea by to relying on appropriate knowledge and adopting a scientific approach to problems. The Joint Monitoring Group (JMG) of OSPAR, with its Joint Monitoring Programme, was unable to tackle the existing shortfall in knowledge about the North Sea since it was not a scientific body and had no authority to install scientific committees. In addition, many observers recognized that the JMG was so involved in administrative matters that preparing overview documents on the health of the Convention waters was out of its reach. Shortcomings in scientific knowledge were particularly apparent for trends in inputs, linking inputs to actual contaminant levels and environmental impacts. A bonafide coordinated scientific program was needed, and in particular a simple, effective monitoring plan to provide consistent and comparable data. Such knowledge was seen as necessary to allow strategic decisions on environmental protection to be made and to assess the effectiveness of measures already taken. As such, the NSTF was created in 1988.

MANAGING THE NORTH SEA: A SCIENTIFIC APPROACH

In the past, most legal initiatives aimed at improving the health of the North Sea have come in response to crises, and thus several management actions continue to coexist.[3] North Sea protection and management are currently undertaken by a number of international agreements and bodies which oversee various aspects of its environmental management and these generally predate other regional marine pollution agreements such as the UNEP Regional Seas Programme. The first International Conference on the Protection of the North Sea in 1984 highlighted the need to scientifically assess the extent to which the North Sea was affected by human activity. This resulted in the production of the 1987 QSR, based on national contributions of information, followed by an interim report in 1990, and the final QSR in 1993.

In 1987, the Ministerial Declaration of the second International Conference on the Protection of the North Sea (known as the London Declaration) identified remaining shortcomings in the scientific knowledge of the North Sea environment. The Conference requested the International Council for the Exploration of the Seas (ICES) and the Oslo and Paris Commissions (OSPARCOM) to jointly take responsibility for developing a research program and to set up an intergovernmental working group in 1988, to be known as the NSTF. By way of background, ICES, founded in 1902, is the oldest intergovernmental marine organization in the world (although not the largest), and it has collected and disseminated extensive literature on marine fisheries, oceanography, and contaminants. The mandate given the NSTF was to carry out work leading, in a reasonable time-scale, to a dependable and comprehensive statement of circulation patterns, inputs and dispersion of contaminants, ecological conditions and effects of human activities in the North Sea."[4] Membership in the NSTF included the eight North Sea states (Belgium, Denmark, France, Germany, the Netherlands, Norway, Sweden and the United Kingdom) and representatives of the Commission of the European Communities. Observers from the Common Wadden Sea Secretariat also took part in the scientific assessment. The NSTF secretariat was based in the OSPARCOM head office in London, and worked in close cooperation with ICES in Copenhagen.

OSPARCOM's policy also evolved and in 1989 the Paris Commission adopted the precautionary principle: contracting parties agreed to reduce at-source polluting emissions of substances that are persistent, toxic and liable to bio-accumulate by the use of the Best Available Technology (BAT) and other appropriate measures. As a result of this policy shift, in 1992 the Commissions decided to merge the two former conventions into one new instrument, the Convention for the Protection of the Marine Environment of the North-East Atlantic. Among the annexes contained in the new convention, one deals with assessment of the quality of the marine environment. It is understood that the relevant annex would continue the scientific work of the NSTF within the new structure, since the NTSF itself was debriefed in 1993.[5] One immediate question is whether the scientific approach specific to the NSTF will be easy to incorporate into a much more complex organization or whether the case of the ephemeral task force will remain unique and difficult to revive within a more political framework.

While OSPARCOM was expanding its scope, a regional organization, the North Sea Commission, was created in 1990. The Commission is made of regional governments within the framework of the 1973 Conference on Peripheral Maritime Regions which deals with particular transnational regions like the North Sea. The objectives of the North Sea Commission are to further partnership between regions which manage the North Sea and to promote the North Sea Basin as a major economic entity within Europe. An environmental group was founded in 1992 in order to further key environmental issues as they affect local authorities bordering the North Sea by influencing future research and future European Union and national policies. It may be possible for this group to take over the scientific work left unachieved by the NSTF.

Although waste generation is unavoidable, the environment must be used in a way which avoids polluting. If marine ecosystems are to be used for waste disposal, surveillance and management must be organized to minimize its impacts. Thus, waste disposal must be conducted as part of a broad holistic approach.[6] The need for such stronger horizontal interconnections of North Sea management policy has recently been recognized, and the NSTF began this task.[7] The Third North Sea Conference invited the

NSTF to attempt, in a holistic QSR, a general assessment of the entire North Sea and to address a number of specific topics.[8] Earlier oceanographic studies demonstrated the need to understand inputs from the Atlantic Ocean and the Baltic Sea. Upon receiving advice from ICES on how to plan a regional study, the NSTF decided to include the northern parts of the North Sea, the English Channel and the regions of the Kattegat-Skagerrak. Furthermore, the NSTF was invited to carry out a number of additional tasks including the elaboration of techniques for the development of ecological quality objectives and the coordination of species and habitat protection plans in order to help assess measures taken to protect marine sites.[9]

From the inception of the NSTF, emphasis was placed on the need to adopt a scientific approach to environmental problems. In essence, the role of the new group was to collect and disseminate the existing scientific knowledge about the North Sea environment and to highlight gaps in existing knowledge and needs for future research. The approach and full participation of ICES as a cosponsor guaranteed a scientific focus for future work to protect the North Sea. Finally, the new Advisory Committee on the Marine Environment (ACME) played a major part in reviewing the text and illustrations of the QSR.

Of course there are limits to scientific assessment. All scientific studies contain elements of uncertainty and may lead to provisional conclusions and predictions. It is very difficult to extrapolate laboratory results to the natural environment: the problem of proving causality is particularly difficult. The precautionary principle, subject of heated debate between policy makers and scientists, illustrates these difficulties well. This principle first appeared at the First International Conference for the Protection of the North Sea, held in Bremen in 1984, when the ministers recognized that the environment is best protected against pollution through timely preventive measures. The ministers declared that coastal states and the European Community (EC) must not wait for proof of harmful effects before taking action.[10]

The level of harm, in terms of biological effects, may be difficult to assess. Synergistic effects between manmade chemicals and unforeseen environmental factors make it hard to focus on any un-expected contaminant. The third International Conference for the Protection of the North Sea in the Hague (1990) went further with the precautionary principle, recognizing the need to take action even where there is no scientific evidence proving a causal link between emissions and effects.[11] The NSTF never dealt with this discussion, remaining focused on the Monitoring Master Plan (MMP). The new Convention for the Protection of the Marine Environment of the North-East Atlantic has improved the definition of the precautionary principle, introducing the notion of "reasonable grounds for concern" as a basis for taking preventive measures.[12] This subjective notion demonstrates that the precautionary approach is a political and policy-oriented doctrine. It takes scientific assessments into account but is not a scientific exercise in itself.[13]

EXPLAINING NSTF SUCCESS

The NSTF "is often cited as a model for how science and decision-making can be effectively connected."[14] The NSTF has based its work on sound scientific knowledge and has used strong supporting scientific evidence to suggest orientations in policy making. Its objective was not to prove specific hypotheses, but to collect convincing information taking into account natural variability and the fact that many environmental factors play a role. When making recommendations for new regulatory decisions, the NSTF relied on policy choices but started from a scientific overview of the problems. Domestic administrative forces rarely prevailed over transnational scientific ones. This was achieved though various initiatives such as establishing expert groups to address a particular issue and prepare advice for consideration by the whole Task Force, and organizing scientific workshops and informing fellow North Sea colleagues of research progress.

However, the political backing and reasoning for the creation of the NSTF seems to have been weak and not well established, thus helping to explain its short life-span. The idea of installing a scientific group to meet issues raised at the North Sea Conference was pushed forward by scientists. The scope of its coverage consisted of monitoring and assessment of a specific area, the North Sea, through a scientific approach. How did the NSTF manage to fulfil this difficult "scientific task?" In the annex to the London Declaration (1987), six elements were proposed for inclusion in its work:

1. agreement on the substances and/or parameters to be measured, the methods to be used to measure or calculate these, the frequency and location of sampling and/or measurement

2. a properly designed and managed quality assurance program covering sampling and analysis for monitoring and research purposes

3. more and higher quality data to be collected in a harmonized manner specifically for the purpose of defining conditions in the North Sea

4. special programs in specific high risk areas such as the Wadden Sea (on seal populations), the Kattegat (on the effects of eutrophication and anoxia), and British estuaries (on chemical contamination)

5. the development of models for assessment purposes, able to make full use of the improved data base, and as management tools to determine the effectiveness of existing or planned control strategies

6. research designed to fill gaps in the knowledge of causal mechanisms needed for the interpretation of the results from elements 1-5 above[15]

The Advisory Committee on Marine Pollution (ACMP, the precursor to the ACME) produced recommendations on how to prepare the assessment. This resulted in the MMP which was a program of environmental monitoring based on an innovative sub-regional approach (see Figure 8.1). Unfortunately, the MMP was only run in 1990 and 1991 and was abruptly interrupted because of a lack of motivation at national level and the need to keep monitoring costs at a minimum level for some countries.[16] The rules established in order to carry out the MMP were simple and clear. In contrast to the Joint Monitoring Programme, they included a short list of factors in a few matrices which were easy to follow.[17] The MMP also helped to structure relationships inside the task force and was typical of the teamwork spirit enjoyed by the group.

The NSTF devoted considerable effort to addressing problems related to improvement of chemical and biological measurements (including biological effects) and it benefitted from the work of groups such as the Marine Chemistry Working Group of ICES. Most of the work, however, was done on a voluntary basis with no real international support. The ICES Data Centre played a key role in collecting and processing the data and providing it for preparation of the QSR. The data was assessed by ICES experts holistically. This difficult and time-consuming work, done by practicing scientists, guarantees that conclusions on the distribution of contaminants are valid and can be regarded as reliable. However, a large quantity of data was not usable because of the lack of intercalibration between laboratories. The data provided by various governments generally suffered from a lack of comparability and missing information on quality assurance procedures. Some laboratories had difficulty adhering to previously agreed protocols regarding sampling and sample processing. Delays in data provision almost sabotaged the work of ICES assessment groups, and in some cases data never materialized. As a result of their experiences with the NSTF, ICES and OSPARCOM, scientists approached the EC with suggestions for funding a "Quality Programme" to address these problems. This resulted in the launching of the EC QUASI-MEME program, a collaborative project among European marine institutes. The project is funded by the Community Bureau of Reference and has developed the use of Quality Manuals in each laboratory. This will improve documentation, reporting, account-

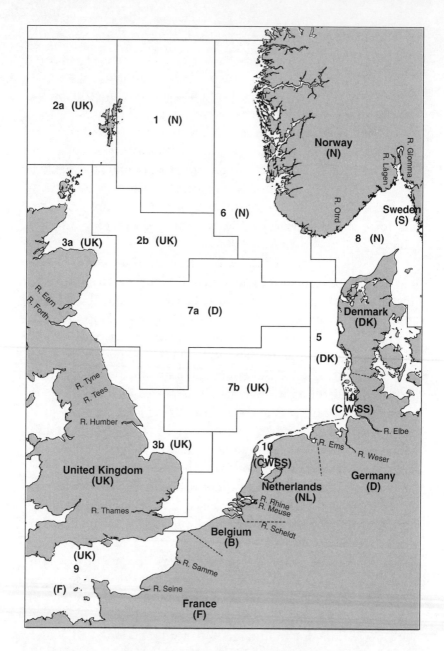

Figure 8.1. Subregions of the North Sea adopted by the North Sea Task Force. The subregions are based on the natural hydrographic variations of the North Sea. Source: See Jean-Paul Ducrotoy, Janet Pawlak, J. Portmann, C.P. Reid, L-O Reiersen. 1991. Scientific activites in the framework of the North Sea Task Force. Source: North Sea Environment Report 4:1-54.

ability and the tracking of information (which was a difficulty experienced by the NSTF). Through a network of laboratories, a Quality Assurance proficiency testing scheme has been launched to improve the performance of inexperienced laboratories and to join the proficiency scheme.[18]

The division of the North Sea into subregions has led to an increased emphasis on sensitive areas. Further work is needed on vulnerable areas and it would be advisable to develop additional studies on, for example, estuaries. In addition, the NSTF prepared an inventory and a comparison of models relevant to its work. Indications of the expected impacts of a reduction of inputs including nutrients and some contaminants were made available. These results were incorporated in the 1993 QSR.[19] In the future, sub-regional modelling techniques need to be developed, including coordinating model verification and validation exercises.

To expand scientific understanding the NSTF undertook two principal activities of research coordination: information dissemination of current research programs via a database, and field studies coordination (see Figure 8.2). Topics developed included eutrophication, biological monitoring programs, ecological quality objectives, the impact of fishing on ecosystems, the protection of habitats and species such as marine mammals and birds, as well as surveys of marine sites and assessments of existing damage and methods for reconstruction. However it is the QSR, prepared through a two-tiered system, which remains the NSTF's crowning achievement. Figure 8.2 demonstrates that holistic assessment, embodied in the QSR, was a essential element in providing policy makers with sound scientific knowledge.

First, the compilation of scientific information was prepared by a group of practicing scientists mostly from universities or research institutes. Nominations were simply "confirmed" by governments so as to ensure participation of "independent" scientists. They were organized into five Drafting Panels for the QSR chapters on geography, oceanography, chemistry, biology, and ecology. As secretary of the NSTF, editing the book was my responsibility with assistance from a "drafting group" led by the Vice Chairman of the NSTF, and comprised of the Environment Secretary of ICES and three scientists nominated by the NSTF.[20] The report was presented to the ACME of the ICES for critical review (see Figure 8.3).

The scientists involved in the preparation of the QSR and various workshops came from diverse scientific backgrounds. The physical, chemical, and biological scientists concentrated on un-

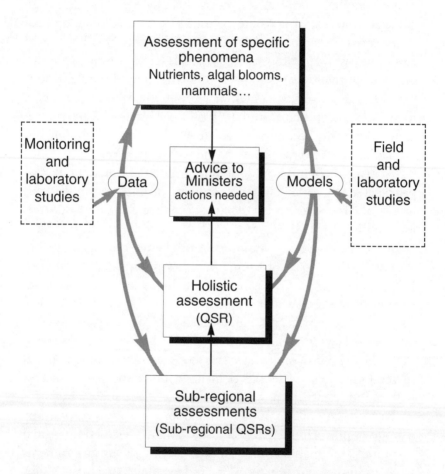

Figure 8.2. NSTF's methodology to prepare the 1993 QSR. Note: The sub-regions are based on the natural hydrographic variations of the North Sea. Source: See Jean-Paul Ducrotoy, Janet Pawlak, J. Portmann, C.P. Reid, L-O Reiersen. 1991. Scientific activites in the framework of the North Sea Task Force. Source: North Sea Environment Report 4:1-54.

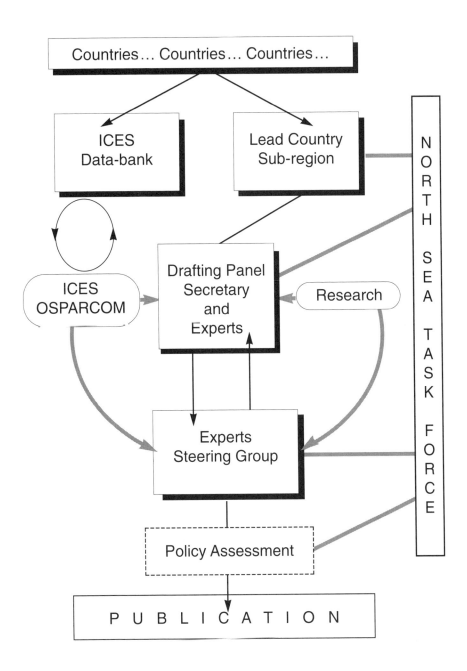

Figure 8.3. Flow of information through the NSTF organization. Source: See Jean-Paul Ducrotoy, Janet Pawlak, J. Portmann, C.P. Reid, L.-O. Reiersen. 1991. Scientific activities in the framework of the North Sea Task Force. Source: North Sea Environment Report 4:1-54.

derstanding the links between inputs and the distribution of substances introduced into the marine environment and the toxicologists and ecophysiologists were crucial for assessments of biological effects. Obvious limits of the exercise included the availability of knowledge and the extent to which scientists could assess and predict the consequences of substance introduction into the marine environment.[21]

Secondly, it was decided by the Experts Steering Group that the report would then go to the NSTF for adoption but that no changes altering the meaning or the content of the report would be allowed. Delegates to the NSTF represented their governments. They had the difficult task of bridging the gap between scientific inputs and policy recommendations.[22] The delegates were responsible for producing the last two chapters of the QSR, incorporating conclusions and recommendations. Leadership in these proceedings came more from individual entrepreneurial delegates than from specific national delegations. In fact, there were passionate and chaotic discussions at the NSTF about issues such as wording, and concentrations of certain substances in seawater and sediment. The conclusions reached by the research scientists were not altered in any significant way.

LESSONS FROM THE NSTF

Due to the fragmentation of North Sea environmental management, it has been difficult to achieve anything approaching ecosystem management. However, the London Declaration (1987) must be interpreted as a suggestion, in the strongest terms, to the Oslo and Paris Commissions that they be more scientific in their work. The NSTF accomplished this mission and serves as an example of the complementarity of scientific and policy-oriented approaches. The NSTF experience suggests a possible list of the categories of scientific knowledge required to support marine environmental protection, including those types which (1) link inputs of contaminants to their distribution in the marine environment, from sources to sinks; (2) expand understanding of the effects of substances introduced into the marine environment on biological systems and other resources; and (3) use an ecosystem approach incorporating the above knowledge into a holistic view of the ecology of animal and plant species in their specific habitats.

The NSTF synthesized considerable knowledge and made it available in clear terms in the QSR.[23] Why, then, was the organization's duration so short? Science is generally understood as synonymous with "progress" and a means to meet many human needs. But science cannot yield certainties on the consequences of human behavior. Science is never able to achieve conclusions beyond the reach of criticism and the scientific approach does not produce copious information (even ordered according to logic) to be used straight away by policy makers. In fact politicians seem to be attracted by the procedure of science itself, i.e., the working methodologies that go into the advancement of learning.[24]

Science can proceed only on a basis of confidence. Fraud exists in the scientific world but it can be quickly relegated to a situation in which disbelief prevents further progress. This may not be the case in politics. Even if the layman is bewildered by the concepts of science, he may be seduced by the simplicity of its reasoning. He may be tempted to confuse the beauty of the idea itself with its abilities to solve problems. The temptation to apply the scientific approach to policy making is great, but political and administrative problems cannot necessarily be translated into scientific terms, nor are they systematically scientific in character. These mistakes can be made easily by groups with weak scientific foundations. Unfortunately, the degree of political learning by the NSTF was low; ultimately, this may be the reason it no longer exists.

How was it possible, in the case of the NSTF, to turn such difficulties into a synergy between science and government? It is not the purpose of science to make the world better, but it can help solve problems which make management more practicable. The role of such bodies as the NSTF is, therefore, to develop applications of available knowledge. Its success lies in its ability to facilitate dialogue between science and politics. Scientists must be consulted, but responsibility remains political. Dilemmas arise when policy makers involved in environmental management are forced to take scientific uncertainties into account. A lesson learned while drafting the QSR is that all uncertainties should be incorporated into any assessment, even if scientific reports look hesitant and pessimistic as a result. Difficulties also arose when scientists attempted to incorporate notions of natural variability and when the NSTF as a whole had to interpret the observed changes in the environment.

The main objective of the group, through its scientific drafting panels, was to give concordant advice from the scientific world. As advised by the Joint Group of Experts on the Scientific Aspects of Marine Pollution shared between the International Maritime Organisation and other organizations, every effort was made by NSTF scientists to better understand the sources of variability and their underlying principles.[25] However, the "pollution approach" is still prominent in the environmental arena. It is hard for governmental bodies to go beyond the discussion of acceptable concentrations in seawater, sediment and organisms. Human activities constitute only a portion of the factors influencing observed changes in marine ecosystems. Thus, scientific advice can serve as only one part of potential solutions for specific problems, not as a final answer in a crisis situation. In this respect, NSTF demonstrated that science can and should help governmental decision-making, but also that science is not and will never be able to correct political uncertainty and incompetence, or balance commercial ambition and greed.

NOTES

1. Gunter Weichart. 1973. Pollution of the North Sea. Ambio 2(40): 99-106.

2. See Peter M. Haas, this volume and Peter M. Haas, Robert O. Keohane and Marc A. Levy (eds.). 1993. Institutions for the Earth. MIT Press, Cambridge.

3. Graham Bennett. 1989. The international control of land-based discharges to the North Sea: a policy review. In Cato ten Hallers-Tjabbes and Auke Bijlsma (eds.). Distress Signals: Signals from the Environment in Policy and Decision Making. Proceedings of the

Third North Sea Seminar, Werkgroep Nordzee, Amsterdam, pp. 55-59; and Haas et al., op. cit.

4. North Sea Task Force. 1993. North Sea Quality Status Report 1993. Oslo and Paris Commissions, London. Olsen & Olsen, Fredensborg, Denmark, p. 1.

5. OSPARCOM. 1993. Ministerial Meeting of the Oslo and Paris Commissions. Paris, 21-22 September 1992, p. 303.

6. GESAMP. 1991. Global strategies for marine environmental protection. UNEP Reports and Studies 45:1-36.

7. Patricia Birnie. 1992. Comparative evaluation in managing conflicts: lessons from the North Sea experience. In Paolo Fabbri (ed.). Ocean Management and Global Change. Elsevier Applied Science, London and New York, pp. 308-324.

8. Peter Hoogweg, Jean-Paul Ducrotoy and Ben van de Vetering. 1991. The North Sea Task Force: the first two years. Marine Pollution Bulletin 22(7):328-330.

9. Jean-Paul Ducrotoy. 1992. The North Sea Task Force: a new approach to assessing the quality of the North Sea. Ocean Challenge 3(1):32-35.

10. Ministerial Declaration. 1984. International Conference on the Protection of the North Sea, Bremen, Germany, 1 November.

11. Ton Ijlstra. 1990. The third International North Sea Conference. Marine Pollution Bulletin 21(5):223-226.

12. Claire Nihoul. 1993. From the Oslo and Paris Conventions to the Convention for the Protection of the Marine Environment of the North-East Atlantic. North Sea Task Force News May 1992:3.

13. A. R. D. Stebbing. 1992. Environmental capacity and the precautionary principle. Marine Pollution Bulletin 24(6):287-295.

14. R. Ferm. 1992. Foreword. In Jean-Paul Ducrotoy, Janet Pawlak, Georges Pichot, John Portmann, Chris Philip Reid, Lars-Otto Reiersen (eds.). Scientific activities in the framework of the North Sea Task Force. North Sea Environment Report 4:1.

15. Ministerial Declaration. 1987. Second International Conference on the Protection of the North Sea, London, 24-25 November.

16. John E. Portmann. 1991. The implementation of the Monitoring Master Plan. North Sea Task Force News. November 1991:4-5.

17. Jean-Paul Ducrotoy, Janet Pawlak, J. Portmann, C.P. Reid, L.-O. Reiersen. 1991. Scientific activites in the framework of the North Sea Task Force. North Sea Environment Report 4:1-54.

18. D. E. Wells. 1993. QUASIMEME — an introduction. QUASI-MEME Bulletin 1:1-5.

19. North Sea Task Force 1993, op. cit.

20. John Portmann, Janet Pawlak, Ben Van de Wetering, Hein-Rüne Skjoldal and Marcel Chaussepied, respectively.

21. M. Elliott and Jean-Paul Ducrotoy. 1991. The future direction of studies on spatial and temporal comparisons of coasts and estuaries. In M. Elliott and Jean-Paul Ducrotoy (eds.). Estuaries and Coasts: Spatial and Temporal Intercomparisons. Olsen & Olsen, Fredensborg, Denmark, pp. 385-390.

22. See also Frieda Taub in this volume.

23. North Sea Task Force 1993, op. cit.

24. See Sheila Jasanoff and Peter M. Haas in this volume for differing discussions of this point.

25. GESAMP, op. cit.

9

Scientific Communities and Multiple Paths to Environmental Management

PETER M. HAAS

Students of environmental politics and policy are typically concerned about the disjuncture between policy advice for the management of coastal and semi-enclosed seas and actual political processes for their management. It is common for environmental policy analysts to contend that the effective management of such seas requires a comprehensive management style using the systematic application of scientific understanding of ecosystems to the management of complex marine ecosystems by all the major current and anticipated users.[1] Such analysts hope for an international political process of social learning where new threats or problems are identified and collective understanding evolves and is mobilized to respond to and collectively manage newly apparent risks.[2] Very sophisticated international cooperation is required.

In practice this process is very rare. Ecological information is seldom translated into comprehensive management for regional and semi-enclosed seas.[3] Domestic and international political systems are typically poorly equipped to adopt and effectively implement such demanding policies. Problems of both information availability and of political power and practice inhibit their rapid and effective application. National regulatory bodies are typically organized to consider and apply management styles designed for discrete problems rather than cross-cutting ones. Timely environmental quality data is often absent, the relevant holistic or ecological models and environmental quality data — when they exist — often remain limited to the purview of the scientific community, while the government administration is ignorant of or indifferent to them.[4]

Politically, users who benefit materially in the short-term from the exploitation of a common resource are generally better represented in the policy process then those who bear costs in the short-term and advocate controls in order to support sustainable development over the longer term. Internationally, governments are often reluctant to commit to elaborate and binding arrangements for collective-action problems such as the management of regional seas, out of a fear that their economies will be saddled with onerous economic costs not be shared by their partners in the area and economic competitors outside.[5] Recent research in international relations suggests the conditions under which different patterns of regional ocean management are likely to occur.

Two reasonably distinct models now exist in the international relations literature about how international regimes for marine environmental cooperation are likely to occur, and the array of plausible policy interventions to promote them. Each model includes a distinctive cluster of features, whose expression varies in each model. These include: (1) the political process by which a regime is created and maintained (i.e., negotiation or leadership); (2) the regime's substance (its scope of coverage and the stringency of its rules); (3) the compliance effects on participating countries (effectiveness); (4) the durability and permanence of the regime (ability to exist beyond the political factors which help account for its creation); and (5) the degree of learning which it fosters. Learning is a political process through which collective behavior is modified in light of new collective understandings. It may be manifest either through more sophisticated policies for the management of a discrete issue, or through the appreciation of linkages between issues which come to be managed in tandem. This chapter examines and applies two recent models of international environmental cooperation to understand the collective management of regional seas and contrasts experiences of international environmental cooperation in the Mediterrranean and the North Seas in order to test the models' predictions and identify possible procedural interventions to improve the quality of the management of regional seas more generally.[6]

INSTITUTIONAL MODELS OF ENVIRONMENTAL REGIMES

Institutionalists focus on interests and analyze the context or setting under which cooperation may be valued and pursued by states out of self-interest. Such analysts typically focus on the institutional context in which decisions are taken, seeking to specify features which may promote the possibility of joint gains being realized through regime creation. Actors are generally portrayed as egoistic, rational utility maximizers, albeit with incomplete information. Their interests are viewed as given, and largely invariant. Alternatively, analysts may take actors' statements of their preferences at face value as accurate depictions of their objectives. Knowledge is generally seen to play a minor role, although it can be a source from which actors recognize new interests, or appreciate a change in institutional context.

Contractual institutionalists who are informed by social choice approaches focus on bargaining structures through which regimes are created and maintained.[7] They assume an area of common interests, and seek to specify institutional factors which may encourage actors to overcome their reluctance to cooperate. Individuals and collective entities are regarded as constructive, information seeking actors. The policy question is how to provide them with sufficient incentives — of which information is one — to ensure outcomes beneficial to the international community, such as preserving the environment. Power is not as important as is the opportunity for finding joint gains from cooperation. States' recognition of their preferences is essential for successfully applying bargaining techniques, as well as understanding states' behavior in collective negotiations. Institutionalists believe that large numbers of parties make regime creation more difficult, and increase the likelihood of very weak and transitory regimes. Conversely, they believe smaller numbers increase the possibility that institutional bargaining could lead to more stringent and durable regimes.[8]

Institutionalists have only minimal expectations about environmental cooperation. They expect to find negotiated regimes whose substance merely reflects the measures tolerable to the least enthusiastic party. Arild Underdal has formulated this behavioral pattern as the "law of the least ambitious program."[9] Consequently, collective measures are often far too diffuse and weak to significantly improve environmental quality, as in the management of international fisheries, and, until 1987, in collective efforts to protect the North Sea and Baltic from pollution.

Least ambitious programs are largely formalizations of the least stringent existing national efforts. Such regimes typically lack serious compliance measures (for either monitoring or enforcement), and regulatory standards tend to be very undemanding. In regions where countries have no or weak standards, the regime will be correspondingly modest. In situations where some states have stronger standards, the weakest one will still serve as the regime norm. Even in these mixed situations compliance is a relatively minor matter. States with weaker standards will not be asked to do more than they are already doing, and backsliding by states with stronger measures is unlikely due to public scrutiny at home and sunk investment costs by firms. Some simple emulatory policy learning may be possible, but more sophisticated institutional learning is unlikely because governments are driven by experience and a reluctance to accept new obligations, and because joint decisions reflect the views of the least enthusiastic party.

Some alternatives to the least ambitious program option exist. Stronger regime patterns are possible if negotiations occur within a setting of institutional bargaining. Oran Young characterizes institutional bargaining as the setting in which regimes are created and maintained through bargaining between several distinct types of actors, including states and NGOs, in an organizational context and subject to uncertainty about the costs and benefits of cooperation.[10] While actors are seeking to obtain their own preferences, they may not be fully certain as to what these preferences are. Under such circumstances Young expects that actors will have only a weak regard for distributional effects. In institutional bargaining, leadership can come from a country, entrepreneurial individual diplomats, or non-state actors — including international organizations, NGOs or epistemic communities. Such a leader can help identify compromises from which everyone else may benefit. With the use of such techniques as stressing uncertainty, monitoring, repeated or "iterated" games, promoting equity and integrative bargaining over debate on distributive and efficiency issues, and the introduction of such "selective incentives" as side payments, political pressure, or education, designers may create and maintain regimes which exceed the least ambitious program.

Robert Axelrod, Robert Keohane, Elinor Ostrom, and Oran Young identify other institutional factors by which negotiated regimes may exceed the limited scope of least ambitious program regimes.[11] They observe that stronger, long lasting regimes are possible when it is easy to monitor and verify actors' compliance with major behavioral obligations, numbers of participants are relatively small, actors are engaged in iterated games, and actors are encouraged to consider long-term effects of their actions (the shadow of the future). Institutionally created regimes may persist if participants come to appreciate the value provided by the regime, and realize that continued cooperation is preferable to a relapse into policy disorder. Regimes established by a hegemon may also persist past hegemonic decline for institutional reasons, as Robert Keohane argues with regard to international economic regimes.[12] Hegemonically inherited regimes may also be regulatory in form, if they were originally designed with regulatory standards.

Environmental regimes concluded in the aftermath of hegemony may aspire to regulatory content, but the regulations are unlikely to initially exceed least ambitious program levels because countries tend to disagree profoundly about appropriate regulatory standards for environmental protection. Regimes are likely to be designed to encourage the provision of information about the quality of the environment (monitoring) and other countries' pollution control activities, administer pollution control facilities, or pay clean up costs from a joint insurance fund. These are international functions which are generally regarded as desirable in the environmental realm both on their own merits and because they backstop a regulatory regime by quickly alerting parties to defections.[13]

Institutional bargaining may contribute to movement away from the least ambitious program over time, subject to domestic level pressures. As national environmental pressures mount, governments are forced to try to persuade their neighbors to adopt stronger measures as well, creating a ratcheting element in the least ambitious program process. Important domestic factors which may result in greater pressures for stronger environmental policy include the division of powers between the federal and state levels, legal traditions, administrative organization and expertise, relations between the judiciary and administration, and a country's research system and its input into public policy.[14] Regimes that exceed the least ambitious program demand stronger compliance from laggards than leaders. Because the regime will probably end up with measures which are weaker than in the strongest country, little accommodation is required by the leader. Laggard countries, however, must beef up their measures to comply with the regime. Leaders may even have their efforts inhibited or retarded by other countries, who may urge them to go slowly in their adoption of more rigorous standards that could introduce new incompatibilities between the national systems they are trying to harmonize. For instance, Sweden's efforts to reduce sulfur dioxide emissions from autos were slowed by up to two years by the European Community's reluctance to adopt similar measures.[15]

Environmental regimes which provide incentives for states to participate are likely to be more effective than ones which do not. Major factors which encourage state compliance include regime features which: create stable bargaining environments, so that on-going negotiations are possible and future expectations of rewards are created; enhance national concern, so governments are held accountable by their populations for complying with international obligations; and offer improvements in state capacity so that states are rewarded for their participation and find it easier to comply with their obligations.[16]

Learning is possible in institutional bargaining. New policies may be identified and adopted, and some issue linkage may occur. Because actors are engaged largely in integrative bargaining involving exploratory forays to determine the exact shape of the bargaining pareto frontier, new scientific findings and consensual knowledge may lead actors to substantively link issues in a regime. Many learning processes are possible within international institutions: through demonstration effects laggard countries may gradually come to emulate stronger policies applied elsewhere; and information may be exchanged by experts leading environment ministers to adopt new measures. While policies may be imitated by other countries, most countries will remain strongly conditioned by the fear of unreciprocated policies and hence fail to adopt new policies which would threaten competitiveness.

Such an approach may have significant value for understanding European environmental negotiations, where many countries have already adopted domestic environmental measures and there are clear reasons for harmonizing national efforts. It is difficult to apply institutional insights to issues where countries with strong domestic environmental protection measures are reluctant to engage in meaningful international discussions, such as the United States during the 1980s. However, there are limits to the applicability of institutional bargaining techniques. If issues are not widely regarded as generating collective outcomes for all, such techniques are unlikely to be effective. Even if actors share common aversions (an assurance game), there will be eventual distributional squabbles — perhaps in a second game — which, if actors rationally anticipate, means that they will also be unwilling to engage in constructive bargaining to resolve the first easier problem.[17]

EPISTEMICALLY INFORMED BARGAINING

Cooperation can also be understood in terms of knowledge. Scholars who stress perceptions, cognitive processes and interpretive approaches to understanding international relations commonly stress the role of ideas and knowledge in shaping the perceptions, beliefs, expectations, and preferences of major actors.[18] Such theorists argue that interests are often unknown, or incompletely specified. Consensus about policy relevant understanding can contribute to shaping regime patterns. Interests are identified subject to consensual knowledge, and the decision to deploy state power is conditioned similarly. Recently, it appears that such explanations have growing utility, as an environmental regime pattern emerges, driven not only by state power, but by the application of scientific understanding about ecological systems to the management of environmental policy issues with which decision makers are unfamiliar. The role of scientific or expert understanding in international policy coordination is documented for security and economic issues as well as environmental ones.[19]

Scientific knowledge may be best operationalized in terms of epistemic communities. Consensual knowledge does not emerge in isolation, but rather is created and spread by transnational networks of specialists. Under conditions of complex interdependence and generalized uncertainty specialists play a significant role in attenuating such uncertainty for decision makers. Leaders and politicians are typically poorly informed about the sources of pollution, extent of contamination, interaction between emissions and water quality, costs of clean up, and likely actions of their neighbors. Such conditions are particularly puzzling in technical issues which possess low probability but high risk outcomes, and in which specific state interests may be hazy.

Under such circumstances perceptions may be false, leaders lack adequate information for informed choice, and traditional search procedures and policy making heuristics are impossible. Information is at a premium, and leaders look for those able to provide authoritative advice to attenuate such uncertainty, and either consult them for policy advice and/or delegate responsibility to them. Subsequent discussions and policy debates are then informed and bounded by the advice which leaders receive. International negotiations may then be viewed "as a process for reducing uncertainty" as well as a process of deferring to specialists.[20] Such experts' influence is subject to their ability to avoid widespread internal disagreement, and it persists through their ability to consolidate political power by capturing important bureaucratic positions in national administrations, from which they may persuade other decision makers or usurp control over decision making.

Epistemic communities are networks of knowledge-based communities with an authoritative claim to policy relevant knowledge within their domain of expertise.[21] Their members share knowledge about the causation of social or physical phenomena in an area for which they have a reputation for competence, and a common set of normative beliefs about what actions will benefit human welfare in such a domain. In particular, they are a group of professionals, often from a number of different disciplines, who share the following set of characteristics:

1. Shared consummatory values or principled beliefs. Such beliefs provide a value based rationale for social action of community members.

2. Shared causal beliefs or professional judgment. Such beliefs provide analytic reasons and explanations of behavior, offering causal explanations for the multiple linkages between possible policy actions and desired outcomes.

3. Common notions of validity: intersubjective, internally defined criteria for validating knowledge.

4. A common policy enterprise: a set of practices associated with a central set of problems which have to be tackled, presumably out of a conviction that human welfare will be enhanced as a consequence.

In environmental issues, many of these experts have been members of an ecological epistemic community. Members of the epistemic community which has dominated technical discussions in environmental regimes have subscribed to holistic ecological beliefs about the need for policy coordination subject to ecosystemic laws. Thus, they promote international environmental regimes grounded on policies which offer coherent plans for the management of entire ecosystems, sensitive to interactions between environmental media (such as air and water), sources of pollution, and contending uses of the common property resource, rather than being limited to more traditional policies for managing discrete activities or physical resources within fairly short term time horizons.

Epistemic communities are likely to be found in substantive issues where scientific disciplines have been applied to policy oriented work and in countries with well established institutional capacities for administration, science and technology. Only governments with such capacities would see the need for the technical skills which epistemic community members command, and such professionals would only be attracted to governmental service when they believe that their policy enterprise can be advanced. Crises or widely publicized shocks are probably necessary precipitants of environmental regime creation, but crises alone are insufficient to explain how, or which, collective responses to a perceived joint problem are likely to develop. Epistemic communities help to identify cause and effect relationships, elucidate linkages between problems, define the consulting state or organization's interests, and formulate policy. Learning will occur in the policy system as new policy relevant knowledge is identified and applied to a common problem.

When epistemic communities are widely spread, even in the absence of leadership by a strong state, environmentally effective regimes are possible. Environmental regimes in this instance emerge through institutional bargaining. Regimes are most likely to be created following widely publicized environmental disasters which mobilize public and experts' demands for governmental action. Regime negotiation and maintenance would be characterized by conference diplomacy, with many countries seeking to resolve shared problems subject to the technical advice which they receive from their own experts, NGOs, transnational scientific networks and from international organizations. Non-state actors play an important role. As epistemic communities obtain and consolidate influence in different governments, national preferences and policies come to reflect the epistemic beliefs. International organization secretariats can play a key role as sources of information and new policy ideas, as well as buffering political differences between the parties. In addition, epistemic communities have often been lodged in international organizations such as the United Nations Environment Program (UNEP) and its Regional Seas Programme.

The negotiated regime would then reflect the causal and principled beliefs of the epistemic community. National positions would vary according to the extent of penetration by epistemic communities, or the sensitivity of policies in that country to policies in a country or international institution already influenced by the epistemic community. In most cases this would make epistemic environmental regimes more stringent and comprehensive than other forms of environmental regimes due to the more sophisticated vision of ecological problems which ecological epistemic communities hold. These regimes will be regulatory and persist until the epistemic community's shared body of knowledge collapses or its institutionalization declines. Both leaders and laggards might modify their policies in light of the new regime as a bandwagoning process develops, leading to gradual, progressively increasing changes in national policies to accommodate evolving scientific understanding of ecosystems. As with other patterns, anticipation of material rewards from the regime (capacity building provisions, for example) would also encourage states to comply with the regime.

Learning would reflect lessons imparted by the epistemic community. Policies and linkages may be quite sophisticated, reflecting the quality of its beliefs. The extent to which such lessons are accepted and converted into new policies in different countries, as well as regime compliance, are subject to the ability of members of the epistemic community to occupy key bureaucratic slots and to persuade others of their preferred policies. They may encourage governments to undertake new patterns of economic development

based on more complex and integrated visions of ecological interactions, organize issues in novel ways, and make decision makers
aware of previously unrecognized possibilities for mutual gain from
cooperation.

Learning in this context may be quite complex as policy makers
reflect on their objectives and recognize or appreciate new substantive connections between issues previously regarded as distinct,
subject to an ecological understanding of global ecological dynamics
and a dawning recognition of extensive interplay between environmental protection and other state concerns. As such actors inter-
cede in policy making, they may change national attitudes towards
environmental protection, thereby overcoming the antipathy to
institutional creation and international cooperation. New institutions would be created by bargaining and the gradual insinuation
of such groups into international secretariats and national bureaucracies, rather than by state leadership.

The epistemic community pattern may well have differential
impacts on advanced industrialized and developing countries. Advanced industrial countries, with greater familiarity and ability to
evaluate external advice will be more likely to defer to transnational scientific recommendations. Conversely, many developing countries are highly suspicious of technical advice and information
from abroad, and will only defer to scientific advice which is provided through domestic channels. The development of indigenous
scientific capability reinforces the authority of those scientists providing advice to decision makers.

COMPARISON OF MODELS

In policy terms, institutionalized cooperation conforming to the
Epistemically Informed Bargaining model is likely to generate more
desirable regimes for managing coastal seas than cooperation
which follows the Institutional Bargaining model, although both
are preferable to inaction. Such models can be assessed in terms of
their conformity to six broadly held and applied norms: (1) a
model's likely contribution to ecological improvement; (2) the
economic efficiency of the anticipated regime; (3) the range of political representation within the regime; (4) the level of equity in

the regime's provisions; (5) the potential for anticipatory action; and (6) the regime's flexibility or ability to promptly develop new measures in response to changes in the policy environment (this ensures that participants are not locked in to costly efforts should their need be challenged). Thus, the models can be appraised in terms of the general features of the regimes they anticipate, and the degree to which the particular environmental policy attributes of the regimes are likely to generate an effective set of arrangements for the environmental protection of a common resource. Not only should the environment be protected, it should be protected in a way which does not seriously threaten other societal goals. The assessment of the two models in terms of these six enumerated norms appears in Figure 9.1.

Pragmatically, epistemic community models are more efficient than institutional ones because they reflect existing political realities about the distribution and availability of technical environmental information. Epistemic communities are naturally favored by decision makers as sources of information and advice, and are likely to be more widely invoked than the multiple, often poorly organized and suspicious groups necessary for a fully specified institutional model to be effective. For those who regard environmental threats as imminent, an epistemic community model is likely to provide policy outputs which more accurately capture the nature of the environmental crisis. The epistemic community models are likely to provide better environmental policy than institutional models because measures will be more closely calibrated to ecosystem realities, and more flexible because they are in tune with consensual understanding of threats to particular ecosystems and the capacity of these ecosystems to withstand such threats. In addition, policy responses are far more likely to be prompt and anticipatory rather than slow and reactive.

The assertion of the technical superiority of epistemically provided information requires support because the knowledge component of the epistemic community's claims are socially constructed.[22] However, the policy advice of the epistemic community is likely to be better because it is not a direct expression of underlying material interests and because it is more likely to be true than advice from other sources. Thus, it is more likely to obtain its desired effect on the policy target. Unlike general political claims, knowledge based claims are grounded on empirical verification and a set of internally derived truth tests. Their application and subsequent learning may promote 'better' policy because the knowledge claims are relatively non-biased and have passed a consensus test for truth.

Comparison of Models

ECOLOGICAL IMPACT: Epistemic community models are more likely to contribute directly to a sustainable level of ecological equilibrium than are institutional models because the ecological epistemic community members may directly apply consensual scientific understanding about ecosystem dynamics to the policy process. Institutional models alone, while open to scientific inputs, are constrained by the need to reach political compromises amongst the participants, leading to lower levels of ecological quality.

ECONOMIC EFFICIENCY: Other things being equal, ecological epistemic communities should be better able to determine economically efficient environmental measures than politicians negotiating through institutional mechanisms. However, ecologists have often focused exclusively on maximizing the environmental quality objectives identified by their disciplinary orientation, as well as preferring regulatory instruments. Economists, including the recent school of ecological economists, often argue that alternative policy instruments may provide more cost efficient ways of achieving environmental quality than regulation. Institutional models may provide more efficient regimes than models of epistemic communities composed solely of ecologists if institutional representation is sufficiently broad and there are institutional provisions for the weighing of all approaches in such a way that least-ambitious programs do not prevail. If the epistemic community is organized or mobilized more broadly, then the epistemic model may generate more efficient regimes.

POLITICAL REPRESENTATION: Institutional models clearly provide for fuller participation and representation of stakeholders in the management of shared resources, although in practice many groups are excluded. The

---

Figure 9.1. Comparison of epistemic and institutional models.

Such evolutionary arguments accept that knowledge is socially constructed, but contend that it cannot be entirely reduced to social influence external to the scientific community.[23] Through careful study of intellectual history it is possible to determine whether the identification of consensually determined views occurred by procedures which were acceptable to the majority of the involved community — and hence regarded as valid judgments of veracity

epistemic community model privileges technocratic decision-making models over more democratic and representative ones based on the argument that such measures are likely to generate regimes which are more likely to improve environmental quality and which are likely to persist beyond the short-term correlation of political forces giving rise to an institutionally-based regime. Over time, regimes designed by ecological epistemic communities may become more representative as a consequence of the community's principled and causal beliefs that the widespread inclusion of local participants contributes more sources of information to a regime and may also contribute to its durability as more supporters are attracted.

EQUITY: Institutional models may generate more equitable regimes which reflect the concerns of all parties because no one party can be forced to unwillingly sustain undue costs once the regimes are adopted and maintained through a process of voluntary compromise. Epistemic models may be equitable if the epistemic community values equity highly.

POTENTIAL FOR ANTICIPATORY ACTION: The involvement of an epistemic community in a regime is likely to encourage anticipatory action by providing a channel for timely environmental information which would be processed much more slowly through an institutional model.

FLEXIBILITY: Epistemic community models would be more flexible than institutional models because they are likely to be more responsive to current understandings of the physical environment. Consequently, because policy is based on consensual knowledge rather than on political compromise it will be easier to modify past choices in light of new information and understanding.

Figure 9.1, continued.

according to the consensus theory of truth — or whether they reflect the introduction of fundamental bias and distortion. Recent reconstructions of the development of plate tectonics, for instance, demonstrate that scientific understanding can progress without being significantly distorted by external social, cultural or political influences.[24] An evolutionary approach does not demolish the truth claims of experts; it scrutinizes the process by which knowledge claims are created and applied. Concretely, the commitments of the epistemic community to truth tests and the degree to which members' specific knowledge base conforms to these criteria must be identified through interviews and studies of specialized publications of technical advisors before their entry into policy making.

Contrary to more general criticisms of the vulnerability of the broader scientific community to political capture and influence, epistemic communities, because of their shared cognitive bonds, are more immune to temptations to temper their beliefs. It is common practice for scientific advice to be subsumed by the political interests of dominant groups or to the bureaucratic exigencies of an institution which may have solicited such advice.[25] The internal belief system of the epistemic community, members' socialized faith in it, and their willingness to subscribe to a code of truth-tests would presumably counterbalance pressures to temper advice to the needs of soliciting institutions. To some extent these bonds create a common sense of community, identity, and belief which community members will not easily reject. Subsequent bureaucratic infiltration and influence by community members could also compensate for institutional pressures to ignore or distort community positions.

Epistemic community models remain elitist models of decision making. They favor a small group of technically (and technocratically) trained individuals who do not speak for all stakeholders in environmental conflicts. Since the late nineteenth century such individuals have been systematically conferred authority by the modern bureaucratic state out of an overarching and historically grounded faith in the application of scientific knowledge and engineering to the management of human affairs (founded in part during the Enlightenment as a reaction to autocratic government based on aristocratic privilege and capricious policy based on religious faith), as well as an instrumental affinity between the social application of these disciplines and the acquisition of prosperity and welfare in modern industrialized societies, on one hand, and between a complex modern administrative state and the provision of advice which is expedient for governance. Originating in Western Europe, these beliefs spread worldwide and are now part of the globalization of international relations.[26]

EXPERIENCE IN THE MEDITERRANEAN

Efforts have been underway since the early 1970s to protect the Mediterranean and the North Seas from pollution. The experiences vary in ways the two models would predict. An epistemic community was involved in managing the Mediterranean, and the Mediterranean regime closely follows the epistemically informed bargaining model. The North Sea, in the absence of an epistemic community, progressed from a least-ambitious program to an institutional bargaining model. The Mediterranean is widely regarded as one of the more effective collective efforts to manage a regional sea.

It is estimated that annually 350 million tonnes of solid material, including about 800,000 tonnes of nitrogen, 500,000 tonnes of hydrocarbons, 320,000 tonnes of phosphorous, 90 tonnes of pesticides, 60,000 tonnes of detergents, 21,000 tonnes of zinc, 100 tonnes of mercury, 3,800 tonnes of lead, 2,400 tonnes of chromium, 12,000 tonnes of phenols, 2,500,000 tonnes of organic material, as well as 2,540 Ci/a of radioactive materials flow into the Sea from human sources.[27]

The regime was established in 1975, with the adoption of the Mediterranean Action Plan, and grew in stringency and scope. In 1976 the umbrella Barcelona Convention was signed, as well as protocols banning dumping of wastes at sea and organizing cooperation in cases of oil spill emergencies. In 1980 a protocol was signed which regulates land-based sources of pollution; banning emissions of a set of widely used toxic compounds, and requiring common standards for the emissions of a broader set of less toxic materials. In 1982 a protocol for specially protected areas was adopted and, in 1993, the parties called for the complete elimination by 2005 of all "toxic, persistent and bioaccumultaive substances directly and indirectly discharged into the Mediterranean...with priority given to organohalogens."[28] All treaties rapidly entered into force. Control measures for 12 pollutants or groups of pollutants have been adopted since 1985, and efforts are underway to develop common standards for all substances in the 1980 protocol.

Coordinated research and monitoring activities have been sponsored by UNEP since 1976, involving the training of hundreds of North African scientists and technicians and the provision of new laboratory equipment. A Regional Coordinating Unit was established in Athens in 1982, which now has a biannual budget of 13.2 million dollars. A Regional Oil Combating Center was set up in Malta in 1976. An integrated planning unit was established in 1977 in France to generate prospective models of regional growth trajectories, called the Blue Plan, and to encourage more comprehensive views of economic planning. A Priority Action Programme was established in 1979 in Yugoslavia to study more concrete projects of immediate interest to the developing countries, including soil protection, water resource management, fisheries and aquaculture management, human settlements, tourism, and 'soft' energy technologies. A Coastal Areas Management Program was established in 1990 to promote development planning in accordance with local environmental conditions. A center for dealing with specially protected areas was established in Tunis in 1985.

This vibrant regime is seen by well regarded local scientists as reversing the decline of Mediterranean water quality. The Mediterranean is probably no dirtier than it was 20 years ago, despite a doubling of the coastal concentration of industry and population. Originally designed to control discrete sources of pollution, by 1990 the regime aimed to encourage more comprehensive coastal zone management. Following the elaboration of the regime, many national pollution control efforts progressed as well, including construction of sewage treatment plants, new environmental legislation, application of environmental impact assessment type procedures to economic planning in five countries, and the introduction of measures that modify existing environmental standards and techniques to control the broader list of substances in the Med Plan.[29]

From 1970 to 1975 France was the regionally predominant power within the regime. It controlled a large proportion of the trade affected by environmental regulations, had the most developed marine science capability, had a strong reputation for diplomacy, and regarded the Mediterranean as a region in which French foreign policy should hold sway. Preparations for the 1972 United Nations Conference on the Human Environment (UNCHE) alerted government officials to the new issue of the environment, and Jacques Cousteau sounded public alarms about the impending "death" of the Sea. Yet decision makers were highly uncertain about their possible range of action. They lacked specific information about the extent of contamination, its causes, and the Sea's ability to sustain pollution, as well as about the range of possible policy responses. National Fisheries Directors approached the General Fisheries Commission of the Mediterranean to collect information about the causes and extent of marine pollution in the Mediterranean, and to draft a treaty for regional protection. The FAO delivered an interim report in 1972 demonstrating that pollution was fairly extensive, and required immediate action.

France convened a conference in 1972 to promote a regional convention to control oil spills which resembled extant French policy commitments. However, many developing countries were suspicious of French motivations, and, together with Italy and Spain, deputized UNEP in 1974 to direct efforts on a draft treaty and regional action plan. The French government consistently opposed including substances or policy instruments in the regime which did not mirror existing French programs, although France was ultimately unable to unilaterally determine the regime. In the absence of an epistemic community and with regime power concentrated in France, little learning occurred during this period, as information on regional pollution was scarce. Few states had yet established national authorities with regulatory responsibilities, and only France, Israel, and Yugoslavia adopted even general marine pollution control laws for oil and dumping. The environment remained isolated from other political issues of regional concern.

French regional dominance persisted until 1980, but the Med Plan's second phase, 1975-1980, was distinguished by the mobilization of a regional ecological epistemic community. France was the primary source of funding for Med Plan activities, and strongly pressed its preferences at international meetings. While France maintained a predominant share of tangible power resources, it was unable to compel others to its preferred policies, and ultimately made concessions to others at negotiations. French efforts at control were stymied by the UNEP secretariat's refusal of French offers to unilaterally conduct monitoring, draft treaties, and house the headquarters. Instead, the secretariat drafted documents endorsing the control of a broader range of pollutants than France preferred as well as supporting monitoring and research in other countries. Developing countries were subsequently much more willing to participate in and support regional talks held under UNEP's auspices. The Land Based Sources Protocol eventually covered radioisotope emissions and pollution transmitted through rivers and the atmosphere, over French and Italian objections. While the quality of regional marine science was surely not as high as that done in France, expanding scientific participation served the political function of expanding the constituency for pollution control.

UNEP's leadership efforts were conditioned by a regional ecological epistemic community. By 1975 UNEP had obtained control over drafting procedures from the FAO, and proceeded to develop a more comprehensive set of policy proposals than the FAO had anticipated. UNEP was staffed much more heavily with ecologists, and the officials responsible for the Mediterranean were members of the ecological epistemic community. They hoped to develop comprehensive regional measures for promoting environmentally sensitive styles of economic development. The members came from a variety of professional backgrounds — engineering, marine science, and law — but all were enamored with the holistic policy philosophy emerging out of UNCHE and galvanized into a common policy enterprise of protecting the environment. They wanted to control a broad range of Mediterranean pollution sources, and incorporate environmental considerations into national economic planning.

Through a consulting mission for UNEP in 1974 and 1975 Stjepan Keckes, a Yugoslavian oceanographer, became familiar with most of the major Mediterranean marine scientists. The epistemic community already existed in the region; Keckes set out to mobilize it through continued involvement in the collective negotiations, by financially supporting monitoring and research, and by disseminating its findings regionally. Through UNEP, this community was mobilized and involved in regional discussions after 1976. Marine scientists worked in many national laboratories throughout the region, but lacked access to their national administrations.

The epistemic community's influence was gradually felt on the negotiations through a deliberate UNEP strategy of concurrent environmental assessment and environmental management. Research on environmental quality occurred while regime negotiations were being conducted. Thus, the scientists involved in the research had improved access to policy makers, and the negotiations were forced to take note of ongoing improvements in technical understanding about the sources and extent of pollution. Moreover, as many of the littoral countries established new environmental ministries or environmental protection agencies, members of the epistemic community were hired to staff these new bodies; in part because few professionals had the relevant experience, and because their professional profile had been enhanced through UNEP's monitoring programs. By providing such resources, UNEP deepened its transnational bond with the region's marine scientists beyond a shared concern about regional pollution. Even those who did not share UNEP's holistic vision, did support the control of specific substances with which they were familiar. Key environmental policy posts in Israel and Greece were already filled by people sympathetic to UNEP's cause, and believed, like UNEP, in the need for coherent, ecologically sound regional development. Through its scientific and monitoring programs UNEP also helped to train and equip more marine scientists to help bolster membership in the ecological epistemic community.

While France remained dominant, it did not prevail in all of its objectives. The regime's substance was regulatory; banning the use of nine proscribed groups of substances and establishing limits and permit setting procedures on the use of thirteen other groups. The actual substances covered reflected the shared understanding of the epistemic community about potential threats to the environment, which was well in excess of the more limited desires expressed by all individual countries. National policy learning also occurred during this phase. Israel, Greece, Algeria, and Spain converted co-ordinative environmental agencies into regulatory authorities, and Greece, Libya, and Morocco adopted new legislation governing oil pollution and marine dumping. Linkages remained weak though, as only France adopted legislation requiring environmental impact assessments for new development projects. Participating states began to consider the linkages between national development activities, population growth, and environmental quality through Med Plan projects such as the Blue Plan, but during this period few countries other than France expressed strong interest in the projects or their conceptual base.

By the early 1980s much of France's dominance had passed, as the North African states were able to diversify their trade dependence from France to the EC and acquire a much greater marine science capability. The regime persisted, as it became self-funding through annual governmental contributions which were proportional to their United Nations assessments. A new protocol establishing marine protected zones for endangered species was adopted in 1982, twelve control measures were adopted for previously targeted pollutants, the parties called for a reorientation from pollution control to coastal zone management in 1985, and a more comprehensive coastal zone management program was established in 1990 to help governments plan for non-environmentally destructive coastal zone developments. Administered by an international secretariat based in Yugoslavia, the Coastal Areas Management Program reflects the institutionalization of epistemic community members as well as their beliefs in the Med Plan's organizational mandate. Its focus follows naturally from the comprehensive scope of the Med Plan, and was approved and developed despite severe budgetary shortfalls for the regime as a whole.[30]

The regime was largely maintained and modified through a process of epistemically informed bargaining. It continued to develop according to the routinized institutional procedures and rules laid out in the Mediterranean Action Plan. While countries continued to engage in institutional bargaining to develop joint measures, national policy making was increasingly shaped by the epistemic community. Its members drafted national policies and, while on delegations, encouraged officials from foreign ministries to endorse UNEP's efforts for more stringent controls. Over time most countries introduced more stringent environmental protection measures, and supported the development of universal regulatory standards for specific polluting substances.

The Med Plan remained significant for both leaders and laggards (defined in terms of the stringency of their national policies). Countries in which the epistemic community consolidated its influence moved toward convergent policies. The effectiveness of the regime is not due entirely to the provision of capacity building equipment and training, as Institutionalists suggest. Countries such as Algeria and Egypt did not come to support the Med Plan until their governments received advice from domestic scientists that coastal pollution was an environmental hazard, even though they had been receiving capacity building assistance from UNEP and other international organizations for several years. The regional leader, France, wound up improving its marine pollution control efforts in accordance with the Med Plan. It also continued to financially and diplomatically support the regime throughout the

1980s. In France and Italy many Mediterranean pollution control efforts preceded the Med Plan, but trajectories of public activity rose following its creation. In each country rates of environmental investment and public enforcement of existing measures grew more vigorous in the late 1970s (for France) and late 1980s (for Italy).

The laggards also improved their environmental protection efforts in light of the Med Plan. Greece, Algeria, and Egypt embarked on new administrative campaigns to integrate environmental considerations into traditional coastal zone development and economic planning. Similar shifts are evident in Israel and Spain, although the data are less thorough. Algeria and Egypt adopted more comprehensive environmental policies. Following their participation in Med Plan discussions and the epistemic community's capture of key environmental policy units within their national administrations, policy reversals occurred in both of these countries in the early 1980s. Algeria strengthened the legal standing of its environmental agency, and passed a sweeping environmental protection law in 1983, requiring environmental impact assessments on new projects. While state infrastructure and capacity to implement such measures remain weak, the legal changes are nonetheless dramatic. Egypt also strengthened the environmental ministry in 1982, and applied more stringent domestic environmental policies in 1983.

Movement since 1990 has been slow, due to the inability of many of the developing countries to actively enforce the measures. The absence of major financial resources and a worldwide recession makes enforcement difficult. In April 1992 the World Bank and European Community announced a new program to promote sustainable development in Mediterranean countries. The division of institutional responsibilities between the Med Plan Regional Coordinating Unit and other organizations is still being worked out, but such an institutional shift may overcome financial bottlenecks which inhibit the North African countries from fully implementing projects to enforce their Med Plan obligations.

THE NORTH SEA[31]

Since the early 1970s, countries bordering the North Sea have tried to coordinate their policies to control marine pollution. Concern was initially triggered by the 1967 *Torrey Canyon* tanker spill and the 1971 meanderings of the Dutch coastal freighter *Stella Maris* as five North Sea governments refused to allow it to dump its load of chlorinated hydrocarbons in their waters. The Oslo Commission was established in 1974 to administer the 1972 Convention for the Prevention of Marine Pollution by Dumping from Ships and Aircraft, and the Paris Commission was established in 1978 to administer the 1974 Protocol to Control land-based sources of pollution in the North Sea. Regular Ministerial Conferences on the North Sea met in 1984, 1987, and 1990. Since 1978, fifty-eight decisions, recommendations, and agreements have been adopted for the North Sea. From 1978-1987 only six Paris Commission decisions were legally binding (adopted unanimously) while eight binding decisions were taken from 1987 to 1992.[32] In 1981 the North Sea received 3 million tonnes of industrial waste, 96 million tonnes of dredging material, and 5 million tonnes of mud from purification plants.[33] Current estimates reveal reductions in the volume of industrial wastes and titanium dioxide dumped in the North Sea. Total oil discharges from offshore installations have declined as well.

Until 1987 these measures were developed and applied on a substance-by-substance basis, leading to a disorganized and incoherent set of policy efforts. Some substances were regulated according to common emission standards and others by common ambient standards. Although the approach reflected scientific consensus about environmental capacity, it was slow and unwieldy. Moreover, because they received little public scrutiny and were subject to pressure from industries, many decisions were delayed or merely reflected a least ambitious program approach which was acceptable to the most recalcitrant government on any particular substance. Since 1987 institutional change has contributed to increased enforcement of environmental protection. Following the establishment of the Ministerial Conferences and the spread of environmental concern in the region, international efforts became more vibrant and stringent through an institutional bargaining approach. At the Third Ministerial Conference in 1990 Environment Ministers approved across the board reductions of 50 percent by 1995 from 1985 levels for 37 significant pollutants, and 70 percent reductions for dioxin, mercury, cadmium and lead emissions. The 70 percent figure was a compromise between the countries with ambitious domestic programs who desired cuts of up to 90 percent and those with less vigorous policies who sought only 50 percent cuts. The list and dates were also reached by compromise.

Because the institutions amplified and reflected domestic environmental concern, many countries have accelerated or broadened national programs for pollution control. Combined with mounting domestic environmental concern, the high profile North Sea Ministerial Conferences made it difficult for environmental ministers from laggard countries to oppose environmental measures by leader countries. Ministers also adopted a Memorandum of Understanding to protect small cetaceans in the North Sea which, in 1991, led the parties to adopt a weak agreement. The current weakness reflects Norway's efforts to protect its fishery interests in the region. Technical and process engineering lessons for specific industries have been circulated around the region as a consequence of meetings convened by leader countries to educate others about best available technologies.

COMPARING CASES AND DRAWING CONCLUSIONS

In the Mediterranean, national and institutional learning has been fairly comprehensive since 1980, reflecting the epistemic community's causal beliefs in linkages between environment and economic development which many of the region's governments have acknowledged. During the 1980s most countries adopted stronger domestic environmental standards for marine pollution, and environmental concerns were increasingly linked to other concerns, both domestically and internationally. Domestically, environmental impact assessments were required in Israel, Greece, Algeria, and Egypt. Internationally, most states became more active in UNEP projects with integrated planning and alternatives to coastal development which threatened marine quality, and endorsed new projects for comprehensive coastal zone management and sustainable development.

These new policies reflect the broader concerns of the ecological epistemic community, involving more comprehensive coverage of pollution sources, and developing more comprehensive planning procedures to harmonize state developmental and environmental objectives. While some governments have borrowed standards from the United States EPA or the World Health Organization, the need for such emulation was prompted by their members, and the information was transmitted through the epistemic community network. In other countries members of the epistemic community were responsible for finding the figures elsewhere and applying them in the countries where they were responsible for formulating and enforcing environmental policy.

Evidence from the Med Plan suggests that insights from each of the approaches are useful for understanding regime patterns. The first phase was largely one of institutional bargaining, with leadership exercised by UNEP, as predicted and explained by Institutionalists. The French failure to control the regime, despite unparalleled control over resources, challenges Neorealist explanations grounded solely on the distribution of power.[34] The second and third phases were periods of epistemically informed bargaining. France continued to support the regime even after its dominance had receded, contrary to Neorealist expectations. The number of substances controlled by the regime is larger than the mere summation of the concerns of individual countries, contrary to Institutionalist predictions. Moreover, the regulatory nature persisted despite the diffusion of power. Compliance by both the leaders and laggards has continued, contrary to the expectations of analysts based on the international distribution of power. Due to the absence of national resources to fully implement national obligations, the full effectiveness of the regime is less than expected based solely on the influence of the epistemic community, however.

Most striking is the rapid strengthening of the regime over twenty years. The evolving regime reflects the altered preferences of the large number of countries in which the epistemic community successfully consolidated bureaucratic power. Knowledge about the behavior of ecosystems, as imparted by the epistemic community, led states to change their preferences for types of environmental protection. As epistemic community members acquired bureaucratic power, they persuaded colleagues of the need for more sweeping national environmental policies and support for coordinated region-wide measures. As the number of countries in which it held influence grew, support for a more comprehensive regime grew as well. Changes in national preferences reflecting more stringent environmental demands occurred during a period of declining systemic concentration of power. The regime's comprehensiveness, successfully imparted despite the opposition of France and a number of developing countries to specific elements, clearly reflects the holistic beliefs of the epistemic community.

A focus on epistemic communities provides the final benefit of endogenizing knowledge based sources of regime change. As a consequence of the regime's activities, new sources of information and new actors became available to states for the articulation of information relevant to the regime's policy domain. The ecological epistemic community was initially found in just a few organizations: Israel, Greece, and UNEP. A weak regime was established through a combination of the epistemic community's influence on its own governments (through diplomatic efforts), through UNEP's organizational actions and regular international bargaining. Once established, the regime helped to identify members of the ecological epistemic community as authoritative sources of information about environmental protection, and helped to strengthen developing countries' scientific capacity, thus deepening epistemic community members' domestic power base, as well as providing institutional incentives for these countries to support the regime.

As epistemic community members consolidated their influence in their respective governments during this later phase, most notably in Egypt and Algeria, their governments came to adopt stronger domestic marine pollution control measures, and to support a more stringent and comprehensive regime. As a sufficiently large power bloc was amassed in the region, the epistemically influenced governments and UNEP were able to press for a more comprehensive regime which reflected their own policy preferences. Through this political process the shared understanding of the ecological epistemic community about the way ecosystems operate was introduced to regional environmental policy making, and institutional learning occurred through the intercession of the ecological epistemic community. The regime's rules became stronger and more sophisticated, and also linked to rules about economic development.

Epistemic communities alone do not fully explain regime patterns. Outcomes are clearly the result of power exercised by parties on behalf of the ideas and preferences imparted by the epistemic community. Institutional resources are also important for an effective regime. Yet, without heeding the knowledge controlled and transmitted by the epistemic community the analyst is unable to capture the change over time in the regime's substance, strength and effectiveness. Learning is a critical process by which regime patterns change over time, and epistemic communities are important actors for shaping what learning occurs and molding the path by which regimes evolve. To a large extent the epistemic community's influence is irreversible, as its involvement in the region's institutions, both in national administrations and on the Med Plan secretariat, will persist unless there is a full-scale purge — and even then their policies would likely endure due to various established patterns of behavior they have induced in domestic industries.

Different regime models yield different patterns of environmental cooperation. Action in both regions was precipitated by well publicized environmental crises but subsequent responses diverged. While in the Mediterranean policies were driven by epistemic consensus and learning occurred, the North Sea trajectory was very different. In the absence of an epistemic community, but with strong institutional pressures, collective measures following the 1987 North Sea Ministerial Conference reflected domestic environmental pressures. Across the board emission standards were invoked for a wide array of pollutants, counter to any scientific understanding about desirable limits, equity concerns for the relative responsibilities of different countries or economic efficiency concerns of setting such high reduction goals. The agenda was also set by public fears and media representations: measures to protect dolphins and porpoises came in response to Greenpeace claims that observed deaths were the consequence of marine pollution despite less categorical medical and biological evidence suggesting a virus as the immediate cause. The stringency and scope of the regime corresponded to pressing political demands. Effectiveness is mixed, varying by the degree of domestic environmental concern. The regime has grown in strength from its inception, but its persistence is solely a function of the continuation of strong domestic environmental concern to which the environmental ministers respond. In the absence of such domestic pressures — and environmentalism may be a faddish movement — the incentives for regime compliance and persistence evaporate. Learning in the North Sea has been limited to the exchange of specific lessons about industrial procedures for managing specific pollutants.

In short, the Mediterranean experience since the late 1970s is consistent with the Epistemically Informed Bargaining model while that of the North Sea, due to the absence of an epistemic community in the area and the lack of consensus about the magnitude and sources of environmental threats, is consistent with the Institutional Bargaining model. The first well regarded systematic summary of North Sea environmental conditions was not released until 1987, and the North Sea Task Force has only recently attempted to organize regional marine scientists into a concerted study of the sea's health.[35]

To some extent the absence of a transnational network of like-minded marine scientists in the North Sea appears surprising, given the high scientific competence of the delineating countries and the substantial regional experience with unilateral and collective efforts to manage technical issues. Yet scientists play only a minor role in the region; virtually no informal policy networks exist. Outside of Scandinavia, most applied marine science in the region is conducted in government laboratories, rather than in universities or independent laboratories. There is no potential for the creation of a community of interest independent of institutional missions. When governments assign experts to international working groups, the scientists are generally chosen from these government bodies and are accountable to the responsible ministry. The International Council for the Exploration of the Seas (ICES) was unable to play a significant role in negotiations due to its overarching fisheries mandate, lack of secretariat autonomy and general subordination to the will of the member governments. Unlike the Mediterranean case, there is a longer historical pattern of state supervision over science in Northern Europe, thus discouraging the mobilization and professional participation of the scientific community in international policy making, as well as inhibiting any formation of collective identity on the part of the region's marine scientific community.

Environmental management of coastal seas appears to vary by a regions' political characteristics. Without the involvement of an epistemic community, efforts are likely to be driven by domestic political currents. They will follow well publicized disasters more quickly than the epistemic model because of the possibility for sidestepping bureaucratic channels, be limited to well publicized environmental threats, stress across the board pollution cuts and they are likely to impose changes for industry if there is powerful domestic political support for environmental protection. In the absence of domestic political support collective efforts will simply confirm status quo measures. Even so, some laggard countries may stiffen their regulations to emulate countries with stronger environmental regulations. With the participation of epistemic communities, policy styles will be more technical, reflecting consensual scientific understanding of ecosystem behavior and carrying capacity. Efforts informed by epistemic communities are likely to be more enduring than institutionally generated ones, as institutions covary with fickle political currents while epistemic communities are likely to create more enduring organizational routines within administrative units responsible for environmental management where they can consolidate bureaucratic power. Epistemically created regimes are likely to be more economically efficient than institutional ones because of the nature of the those communities which actually receive governmental attention; however such regimes may be less easily enforced.

Some effort can be taken to identify and mobilize epistemic communities in order to expand their influence. Epistemic communities can be fostered by international institutions, as UNEP has done in its Regional Seas Programme. Regional institutions should be encouraged to foster the development of epistemic communities through enhancing regional marine science cooperation. In areas where epistemic communities may already exit, institutions should be encouraged to mobilize their participation and include them in decision making. The inclusion of epistemic communities in regional environmental institutions may broaden the substantive base of the regime and enhance its longevity.

ACKNOWLEDGMENT

I am grateful to M. J. Peterson and Henry Regier for comments on an earlier draft of this chapter. This chapter draws from Epistemic Communities and the Dynamics of International Environmental Cooperation in Volker Rittberger et al. 1993. Regime Theory and International Relations. Oxford University Press, Oxford.

NOTES

1. Adalberto Vallega. 1992. Sea Management: A Theoretical Approach. Elsevier Applied Science, London; Robert Costanza, Bryan G. Norton and Benjamin D. Haskell (eds.). 1992. Ecosystem Health. Island Press, Washington, D.C.; UNCED Agenda 21 Chapter 8. 1992. Integrating Environment and Development in Decisionmaking; and Chapter 17. Oceans and Their Living Resources.

2. Kai Lee. 1993. Compass and Gyroscope. Island Press, Washington, D.C. and Lester Milbrath. 1989. Envisioning a Sustainable Society. State University of New York Press, Albany, New York.

3. Gerard Peet. Ocean management in practice, and Edward L. Miles. Future challenges in ocean management. Both in Paolo

Fabbri (ed.). 1992. Ocean Management in Global Change. Elsevier, London.

4. Viktor Sebek. 1983. Bridging the Gap Between Environmental Science and Policy-Making. Ambio 12(2):118-120 and Martin W. Holdgate. 1982. The environmental information needs of the decision-maker. Nature and Resources 38(1):5-10.

5. Mancur Olson. 1965. The Logic of Collective Action. Harvard University Press, Cambridge; Kenneth A. Oye (ed.). Cooperation Under Anarchy. 1986. Princeton University Press, Princeton; Peter M. Haas, Robert O. Keohane and Marc A. Levy (eds.). 1993. Institutions for the Earth. MIT Press, Cambridge.

6. See also Ducrotoy in this volume; on general efforts by UNEP see Peter M. Haas. 1991. Save the Seas. In Elisabeth Mann Borgese, Norton Ginsburg, and Joseph R. Morgan (eds.). Ocean Yearbook 9. University of Chicago Press, Chicago, pp. 186-212.

7. See Robert O. Keohane. 1984. After Hegemony. Princeton University Press, Princeton; Robert O. Keohane. 1989. International Institutions and State Power. Westview Press, Boulder; Robert O. Keohane and Robert Axelrod. 1986. Achieving cooperation under anarchy: strategies and institutions. In Kenneth Oye (ed.). 1986. Cooperation Under Anarchy. Princeton University Press, Princeton, pp. 226-254; Elinor Ostrom. 1990. Governing the Commons: The Evolution of Institutions for Collective Action. Cambridge University Press, Cambridge; Arild Underdal. 1982. Causes of negotiation failure. European Journal of Political Research 11: 183-195; Oran R. Young. Summer 1989a. Politics of international regime creation. International Organization 43(3):349-376; and Oran R. Young. 1989b. International Cooperation: Building Regimes for Natural Resources and the Environment. Cornell University Press, Ithaca; Oran R. Young. 1993. Negotiating an international climate regime: institutional bargaining for environmental governance system. In Nazli Choucri (ed.). 1993. Global Accord: Environmental Challenges and International Responses. MIT Press, Cambridge, pp. 431-452.

8. William J. Baumol. 1971. Environmental Protection, International Spillovers, and Trade. Almqvist & Wiksels, Uppsala; Mancur Olson. 1965. The Logic of Collective Action. Harvard University Press, Cambridge.

9. Underdal 1982, op. cit.

10. Young 1989a and 1993, op. cit.

11. Ostrom 1990; Keohane and Axelrod 1986; and Viktor A. Kremenyuk (ed.). 1991. International Negotiation. Jossey-Bass, San Francisco.

12. Keohane 1984, op. cit.

13. The general economic or social functions which these activities fulfill can be found in Robert O. Keohane. 1982. The demand for international regimes. In Stephen D. Krasner (ed.). International Regimes. Cornell University Press, Ithaca, pp. 141-172; Keohane 1984, op. cit.; and Keohane and Axelrod, op. cit.

14. Ronald Brickman, Sheila Jasanoff and Thomas Ilgen. 1985. Controlling Chemicals: The Politics of Regulation in Europe and the United States. Cornell University Press, Ithaca; and George Hoberg, forthcoming. Governing the environment: Comparing policies in Canada and the United States. In Keith Banting and Richard Simeon (eds.). Canada and the United States in a Changing World. Vol 2.

15. Boehmer-Sonia Christiansen. January 1984. Marine pollution control in Europe. Marine Policy 8(1):44-55.

16. Haas, Keohane and Levy, op. cit.

17. Ostrom. 1990, pp. 42-43 and Robert Bates. 1988. Contra contractarianism. Politics and Society (16):387-401.

18. Peter M. Haas (ed.). 1992. Knowledge, power and international policy coordination. Special issue of International Organization 46(1).

19. Ibid.

20. Gilbert R. Winham. October 1977. Negotiation as a management process. World Politics 30(1):96.

21. Haas (ed.) 1992, op. cit.

22. My position falls between that of Ducrotoy and Jasanoff in this volume.

23. Stephen Toulmin. 1972. Human Understanding. Princeton University Press, Princeton; Imre Lakatos. Falsification and the methodology of scientific research programmes. In Imre Lakatos and Alan

Musgrave (eds.). 1974. Criticism and the Growth of Knowledge. Cambridge University Press, Cambridge, pp. 91-196; Donald T. Campbell. 1974. Evolutionary Epistemology. In Paul A. Schilpp (ed.). The Philosophy of Karl Popper. Open Court Publishing, LaSalle, Illinois, pp. 413-463; Jon Elster. 1985. Sour Grapes. Cambridge University Press, Cambridge; and Jurgen Habermas. 1979. Communication and the Evolution of Society. Beacon Press, Boston.

24. Ronald N. Giere. 1988. Explaining Science. University of Chicago Press, Chicago; and H. E. LeGrand. 1988. Drifting Continents and Shifting Theories. Cambridge University Press, Cambridge.

25. Sheila Jasanoff. 1990. The Fifth Branch. Harvard University Press, Cambridge; see also chapter by Jasanoff in this volume. Jasanoff focuses more closely on the distributional tradeoffs which are implicitly sacrificed under the rubric of technical decision making, while I focus on potential options created through technical decision making which would otherwise be politically difficult and unlikely.

26. Peter M. Haas. 1992. Introduction. In Haas (ed.), op. cit., pp. 7-12; Jean-François Lyotard. 1984. The Postmodern Condition. University of Minnesota, Minneapolis; and Anthony Giddens. 1990. The Consequences of Modernity. Stanford University Press, Stanford.

27. UNEP/WG.18/INF. 4, p. 24; and Council of Europe. 1991. The State of the Environment in Europe. Report of International Conference, Milan, 12-14 December p. 20. It is not known what percentage of radioactivity found in the Mediterranean occurs naturally as part of the background range.

28. Texts of the Barcelona Convention and its Protocols are in: United Nations. 1982. Convention for the Protection of the Mediterranean Sea Against Pollution and Its Related Protocols. United Nations, New York; United Nations. 1984. Protocol Concerning Mediterranean Specially Protected Areas. United Nations, New York; and UNEP(OCA)/MED IG.3/5. October 1993. Report of the Eighth Ordinary Meeting of the Contracting Parties to the Convention for the Protection of the Mediterranean Sea Against Pollution and Its Related Protocols. For the 1993 decision, see note 30.

29. Peter M. Haas. Summer 1989. Do regimes matter? Epistemic communities and Mediterranean pollution control. International Organization 43(3):377-404; and Peter M. Haas. 1990. Saving the Mediterranean: The Politics of International Environmental Cooperation. Columbia University Press, New York. Chapter 5.

30. UNEP(OCA)/MED IG.3/5. 1993. Report of the Eighth Ordinary Meeting of the Contracting Parties to the Convention for the Protection of the Mediterranean Sea Against Pollution and Its Related Protocols, October; and Arsen Pavasovic. 1993. Experiences and Results of the Mediterranean Action Plan of UNEP in Integrated Coastal Management in the Mediterranean Region, September. Split, Croatia.

31. The account in this section is drawn from Peter M. Haas. 1993. Protecting the Baltic and North Seas. In Haas, Keohane and Levy (eds.), op. cit., pp. 133-181.

32. J. Wettestad. 1992. The "effectiveness" of the Paris Convention on marine pollution from land-based sources. International Environmental Affairs 4(2):101-121.

33. Council of Europe, op. cit., p. 20.

34. Neorealism is one of the major contemporary research programs in international relations in the United States. It focuses on the interaction of states which are treated as unitary actors which behave rationally. For a summary of the propositions by one of its major proponents, Kenneth Waltz, and a collection of critiques, see Robert O. Keohane (ed.). 1986. Neorealism and its Critics. Columbia University Press, New York.

35. See Ducrotoy, this volume, for recent and detailed appraisal of the Task Force.

10

Compelling Knowledge in Public Decisions

SHEILA JASANOFF

As if revealing the world in a grain of sand, the widely cited phrase "speaking truth to power" conjures up a tightly-knit universe of assumptions about the proper relationship of science to social order.[1] Predicated on an unswervingly realist view of the nature of scientific knowledge, this curiously impersonal phrase implies that truths about the natural world arise without meaningful human agency or intervention, in an autonomous domain of endeavor that is cleanly separated from the uses of political power. Facts, the results of scientific inquiry, are assumed in this standard account of science in public policy to be distinct from values, which are seen as the primary medium of exchange in the political realm. Values are thought to play no significant role in the creation of scientific facts. Realists believe that productive discussion of norms and values stops at the point where public choices come to depend on chiefly on experts' objective assessments of the facts.[2] By extension, it is the duty of expert policy advisers to bring facts to bear on the processes of political evaluation and judgment, and so to keep public actions from falling prey to passion and irrationality.

Historically, the realist account of the science-policy relationship was grounded in two well-established strands of scholarship:

logical positivism in philosophy and, in postwar sociology of science, a perspective that associated scientific activities with special normative commitments designed to promote objectivity. Robert Merton's work, which coupled science uniquely with the norms of communalism, universalism, disinterestedness, and organized skepticism, framed the public rhetorical posture not only of scientists themselves, but also of policymakers who increasingly turned to science for legitimation of complex social choices.[3] It was comforting to imagine a neutral space from which scientists could objectively influence political outcomes because of their privileged ability to describe present realities and predict plausible futures. More recently, however, theoretical and empirical investigations of science policy have begun to question the boundaries that were so easily taken for granted by mid-century writers on science and the state. In this chapter I present two important competitors to the standard account of the science-policy relationship and argue that a more complex formulation, combining elements of both, is needed to explain the patterns and outcomes of policymaking based on science, and, increasingly, on scientific uncertainty.

One point of departure is the *radically relativist* critique of the standard account that emerges from studies of technological and environmental controversies over the past quarter century. Science has come to be seen in this line of research as chronically incapable of rationalizing policy because outcomes are always determined by social relations, such as the competing values of political actors. Scientific knowledge serves only to underpin particular group or class interests, lending them the appearance of objectivity, even though each side's claims of knowledge are thoroughly contingent on the purposes for which they were produced. Scientists themselves are often characterized as a captive resource in the political arena, available to be mobilized in the service of other actors.[4] Since interests shape the framing and resolution of issues, including the conduct of scientific research, science contributes no independent direction to the policy discourse. At best, one side or the other in a policy debate gains temporary advantage by claiming access to superior knowledge, but such gains are eventually wiped out as the opposing side learns to generate competing and equally authoritative scientific claims.

Growing scholarly interest in transnational policy debates has given rise to a rather different account, which also seeks to avoid the pitfalls of scientific realism. In this account, which I call *mediated realism*, science continues to be seen as the repository of a distinctive form of knowledge with the power to compel political action, but this approach incorporates the recognition that policy decisions are always made under conditions of imperfect knowledge and political contestation. Under these circumstances, it is difficult to demonstrate that actors agree to policy choices because they are persuaded by irrefutable scientific claims. Instead of focusing on the *truth* of scientific ideas, therefore, the advocates of mediated realism emphasize the role of expert groups — often termed "epistemic communities" — in producing authoritative interpretations of scientific evidence. Scientists are seen in the literature on epistemic communities as critically important players in decisionmaking, particularly in the context of international environmental regimes.[5] It is their communal work of consensus building that gives scientific knowledge and beliefs the power to cross political boundaries and influence policy; scientific accounts of reality must, in other words, be mediated by scientists in order to command general political assent. Yet, relatively little attention has been paid to the means by which scientific communities secure either their internal cohesion or their authoritative positions in the policy process. Most of the work on these coalitions uncritically assumes that they are held together by nothing more than their shared consensual understandings about the natural world.

While avoiding the naive simplicities of the standard account, neither radical relativism nor mediated realism have proved able to capture the complexity of science's place in the formation of environmental policy. By denying the independent authority of science, the radically relativist view founders against cases where scientific findings appear to have reframed policy agendas, redirected the focus of debate, and even closed ongoing controversies. By contrast, the focus on epistemic communities fails to explain how groups of experts can overcome the resistances of politics and culture to impose a commanding vision of political action on skeptical policy audiences. Missing from the science policy literature are convincingly elaborated accounts of the processes by which locally contingent or contested knowledge wins the assent of wider communities and is taken up into political decisions.

The central argument of this chapter is that, in order to influence public policy, science must achieve moral as well as epistemological authority — indeed, that the latter cannot be attained except in conjunction with the former. For scientific claims to carry weight in the policy arena, they must be harmonized with prevailing frameworks for legitimating political action; put differently, scientific discourse and political discourse must be brought into a mutually sustaining relationship. It follows from this analysis that neither science nor scientists can be counted on to *resolve* scientific uncertainty on their own. Uncertainty about facts in the political arena is almost inevitably a product of social as well as scientific indeterminacy. At best, then, scientists can work with other social actors to *repair* uncertainty.

Using examples from U.S. environmental decisionmaking, I illustrate three pathways by which the repair of scientific uncertainty may come about in the American political context: scientific ideas may prove influential because they (1) converge with prevailing cultural ideas about responsibility and fault; (2) support politically accepted forms of discourse and reasoning; or (3) are ratified by communities that have established, within well-defined boundaries, a privileged right to formulate policy. I conclude by speculating on how science may acquire similar prescriptive power even when policy issues cut across the cultural and political divisions among nation states, as they do in international environmental regimes.

THE PROBLEM OF RELATIVISM

Controversies about environmental issues multiplied in America during the 1970s, posing serious challenges to the realist view of science as an impersonal force "speaking truth to power." On a host of issues from nuclear power to hazardous waste disposal, science proved incapable of mustering a unified consensus as to what counts as truth. Instead, knowledge claims frequently fractured along lines of political interest. Thus, on the basis of scientific evidence, the nuclear industry argued that it was possible to store high-level radioactive wastes over long periods of time with minimal risk to populations or ecosystems. The chemical industry vehemently contested the claims that chemical herbicides such as DDT or 2,4,5-T presented serious risks to health or, subsequently, that bio-engineered products posed long-term threats to ecological sustainability. The building industry evaluated the threats of asbestos and formaldehyde-based insulation materials as too small for regulatory concern. In each case, environmental and consumer groups disagreed with industry's assessments and fought successful battles to translate their countervailing perceptions into tough regulatory mandates. Both sides in this way tied their political agendas to expert assessments, although they extracted from the same scientific studies vastly different estimates of risk to health and the environment.

Troubled by their failure to close these spiraling techno-political debates, scientists sought refuge in explanations that attributed all conflicts to uncertainty, that is, to lack of sufficient knowledge. Alvin Weinberg's assertion that there are scientific questions which science cannot answer struck a deeply responsive chord with fellow scientists.[6] By committing contested issues to a region labeled trans-science, Weinberg and his followers kept alive the realist conviction that science, when properly interrogated, remains capable of delivering definitive conclusions. Special decision rules are needed only in those trans-scientific situations where scientists cannot reasonably be asked to provide policymakers with the truth. Weinberg identified three such situations in his influential 1972 article on trans-science: (1) where more research would be prohibitively expensive; (2) where estimates would be required for extremely low-probability events; and (3) where inquiry would be ethically impermissible.

Scientists, however, did not long remain content with an analytic framing that took many types of "uncertainty" out of the reach of science and so reduced their power to play an active part at the nexus of science and policy. From 1970 onward, scientific inputs to environmental decisionmaking turned increasingly to developing techniques for objectively measuring and representing uncertainty. Quantitative risk assessment, in particular, emerged as a widely hailed basis for estimating the likelihood of harm in just those zones of small probability that Weinberg had once relegated to trans-science. Confident scientists declared these mathematically disciplined calculations of the unknown to be a sphere of purely technical activity (risk assessment), to be kept apart from the political world of decisionmaking (risk management).[7] The uncertainty-acknowledging abstinence of Weinberg's trans-science was replaced within a generation by a resurgence of the realists' more imperialist vision that science could represent even uncertainty as relevant to public policy.

Work in the social studies of science has provided useful correctives to scientists' naive assumption that there is a clear boundary between the technical and the non-technical aspects of science policy, but such scholarship has led, in the end, to its own simplifications. A growing body of research has shown scientific facts to be socially constructed — to be, in other words, the products of complicated negotiations among scientists over how to make and how to construe observations about the natural world. Social scientists have been able to show that in natural science fields far removed from politics closure occurs around particular descriptions of natural phenomena by intrinsically social pathways.[8] Controversies over facts are closed, for instance, through experimental replication carried out in accordance with conventions that were themselves the products of prior negotiation; through the provisional incorporation of contested facts into broader, ongoing research programs; or through tacit agreements within a research community not to disagree about poorly understood elements of a dominant research paradigm. None of these avenues are normally as effective in closing political debates about science, where combatants lack the incentives to bury their disagreements in favor of superarching professional goals, such as the continuation of productive research programs.

Confronted by the pervasive social construction of science, some analysts speculated that science is competent to guide policy only in areas where the participants are already in substantial agreement on relevant normative issues: for instance, how deeply and in what forms the state should intervene in market arrangements; what rights are due to specially vulnerable populations; or what value is accorded to an ecological resource or human life. Such overriding value choices, analysts have argued, must always hinder science from playing a completely autonomous role in policy debates. In one particularly stark formulation of the relativist position, science is always doomed to encounter either an under-critical or an over-critical policy environment — in either case it proves irrelevant to actual decisions.[9] In under-critical situations, policy actors are already in agreement with respect to values, and scientific claims will uncritically be accepted as supporting the pre-existing consensus. In over-critical settings, disagreement over values permeates scientific deliberations, so that technical issues remain contested and unresolved under intense partisan scrutiny.

This radically skeptical view plausibly accounts for many controversies over policy-relevant science, but, as noted earlier, it fails to do justice to the wealth of empirical data on episodes where protracted conflict over science-based policymaking eventually led to closure. Scientific claims seem frequently to function as effective motors for determining policy choices as well as for prolonging disputes. Thus, the recognition of the bioaccumulation of pesticides arguably gave birth to the modern U.S. environmental movement, especially after Rachel Carson, in *Silent Spring*, found a compelling narrative voice for expressing the scientific community's nascent ecological concerns. More recently, the detection of the ozone hole and the recording of increased carbon concentrations in the earth's atmosphere have been credited with arousing worldwide concern and motivating political action. Finally, the relativist position seems incapable of explaining why science remains such a potent resource for policymakers if it is entirely powerless to influence decisions.

MEDIATED REALISM AND EPISTEMIC COMMUNITIES

If radical relativism accords too little respect to science as a force in policy, the move to epistemic communities tends to err in the opposite direction. Writers on epistemic communities appear at first glance to avoid the straitjacket of realism by focusing on the bearers of claims rather than on the claims themselves. Knowledge, in this line of analysis, ceases to be a mere collection of factual assertions whose truth is guaranteed by theory and experiment. Science appears instead as a system of beliefs supported and maintained within a network of social relationships — in short, within communities that both constitute and are constituted by their common cognitive and normative commitments. For epistemic communities, according to one current definition, are groups of professionals united by (1) a shared set of normative and principled beliefs which provide a rationale for social actions; (2) shared causal beliefs, which serve as the basis for linking policy actions to desired outcomes; (3) shared criteria for weighing and validating knowledge; and (4) a common policy enterprise.[10] These like-minded professionals gain influence in the policy system through their capacity to make authoritative knowledge claims which lay the groundwork for policy prescriptions. Epistemic communities restore, in this sense, the invisible though functionally indispensable agent to the otherwise agentless aphorism of "speaking truth to power."

The difficulty of this approach for political analysis, however, is that it leaves unanswered the very question that most cries out for explanation when science is engaged in serving policy. What gives epistemic communities their peculiar staying power in the contested and deconstructive domains of politics?[11] If we assume that the cause-effect claims advanced by epistemic communities are unproblematically correct, then we are back in the world of scientific realism where facts alone are sufficient to produce actions and scientists themselves are politically superfluous. If, on the other hand, it is a set of shared values that holds epistemic communities together and empowers their instrumental role, then their claims-making activity becomes just another form of political expression designed to advance particular social ends. In this latter case, it is hard to understand why scientists — as producers of politics by other means — command higher cognitive authority than any other interested actors in the political process.[12] As in the relativist account, scientists now appear as one among many contending voices, and one must look to politics itself to see why their voices nonetheless win a privileged place in policy.

These unresolved tensions within the epistemic communities approach point toward the need for supplemental theorizing about the mechanisms by which scientific knowledge, even when contested, may be able to exert a determining influence on environmental policy. Put differently, we need ways of accounting more completely for the apparent successes of epistemic communities in connecting their causal beliefs about the environment to selected prescriptive agendas. Let us turn for further elucidation to the discursive and institutional contexts within which U.S. environmental scientists have normally sought to link their epistemological claims to social action.

RESPONSIBILITY AND CAUSATION

Controversy over the Reserve Mining Company's discharge into Lake Superior of wastes ("tailings") from the processing of taconite, a low-grade iron ore, marked a turning point for modern environmental policy in the United States. From about 1963 to 1978, the company and its opponents waged Byzantine battles in state and federal courts over the most appropriate means of controlling the potentially adverse impacts of these discharges.[13] Scientists and lawyers crossed swords over the nature and severity of the impacts, as well as over the standard of evidence that courts should insist on before ordering the cessation of productive economic activity. Reserve Mining's legal travails coincided with a shift in public thinking that eventually reduced the quantum of proof needed to justify protective environmental regulation. But the case in retrospect stands for more than a milestone in the changing consciousness about risk. It illustrates the complex processes by which social presumptions about causation and responsibility can repair uncertainty about physical causes and lead, in time, to publicly accepted decisions.

The first phase of the Reserve Mining controversy centered on the possible effects of the taconite discharges on the aquatic environment of Lake Superior and their implications for the region's commercial and recreational development. Experts argued in skirmishes before a state trial judge about whether the tailings would increase the turbidity of the lake, promote algal growth, and harm fish life or drinking water quality. By 1973, however, a new and encompassing scientific issue had appeared on the agenda: were the taconite fibers sufficiently similar to asbestos, a known carcinogen, to endanger those drinking the waterborne residues of Reserve's mining process? According to the political scientist David O'Brien, this question shifted the controversy "from that revolving around the ecological risks to Lake Superior to one over public health and safety."[14] Indeed, the public health issue completely eclipsed earlier ecological concerns and became the focal point of a 139-day trial held in the latter half of 1973.

Linking taconite with asbestos did not resolve the scientific uncertainties that had plagued decisionmakers for nearly a decade — rather, new grounds for expert disputation arose around such issues as the functional similarity of taconite and asbestos fibers, the relative risks of ingested and inhaled fibers, and the explanation for the carcinogenicity of asbestos itself. At the same time, what seemed at first a scientifically and politically isolated inquiry into the effects of taconite became intertwined with stories of responsibility and blame carrying more expansive moral overtones. Asbestos by now was emerging as America's leading symbol of death through policy neglect.[15] Cancer caused by exposure to asbestos, was already entrenched in the public mind as the most dreaded of environmental illnesses, and the fear of cancer had begun to exert its insidious influence on notions of prudent environmental management. Compensation claims by injured asbestos workers led in 1973 to a major change in judicial policy permitting workers to sue third-party manufacturers.[16] The image of asbestos as hidden killer would eventually help fuel the passage of the Toxic Substances Control

Act in 1976.[17] Associated with the deadly resonances of asbestos, taconite became in the 1970s a more politically consequential, if no less scientifically controversial, emblem of environmental concern.

Judicial attitudes, too, were changing throughout this period in response to the combined demands of new social movements and formal legislative enactments. Reduced burdens of proof for regulating risks to health and the environment were gaining support in the federal courts, most notably in the influential Court of Appeals for the District of Columbia Circuit.[18] Courts, like the activists who petitioned them for aid, had begun to accept that the changeover from a harm-based to a risk-based system of environmental management could only be achieved by requiring less than definitive evidence of risk. Judge Miles Lord, the populist trial judge in charge of the Reserve Mining case, was an early convert to this position. The Eighth Circuit, as O'Brien notes, was at first reluctant to ratify Lord's relaxation of the common law standard of proof but later approved it in response to developments in other circuits and pressure from the Supreme Court.[19]

Reserve Mining agreed in 1978, after almost fifteen years of legal conflict, to stop discharging taconite into Lake Superior. Since the carcinogenicity of taconite tailings was never firmly established, it could hardly be said that this action was prompted either by scientific consensus or by pressure from a knowledge-based epistemic community. Rather, the cessation of the discharges became the only reasonable policy choice once there was convergence between an epistemic order that gave credibility to claims of future health risks from invisible, asbestos-like fibers and a moral order that validated, in the name of environmental stewardship, precautionary actions even in the absence of definite proof of harm. Within this new cognitively and morally bounded space, predictive environmental science and preventive health policy sustained each other completely at relevant points, although there was no discernible community of actors that knit together the science and the social response.

DISCOURSES OF LEGITIMATION

As governmental decisionmakers around the world accepted the need for preventive policymaking, founded on evidence of risk rather than harm, pressure grew on the scientific community to supply plausible, quantitative estimates of impacts under various possible scenarios.[20] Modeling replaced direct perceptual experience as the basis for decisions in many fields of environmental management, from the control of carcinogenic pesticides to emissions trading policies for greenhouse gases. Regulatory scientists in the United States spearheaded the move to create and disseminate environmental models, in part because U.S. political culture strongly encourages explicit justification of regulatory decisions, grounded where possible on seemingly impartial, quantitative assessments of the evidence.[21] In an address to his disciplinary peers, a leading American ecologist expressed an attitude widely shared by scientists sensitive to policy needs: "Scientists must make clear that uncertainty is an essential part of prediction, and that decisions must be made in the face of uncertainty."[22]

What happens, however, when predictive models incorporating divergent ways of understanding the unknown are brought into conflict within a specific policy proceeding? The metaphor of "dueling" is often heard in the world of regulatory modeling, where disenchanted participants bemoan the stalemate arising from apparently unresolvable conflicts between alternative models and the divergent numerical estimates they generate. How, if at all, does scientific and political closure occur under these circumstances?

An instructive example derives from the protracted controversy between the U.S. Atomic Energy Commission (AEC) and Consolidated Edison (Con Ed), a major New York utility company, concerning the environmental impacts on the Hudson River from a planned facility at Storm King Mountain.[23] Competing teams of scientists working for the AEC and Con Ed sought to model the possible effects of water withdrawal for the plant's cooling system on striped bass populations in the river. The result, almost inevitably, was a lengthy technical confrontation between "dueling models": scientists for the major parties refined their assumptions, yet continued to differ about which assumptions best corresponded to reality. Mutual deconstruction proved to be the order of the day, since each party's model was seen by the other as an interest-driven and essentially unverifiable surrogate for direct empirical knowledge, which under the circumstances was impossible to acquire. The Atomic Energy Licensing Board observed in 1973, in near-poetic despair, "No one knows in detail what activities of life go on in the unseen depths of the Hudson River nor what the future response to changing inputs is going to be."[24]

The differences between the agency's and the utility scientists' simulations could not be resolved on the basis of universally accepted facts. Only arbitrary or implausible figures could be provided for crucial parameters, such as the magnitude of biological compensation, without which no reasonable projections could be made of long-term population effects. In the end, a greatly simplified model had to be constructed to win the assent of the involved parties and produce the 1980 "Peace Treaty for the Hudson." Relying on a technique called "direct impact assessment," this model stuck more closely to easily observable phenomena than the sophisticated but untestable alternatives that agency and utility experts had constructed during the life of the controversy. Relatively unproblematic data on the annual abundance and distribution of fish populations laid the foundation for an eventual convergence in expert calculations. Once they decided to accept these common baseline data, the experts came to roughly similar conclusions when they modeled specific biological endpoints (for example, the likely reduction in several vulnerable species through entrainment and impingement of individuals).

Science, in this case, contradicted the expectations of extreme relativists by producing a new data-driven approach to biological modeling that helped bring closure to the protracted Hudson River controversy. As in the Reserve Mining case, however, experts gravitated toward closure (in this case, the acceptance of direct impact assessment) only when the underlying policy debate shifted away from an absorption with long-term biological effects, and the merits of cooling towers, toward a focus on mitigating short-term detriments to fish populations. Scientific knowledge achieved political authority when the boundaries of the relevant moral-political space were redrawn so as to accommodate the interests of all parties. In particular, a consensus developed that entrainment was the process of greatest environmental concern, and, with this endpoint in place, the negotiating parties eventually worked out a proposal that provided a degree of mitigation acceptable to the agencies at a cost acceptable to the utilities.[25]

In a similar vein, Baruch Boxer has argued in his work on marine pollution science that even the most productive scientific research programs may have no power to sway policy unless they are integrated with, and interpreted within, a coherent framework of values and social expectations. "Sophisticated models of water circulation, ecosystem dynamics, and pollutant migration paths have been developed to describe and simulate local and regional conditions in the Hudson-Raritan estuary," Boxer observes, but it is difficult "to relate this information to ill-defined public concerns about health and the environment, given the vagueness of statutory mandates, and the overlap and imprecision of regulatory goals."[26] And shifts in the way institutional and social factors structure the use of science can undermine or offset a shared scientific sense (that is, an epistemic community's vision) of what the problem is or how it should be addressed.

KNOWLEDGE AND INSTITUTIONS

Both committed scientific realists and researchers working in the more skeptical social constructivist paradigm agree that expert institutions, such as scientific advisory committees, are capable of stabilizing the knowledge base for policy, protecting it against unlimited deconstruction. For realists, this phenomenon is quite unproblematic and hardly requires further explanation. Advisory committees are selected for their command of the "best science"; they are trustworthy because they comprise the most qualified experts in a given policy domain, and they set the stamp of validity on policy-relevant science through informed peer review and impartial assessment.

For social constructivists, who recognize that "best science" is not given but is contingent upon particular constellations of local practices and conventions, the picture is significantly more complicated. The authority of expert committees flows from their ability to demarcate their own claims as "science," as impartial, and as the best available knowledge about a given domain of inquiry. Numerous studies of expert advice and technical policymaking, have shown that bodies which fail to shore up their trustworthiness in the public domain are equally unsuccessful in articulating compelling pictures of the natural world, no matter what "objective" credentials they may have brought to their tasks.[27] An advisory committee's ability to validate knowledge claims is thus invariably bound up with the robustness of its own moral authority as constituted within the prevailing social and political culture.

The controversy over the ill-fated Westway project in New York City illuminates the subtle connections between institutional and epistemological credibility in the context of a dispute over fisheries assessment. The focus of contention in this case was a plan to construct a US$4 billion highway and waterfront development project along the Hudson River, creating prime new residential and commercial real estate but also changing the river's course, permanently altering the shape of lower Manhattan, and (most important for our purposes) influencing in unknown ways the striped bass population in the river. The attempt to assess the biological impact of Westway engaged the attentions of two groups of expert agencies: on the side aggressively favoring construction were state and federal "project agencies," the U.S. Army Corps of Engineers, the Federal Highway Administration (FHWA), and the New York State Department of Transportation; on the side urging caution were three federal "resource agencies," EPA, Fish and Wildlife Services, and the National Marine Fisheries Service. Differences among these agencies crystallized most clearly around an environmental impact statement (EIS) prepared under FHWA's direction, which declared the proposed project area to be "biologically impoverished" and hence presenting no environmental barriers to the massive Westway landfill.[28]

Between 1977 and 1981, the federal resource agencies repeatedly criticized the adequacy of the FHWA's biological assessments, commissioning at least one new scientific study for the purpose, but the project agencies pushed ahead in spite of these challenges and, in March 1981, the Army Corps finally issued a landfill permit for Westway. It was an unstable victory for supporters of the project. The entire process was reviewed first by a hostile federal court and later in a 20-month investigation by the House Committee on Government Operations. The outcome can only be described as a rout for the project agencies; the Westway EIS, in particular, failed to withstand the double-barreled scrutiny by court and Congress.

That the investigators uncovered various methodological deficiencies in the EIS under these circumstances was hardly surprising. Indeed, several of the problems identified in the initial field survey of fish in the proposed construction zone exactly followed the well-attested pattern of "experimenters' regress" described by the sociologist of science H.M. Collins.[29] In this disputing strategy, scientists attack each other's experimental techniques, proposing methodological improvements. The result is a potentially infinite regress of "tests of tests of tests," since there is no possibility of an appeal to a mutually agreed external reality that can save the original claim. Thus, the survey that FHWA had relied upon was held to be insufficient because:

> (1) sampling efforts spanned a period of less than two months; (2) stationary 'fish traps' with entrances of two inches in diameter were used to capture fish; and (3) fish sampling was not conducted in the winter, when young striped bass and other fish were known to heavily utilize the lower Hudson for protection from predators and the cold.[30]

Yet, when EPA proposed a new study to test the results of the earlier survey, the concerned agencies still could not agree on the appropriate length of time to be covered. They ultimately settled on a compromise of eight months, requiring no sampling in the winter months, although the wintering habits of striped bass had already been identified as a contested issue.

More interesting from the standpoint of policymaking was the transmutation of what was on the surface an inquiry into the (scientific) integrity of the Westway EIS into a probing critique of the moral and institutional integrity of the project agencies, particularly FHWA and the Army Corps. Congressional investigators concluded that both agencies had violated basic canons of independent review and analysis. Their science was flawed, the critics concluded, because their methods had not been sufficiently virtuous to ensure credible results. In this vein, the House report focused especially on instances where the project agencies had defied what the legislators took to be the established norms of scientific peer review. The criterion of independence, for example, was found to have been violated when the Army Corps turned to the New York Department of Transportation, "the very entity seeking the permit," for critical comment on the EIS.[31]

The inquiry also revealed suggestive failures of communication between ecological experts and other decisionmakers *within* the challenged agencies. Charles DesJardins, senior ecologist at FHWA, cited intra-agency rivalries as the explanation for his relatively late and ineffectual entry into the review process: "People in the [FHWA regional offices] back then were sometimes reluctant to share things with us at headquarters."[32] The Army Corps, too, was shown to have ignored the assessments of its own staff biologists and ecologists, some of whom had questioned whether the proposed landfill site was really as biologically inactive as determined by the FHWA.[33] A majority of the House committee concluded from this evidence that only the federal resource agencies could properly guarantee the integrity of environmental impact assessments for large federally-funded projects. Their report recommended that the design and conduct of such scientific studies should in the future be supervised by the appropriate resource agency.

In the Westway EIS controversy, then, both the cognitive and the moral authority of the project agencies were simultaneously under attack, and both crumbled under the weight of the project's unresolved political tensions. Westway's opponents were never called upon to prove their contention that the interpier landfill zone was actually teeming with important, if unmeasurable, marine resources. Doubts engendered by the size, cost, irreversibility, and questionable social value of the proposed development plan helped leverage the quite ordinary scientific skepticism of the anti-Westway forces into an effective engine of deconstruction. Under assault, the project agencies could not even safeguard their institutional identity. Rifts were exposed between ecologically-minded and project-minded experts within the same agency. Integrity in the sense of scientific probity was forfeited along with integrity in the sense of structural wholeness, showing once again how complex are the dynamics by which public assent is secured for knowledge claims used in policy.[34]

PROTECTING THE UNSEEN DEPTHS

What lessons can we reasonably draw for managing the invisible biological resources of our seas and oceans from the faltering and often inconclusive experiences of national policymaking discussed above? In particular, what are the implications of these cases for the persuasiveness of science when policy issues cut across cultural and political boundaries, as in regimes governing international marine environments? Here, as against in the nation state context, there are no long-established, culturally sanctioned institutional forms or shared discursive practices around which scientists and policymakers can coalesce into credible, trustworthy epistemic communities. Without the ordering frameworks which help in more bounded political settings to repair uncertainty and rationalize action, how can scientific knowledge play a reliable and useful role in shaping international environmental policy?

In reaching for answers, I have suggested that we may need to turn on its head the normal formulation of the science policy problem. The question before us is not how to produce the "best" possible science for policy, a problem definition that falsely presupposes the autonomy of scientific inquiry. Rather, we must ask how to achieve the moral certainty needed for real-time political decisions, given that most knowledge about the environment, such as our understanding of the processes of life in the unseen depths of the seas, will continue indefinitely to elude the firm grasp of science. A generation of precautionary environmental decisionmaking points toward the central proposition that scientific knowledge needs a sustaining and supporting social order — in short, a living, vibrant community — in order to reassure skeptical publics and serve as a compelling basis for policy decisions.

The community in question may be as localized as a research laboratory or as widely distributed as an interest group, a political institution, a social movement, or a nation state; authoritative knowledge can be generated in micro as well as macro-political settings. Whatever the level of organization, however, some collective activity is needed to define meaningful goals for scientific research, establish discursive and analytic conventions, draw boundaries between what counts and does not count as reliable knowledge, and provide morally acceptable principles for bridging uncertainty. Science, in other words, has to be produced and interpreted within a pre-existing epistemic community — a community already committed to the joint production of epistemological and moral order — in order to have meaning for policy. It is this community of knowledge and belief that validates the policy-relevance of new scientific findings, not (as is assumed by the mediated realists) shared scientific knowledge that binds together the relevant political community. The analyst's challenge is to discover how such communities come about, how they sustain and propagate their views, how they repair their cognitive and social uncertainties, and how their contributions should be assessed if we give up the notion that their power derives from a privileged access to the truth.

The growing number and variety of international environmental accords in recent years hold out the hope that politically effective epistemic communities can arise under a variety of circumstances and influence action across geopolitical boundaries. In the case of bounded environmental resources, such as rivers, lakes, and seas, the resource itself may promote community-building among those who claim to know it best. The formal, universal knowledge of science may combine powerfully in these settings with the informal, but no less significant, local knowledge and local community practices of those who experience the resource for recreation, esthetics, livelihood or commerce — producing in the end a common normative and epistemological vision. The early successes of the U.S. anti-nuclear movement, for example, were often achieved through alliances between local residents with a stake in the preservation of a bay or a lake and scientists who helped their cause by giving formal evidence of the complexity of biological processes in these bodies of water.[35] Scientists in these cases shared a kind of custodial right with local residents over the resource, and therewith earned the right to speak compellingly on its behalf.

The power of science to influence policy emerges from the foregoing discussion as less mythic but more human and, finally, more worthy of respect and political assent. For science now can be seen as an important contributor to policymaking even when it is not capable of delivering complete or certain knowledge about natural phenomena. To say that science (most especially environmental science) only makes sense for policy within an enveloping moral and social order is not to deny the value of scientific knowledge. It is to reaffirm that science is but one of the productions of the human imagination, and scientific beliefs cannot operate independently of other forms of social production if they are to undergird our conceptions of the good society or the good environment.

NOTES

1. See Sheila Jasanoff. 1992. Science, politics and the renegotiation of expertise at EPA. Osiris 7(8):196; see also Carnegie Commission on Science, Technology and Government. 1992. International Research and Assessment: Proposals for Better Organization and Decisionmaking. Carnegie Commission, New York.

2. Peter Singer. 1972. Famine, affluence and morality. Philosophy and Public Affairs 1:229-243.

3. Robert K. Merton. 1973. The Normative Structure of Science. Reprinted as Chapter 13 in The Sociology of Science. University of Chicago Press, Chicago, pp. 267-278.

4. Chandra Mukerji has argued, for instance, that oceanographers in the United States should be seen as an elite reserve labor force for

the state. Soft-money scientists, in her view, enjoy the illusion of autonomy through the freedom to design their immediate research programs, but the state maintains them, often at considerable expense, so that their "honed skills" can be drawn upon by "the military in case of war, by industry in case there are major changes in the direction of the economy, or by the medical community if there is an outbreak of some new and threatening illness." Chandra Mukerji. 1989. A Fragile Power: Scientists and the State. Princeton University Press, Princeton, p. 6.

5. See Peter Haas, this volume.

6. Alvin Weinberg. 1972. Science and trans-science. Minerva 1:209-222. For a deconstructive critique of Weinberg's position, see Sheila Jasanoff. 1987. Contested boundaries in policy-relevant science. Social Studies of Science 17:195-230.

7. See, for example, National Research Council. 1983. Risk Assessment in the Federal Government: Managing the Process. National Academy Press, Washington, D.C.

8. A particularly influential modern study in this genre is Bruno Latour and Steve Woolgar. 1979. Laboratory Life: The Construction of Scientific Facts. Sage Publications, Beverly Hills. An important historical antecedent was Ludwik Fleck. 1979. Genesis and Development of a Scientific Fact. University of Chicago Press, Chicago. Originally published in 1935 as Entstehung und Entwicklung einer wissenschaftlichen Tatsache. Benno Schwabe, Basel.

9. David Collingridge and Colin Reeve. 1986. Science Speaks to Power. St. Martin's Press, New York.

10. Peter M. Haas. 1992. Introduction: epistemic communities and international policy coordination. International Organization 46: 3.

11. On the factors that lead to the deconstruction of science in the political realm, see, for example, Sheila Jasanoff. 1986. Risk Management and Political Culture. Russell Sage Foundation, New York; Jasanoff 1987, op. cit., pp. 195-230; and Dorothy Nelkin (ed.). 1991. Controversy. Third ed. Sage Publications, Beverly Hills.

12. For an application of this argument to the international community of experts on climate change, see Sonja Boehmer-Christiansen. 1994. Global climate protection policy: the limits of scientific advice. Global Environmental Change 4:140-159, 185-200.

13. David M. O'Brien. 1987. What Process Is Due? Courts and Science-Policy Disputes. Russell Sage Foundation, New York, pp. 81-106. Many dates and other factual details in the following paragraphs are drawn from O'Brien's description of the case.

14. Ibid., p. 90.

15. This case would be made most forcefully in books and articles published in the mid-1980s. See, in particular, Paul Brodeur. 1985. Outrageous Misconduct. Pantheon, New York and David Rosenberg. 1986. The dusting of America: Carnage, cover-up and litigation. Harvard Law Review 99:1639-1706.

16. Borel v. Fibreboard Paper Products Corp. 493 F.2d 1076 (5 Cir. 1973).

17. See, for example, the statement by Senator John Tunney (D-NY) on March 26, 1976:

    "I was horrified to learn that we have asbestos in many of our body powders, and that when youngsters' mothers put powder on them, this can be inhaled into their lungs and that asbestos sits in the follicles of the lung and can produce cancer 20 years later.

    In the late forties or early fifties, we used to spray the ceilings of our schools with asbestos and now this asbestos is flaking off and can get into the atmosphere of the school, the classroom, and children can inhale it and, 20 or 25 years later, die of cancer."

    U.S. Congress, House Committee on Interstate and Foreign Commerce. 1976. Legislative History of the Toxic Substances Control Act. U.S. Government Printing Office, Washington, D.C., p. 211.

18. For a fuller review of these developments, see Sheila Jasanoff. 1990. The Fifth Branch: Science Advisers as Policymakers. Harvard University Press, Cambridge, pp. 49-57; see also Sheila Jasanoff. 1995. Science at the Bar. Twentieth Century Fund Books, New York, especially Chapter 2.

19. O'Brien, op. cit., p. 103.

20. This change in the basis for regulation is reflected in the United States in major laws mandating prevention of unreasonable risks to health or the environment, or, in some cases, any endangerment of public health. In Europe, the adoption of the "precautionary principle" reflects a similar move.

21. See, for example, Sheila Jasanoff. 1991. Acceptable evidence in a pluralistic society. In Deborah Mayo and Rachelle Hollander (eds.). Acceptable Evidence: Science and Values in Risk Management. Oxford University Press, New York, pp. 29-47.

22. Simon A. Levin. 1992. Sustaining ecological research. Address of the Past President. Bulletin of the Ecological Society of America 73:217.

23. L. W. Barnthouse, J. Boreman, S. W. Christensen, C. P. Goodyear, W. Van Winkle and D. S. Vaughan. 1984. Population biology in the courtroom: The Hudson River controversy. BioScience 34:14-19.

24. Extract from the ASLB's initial licensing decision, Ibid., p. 17.

25. Ibid., p. 17.

26. Baruch Boxer. 1991. Societal contexts of ocean pollution science: cross-national comparisons. Global Environmental Change. March, pp. 139-156.

27. See, in particular, the discussion of EPA's Scientific Advisory Panel for pesticides in Jasanoff 1990, op. cit. The relationship between social and epistemological trustworthiness has been most powerfully elaborated in Steven Shapin. 1994. A Social History of Truth. University of Chicago Press, Chicago. For further insights into the relationship between trust and scientific credibility, see Stephen Breyer. 1993. Breaking the Vicious Circle. Harvard University Press, Cambridge; Nicholas A. Ashford, C. William Ryan and Charles C. Caldart. 1983. Law and science policy in federal regulation of formaldehyde. Science 222:894-900; and Brian Wynne. 1987. Risk Management and Hazardous Wastes: Implementation and the Dialectics of Credibility. Springer, Berlin.

28. House Committee on Government Operations. 1984. The Westway Project: A Study of Failure in Federal/State Relations. 98th Congress, 2d Session, p. 11.

29. H. M. Collins. 1985. Changing Order. Sage, London, p. 2.

30. House Committee on Government Operations, op. cit., p. 10.

31. Ibid., p. 13.

32. Ibid., p. 10.

33. Ibid., p. 24.

34. For an extended study of EPA's difficulties in maintaining its credibility as an expert agency, see Jasanoff 1992, op. cit.

35. See, for example, Brian Balogh. 1991. Chain Reaction: Expert Debate and Public Participation in American Commercial Nuclear Power 1945-1975. Cambridge University Press, Cambridge, pp. 240-244 (describing alliance between scientists and grass-roots citizen activists at Bodega Bay, California) and Dorothy Nelkin (ed.). 1984. Controversy: Politics of Technical Decisions, 2d ed. Sage Publications, Beverly Hills, pp. 61-70 (describing successful coalition building between Ithaca residents and Cornell University scientists to block construction of nuclear power plant at New York's Cayuga Lake).

Part III

International Governance, Actors, and Institutions

11

Leadership and International Environmental Policy Making

CRAIG N. MURPHY

In many ways, the international environmental issues of the late twentieth century demand to be treated as fundamentally new problems of public policy. While Thomas Malthus worried about the potential for human overpopulation and Alexander von Humbolt promoted the scientific study of the whole earth in the early nineteenth-century, not until after the Second World War, when the eminent British biologist, Julian Huxley, became UNESCO's first Executive Director, did environmental issues became a regular topic of intergovernmental conferences and the subject of international public policy making.[1] Yet, when larger-scale environmental issues became a focus of regular international discussion they initially did so without widespread comment among students of international administration, and without the parties involved saying that they had engaged in any fundamentally new form of intergovernmental cooperation. Governments found it easy to include these new issues in what I have called the "meta-regime" under which most intergovernmental agreements dealing with civil matters have been created since the middle of the nineteenth century.[2]

This chapter begins with the premise that something about the prospects for effective international environmental regulation can be learned by considering the process through which intergovernmental agreements have been formed in other realms over the last century and a half. I begin by identifying the similarities between current international environmental issues and the civil matters that have been the focus of effective intergovernmental agreements in the past. Then I consider the three types of leadership that have characterized the meta-regime under which these agreements have been established, as well as the available sources of each type of leadership relative to current international environmental issues.

Many analysts argue that international regimes which require redistribution of property or property rights in order to be effective will be particularly difficult to negotiate. In the terminology of the argument outlined here, this difficulty should be treated as a likely deficit of one of the three types of leadership: few potential *benefactors* of intergovernmental cooperation are likely to be willing to bear the burden of underwriting new international institutions that provide significant property or property rights to the less advantaged. This problem characterizes many North-South environmental issues. However, in the environmental realm the potential deficit of this form of leadership can be mitigated due to the political and technological characteristics of the issues involved. In fact, many international environmental issues may actually be made more tractable if they are connected to North-South divisions. I suggest real and hypothetical examples and then conclude by turning a final lesson from the longer history of international civil cooperation: we should not expect widespread, effective agreement on international environmental issues without concurrent agreements to manage other conflicts that arise from industrialism.

INTERNATIONAL ENVIRONMENTAL ISSUES AND GOVERNANCE WITHOUT GOVERNMENT

Policy analysts who focus on environmental problems confined within the boundaries of a single country do not have to consider the central problem faced by those trying to devise effective intergovernmental environmental regulation: the need to concentrate on devising relatively inexpensive, cooperative instruments. Within a sovereign state analysts can focus on the politics of convincing legitimate authorities to legislate wise air, water, land-use, and resource policies and then to enforce them using appropriate, legitimate coercive sanctions and economic inducements in addition to less-expensive cooperative instruments such as (1) monitoring prior pro-environment contracts made among citizens and firms, (2) helping different social groups recognize interests in preserving the environment that they share, and (3) working with the same groups to design new regimes (contracts) that favor the environment — contracts based on shared interests that have already been recognized. Most intergovernmental activity associated with the environment has used only these three cooperative instruments.

The division of sovereignty among states makes the effective use of other instruments quite a bit harder. The problem is not, as many analysts argue, that the international system lacks coercive authorities.[3] The difficulty arises because even when such authorities exist, their actions can always be treated as suspect; to some states, those actions are bound to be illegitimate. A preponderant military power may be able to force many other states to do its bidding, and so can an intergovernmental organization whose approval is needed to keep severely dependent states afloat. In either case analysts might argue that the sovereignty of the target states should be understood as "merely juridical." Nevertheless, even the "merely juridical" sovereignty of the many entities that Robert H. Jackson calls "quasi-states" assures that the external authority's action will be viewed as illegitimate by those it commands.[4] This lack of legitimacy makes such international coercive authorities a rather tenuous basis for the long-term public policies that most environmental problems demand.

Moreover, unlike the legitimate political authorities that exist in states where a regular political process assures that the central authority responds to some version of the collective interest, the authorities that exist at an international level generally have their own particular interests foremost. The U.S., for example, may speak of the global good whenever it replaces a dictatorship in

Panama, but no one would assume that the U.S. will use its authority to foster the "global good" by replacing all dictators, including those who happen to be U.S. allies. Similarly, the IMF, like any successful bank, is designed to serve the good of the financial markets before any other interest.[5]

Despite the lack of legitimate coercive authority at the international level, governments have created effective and legitimate intergovernmental regulatory institutions in a host of fields, from accounting to zoology. Typically, these institutions carry out research and hold meetings aimed at discovering and promoting common interests among potentially antagonistic social forces. These have not been limited to national governments, but have included class, sectoral, and economic-regional interest groups. When governments formally agree with one another to pursue some form of intergovernmental regulation (which usually means pledging that private interests within their societies will be convinced or compelled to act in certain ways) international institutions are often given the task of monitoring adherence to the intergovernmental agreements. Occasionally the intergovernmental bodies are given the right to demand that member states impose coercive sanctions when prior agreements are violated. Much more frequently an international executive body is given the responsibility to provide specific services to some or all members, for example, the technical assistance to Treasury Departments and central banks provided by the IMF. In many cases, the ultimate recipients of these services are not states themselves, but economic interests that most national governments treat as important constituencies.[6]

Thus, the oldest of the global-level international institutions, which date back to the middle of the nineteenth century, originally provided accounting, security, and technical services that made it possible for an international telegraph and railroad network to be created. The primary beneficiaries of that network were the large firms involved in the international sale of industrial goods. Similarly, today some of the most active global intergovernmental organizations provide services to the air transportation and satellite telecommunication industries, which, in turn, create the physical infrastructure of the markets used by today's global corporations. Very early on, global level international institutions also began providing services that helped manage conflicts between labor and capital, and between newer and older economic sectors. Later, international institutions concerned with regulating conflicts between the more industrialized, and less industrialized world were added.[7]

Conflicts dealt with by international institutions before the Second World War resemble most post-war international environmental problems of resource depletion and pollution in at least five ways:

1. All are problems that have been caused by, or greatly exacerbated by, the industrial system.

2. In each case, decisions about long-term investments in industry have a great deal of influence, perhaps a determining influence, over the degree to which the problem can be managed.

3. As a consequence, in each case one productive aim of governmental and intergovernmental regulatory efforts is to shape investment decisions toward more benign ends.

4. The investors who first move toward these more benign ends can become major allies in the larger regulatory effort because they have an interest in imposing similar investment costs on competitors, as long as that does not mean that the first-movers lose the advantages conferred on them by their early investment.

5. Once in place, regimes regulating each of these problems may require little enforcement. The stickiness of long-term investments makes the actions required by the regimes a matter of habit, at least until replacement investments need to be made.

Relative to the problem of the pollution of rivers, lakes, and seas the key large investment decisions include choices among different designs and different locations of sewage and waste disposal systems, industrial plants, and refineries whose effluent may enter the waters. Key decisions also include choices among different designs of ships as well as investment decisions regarding designing and marketing fertilizers and pesticides used on lands that drain into waters. Of course, the list is much longer, but it is reasonable to assume that the larger and more long-term investments — in sewage plants, fertilizer factories, or tankers, any of which may be from 40 to 60 years — will have the most impact. Even the most-significant of these decisions can be shaped by the governmental and intergovernmental regulatory environment simply because wise firms (whether public or private) always take projections about the regulatory environment into account before making investments.

Shell Oil, for example, has a 50-year planning horizon. In one of the firm's latest exercises, strategists concluded that the company's decisions should be made so that it could thrive in two, equally probable, future worlds:

> In one...regional conflicts plague the world, environmental problems are attacked piecemeal, and low prices shape energy use. In the other, sustainable development takes hold. International cooperation blossoms to combat environmental damage and global warming. Governments discourage fossil fuel use and promote renewable energy.[8]

A critic of Shell's planning process might complain that its own decisions to explore, refine, and transport fossil fuels will have a major effect on which of these two scenarios becomes a reality, but it may be more fruitful for environmentalists to concentrate on designing public policies that could convince Shell planners that their second, more benign world is the one in which the firm will have to act. The relevant variables identified by the planners are, after all, familiar matters of government action or intergovernmental cooperation. If governments institute policies toward those ends, Shell would not only respond with its own investments that would help make the goal a reality, the firm would have reason to advocate that all other firms be held to the same, or stricter, environmental standards. This interest is characteristic of all the companies that have become "first movers" on environmental issues, the firms that have been the first to make massive investments in technologies that may reduce environmental damage.

Recent policy innovations triggered by the Business Council on Sustainable Development (BCSD) exemplify this process. The BCSD brings together the leaders of a host of the world's largest firms, including Shell, Dow Chemical Company, Nippon Steel, India's giant TATA, and Volkswagen. These companies have learned from experience that it can pay to be an environmental first-mover. Generalizing from their individual experiences, they have convinced the International Organization for Standardization (ISO) to establish a Strategic Advisory Group on the Environment (which, like most ISO groups, essentially represents key companies) to prepare international standards for the "eco-efficiency" of industrial products and services. The aim is to assure that products have standard "eco-labeling" and that public entities purchasing goods and products look at life-cycle analyses and environmental audits.[9] The self-interest of the BCSD firms is transparent, but it is enlightened. They believe that in a global market of Green consumers and of governments increasingly influenced by the environmental concerns of their publics, ISO standards labeling the environmental desirability of every product and service will benefit environmental first movers over all their competitors.

ISO standards that play to green consumer preferences represent only one of many ways that the self-interest of firms acting as environmental first movers can be enlisted to extend the impact of cooperative international institutions involved in environmental regulation.[10] Perhaps most significantly, the first large investors in progressive environmental practices have every interest in becoming the eyes and ears of the regulators, thus strengthening the typically inadequate monitoring systems established through intergovernmental agreement. Moreover, the longer history of international industrial regulation suggests that once the investment costs associated with a new regulation have been absorbed, the need for monitoring and for taking sanctions against violators diminishes. Conforming with the regulations becomes a matter of habit; after all, the major decisions, the decisions to make large investments in the cleaner of the available technologies, have to be made very rarely. Even if a period of economic stagnation gives firms temporary incentives to cut costs by cutting corners, the older habit of investment in conformity with "high cost" regulations is likely to return along with the prosperity that would make a new round of big investments possible.

The reinforcing process of intergovernmental cooperation influencing the large investment decisions of corporate first-movers who in turn become the advocates, eyes, and ears of the international regulators has been central to many even more effective forms of intergovernmental regulation for over a century. The creation of international transportation and communication networks have convinced firms to invest in plants large enough to serve the new market areas, and to become advocates of international agreements on industrial standards, intellectual property, and rules of trade that facilitate trade within the market area just as international agreement on high labor standards have convinced companies to invest in plants that make adherence to those standards possible, and they have helped assure that the companies that became first-movers on higher labor standards pushed to see them extended to all their international competitors. The very existence of the BCSD suggests that this same process has begun in the area of international environmental standards as well.

INTELLECTUAL LEADERSHIP

Intergovernmental cooperation can convince investors to choose cleaner technologies either through incentives, disincentives, or outright bans. Most international environmental regulations ban some actions or rest upon the possibility that actions can be banned. As many scholars, perhaps most notably Peter M. Haas, have pointed out natural scientists have played a key role in the formation of all international environmental regimes.[11] Whether the problem at hand is the depletion of the "living resources of the sea," an issue that has been the focus of international regulatory efforts for almost a century, or the more recent efforts to end depletion of the ozone and control greenhouse gases, scientists' projections of the cumulative effects of continuing certain practices have convinced some governments of the need for international prohibitions.[12]

Natural scientists have not been the only intellectual leaders who have influenced international environmental regulation. As Robert Keohane argues, designing effective international institutions involves fostering new forms of cooperation between states.[13] The intellectual task involves demonstrating to governments that they have shared interests in the outcomes that would be "assured" by some proposed new international regimes.[14] The intellectual task is one of designing a regime that will avert the disasters that the natural scientists foresee, or at least will convince governments that they are doing what they can to avoid those disasters that could harm their constituents. This work of proposing institutions is done by economists, lawyers, and diplomats, who, the scientists are apt to complain, oversimplify, ignore interaction effects, and refuse to recognize the pervasive uncertainty associated with all predictions in the environmental sciences.[15] There is nothing new about such conflict-ridden collaboration between natural and policy scientists. Similar cooperation between intellectual leaders, and similar tensions, have characterized the first stage in the formation of international regulatory institutions (and, one could add, the public policy process as a whole) since the middle of the nineteenth century.

The differences between the two types of intellectual leaders have always proved less significant than the values that they typically share. These can be summarized as preferences for (1) order and control, a desire to make society more structured and predictable; (2) economic efficiency; and (3) what might be called the political efficiency that comes from de-emphasizing potentially divisive aspects of new regulatory regimes.[16] These ideas may be essential goals of any policy analyst attempting to discover previously unrecognized grounds for cooperation between sovereign states, but they also help explain why one ecological paradigm — what Peter Haas calls "scientific holism" — rather than the available alternatives, has come to underlie the international environmental policy discussion.[17] On the one hand, "scientific holism" directs attention toward the "politically efficient" environmental problems that "threaten global survival," a set of problems that, to the extent that we believe they exist, leave us little room to see differences in interest in the way that problems of wildlife management or some of what Haas calls "Malthusian paradigm" problems of pollution control might.[18] Yet, the "scientific holists" still believe that more complete planning, greater attention to imposing order, can avert the key ecological problems, something not accepted by what Haas calls the "philosophical holist" paradigm.

The convergence around the global problems encouraged by scientific holism has meant that it has been somewhat easier to focus international attention on problems associated with pollution of the atmosphere — ozone depletion and the emission of global warming gases — than on the typically less-threatening, regional problems of international pollution of shared bodies of water. As Haas's study of the Mediterranean suggests, the levels of the various harms caused by pollution of an international waterway have to be fairly high before there is a large and cohesive community of intellectual leaders, including both natural scientists and policy scientists, ready to propose designs of international institutions that will try to limit further damage in a comprehensive way.[19]

Given the history of international institutions, it is not surprising that the first international water pollution regimes were associated with petroleum transportation and the International Maritime Organization rather than with a new organization concerned with environmental issues. The relevant pattern was initiated a century earlier by social movements that pushed for the first international health institutions. They convinced shippers that communicable disease could become a problem that would impede shipping, i.e., that social movements concerned with public health would sometimes raise such a hue and cry about ships entering from disease-ridden areas, that it would be better to support a regularized, predictable intergovernmental system of quarantines, even though many shippers (and, initially, many medical professionals) were not convinced that the need for such measures had been demonstrated by the best existing science. The science promoted by the social movements advocating quarantine quickly triumphed among all health scientists, in part due to the research carried out under the initial international health regimes.[20] Similarly, in a number of cases where international institutions regulating environmental problems began with issues that not all scientists saw as threatening, the research carried out as a result of preliminary international agreements quickly led to a stronger international consensus on what needs to be done.

SPONSORSHIP

No matter how intellectual leaders advocating international environmental agreements begin, they always face an uphill struggle to turn any vision of international regulation into reality. This is true for designers of all international regimes. Governments, like all habit-driven actors, resist pressure to do new things, especially when the new things require cooperation with foreign actors over whom they have no control. Keohane's image of active international cooperation as something that comes about when states pay attention to the possibility that they may have shared interests is telling.[21] For the most part, intellectual leaders who propose international regimes feel that their designs are in the interest of all the states they would like to see involved. The problem comes in getting the attention of state leaders, in getting them to sit down, focus on, and discuss the various proposals in order to recognize their shared interests.

Standard diplomatic practice provides one generic institution suitable for achieving that end, the international conference. Ever since the middle of the nineteenth century issue-oriented, functionally-specific international conferences have been central to global and regional governance. Under the nineteenth century conference system the problem of getting governments to focus on proposals for new international regimes to serve previously-unrecognized shared interests was solved by an institution that many political scientists might consider atavistic: Europe's princes. When Baron Pierre de Coubertin created the modern Olympics in 1900 he was simply following the fashion of Europe's most powerful aristocrats. Most often acting on their own behalf, often motivated as much by a nineteenth-century progressive version of liberalism as by aristocratic *noblesse oblige*, Europe's crowned heads called governments together to form almost all of the first generation of international organizations, including the International Telegraph Union, the original Europe-wide trade organization, the FAO's predecessor (the International Institute of Agriculture or IIA), the International Labor Office, and the international police union, Interpol, which were sponsored by Napoleon III, the Kings of Belgium, Italy, and Germany, and the Prince of Monaco, respectively.[22]

In the first quarter of the twentieth century what might be called "democratic *noblesse oblige*" began replacing the aristocratic version. Woodrow Wilson's promotion of the League of Nations had been anticipated by a half-dozen major international conferences sponsored by his immediate predecessors and by the presidents of France and Switzerland. All three countries, even the "isolationist" U.S., continued to play similar roles through 1929, always justifying the effort involved by referring to responsibilities for fostering international cooperation of progressive states that already enjoyed republican constitutions.[23]

Immediately after the Second World War the major allied victors, countries that either eventually enjoyed or were considered for permanent memberships on the UN Security Council — Brazil, China, France, the U.K., U.S., and U.S.S.R. — split the task of hosting the international conferences needed to create the global institutions of the post-war era. Then, beginning in the late-1940s, world organizations, and, at a regional level, older organizations, became the typical sponsors of international conferences designed to create new international institutions, with the General Assembly hosting the conferences that created UNCTAD and UNIDO and the Organization for European Economic Cooperation (OEEC) sponsoring the first moves toward a European Community.[24]

The last two decades, when international institutions involved with environmental issues began to proliferate, have seen a period in which many global organizations that had earlier acted as sponsors of new international regimes no longer had the legitimacy to do so. Third World governments often perceived the World Bank as partisan toward Northern economic interests, while many Northern governments made similar complaints about the General Assembly and other organizations in which the Third World had a clear majority.[25] As a result, major environmental conferences have been sponsored both by one or more international organizations and by states willing to take a lead in some environmental matters, such as the roles of Sweden relative to the Stockholm Conference, Germany and France in institutionalizing the World Bank's Global Environmental Facility, and Brazil in hosting the 1992 conference on development and the environment.

For the international organizations the motivation for sponsoring such conferences is clear; it is their mandate. Moreover, institution-building is one of the few ways that political entrepreneurs within the world organizations — from Raul Prebisch to Maurice Strong — have found to put their mark on international affairs, and sponsoring international conferences is one of the tools of institution-building that they have had at hand. On the other hand, the motivations of national sponsors of international conferences may be less clear. They appear to involve something more than short-term national self-interest, some current equivalent of *noblesse oblige*. In the environmental realm it may best be understood as a desire to appear as a national "first-mover" in environmental affairs either to some national constituency (for example, voters influenced by the Green politics of Germany or France) or to the international community as a whole (a likely part of the Brazilian calculation at different stages in the planning for the 1992 conference).

As we approach the twenty-first century there is little difficulty in finding adequate sponsors for international conferences that encourage states to recognize and attend to shared global environmental interests. Although financial problems remain chronic, the organizations of the UN system currently have more legitimacy vis-a-vis the environment (they are less likely to be seen as "politicized") than in the 1970s and 1980s. Perhaps more significantly, a relatively large number of governments have some interest in being considered first movers on international environmental regulation and there is enough overlap that most topics can be covered. For example, while it may be difficult to imagine Japan or Norway sponsoring international conferences to strengthen international bans on the hunting of sea mammals, it is easy to imagine the U.K. or the U.S. doing so, even though they might rarely be leaders in other environmental realms.

Even at a regional level analysts can identify states that are likely to sponsor international discussions due to a desire to be seen as first movers. The tourist industries of southern Europe give their countries such an interest relative to problems of the Mediterranean. A similar interest is shared by the tourist nations of the Caribbean and by Australia. The power of Green movements give similar motivations to the Nordic countries and Germany relative to the Baltic and the North Seas and Japan concerning the waters on its western coasts.

BENEFACTORSHIP

It is one thing to pick up the bills for a big global meeting, but it is quite another to underwrite international environmental regimes for any length of time. Benefactors willing to pay for costs of international cooperation over many years have been essential to institutionalization of many international regimes in the past. In the nineteenth and early twentieth centuries many of the first generation of major international organizations relied on their original sponsors to pay for the secretariat that carried out research, monitored prior international agreements, and prepared periodic international conferences. In fact, the presence of such a benefactor often was what convinced habit-bound governments to create new international regimes, at least as experiments. After all, if Napoleon III was willing to pick up most of the bill for the Telegraph Union, the Kaiser was willing to pay for the Labor Office, and Italy's Victor Emmanuel III was willing the underwrite the work of the IIA, no one was willing to object.

In fact, in these cases one could argue that the organizations and the regimes to which they contributed only became truly institutionalized as forms of intergovernmental cooperation after political or economic crises destroyed the capacity of the original benefactor to help underwrite the institution. When the noble benefactor disappeared, member governments had to put up or shut up. In the case of these organizations, the experience of five or more years of international cooperation made members quite willing to pay all the costs of linking the international telegraph system, collecting information on labor and agriculture, and linking national police forces.

Since the Second World War many of the initial costs of new international institutions have continued to be borne by the institutions' original sponsors. International organizations have acted as the benefactors of international organizations, by providing staff, space, and operating funds for months or even years. Thus, the UN Relief and Rehabilitation Organization provided much of the initial support for UNICEF, the UN Secretariat underwrote much of the UN's early work on population planning, and the World Bank provided the initial funding for hybrids like the International Fund for Agricultural Development. In many other cases a single state, the U.S., acted as the key benefactor. This has been especially true when international cooperation demanded large transfers of funds, as in the case of European recovery under the OEEC and the Marshall Plan, as well as with the IMF and World Bank, whose earliest subscriptions in internationally negotiable currencies came from the United States.

Various theories of hegemony have been used to explain American benefactorship of Western cooperation in early post-war years. Some of the most convincing are those that rely on Antonio Gramsci's ideas about consolidation of power over large populations and territories.[26] America's post-war leaders, the argument goes, were not pursuing the short-term self-interests that underlie so much foreign policy behavior. Instead, they were pursuing a more long-term aspiration for a world structured under American leadership, an aspiration at the heart of American elite ideology for generations, but one that had never before been a realistic option for a New World country so isolated from most of the world's popuation and territory.[27]

To construct that world, and create American hegemony (in Gramsci's sense of the word) required that U.S. policy-makers forgo narrow, short-term advantages in order to pursue the collective interests of the Western bloc. Arguably then, from this point of view, the entire problem of the "decline of American hegemony" stems from the from the fact that the accumulated debt of the U.S. government and the long-unattended concerns of many U.S. citizens mean that now no U.S. government is in the position to act as a major benefactor of international cooperation. Moreover, no other state is in the position that the U.S. was in 1945.

Unfortunately, in the absence of a state willing and able to seek a Gramscian sort of hegemony, it can be extremely difficult to build international institutions that require significant funding. This is one reason that the so-called North-South "dialogue" of the 1970s and early 1980s got so bogged down. It may very well have been the case, as the authors of the second Club of Rome Report and the Brandt Commission argued, that there were international institutions that could have served Northern and Southern collective interests in returning to the rapid economic growth of the 1960s, but such institutions could not be formed in the traditional way of getting governments to agree to something as an experiment and then relying on a benefactor to keep them operating for as long as was needed to prove that the experiment was worthwhile.[28] Taken together, the experiments proposed by both groups would have required something on the order of a five or six fold increase in aid funds from the U.S., Japan, the U.K., and a number of other donor countries. If one thinks about the size of the lobbying effort needed by any group that secures the equivalent of say, a 50 billion dollar allocation in the U.S. budget each year, one might get a sense of how unrealistic such a call was, especially since this was not the "experimental" amount to be borne by a benefactor over a short period of time, but the "regular dues" to be expected each year. Unfortunately, the UNCED Conference made the same unrealistic call for a similar level of ongoing new redistributive funding as part of its proposed global compact.[29] Because there is no state that would be able to bear that cost, especially as a benefactor, the longer experience of the creation of effective international regulation suggests that it may be unrealistic to imagine that the regimes that would rest on that compact will ever be formed.

Perhaps the best that can be hoped for in international environmental cooperation is agreement on the relatively cost-free kind of eco-labeling encouraged by the BCSD. After all, in most recent UNEP trade talks, which focused on just those sorts of measures, officials were delighted to find that the agenda was one in which, "there was so much agreement between industrialized and developing countries." By focusing on the kind of measures that have been typical of international regulation for over a century, the meeting became one of the few recent international environmental forums that, "did not degenerate into North-South conflict."[30]

CREATING RESOURCES

Nonetheless, the longer history of international civil cooperation suggests that something more may be possible. Many of the international civil institutions constructed in the last century can be thought of as having *created* resources that were then allocated by "politically efficient" means that often hid the redistributive element. For example, the traditional international intellectual property regime not only created a form of property in the monopoly rights given to inventors, authors, and trademark owners, it also created a duty on the part of patent owners to "work" their patents in every international market, or else lose the right to maintain them. Thus, if Thomas Edison had not produced his light bulbs in Denmark, or, at least, sold his rights so that a local firm could produce Edison bulbs, the invention would have been public property.

Compared to an "absolute" system of patents (the kind of system that always seems to be advocated by the technology leaders, whether it is Britain in the 1850s, Germany in 1910, or the U.S. today), the actual international regimes have, through the requirement that patents be worked, lowered the price of technology to industrializing nations. The current Biodiversity Treaty with its sections on intellectual property, which will be subject to a great deal of interpretation, also may eventually serve to create similar resources for industrializing nations, at least as compared to absolute system of intellectual property envisioned under the Uruguay Round of the GATT.

Two generations after the first global intellectual property regimes were put in place, international institutions also "created" resources through the drawn-out process of renegotiating Germany's war debts. Resources created by fiat, the war debts themselves, were reduced by fiat, although with much hand waving about responsible international financial practices and with the agreement of international bankers and captains of industry. It was, nonetheless, a "politically efficient" move that obscured the (new) redistributive elements from the mass publics within Belgium, France, Italy, and the U.S., and (more significantly) from their elected representatives, many of whom most certainly would have objected.

In 1991 the distinguished Mexican economist Victor Urquidi argued that something similar should be done in order to assure some level of redistribution to the less-industrialized world: "The essence of the [current] problem, so clearly foreseen by Keynes at the time of the German reparations...is that for the debt to be repaid...the debtors must develop a sufficiently large export surplus."[31] In the 1980s the recession-induced collapse of world markets for Third World goods made that impossible. Therefore,

> many countries went into default, which made them ineligible
> for loans or other forms of financial assistance. Others kept on
> meeting their interest payments at the expense of growth and de-
> velopment. What came to be termed the 'reverse transfer,' that is
> the net out-transfer of financial resources from the developing to

the industrialized countries, was the equivalent of reparations payments as if a war had been lost. In fact, the war on poverty, the great struggle for development, had to be given up.[32]

Urquidi's position has not been taken up in this wholesale form by advocates of North-South compromises on environmental issues; although those relatively small attempts at "debt for nature" swaps that leave the less-industrialized country effective sovereignty over the new nature preserves reflect the same logic.

Other cases where international institutions have created resources and then redistributed them also exist. For example, the Bretton Woods institutions used the initial deposits of gold and hard currencies by the U.S. (and the very few other original members whose money was convertible) to create a pool of loan money that the IMF and World Bank immediately were able to expand both by fiat and by borrowing. As a result of this precedent, the Keynesian proposal to use additions to IMF reserves as a pool of funds for development assistance remained a hardy perennial in discussions of international public finance until the floating exchange rate system appeared in the early 1970s. The new system made this "reserve-expansion/foreign assistance link" proposal somewhat irrelevant in recent discussions of North-South environmental issues. Nevertheless, it might be a better use of UNEP analysts' time to concentrate on developing proposals of this sort rather than on finding new ways to importune reluctant donors and point out their inconsistency in endorsing multilateral programs without providing the necessary financing.

Analogous programs would establish regular, even if initially small, sources of development finance linked to some growing aspect of the world economy.[33] The most interesting possibilities are those that could be connected back to the traditional, proven way in which benefactors have played a role in extending the activities of world organizations by allowing new programs to be demonstrated in practice before all states are required to bear their part of the burden. A recent Norwegian initiative to impose a carbon tax on North Sea oil is a case that could be easily be linked to such a process.[34]

States that might be willing to impose such a carbon tax include the "like minded" pro-development oil producers such as Canada and Mexico as well as Norway, similar countries with significant roles in the oil trade such as the Netherlands and Finland, and perhaps those OPEC members that do not have a strong interest in maximizing current production. They might be joined by the oil companies with executives on the BCSD like Chevron, ENI, and Shell. All might agree to impose a small unit fee on the oil they process and then give the funds to the GEF. The retail vendors of oil thus "taxed" would be able to advertise to Green consumers, explaining the major benefit to the environment that derives from a slight increase in price. If some firms' expectations about the significance of the Green segment of the market are correct, then market forces would generate significant development funds. Moreover, governments committed to a Green industrial development path would have an incentive to join in imposing the tax on all the oil sold in their countries. This, along with the pressure of consumers, might initiate the kind of bandwagon effect that has never started relative to the 0.7 percent aid target, the unrealistic target that the Club of Rome, the Brandt Commission, and the UNCED all embraced.

Of course, one thing that should be noted about such a proposal — which is also true about all the ways in which international institutions have "created" resources — is the reliance on the special power of some social group, a power that is amplified at the same time that it is somewhat hidden by the international institution. In this last example it is the (hypothetical) power of Green consumers. In the case of the renegotiation of war debts and the original funding of the Bretton Woods institutions it was the power of international financial interests, a power that was never there to back the "reserve-expansion/aid link proposals." In the case of the original intellectual property regimes it was a balance of the powers of inventors (more concretely, firms with high research and development budgets) with those of the governments of industrializing countries in which those firms expected to develop new markets. We might hypothesize that one of the most reliable sources of power that could be amplified by international institutions concerned with environmental issues is that of environmentalist social movements and environmentally-concerned citizens and governments. It may be worthwhile to speculate about all the possible international institutions that could help solve the "redistribution" problem associated with creating effective North-South environmental regimes by thinking of ways to use that power to "create" resources.

"ABSOLUTE" GREENING AT HOME VERSUS GREATER (GLOBAL) GREENING ABROAD

Current Norwegian policy can again provide a starting point for thinking about such policy innovations that rely on more than the power of Green consumers. Under current Norwegian air pollution standards a number of firms are faced with the problem of making major investments to eliminate the last five to ten percent of various greenhouse gases discharged from plants that are already some of the cleanest in the world. As is often the case with the economics of reducing effluent, the marginal cost of cleaning up these pollutants increases markedly with the percentage of pollutants already eliminated. Consequently, the Norwegian firms have negotiated with their government to transfer technology and help build plants in China that will reduce substantially more of the same greenhouse gases than similar levels of investment at home.[35]

Economists might note that this could be understood as one of many types of schemes to reduce effluent that could be thought of as involving some kind of exchange of "rights to pollute." Usually, however, that idea applies within a sovereign entity where all polluters can be sure that they will be forced to abide by some standard. In most international cases, in contrast, we would expect industrializing states to reject international pollution standards unless wealthy countries compensate poorer ones for the opportunity costs of compliance. In this case, we would expect that the Chinese plants would have continued to use older, more-polluting practices if the Norwegians had not assisted.

The lesson can be generalized, at least as long as environmental movements are willing to exchange a higher pollution reduction abroad for a lower of reduction than they could otherwise get at home. This probably would not be seen as a reasonable exchange if the region in question was wholly within the country where environmental movements were strong: U.S. Audubon Society members probably would not campaign to have the U.S. government sell the Cape Cod National Seashore to developers in order to buy and preserve ten or twenty times the length of pristine shoreline in southern Mexico. Yet, it would be reasonable for Northern environmentalists to promote schemes affecting common resources that both "Northern" and "Southern" countries pollute.

Many international seas, lakes, and rivers fall into this category. Finnish, Swedish, and German environmentalists, for example, would have reason to support national legislation that would allow companies in their countries to invest in cleaning massive amounts of Estonian, Latvian, Lithuanian, and Russian effluent into the Baltic in lieu of completely eliminating effluent from their own, already much cleaner, ships and plants.[36] In fact, one might argue that the North-South logic of such exchanges is so compelling that it may be *easier* to negotiate effective international regimes for cleaning up bodies of water that lie across North-South divides than to negotiate effective regimes to clean up bodies of water bordered only by states that share a high degree of privilege. For example, effective regimes for the Baltic or the east Asian seas may be easier to achieve than a regime for the Arab/Persian Gulf. On the other hand, in cases where the wealthy states on both sides of a body of water have strong environmental movements and — usually as a result — a national commitment to being a "first mover" in environmental regulation, the process of negotiating international regulations should be easier.

In the many North-South situations the Northern governments, and the Northern environmental movements willing to make the required trade-offs would, by their actions, contribute to what Daniel Duedney has dubbed the "world domestic politics" of "global environmental rescue" in a very concrete way.[37] Rather than just "thinking locally and acting globally," worrying about the pollution of common resources and reducing their local contribution to it for example, they would be thinking about a global (or regional) international problem with the logic of domestic politics, the logic of optimal feasible compromises and of getting the greatest "good" for each expenditure of political resources.

CYCLES OF EFFECTIVE INTERNATIONAL POLICY

Even after I have invoked this kind of benign *Realpolitik* that would have Northern environmental groups husbanding their power carefully and targeting it to sites around the world, a critic might still charge that the bulk of my argument is too congruent with various rosy liberal scenarios about the interaction between the concerns of industrialists and environmentalists painted by groups like the BCSD and the Japanese Ministry for International Trade (MITI) when it concluded that, "environmental concerns will drive the next generation of economic growth," and, therefore, more government money had to be spent in the "strategic repositioning of Japanese industry" to take advantage of this development.[38] This kind of argument rests on the assumption that economic growth occurs in "waves" and that initial investment environments created by governments influences the nature of successive waves.

Of course, many economists do not accept this view of economic growth. For example, while Richard Cooper, who served on the U.S. National Academy of Sciences panel that prepared the U.S. response to UNCED, agrees with his colleagues at the BCSD and MITI that some of the actions needed to diminish global warming might provide a net economic gain in the short-run as well as the long-run, he does not believe that all the costly investments required in the short-run will "pay off" simply by "returning the world economy to a high-growth phase."[39] Because Cooper does not see growth as occurring in cycles, he sees some of the actions demanded at UNCED as requiring unacceptably large short-run costs.

My own work on the longer history of international institutions makes me believe that there is some validity to arguments about long waves of economic growth. Twice in the past, in Europe in the 25 years before the First World War and throughout the OECD world in the 25 years after the Second World War, there appear to have been waves of economic growth and industrial transformation that appear to correspond to the predictions of liberal internationalists going back to Adam Smith: international cooperation helped create larger market areas which, in turn, encouraged investors to develop new and much more productive technologies (and whole new industries) that led economic growth in these periods of relative peace and prosperity.

Unfortunately, the same research suggests that the problem of creating the regulatory environment for a new cycle of growth is not just one of establishing a few clever international agreements and priming the pump with some public investment. Before each of the prior growth phases could begin a whole host of conflicts associated with industry had to be managed. New institutions, many of them international, had to be created to mitigate the conflicts over the control of industry that divide labor and capital, the conflicts over compensation in sectors of waning importance that divide older and newer industrial regions, the conflicts over investment opportunities and local autonomy that divide the industrialized and the non-industrialized world, and the conflicts of prestige that divide industrial centers. Long wave theorists would argue that international environmental issues have come to the fore in a period of relative stagnation, the period of slow growth that began almost simultaneously with the Stockholm Conference. It certainly may be possible to imagine scenarios that are both rosy and reasonable in which international environmental management improves along with the world economy, but we should recognize how broad the international policy agenda must be if we are to make that imagined world real.

NOTES

1. Peter M. Haas. 1992. From Theory to Practice: Ecological Ideas and Development Policy. Harvard University, Center for International Affairs. Working Paper 92-2.

2. Craig N. Murphy. 1994. International Organizations and Industrial Change: Global Governance Since 1850. Oxford University Press, New York.

3.	I understand "authority" in the way that David Bell does, as a political actor able to issue imperative commands with the expectation that they will be followed. Bell defines the exercise of authority by distinguishing it from two other forms of persuasive action, the exercise of power and the exercise of influence. The exercise of power takes the form, "If you do X, I will do Y," where X is the desired action and Y is some positive or negative sanction. The exercise of influence takes the form, "If you do X, you will feel or experience Y," which is a claim to knowledge. I would extend Bell by arguing that in illegitimate exercises of authority, the force of the authority's command rests upon its preponderant power rather than on some mutually-accepted structure that binds the commander and commanded into a single community. See David V. J. Bell. 1975. Power, Influence, and Authority: An Essay in Political Linguistics. Oxford University Press, New York.

4.	For a discussion of such states, see Robert H. Jackson. 1990. Quasi States: Sovereignty, International Relations and the Third World. Cambridge University Press, Cambridge. See also VanDeveer, this volume.

5.	However, IMF officials can pursue the interests of financial markets in ways that are more, or less, in accord with wider interests. See, for example, John Loxley. 1986. Alternative approaches to stabilization in Africa. In Gerald K. Helleiner (ed.). Africa and the International Monetary Fund. International Monetary Fund, Washington, D.C. and Victor L. Urquidi. June 1991. Can the United Nations System Meet the Challenges of the World Economy? The John W. Holmes Memorial Lecture to the annual meeting of the Academic Council on the United Nations System, Mexico City.

6.	Murphy 1994, op. cit., pp. 108, 219, and 285-92 provides some detailed data on these means.

7.	Murphy 1994, op. cit. and Craig N. Murphy and Enrico Augelli. 1993. International institutions, decolonization, and development. International Political Science Review 14(1):71-85.

8.	Emily T. Smith. 1993. Growth vs. environment. Business Week 3265(May 11):66-75.

9.	Stephen Schmidheiny (ed.). 1992. Changing Course: A Global Perspective on Development and the Environment. MIT Press, Cambridge, p. 95.

10. See Haufler, this volume, for further discussion of "greening" in the private sector.

11. Peter M. Haas. 1990. Saving the Mediterranean: The Politics of International Environmental Cooperation. Columbia University Press, New York; Haas 1992, op. cit. and see also Haas in this volume.

12. The scientists sometimes have convinced governments themselves. In most cases, however, their impact has also been through the pressure of social movements activated by or, at least, willing to use, the scientists' results. See Murphy 1994, op. cit., p. 80.

13. Robert O. Keohane. 1984. After Hegemony: Cooperation and Discord in the World Political Economy. Princeton University Press, Princeton, pp. 51-57.

14. If we accept the more complex ideas about human motivation offered by Antonio Gramsci, we would have to add that the intellectual task could also be one of convincing governments that they have a shared aspiration to be the builders of the social order that the new regulations would help create.

15. See, for example, Mario J. Molina. 1992. Science and policy interface. In Nazli Choucri (ed.). Global Environmental Accords: Implications for Technology, Industry, and International Relations. Massachusetts Institute of Technology, Cambridge, United Nations Environmental Programme, United Nations Development Programme, the World Bank, and the Business Council on Sustainable Development.

16. Murphy 1994, op. cit., pp. 64-67.

17. Haas 1992, op. cit.

18. Ibid., p. 9.

19. Haas 1990, op. cit.

20. Murphy 1994, op. cit., p. 65.

21. Keohane, op. cit.

22. Murphy 1994, op. cit., pp. 77-79.

23. Ibid., pp. 181-182.

24. Ibid., pp. 185-186.

25. This development parallels a similar set of fears about the "politicization" of the sponsorship of international conferences from

about 1907 until the outbreak of the First World War. The Kaiser's sponsorship of meetings on such "non-strategic" matters as international labor legislation and geodesy could be read by Germany's potential enemies as a way of promoting German interests. Similarly, a planned 1914-15 reunion of the 1899 and 1907 Hague Conferences could not be held because the Central powers feared the politicization that might result from the traditional sponsorship by the Czar, even if he were joined by the American president.

26. The best one-volume introduction to the wide range of such theories is Stephen Gill (ed.). 1993. Gramsci, Historical Materialism, and International Relations. Cambridge University Press, Cambridge. Excellent complements to this are provided by Henk Overbeek (ed.). 1993. Restructuring Hegemony in the Global Political Economy: The Rise of Transnational Neo-liberalism in the 1980s. Routledge, London and David P. Rapkin (ed.). 1990. World Leadership and Hegemony. Lynne Rienner Publishers, Boulder, Colorado.

27. Augelli and Murphy, op. cit., pp. 58-70.

28. Jan Tinbergen (coordinator). 1976. Reshaping International Order: A Report to the Club of Rome. Dutton, New York; Brandt Commission. 1980. North-South: A Program for Survival. MIT Press, Cambridge; and Brandt Commission. 1983. Common Crisis North-South: Cooperation for World Recovery. MIT Press, Cambridge.

29. Murphy 1992, op. cit.

30. UNEP. 1994. A Successful Start to Informal Trade-Environment Talks. UNEP Press Release, Geneva. 18 February.

31. Urquidi, op. cit.

32. Ibid.

33. The work of Mendez, of the U.N. Sudano-Sahelian Office, suggests some possible directions. See Ruben P. Mendez. 1992. International Public Finance: A New Perspective on Global Relations. Oxford University Press, New York.

34. Richard N. Cooper. 1992. Public Policy Towards Global Warming. Lecture presented to the Wellesley College Department of Economics. 12 March.

35. Haakon Sandvold. 1993. Industry-Environment-Sustainability. In Choucri, op. cit.

36. See Thompson and Trisoglio, and Serafin and Zaleski in this volume.

37. Daniel Deudney. 1993. Global Environmental Rescue and the Emergence of World Domestic Politics. In Ronnie D. Lipschutz and Ken Conca (eds.). The State and Social Power in Global Environmental Politics. Columbia University Press, New York.

38. Bhaskar Menon. 1992. International Documents Review: The Weekly Newsletter on the United Nations. 6 March, p. 5.

39. Cooper, op. cit.

12

Sea Changes and State Sovereignty

STACY D. VANDEVEER

For decades regional seas such as the Baltic and Mediterranean have been the focus of growing efforts, with mixed results, to protect their ecological quality and ensure their continued production of marine resources. In addition, they have served as arenas for the military, economic, and ideological conflicts which have shaped European and global history throughout the twentieth century. The implications of any transnational cooperation in pursuit of marine environmental protection which occurs across these "high politics" fault lines are worth exploring.

This chapter argues that transnational norms shape state action by changing incentive structures and constraining state autonomy through subtle, so called, "suprarational" influences on processes such as categorization, interest definition, bargaining, negotiation, and perception. As such, the concept of state sovereignty — best understood as a dynamic set of related transnational norms — changes over time, influencing states and their behavior. These processes are especially clear in international environmental issue-areas such as the environmental protection of international regional seas. This is a substantial critique of the current "hegemonic discourse" within international relations. Rather than arguing that state actions and autonomy are dependent only on the power of other states and/or rationally determined interests, this argument suggests that the definitions of interests and the processes by which they are determined change over time, sometimes quite substantially, at least partially as a result of changing transnational norms (and, therefore not just as a result of changing capabilities and incentive structures). Simply put, I posit that state policies, autonomy, and concepts of sovereignty are shaped by changes within the realm of transnational norms resulting, over time, in qualitative differences in all three.

The international system of sovereign states that characterizes the global organization of our species has been constructed by centuries of social interaction and has undergone continuous, and at times dramatic, reconstruction. However, one rarely finds this point reflected in international relations theory. This chapter briefly discusses the contemporary international relations discourse and attempts to bring a social constructionist approach to bear on it. Utilizing these approaches, the chapter focuses on the influence of transnational norms for the protection of coastal sea environmental quality on state behavior and autonomy. Individuals and organizations interested in promoting and pursuing policies aimed at protecting the environment often view the state system as an impediment to their goals, and literature on these issues, when it discusses international politics and institutions, frequently makes reference to "problems" or "challenges" presented by the system of sovereign states. Why is this? Is it true? The final section of the essay suggests some answers to these questions if they are approached through the perspective of the subtle influences of socializing institutions on state action and autonomy and reigning conceptions of sovereignty.

First, an important distinction must be made between influences on state action and influences on state autonomy. Simply put, a state action is merely the policy course pursued by the state, or what the state actually does. State autonomy, as the term is used here, refers to the general ability of the state to act on the basis of its capabilities and pursuant to its policy objectives free from control by exogenous institutions or organizations.[1] My use of the term makes it analogous to human free will (to choose a course of action). This usage allows for examination of the ways in which state policy preferences are shaped by more subtle and diffuse influences — the influence of norms. Neither theory nor practice in international relations offers significant guidance on these issues.

NEOREALISTS, NEOLIBERALS, AND SOCIAL INSTITUTIONS

Much recent analysis of state action within the international system falls into the debate between two general areas of scholarship: so called "neorealism" and "neoliberalism." Both are grounded in the rational self-interest assumptions of traditional international relations literature and both rely heavily on analyses of bargaining processes; interests are generally viewed as given and invariant. The debate within this body of scholarship centers primarily around whether interests are generally thought to be in conflict or shared.[2] Neorealists tend to concentrate on conflicting interests, relative gains, and power politics. The neoliberals and most "international regime theorists," whom Peter Haas has aptly called "contractual institutionalists," tend to focus their examinations on explaining, and at times attempting to expand, cooperation within the international arena.[3] Realist and neorealist theorists have traditionally rejected, or had difficulty explaining, any significant influence of normative factors such as values, norms, and expectations on state action and autonomy. In addition, they generally view state sovereignty as a universal and unitary concept. It is assumed (or "given") because states, by definition, possess it.

Neoliberals and regime theorists, however, have argued that institutions and, by implication, transnational norms, can play a role by changing incentives for states, thereby helping to produce compliance with international environmental agreements in the absence of strict enforcement.[4] Neoliberals have been more willing than neorealists to treat sovereignty as a conceptual moving target. In general, however, they continue to treat it as a universal and largely unitary concept. The neorealist-neoliberal discourse is by no means a simple two-sided debate; there is substantial variety.

Yet most of the participants are informed by assumptions of rational actor models and continue to treat interests as exogenous.

Mainstream theories of international relations suggest that although the sheer number of policy options available to a given state may be reduced by institutions, the state's ability to chose between these options is not constrained. The regime literature argues that actions are often guided by institutionalized habit, routinization, or accepted behavioral and social norms. However, anthropologists such as Mary Douglas argue that institutions help individuals and collectives code experiences and shape the meanings ascribed to their pasts and futures, thereby helping to shape criterion for judgements of what is "appropriate."[5] Thus, given that norms are social institutions, one can ask what role transnational norms associated with the concept of sovereignty play in processes which confer appropriateness or impart meaning[6] on certain policies or regime structures. That is, what role do they play in socially constructing interests, debate, negotiation, and bargaining?

Social constructionist literature emphasizes the constraints on autonomy presented by such factors as limited human cognition, categorization, institutionalized roles and identities, and other forms of socialized behavior. It unpacks and reveals processes which operate "all around" and permeate interest bargaining, a *supra* rational process if you will, influencing assumptions, expectations, definitions, preferences, and so on. Robert Jackson put it this way: "Social and political ideas can become institutionalized as normative frameworks of human relations — like the rules of a competitive game — within which utilitarian interests and purposive activities are played out."[7] Thus ideas and the institutionalized norms they beget are a significant force in world politics.[8] Interest in the normative influences on international relations appears to be growing. For example, Robert Keohane acknowledges the value of so called "reflective approaches" in identifying important contextual influences such as history, culture, and learning which are not well captured in rationalistic approaches. John Ruggie argues for the recovery of "principled meanings [which] have come to be institutionalized throughout history."[9] These lines of inquiry treat interests as endogenous and historically contingent.

TRANSNATIONAL NORMS

Transnational norms serve as models for expected behavior or practice. Generally, norms "simplify choices of actors with non-identical preferences facing each other in a world characterized by scarcity."[10] They are of a "problem-solving character."[11] As such, transnational norms serve as relatively specific models for practices intended to accomplish certain tasks. As discussed here, a transnational norm is more than a practice which happens (through coincidence or ad hoc replication) to exist in more than one country. In order to be "transnational" a norm must be institutionalized across boundaries as well as within more than one country. Thus, the norm itself is associated with transnational activity intended to encourage the continuance and/or expansion of its practice and is rationalized by a consistent and similar, if somewhat differently organized, set of values.

Transnational norms have a normative component; they possess, as I refer to it, *normative force*. In other words these norms become guides for how specific tasks *should* be accomplished. Krasner states that "norms are standards of behavior defined in terms of rights and obligations."[12] As used here, the term "norm" differs from Kratochwil's. It incorporates behavior, practice and justification. Including both a normative component of values and expectations and an applied one of actual practice within the discussion of norms, affords opportunities for examination of the differences between the two. This distinction is especially important in the transnational realm because well-developed legal norms and principles can be observed in the absence of institutionalized practices which reflect them at regional, domestic, or local levels.

Transnational norms can influence many types of relevant actors including states, international organizations, and NGOs.[13] The distinction between institutions and organizations relied upon in this chapter is borrowed from Oran Young:

"Institutions are social practices consisting of easily recognized roles coupled with clusters of rules or conventions governing relations among the occupants of these roles" while organizations are defined as "material entities possessing physical locations (or seats), offices, personnel, equipment and budgets..."[14]

Transnational norms are distinct from regimes and international organizations. Norms are more diffuse, becoming embedded in these other institutional arrangements. In fact, standard definitions of regimes identify norms as only one component of these "larger" social institutions.[15]

Norms can be distinguished from international law and legal principle. Like norms and regimes, these international laws are social institutions. However the differences are best seen after distinguishing between "hard" law and "soft" law. Hard law, generally laid down in treaties, imposes binding obligations on states to enforce such law domestically.[16] Soft law, on the other hand, is vague and open to greater discretion. It usually helps guide implementation and it emerges from resolutions, declarations, and state practice.[17] Although transnational norms can be codified through treaty into international (hard) law, this is not necessarily done. Norms can also become legally binding through state custom if states believe that they must abide by the custom.[18] This process generally takes many years, whereas transnational norms can influence state action and autonomy without being legally binding and can emerge, at least regionally, in relatively short periods of time.

Transnational norms and customary law do overlap, however. In areas where there is ongoing scholarly debate regarding whether a specific custom is or is not yet part of international law, one is probably in the presence of a transnational norm which may or may not be in the process of becoming binding in international law. Common regional practices can be better accommodated by the discourse of transnational norms. While regional (hard) international law is binding, the binding nature of regional custom, unless declared law by some form of regional judicial authority, is much less certain.[19] Thus one can better understand the significance of transnational regional practices through the analytical lens of norms.

Soft law is similar to transnational norms, however it tends to be less specific and open to greater discretion.[20] In general, however, the debates about soft law and custom tend to center around whether or not they are legally binding (that is, on whether or not they constitute law), how they can be made so, and how they might serve the implementation of law which is binding. While these are interesting discussions, underlying them is a sense that international or transnational "rules" must be legally binding if they are to shape state action. This assumption obscures other ways state action and autonomy are influenced.[21] Lastly, such norms can also be differentiated from general principles of international law, which provide the basic assumptions upon which norms and rules (laws) are elaborated. These principles are the foundations for whole bodies of law. They are more diffuse, vague, and grandiose than transnational norms and they do not concern relatively specific models for certain practices intended to accomplish specific tasks.

Much of the transnational activity associated with the protection or restoration of environmental quality of coastal seas such as the Baltic, Mediterranean, and Black Seas and major lakes such as the Great Lakes evokes relatively new issue areas for international relations, involving concerns once considered the sole purview of domestic or "internal" authorities such as resource use, development planning, regulatory structure, and waste disposal and treatment. Many coastal seas protection regimes have moved from the regulation of a common resource to advocating, facilitating, and at times requiring fairly extensive changes in land use policies, scientific research and monitoring, economic development, and other state and societal practices "on land."[22] Such arrangements, and the norms they entail, are being used as models for other regional seas such as the Black Sea.[23] Thus, many states and subnational governments are becoming increasingly bound by transnational norms associated with certain practices which have acquired normative force; that is, they are viewed as the ways in which regional seas research, monitoring, management, or administrative enforcement should be accomplished.

CONSTRUCTING SOVEREIGNTIES

Having both internal and external dimensions, "sovereignty" has long been the conceptual intersection between that which is "inside" the territorial state, and thus subject to its authority, and that which is "outside." This concept remains the base around which theory and empirically observable institutions and organizations have been constructed. Sovereignty is said to accord all states equal juridical status within the international community as each state recognizes the internal authority of the others. I argue that sovereignty is best viewed as a socially constructed concept constituted by a set of norms which change over time through the constant interplay of state actions with one another and with other domestic, international, and transnational norms and actors.

This approach alters traditional understandings found in the dominant theoretical approaches of international relations. For example, theorists and practitioners of international relations and political economy have traditionally discussed international cooperation in terms of a state's willingness to "give up" or "preserve" its sovereignty. However, understanding state sovereignty as a set of socially constructed norms suggests that state and transnational actors are instead engaged in ongoing processes which reconceptualize or reconstruct the concept of sovereignty and the set of norms associated with it. Thus, sovereignty is more than a legal convention which organizes territorial units and their inhabitants into separate jurisdictions.

Debate regarding what, if anything, is "happening to state sovereignty" has become commonplace. Much of this debate "has turned on a ritual of affirmation and denial."[24] There are those, realists and neo-realists in particular, who insist that the state remains the central organizational component in world politics and that it may even be strengthened, and its sovereignty enhanced, by forces such as technological development, multinational business, global markets, environmental problems, and the protection of human rights.[25] Others argue just as strenuously that sovereignty is "decaying" or "eroding."[26] As Ken Conca points out, much of this discourse, at least with respect to the "ecology-sovereignty debate," reflects an "essentially functionalist" approach based on a very simplistic and general view of sovereignty.[27] A view reflected in much of the neorealist-neoliberal literature.

Sovereignty has a long and exceedingly complex conceptual and empirical history. It is not one coherent and consistent whole. Sovereignty is a set — the contents of which is not entirely uncontroversial — of interrelated and interdependent norms. Although numerous ways to articulate sovereignty's constituent norms exist, those most often identified are the following: equity among states, nonintervention, exclusive territorial jurisdiction, the presumption of states' competence or capacity, prohibition of binding jurisdiction without consent, exclusive (and largely unrestricted) use of force, and a (positivist) conception of international law as rooted in the free will of states.[28]

Sovereignty is embedded or "nested" within a larger framework consisting of other institutions with which it has a dynamic relationship.[29] For example, treaties and regimes concerning the use and ecological protection of regional seas are embedded in larger bodies of law concerning such issues as boundaries, the use of common resources and treaty making.[30] As norms change within the international system, those associated with sovereignty are also altered. In addition, some of the norms associated with state sovereignty, such as exclusive territorial control, non-interference in internal politics and "self-help" (or the right of the state to conduct its foreign policy pursuant to its interests) are in contradiction with one another.[31] These contradictions create tension and add to the dynamism within the set of norms. Theoretically, this argument is consistent with those in the social constructivist work on institutions. Empirically, these processes are illustrated by historical cases such as the collapse of colonial empires.

The European state system spread around the globe through trade, colonialism, and domination. During this period a positivist conception of sovereignty reigned. In other words only those states which demonstrated, through observable behaviors and institutions, that they were sovereign (i.e., possessing a relative amount of internal authority and external autonomy of action as well as juridical recognition) were considered so. This view of sovereignty served as the conceptual justification for the view that only "civilized" countries were sovereign.[32] Consequently, only colonial powers and a handful of small, mostly European states were seen as sovereign.

The norms of sovereign authority changed as it became clear that many of those under colonial rule desired some form of self-determination. Movements of decolonization or independence and resistance vis-a-vis imperial powers altered the values and norms of sovereignty. No longer could "uncivilized" societies be denied recognition as "sovereign" states as the principle of self determination (which also has a long and varied history of normative and practical changes) became institutionalized within the international system giving *de*colonization great normative force.[33] Limited resource capabilities and normative constraints on the legitimacy of continuing to use force to maintain colonial rule combined to produce a relatively rapid global decolonization.

Colonial systems built over 300 years came to be seen within 30-40 years as illegitimate and not worth the resources demanded to maintain them. Newly independent colonies became sovereign states after being recognized as such by other states.[34] The importance of recognition remains as the number of "sovereign states" increases and debates rage as to whether and when new territorial units should be recognized as states. This further illustrates movement away from a narrowly positivist conception of state sovereignty to one which relies more heavily on juridical recognition and the "meanings" assigned by international society. Thus, core values and norms of the international system experience fundamental change producing changes in the reigning conception of state sovereignty somewhat analogous to Kuhnian paradigm shifts.[35]

"Unbundling" sovereignty's constituent norms helps to illustrate the concept's bases in both empirical realities and normative constructions. Robert Jackson states that sovereignty is both a norm and a fact.[36] However, it is probably more accurate to say that sovereignty is both norms and facts. As Jackson points out, territorial jurisdiction is an international legal condition — a norm — rather than a sociological given.[37] Physical control of a piece of land is a fact, but from a sociological perspective, a social institution might possess many or all of the empirical characteristics of a state; however, without the juridical components (the norms), such an institution would not be a state. In short, state sovereignty is conceptual as well as organizational and it need not be necessarily or essentially defined and operationalized as a singular and specific practice or concept. If simply demonstrating material capabilities or "the facts of sovereignty" were sufficient for identification as a sovereign entity (a strictly positivist notion of sovereignty), then there would certainly be at least a few ethnic groups, indigenous peoples, and multinational corporations or criminal organizations which could qualify. These entities are not sovereign because they are not recognized as such by other states.

Sovereignty must also be understood to have both internal and external dimensions.[38] Sovereignty is said to denote the state's internal authority over "its" citizens and territory and external autonomy from interference by other states and from the control of any form of higher governing authority. These two dimensions and their mutual dependence can also be seen in the list of norms above. In fact, in order for the norms to make sense there must be an "inside" and an "outside."

Lapidoth argues that the internal dimension of state sovereignty has experienced a "loosening" over the past two centuries — largely the result of changes produced by varying forms of democratic governance.[39] There are now a host of different and sometimes divergent notions of sovereignty within the state which, at minimum, suggests that sovereignty can no longer be treated as monolithic in nature.[40] Of particular interest for this paper is the notion of "functional sovereignty" of states over the natural resources and continental shelf off the coasts of their territory and within their exclusive economic zones (EEZs).[41] Others notions of sovereignty include "quasi-sovereignty" and "impaired sovereignty."[42] Patricia Birnie suggests that the ways in which international law is evolving in response to environmental issues might best be called "responsible sovereignty," presumably because states have begun to recognize some ecological limitations and some of their responsibility to ensure that such limits are not exceeded.[43] Such empirical and conceptual changes, Lapidoth states, suggest that "sovereignty is not indivisible, and that two or several authorities may have limited, relative, differential, or functional sovereignty over certain areas, groups, or resources."[44] Such a multidimensional, complex and particularistic view of sovereignty is not generally reflected in the mainstream international relations scholarship outlined above.

State sovereignty, therefore, is conceptual as well as organizational and it need not be necessarily or essentially defined and operationalized as a singular and specific practice or concept. The state finds itself and its sovereign authority (internal) and autonomy (external) functionally and normatively "nested" within various levels of interaction. These processes influence state autonomy and policy choice because the meanings, or normative perceptions, of certain state actions change over time. In addition, norms frame political debate in the same way international law often does. Like international law, for example, when norms do not restrain practices they were intended to curb, they delineate concerns which must be addressed; they influence the discourse.[45]

SOVEREIGNTIES AND COASTAL SEAS

What is true of sovereignty is also true for norms associated with environmental protection of coastal seas. Norms within the communities concerned with coastal seas protection, for example, exist within larger normative frameworks of marine science and environmental protection. Changes in the guiding principles and norms of these frameworks produce changes with respect to coastal seas norms and policy. For example, Peter Haas has identified the effects on the Mediterranean protection regime of the changes in the field of ecology over time. As the field embraced so called "ecosystem management" and then "holistic" approaches to the human-environment relationship, the regime was altered to reflect these views.[46] Mark Sagoff similarly argues that a primary cause for the growing interests in "saving" regional seas is that their value or meaning for humans has changed from one based on utility to one grounded in moral and aesthetic concerns.[47] In other words, their meaning has been reconceptualized; it has been socially constructed in a new way.

To further complicate the picture, different states and groups of states possess different resource capabilities, institutions, histories, social norms, and hierarchies of societal values. Thus, in addition to changes over time in the reigning general conceptualization of state sovereignty, the concept turns out to be different in theory and in practice for different states. That is, it takes on different meanings and is associated with different practices and goals from one state or group of states to another. This is in sharp contrast to most international relations theory which assumes sovereignty to be constant and universal for all states.

Today, the state is far from the only organization which interprets the "outside" world for domestic polities. Global markets, communications and travel, and a vast array of inter-governmental and non-governmental organizations make up what Ronnie Lipschutz calls "emerging global civil society."[48] In the contemporary world greater numbers of domestic and transnational groups, with their own norms, rules, and values, have the capacity and the desire to influence state policy and autonomy through incentives, definitions of interest, and determinations of policy appropriateness. As a result, the state is not "free" to define or conceptualize an idea of sovereignty on its own. This point casts doubt on the contemporary applicability of Krasner's argument that ideas and norms regarding sovereignty have generally been employed by the state to construct the concept in service of its interests.[49]

These processes have been accompanied by a diffusion of authority, allegiance, and identity which by no means guarantees a more environmentally sound, democratic, and peaceful world because the norms, values, and interests of different transnational and local communities often do not correspond.[50] Transnational environmental cooperation for regional seas protection illustrates the importance of norms as factors which limit state autonomy and shape state policy options and actions, and thus shed light on tensions between globalizing and particularizing forces, further revealing limitations of the domestic-international dichotomy. The diffuse process of "constructing sovereignty" involves institutions and interests at the state level as well as those from "inside" and "outside," or all around, the state. Norms and ideas do not influence state action, autonomy, and sovereignty only by reining them in. Rather, the state is porous to norms and ideas; they become institutionalized within the state. In short, if sovereignty is socially constructed, then it is constructed at more than one "level" of social interaction.

Thus, processes of constructing sovereignties include states, international organizations, regimes, NGOs, transnational communities, and so on. Peter Haas' discussion of epistemic communities is an excellent example; membership in such a community is not contingent upon one's "level" or position vis-a-vis the state, but on a set of "shared values" and a "common policy enterprise."[51] Community members not only directly influence policy in advisory capacities, they can move into the employ of the state, taking their values, norms, and policy enterprises with them.[52]

As mentioned above, some perceive state sovereignty to be incompatible with attempts to address international environmental issues. I suggest some strategic approaches which might be useful to those interested in protecting and restoring ecological quality by constraining and shaping state action and autonomy and altering reigning conceptions of sovereignty, in ways which might be more compatible with such goals. These general strategies suggest numerous opportunities for the protection of enclosed coastal seas through international and transnational cooperation, where environmentalists tend to assume there are few, as well as challenges, which international environmental policy makers and activists have often overlooked.

INTERNATIONAL PLURALISM

The first and most obvious strategy amounts to suggesting more of the same: those interested in ecological protection must further engage the growing international pluralism. Already the international agenda has taken on more a "pluralized" character. Efforts to protect regional seas serve as excellent illustrations of both possibilities and limitations of this "international pluralism" of interests. Citizen and professional groups have succeeded in raising coastal sea protection issues in areas such as the North, Black, Baltic, and Mediterranean Seas, the Great Lakes, the Sea of Japan and the Seto Island Sea.[53] As several contributions to this volume have made clear, scientific and other "knowledge-based" groups have played key roles in these policy processes and citizenries possess a rapidly growing capacity to affect international relations and foreign policy.[54]

These pluralizing trends were at work before the collapse of the Communist Bloc. However, the end of the East-West division offers opportunities to expand international and transnational environmental cooperation in areas were it was previously constrained. In the Baltic, for instance, environmental cooperation across the East-West divide was fairly extensive before 1989. This cooperation appears to have helped set the stage, through confidence building, for cooperation on other issues.[55] Since 1989, though, there has been a dramatic increase in Baltic cooperation on all fronts. Now it is funding and imagination, not ideologically determined national security concerns, which constrain Baltic environmental action. In an equally inhospitable political environment, the formulation and implementation of the Mediterranean Action Plan managed to achieve a relatively high degree of agreement and cooperation even though a number of the participating states saw one another as enemies.[56]

Pluralist interest group articulation is generally found in greater frequency in the so-called advanced democracies. This is not surprising, but it does bear noting. For state and non-state actors, participating in international relations either through influencing a state or the international agenda requires a minimum amount of institutional access and reasonably high levels of resources. That wealthy democratic states are a main focus of pluralist activity is not entirely detrimental to the promulgation of environmental norms. These states with higher levels of material capability are essential for institutionalization and enforcement of ecological norms in international politics. However, telecommunications, information, and travel technologies are lowering transaction costs and increasing access between localized environmental groups from less wealthy societies.[57]

In this more pluralist organization of international and transnational relations that intergovernmental organizations (IGOs) and NGOs have begun to play significant roles. UNEP, for example, has been an extremely important player in transferring norms and establishing cooperative arrangements designed to protect coastal sea environmental quality. Similarly, UNESCO has been a centrally important force in the global promulgation of norms associated with science policy.[58] Transnational environmental NGOs such as Greenpeace and Coalition Clean Baltic have also gained prominence in seas-related politics and governance in Northern Europe. Those organizations and institutions which aid in the transfer of the resources and expertise which allow for participation are already contributing to the redefinition of sovereign authority and autonomy. They, and the values and norms they embody, give voice to previously unarticulated interests and groups.

CONFRONTING DIFFERING SOVEREIGNTIES

Secondly, environmentalists must confront problems associated with the existence of differing ideas and norms regarding sovereignty, in addition to challenges presented by variances in institutional capacity among states. Positing state sovereignty to be a universal reality masks a number of challenges to effective multinational environmental cooperation. Empirical evidence and institutional theory support the contention that "state sovereignty" is very different in both theory and practice for different states or types of states. Failure to take this into account when designing "regimes" for the protection of enclosed coastal seas presents serious challenges to their success. That states possess dramatically different levels of institutional capability has often hampered such environmental cooperation.[59] The myth of universal sovereignty does not admit the possibility that some states are not in possession of either internal authority or external autonomy. For example, it may be that the state does not have sufficient authority over large private corporations or parts of its territory or citizenry to force compliance with environmental regulations.

On the other hand, environmental policy may expand the authority of the state by affording it the opportunity to conduct policy in an area in which it was not previously involved.[60] Environmental regimes which augment the states' institutional capacities for environmental protection in ways which open these institutions to greater participation appear to be the most effective.[61] These are the types of country-specific differences which are often overlooked by assuming a traditional, universal conception of state sovereignty. Jackson's work on less developed states demonstrates that many do not possess internal order (indeed many do not even have control of the territory which is ostensibly within their borders).[62] For these states, it is the perpetuation of concepts of sovereignty or "quasi-sovereignty" by other states which maintains their existence.[63] In addition, it has been suggested that some states exist in an arena of normative conflict with "their" societies — that they struggle for decades to extend their authority, gain "social control," over the rules, values, and norms of their societies.[64] Thus, if sovereignty consists of the ability to impose internal order and to act freely in relation to other states, then many "quasi-sovereign states" are maintained only by the latter.

Such concerns directly impact the ability of cooperative arrangements to address coastal sea degradation. For example, in the Black Sea ecosystem countries have agreed to conduct environmental impact assessments for major developments. However, a new Ukrainian oil terminal is being constructed near Odessa without one. Valeriy Mikhailov, director of the Ukrainian Scientific Center of Marine Ecology, said of the project, "It is technically illegal, but we don't have laws here anymore."[65]

RECONSTRUCTING SOVEREIGNTIES

Lastly and perhaps most importantly, viewing sovereignty as an evolving set of norms alters traditional discourse about state capacities, policies, and autonomy, allowing sovereignty to be seen as a concept amenable to "reconstruction." This understanding of state sovereignty offers opportunities for the development and strengthening of international norms which are more compatible with environmental cooperation. Environmentalists must engage debates about state sovereignty and attempt to participate in its reconceptualization, instead of allowing it to be used as a rhetorical weapon against international actions to protect environmental quality. Environmental interests are already playing a role in this reconceptualization. The transnational nature of these issues necessitates transnational cooperation if they are to be addressed. This is certainly true of protecting coastal seas. However, regional cooperation is often not enough. Even if a group of countries that share a sea agree to act to preserve its ecological integrity, international shipping, dumping, or fishing activities may continue to have serious adverse environmental impacts. This is becoming more important as markets, and the organizations which regulate them, become increasingly global in scale.

If states are to view seriously the maintenance of environmental quality as a norm which contributes to shaping state policy, sovereignty must be reformulated in ways which afford opportunities for norms associated with state sovereignty and environmental protection to coexist compatibly. The interaction of the two would influence the development of both. To a limited extent this has already begun. There exists a growing body of international environmental law and legal principle which did not exist a few decades ago.[66] It is important to note, however, that international law is state-centered. It depends on state actions for its creation and enforcement. The strategies outlined above are important because environmentalists often turn to the state for help in addressing environmental problems. There are, however, many problems the state can not or will not attempt to solve. Thus, engaging debates regarding state sovereignty must also mean building and strengthening norms which make more room for non-state actors at all levels and in all stages of ecosystem protection.

Reconceptualizing sovereignty can cut both ways, however. Other norms are already becoming extremely influential in the debate and process by which state sovereignty is reformulated — some may be compatible with environmental protection and some may not. The list of justifications for "violating" so-called traditional concepts of sovereignty continues to grow. In addition to the challenges of environmental problems, the list includes universal human rights, regional and global "free trade," installing or re-installing democratically elected officials, humanitarian and/or "peace-keeping" interventions, and economic growth and development. While some are more controversial then others, all of these issue areas are likely to influence the future development of the norms associated with state sovereignty and shape state action and autonomy. There is already a widespread movement to define economic competitiveness and development goals as the justification for the state. For example, the evolution of the European Union and the substance of the Uruguay round of the GATT negotiations and the NAFTA agreement are clearly engaged in redefining the relationship between liberal trade norms and sovereign autonomy.

Some may argue that another possibility exists; that more traditional concepts of sovereignty could be reasserted.[67] This is true of course, but only to a limited extent. Like many contemporary "reassertions" of nationalism, if an older conception of sovereignty makes a comeback it will still be different than any formulation which has come before. Contemporary empirical and normative contexts are historically unique. Thus, sovereignty, in that it is centrally related to both of these contexts, cannot be the same as it was before. As the old cliché says, "you can never go back."[68]

If state sovereignty is to be reconceptualized in ways that constrain state autonomy, influence state action, and refocus both toward more environmental protection, then scientists, citizen activists, and academics must engage the normative debate, not give it up as a lost cause. Institutional change and reform can follow conceptual innovation as new norms are created and old ones evolve. It is these types of dynamic ideational processes that help to determine the possibilities for institutional solutions for protecting coastal seas. If whole marine ecosystems are to be kept from ecological degradation, environmentalists must engage the conceptual transformation of sovereignty and its associated norms, making ecological norms a more central concern of the state.

These strategies do not guarantee any single or certain end. "New" ideas and norms associated with sovereignty will never be set in stone either. Perhaps it is the possibilities created by all this uncertainty that encourages people to even attempt to "save" things like regional seas.

ACKNOWLEDGMENT

I am grateful for financial support from the Department of Government and Politics and the Institute for Philosophy and Public Policy at the University of Maryland, College Park, and for the many helpful and enlightening comments on various drafts of this chapter from L. Anathea Brooks, Ken Conca, Virginia Haufler, Martin Heisler, Ronnie Lipschutz, M. J. Peterson, Don Piper, Dennis Pirages, Mark Sagoff, Vladimir Tismaneanu, and Diana Zoelle.

NOTES

1. This usage of "state autonomy" is more general than that found in comparative politics literature (i.e., the degree of autonomy held by the state vis-a-vis certain domestic social and economic classes). See, for example, Theda Skocpol. 1979. States and Social Revolutions. Cambridge University Press, Cambridge.

2. For in-depth discussions of the differences between these schools of thought, see David Baldwin (ed.). 1993. Neorealism and Neoliberalism: The Contemporary Debate. Columbia University Press, New York; and Robert Keohane (ed.). 1986. Neorealism and Its Critics. Columbia University Press, New York.

3. Peter M. Haas in this volume. This school includes, for example, Robert O. Keohane. 1984. After Hegemony: Cooperation and Discord in the World Political Economy. Princeton University Press, Princeton; Robert O. Keohane. 1989. International Institutions and State Power. Westview Press, Boulder, Colorado; Martin List and Volker Rittberger. 1992. Regime theory and international environmental management; and Lawrence Susskind and Connie Ozawa. 1992. Negotiating more effective international environmental agreements. In Andrew Hurrell and Benedick Kingsbury (eds.). The

International Politics of the Environment: Actors, Interests and Institutions. Clarendon Press, Oxford; Elinor Ostrom. 1990. Governing the Commons: The Evolution of Institutions for Collective Action. Cambridge University Press, Cambridge; and Oran Young. 1989. International Cooperation: Building Regimes for Natural Resources and the Environment. Cornell University Press, Ithaca and London.

4. Abram and Antonia Chayes. 1991. Compliance without enforcement: state behavior under regulatory treaties. Negotiation Journal. July: 311-30; Arthur A. Stein. 1983. Coordination and collaboration: regimes in an anarchic world. In Stephen D. Krasner (ed.). International Regimes. Cornell University Press, Ithaca; Oran Young. 1977. Resource Management at the International Level. Pinter and Nichols, London and New York; Oran Young. 1979. Compliance and Public Authority. Johns Hopkins University Press, Baltimore; and Oran Young. 1982. Resource Regimes: Natural Resources and Social Institutions. University of California Press, Berkeley.

5. Mary Douglas. 1986. How Institutions Think. Syracuse University Press, Syracuse, NY.

6. James March and Johan P. Olsen. 1989. Rediscovering Institutions. Free Press, New York.

7. Robert H. Jackson. 1993. The weight of ideas in decolonization: normative change in international relations. In Judith Goldstein and Robert O. Keohane. 1993. Ideas and Foreign Policy: Beliefs, Institutions and Political Change. Cornell University Press, Ithaca, pp. 111-138. Quotation p. 111.

8. Goldstein and Keohane, op. cit.; Ronnie Lipschutz and Ken Conca (eds.). 1993. The State and Social Power in Global Environmental Politics. Columbia University Press, New York.

9. John G. Ruggie (ed.). 1993. Multilateralism Matters: Theory and Praxis of an Institutional Form. Columbia University Press, New York, p. 7.

10. Friedrich V. Kratochwil. 1989. Rules, Norms and Decisions. Cambridge University Press, Cambridge, p. 14.

11. Ibid.

12. Stephen D. Krasner (ed.). 1983. International Regimes. Cornell University Press, Ithaca, p. 2.

13. Actors generally become "relevant" through a combination of material capabilities and legitimacy levels vis-a-vis a particular issue area.

14. Oran Young. 1989. International Cooperation: Building Regimes for Natural Resources and the Environment. Cornell University Press, Ithaca and London, p. 32.

15. See, for example, Stephen D. Krasner (ed.). 1983. International Regimes. Cornell University Press, Ithaca and Young 1989, op. cit.

16. Patricia Birnie. 1992. International environmental law: its adequacy for present and future needs. In Andrew Hurrell and Benedict Kingsbury (eds.). The International Politics of the Environment. Oxford University Press, Oxford, pp. 52- 84; see also, Kratochwil, op. cit.; and Paul Szasz. 1992. International norm-making. In Edith Brown Weiss (ed.). Environmental Change and International Law. United Nations University Press.

17. Ibid.

18. Ibid.; see also, M. N. Shaw. 1991. International Law. Third Edition. Grotius Publications Limited, Cambridge, UK; and Michael Akehurst. 1974-75. Custom as a source of international law. British Year Book of International Law.

19. For a discussion of the complex debate regarding the frequency and type of state practice as they concern customary law, see Akehurst, op. cit.

20. Szasz, op. cit., treats norms and soft law as one and the same. The meaning he uses, however, is less task-specific than my use of "norm." Though Szasz uses the terms interchangeably, his meaning is generally the same as that of soft law in this chapter.

21. Here I am in agreement with Kratochwil 1989, op. cit.

22. See chapters in this volume by Ducrotoy; Francis and Lerner; Haas; and Shimizu et al.

23. John Pomfret. 1994. Black Sea, strangled by pollution, is near ecological death. The Washington Post, June 20, pp. A1, A10; Frank J. Gable. 1993. The Black Sea: an environmental and ecological profile with a view towards UNCED. Paper presented at the inter-

national conference of Environmental Management of Enclosed Coastal Seas. Baltimore, Maryland. November 10-13.

24. R.B.J. Walker and Saul H. Mendlovitz (eds.). 1990. Contending Sovereignties: Redefining Political Community. Lynne Rienner Publishers, Boulder, Colorado, p. 2.

25. In general, such scholars argue that, through these "new" issue areas and the policies designed to address them, the state acquires more authority in the domestic sphere and/or more autonomy from international and/or domestic interests. See, for example, Janice Thomson and Stephen D. Krasner. 1989. Global transactions and the consolidation of power. In Ernst-Otto Czempiel and James Rosenau (eds.). Global Change and Theoretical Challenges. Lexington Books, Lexington, Massachusetts.

26. These types of arguments generally focus on the degree to which state authority and/or autonomy are being limited or constrained vis-a-vis domestic and/or foreign policy arenas. See, for example, Joseph Camilleri and Jim Falk. 1992. The End of Sovereignty? Edward Elgar Publishing Limited; Eugene B. Skolnikoff. 1993. The Elusive Transformation. Princeton University Press, Princeton, NJ; and Mark Zacher. 1992. The decaying pillars of the Westphalian Temple. In James Rosenau and Ernst-Otto Czempiel (eds.). Governance Without Government: Order and Change in World Politics. Cambridge University Press, Cambridge, pp. 58-101.

27. Ken Conca. 1995. Rethinking the ecology-sovereignty debate. Millennium 23(3):1-11.

28. This list is taken from Ruth Lapidoth. 1992. Sovereignty in transition. Journal of International Affairs. 45(2):325-346. This list is also cited in Conca, op. cit.

29. On the concept of nested games see George Tsebelis. 1990. Nested Games: Rational Choice in Comparative Politics. University of California Press, Berkeley.

30. See, for example, Don Courtney Piper. 1967. The International Law of the Great Lakes. Duke University Press, Durham, North Carolina.

31. Stephen D. Krasner. 1993. Sovereignty, regimes and human rights. In Volker Rittberger (ed.). Regime Theory and International Relations. Clarendon Press, Oxford, pp. 139-167.

32. Kratochwil, op. cit.; Jackson, op. cit.

33. Watson, op. cit.; and Jackson, op. cit. For an analogous discussion of the end of the slave trade, see Ethan A. Nadelman. 1990. Global prohibition regimes: the evolution of norms in international society. International Organization 44(4):479-526; See also, Krasner 1993, op. cit.

34. The smaller and "weaker" the state (or "quasi-state") the more important recognition becomes. See Robert H. Jackson. 1990. Quasi-states: Sovereignty, International Relations and the Third World. Cambridge University Press, Cambridge.

35. Thomas Kuhn. 1970. The Structure of Scientific Revolutions, Second edition. University of Chicago Press, Chicago.

36. Robert H. Jackson. 1990. Quasi-states: Sovereignty, International Relations and the Third World. Cambridge University Press, Cambridge.

37. Ibid. Introduction.

38. Conca, op. cit. refers to these as the "inward looking" and "outward looking" dimensions of sovereignty.

39. Lapidoth, op. cit., p. 332.

40. The list of notions of sovereignty includes the following: "popular" sovereignty, "national" sovereignty, "dual," "de facto," "residual," or "de jure" sovereignty, as well as "negative," "positive," and "pluralist" sovereignty. Cites for which can be found in Lapidoth, op. cit., pp. 332-334.

41. Ibid.

42. See, Jackson, op. cit. and Steven E. Goldman. 1994. A right of intervention based on impaired sovereignty. World Affairs. 156(3): 124-129.

43. Birnie, op. cit.

44. Lapidoth, op.cit., p. 334.

45. See David P. Forsythe. 1990. The Politics of International Law. Lynn Reinner Publications, Boulder, Colorado, especially chapter 7.

46. Peter M. Haas. 1993. Protecting the Baltic and North Seas. In Peter M. Haas, Robert O. Keohane and Marc A. Levy (eds.). Institutions for the Earth. MIT Press, Cambridge and Haas, in this volume. Similar arguments regarding Great Lakes management are

made in contributions to this volume by Shimizu et al. and by Francis and Lerner. Similar process may be occurring regarding environmental norms and values and private sector activities. See, for example, Haufler, this volume, and Alan Miller. 1994. Corporations as agents for sustainable development. Revised version of paper presented at Footsteps to Sustainability Conference, Harrison Program for the Future Global Agenda, Washington, D.C., October 1993.

47. See the contribution by Sagoff in this volume.

48. Ronnie Lipschutz. 1992. Restructuring world politics: the emergence of global civil society. Millennium 21(3):389-420.

49. Stephen D. Krasner. 1993. Westphalia and all that. In Goldstein and Keohane, op. cit., pp. 235-264

50. Ibid. See also, Benjamin Barber. 1992. Jihad vs. McWorld. Atlantic Monthly. March; Furio Cerutti. 1992. Can there be a supranational identity? Philosophy and Social Criticism 18:2; Mike Featherstone (ed.). 1990. Global Culture: Nationalism, Globalization and Modernity. Sage Publications, London; Gidon Gottlieb. 1993. Nation Against State. Council on Foreign Relations Press, New York; Lipschutz and Conca, op. cit.; and Michael Walzer. 1993. Between nation and world: welcome to some new ideologies. The Economist. September: 11-17.

51. See Haas in this volume. Douglas' "cognitive communities" are conceptualized in much the same way. See Douglas, op. cit.

52. Haas, this volume. See Jasanoff in this volume for a discussion of why scientists need institutions like epistemic communities.

53. For in-depth analysis of the ways in which growing citizen access and participation is altering transnational politics, see Rosenau, this volume; James Rosenau. 1990. Turbulence in World Politics: A Theory of Change and Continuity. Princeton University Press, Princeton; and James Rosenau. 1992. Citizens and a changing global order. In James Rosenau and Ernst-Otto Czempiel (ed.). Governance Without Government: Order and Change in World Politics. Cambridge University Press, Cambridge. pp. 272-294.

54. See also, Peter M. Hass (ed.). 1992. Knowledge, Power and International Policy Coordination. Special issue of International Organization. 46(1).

55. Martin O. Heisler (ed.). 1990. The Nordic Regime: changing in international relations. The Annals of the American Academy of Political and Social Science. Sage Publications, Newbury Park, California; Arthur Westing. 1989. Comprehensive Security for the Baltic: An Environmental Approach. Sage Publications, London.

56. Peter M. Haas. 1990. Saving the Mediterranean: The Politics of International Environmental Cooperation. Columbia University Press, New York.

57. See both Lipschutz and Rosenau, this volume.

58. Martha Fennemore. 1993. International organizations as teachers of norms: the United Nations Educational, Scientific and Cultural Organization and Science Policy. International Organization. 47(4):565-597.

59. Haas et al. 1993, op. cit.

60. Nancy Peluso. 1993. Coercing conservation: the politics of state resource control. In Lipschutz and Conca, op. cit.

61. Haas et al. 1993, op. cit.

62. Jackson. 1990, op. cit.

63. Ibid.

64. Joel Migdal. 1988. Strong Societies and Weak States. Princeton University Press, Princeton.

65. As quoted in Pomfret, op. cit.

66. See, for example, Birnie, op. cit.; Brown Weiss, op. cit.; and Shaw, op. cit.

67. This is one of the messages of American opponents of the recent GATT agreement and the World Trade Organization it establishes.

68. Clearly, however, the impossibility of recreating the past does not keep people from trying.

13

Dancing with the Devil: International Business and Environmental Regimes

VIRGINIA HAUFLER

Environmental activists, and indeed many environmental policy-makers, tend to demonize business as the prime enemy of Mother Nature, and try to force it to "behave" through coercive regulation. At the same time, environmentalists today call for extensive investment and technology transfer for sustainable development projects. Given economic recession and popular resentment against high taxes in many of the wealthiest countries, it seems unlikely that the large sums of money needed for these projects will be forthcoming from government budgets. "Deep pockets" can be found only in the corporate community. This poses a difficult problem for environmental policymakers: how can corporate assets be mobilized towards environmentally benign ends?

Many people fear a rush by multinational corporations toward the least environmentally regulated markets, since today's increasingly deregulated financial markets and open borders make the decision to move investment dollars relatively easy. In response, government leaders may perceive a need to weaken existing regulations in order to compete with other countries to attract and retain corporate investment, leading to a process of downward global regulatory arbitrage. Ultimately, under this scenario, states will lose or voluntarily relinquish their autonomy to pursue socially desirable policies such as sustainable development when these conflict with the pursuit of economic competitiveness. This dilemma seems particularly acute for the less developed nations, which generally find it difficult to attract capital, but we can also see this concern in the recent heated debate in the U.S. over the potential for Mexico to become a "pollution haven" under the North American Free Trade Agreement (NAFTA).[1]

One can construct a more optimistic scenario, however, based on the evidence that certain major corporations today invest millions of dollars in new environmental products and processes. These firms see sound environmental management as a way to cut costs and meet the demands of an evolving global market for ecological goods. The Japanese government recently identified so-called "green markets" as the cutting edge of competitiveness, and therefore a priority for Japanese corporations to pursue. Some business managers and policymakers believe the economic goals of corporate profit and national economic development are compatible with environmental protection. Therefore, the fear that corporations will not invest in countries with tough environmental regulations may be an over-reaction, especially if investors can be convinced of the profitability of sustainable products and processes. The question, then, is how to institutionalize and expand environmental consciousness in the business community, in order to avoid the potential for regulatory arbitrage and increase the opportunities for sustainable development.

In this chapter, I argue that international organizations may provide services which can support the goal of sustainable development, but they need to be designed in ways that minimize the obstructionist impulses of major corporations (and international development organizations) and reinforce an emerging consensus on environmental efficiency. The argument proceeds in three sections. First, I argue that we are witnessing profound changes in business norms and practices, particularly among the most globally competitive industries. Second, these changes can and should be reinforced and expanded through the activities of international environmental regimes. Third, the international and national organizations that make up environmental regimes can implement policies which provide incentives for changing corporate behavior, such as monitoring and information, harmonization, and risk reduction. Ultimately, the goal of environmentally sustainable development can be reached successfully only through transforming the management perspectives of business leaders.[2]

GLOBAL CAPITAL AND SUSTAINABLE MANAGEMENT

What do we mean by "sustainable development," "sustainable practices," or "sustainable management"? The Brundtland Commission Report defined sustainable development as development that "meets the needs of the present without compromising the ability of future generations to meet their own needs."[3] Sustainable practices or processes minimize their impact on the depletion or degradation of natural resources. In the case of coastal seas, sustainability requires practices which reverse ecosystem degradation and loss, and maintain the amenity value (or "place") of the area for future purposes we may not anticipate today.[4] The leaders of the 1992 United Nations Conference on Environment and Development (UNCED) accepted and publicized the proposition that sustainable development and economic growth can be pursued simultaneously.

Some people consider sustainable development to be a contradiction in terms, and others consider it more a hope than a practical ambition. That sustainable development is impossible implies only two kinds of policy choices: reversion to a pre-industrial politico-economic system, or total inaction. Even those who agree that sustainable development is possible may not believe the current system can be transformed quickly enough to prevent disaster. This possibility, however, does not excuse society from the moral obligation to at least attempt the pursuit of a more sustainable future. Regardless of one's beliefs, clearly the feasibility of pursuing even minimal steps towards sustainability within the current political-economic system hinges upon our ability to develop new technologies, products, and manufacturing processes which have the least negative repercussions on our resource base. We can imagine an authentically post-industrial society which would apply technology towards low-intensity resource use in production, and probably would require a complete retooling of the economy at every step from the design and development of a product or service, to its manufacture and marketing.

The financial costs of such change could be enormous. For this reason, the less industrialized nations demanded monetary compensation as part of their agreement to the Montreal Protocol on Ozone Depletion, and negotiated the establishment of a Global Environmental Facility as one outcome of the UNCED. However, the financial resources of the industrialized nations which contribute to such global funds are limited, particularly by domestic political resistance to increases in foreign aid expenditures. Even in those countries with strong environmental movements, the public believes the costs of government environmental policies are almost unbearably high.

The public money available for environmental funds is literally a drop in the bucket compared to the resources available to major corporations and institutional investors. For example, the core of the Global Environmental Facility totals approximately US$825 million over three years to fund investment projects, technical assistance, and research in the developing countries.[5] By comparison, daily turnover in exchange markets around the world is approximately US$650 billion,[6] and one estimate indicates that the recessionary 1980s witnessed more than US$3.5 trillion in global foreign direct investment.[7] Therefore, multinational corporations and institutional investors must become major participants in sustainable development efforts.

Environmental associations are extremely reluctant to tackle this issue. For example, a recent World Wildlife Fund position paper argued for more investment from governments and international development banks in natural resource sectors for sustainable development.[8] The policy section did not mention business contributions, and the body of the paper contained only one sentence on the need to mobilize the business sector, with no details on how to do so. However, some have recognized the necessity to connect private sector actors to the sustainable development discourse. UNCED Chairman Maurice Strong, when accused of being a supporter of business interests, reportedly replied: "How can we achieve [sustainable development] without the participation of business?"[9]

Economic downturn in the industrialized nations, increasing competition from newly industrializing countries, and the existence of burdensome debt in developing states has put extreme pressure on government policymakers to consider every possible means of attracting investment capital to stimulate economic growth. Business interests have often pointed to strict environmental regulations as a negative element which affects their decisions on where to invest.[10] Concern over whether investment capital will move to the least regulated market is not a new phenomenon, but has been heightened by the revolutionary deregulation of national financial markets and the loosening of capital controls that occurred in the 1980s.[11] Thus, government leaders may picture themselves in a terrible bind: to attract capital, even for sustainable development projects, may require them to weaken environmental regulations.

The following sections of this chapter detail two points. First, the fears about investment bypassing the environmentally most regulated locations may be overstated, especially considering recent trends in corporate culture. The most progressive corporations and investors might be labelled "green leaders." They tend to be in industries which are close to the customer and therefore susceptible to consumer demand for ecological products. A recent EPA analysis of three forward-looking companies indicated a shared commitment to environmental goals beyond simply complying with regulations, essentially making environmental performance one of the firm's products.[12] Second, the incentives to pursue individual policies potentially leading to a downward spiral of regulation may be mitigated through inter-state cooperation in global resource management regimes.[13] These are likely to be found in industries where savings can be obtained from energy- and resource-efficient practices, but where lack of information, competing regulatory environments, and a perception of high risk discourage change. There is, of course, a third category of incorrigibles which require strict governmental regulation to enforce sustainable development goals.

CHANGING BUSINESS NORMS AND PRACTICES

The popular environmental view of business is that it is a monolithic community intractably opposed to change. For instance, one analysis of the Earth Summit argues that the multinational corporations should have been confronted, and not included in the negotiations.[14] It identified the many points of contact between UNCED leaders and leaders of the business community, assuming that such interaction was bad for the negotiations, and it notes approvingly that the non-governmental organizations (NGO) dismissed one NGO leader who wanted to pursue business consciousness-raising, preferring confrontation and regulation instead.[15] This narrow view of business ignores the wide variety of interests and approaches among different firms and industrial sectors. Furthermore, it glosses over evolutionary changes in the norms and practices of corporate leaders. Two notable trends in behavior may indicate that popular concern over attracting investment by weakening environmental protection may be misplaced. First, not all corporations immediately flee strict regulatory environments, and in some cases the business community has been directly involved in the development of government policies. Second, a significant number of business leaders are beginning to view sustainable practices as a contribution to bottom-line profits, instead of an extra cost. These indicate that there is much more room for shaping the direction of investment in environmentally favorable ways than is popularly supposed.

A multitude of factors affects corporate decisions regarding where to locate new production facilities and in what businesses to invest. These include, among others, local labor skills, tax codes, resource costs, diversification, size of the local market, and political stability. In other words, modifying environmental regulations probably will not attract foreign investment if other factors are unfavorable. Charles Pearson's research indicates there is no significant relationship between trends in environmental regulation and trends in investment relocation.[16] Note that the majority of investment today occurs in OECD member countries, which have some of the highest regulatory standards in the world.[17]

Recently, a spate of popular books has reflected the development of new ideas and new perceptions in the business community. The most prominent of these has been *Changing Course: A Global Business Perspective on Development and the Environment*.[18] The authors of this and other books present evidence and persuasive claims that business profits can be enhanced by the search for sustainable products and processes. The World Resources Institute recently published a book designed to highlight and directly encourage what its editor views as a "sea change" in corporate environmental understanding and response by presenting information on a number of company environmental programs.[19]

This change in attitude can be attributed in part to the increasing demand by consumers for ecologically acceptable products. Evidence suggests that consumers today are less likely than previously to trade off environmental values for other values.[20] Being able to anticipate this type of changing global demand can contribute to competitive advantage. For instance, the contemporary clothing retailer Esprit is launching a "green" product line, which will be marketed as fashionable, environmentally friendly, and cutting-edge in the use of new technologies.[21] Large numbers of businesses are jumping on the green bandwagon, although sometimes in the most superficial ways.[22]

Evidence from the past few years indicates a surprising increase in the pace of change in corporate culture. For example, the chemical industry eventually participated in developing strict international notification procedures for toxic exports, a significant break from their earlier unyielding negotiating position.[23] In agriculture, some major growers formerly wedded to chemical-intensive farming practices are beginning to implement organic farming. For instance, some California grape growers originally pursued organic farming only to appeal to customers concerned about toxins in the food supply. They discovered, after initial investments and a move up the learning curve, that organic methods are both productive and cost-effective.[24] Various world industry associations now recommend that their members use environmental technologies and develop procedures for ecological audits and life cycle analysis.

A recent United Nations Centre for Transnational Corporations survey indicated that many businesses have established corporate environmental policies that actually exceed national standards.[25] Regulation can in fact be a driving force behind changing relative competitiveness in global markets.[26] But some corporations have rectified their practices prior to any government regulation or environmentalist pressure. For instance, Northern Telecom of Canada completely eliminated CFCs in its facilities long before the target dates set by the Montreal Protocol on Ozone Depletion. More importantly, the process of change convinced upper management that this policy had economic benefits, since they eliminated $50 million in costs along with the CFCs.[27] Traditionally, efficiency meant the maximum consumption of the least costly factor in the production process, which generally is resource commodities. However, true efficiency entails the minimum consumption of all factors per unit of output. The businesses most aggressively pursuing environmental practices have discovered this truth.

INTERNATIONAL REGIMES AND CORPORATE COOPERATION

Originally, the literature on international regimes focused only on sovereign states as legitimate participants, and not corporations.[28] Regimes are defined in terms of the norms, principles, rules, and practices which help member-states agree on what to expect from each other in dealing with a particular policy issue. They provide services which might be called "collective goods" to their participants by reducing transaction costs, increasing available information, and decreasing uncertainty about the operation of the system.[29] Through repeated interaction among participants in a regime, common concerns and obligations can be elucidated. Most importantly, once a regime is negotiated it encourages further bargaining over a range of issues, thus expanding the potential for cooperation.

Environmental issues have brought non-governmental organizations to the fore as important participants in regime dynamics. For example, the UNCED process deliberately reached out to the environmental community, giving it standing in international negotiations. Environmental associations provided original, empirical research to guide the deliberations of the Rio Conference, and helped establish norms and principles upon which inter-state negotiations proceeded. The business community also plays a role in generating behavioral rules and preferences within regimes, but its role in inter-state negotiations has been somewhat obscured. For example, national delegations to European Union negotiations over environmental rule-making explicitly include business representatives although technically the Union has only states as members.

There are three main ways in which corporations interact with regimes. First, they may simply be the target of regulation by international agreements, which is the traditional model of regime-corporate interaction. The national government is expected to implement international agreements by regulating corporate behavior.[30] It implies that governments must continuously monitor and enforce the rules in order to establish compliance with their environmental goals. It should be noted, however, that the literature on regimes focuses on monitoring and enforcement with respect to state behavior, and not corporate behavior directly. In fact, the ultimate target of international environmental regulation is usually corporate behavior, with the national government as cop.

The other two types of relationships between corporations and regimes are more relevant to this discussion. Corporations may be independent of any international regime, and may in fact develop their own conventions with regard to a particular issue area. For instance, in the 1960s private shipping interests developed commonly accepted behavior with regard to oil pollution of the oceans.[31] Usually, such industry norms are most likely to develop in the absence of strong government preferences. Finally, the relationship between a regime and non-state actors may be instrumental in nature. The goals of the regime may be carried out by non-governmental organizations and/or corporations. For instance, the international regime for family planning, centered on the United Nations Fund for Population Activities, implements many of its objectives through non-governmental organizations such as the International Planned Parenthood Federation.[32] These two types of regime/corporate interaction may provide access for international organizations to influence the ways in which the private sector defines its interests.

CARROTS INSTEAD OF STICKS IN ALTERING CORPORATE BEHAVIOR

International regimes can act as catalysts for a genuine development of sustainable practices. Agreements reached at the global level can be designed to ensure that "policies are mutually reinforcing and no country is penalized for unilateral efforts to move towards sustainable development."[33] These agreements should provide incentives for changes in corporate behavior, directly or indirectly via home government policies. There are three main ways in which international regimes can influence the business community: through provision of information, harmonization of national regulatory practices, and mitigation of risk.[34]

Provide Information

One of the most important barriers to change is the lack of usable information. Many international organizations produce reams of research and analysis, but this is usually tailored to governance problems. Three kinds of information can be provided by international organizations that would be relevant to corporations: information about current technologies, products and processes; information about regulations and patterns of compliance; and, most interestingly, a process of information gathering and debate among participants that could lead to the generation of new norms of business behavior.

An important responsibility of international organizations should be to persuade business managers that environmental policies do not necessarily increase costs, reduce or eliminate markets, or decrease corporate autonomy. They can provide empirical evidence that anticipating problems and building environmental practices such as waste reduction into the production process can be extremely efficient. For example, the petroleum and shipping industries eventually supported strict international standards in order to decrease the costs of accidental oil loss and to obtain better insurance ratings and thus lower premiums, contributing both to their profitability and to collective anti-pollution goals.[35] While a pollution-free environment is a public good, the benefits of corporate policies of reduction or elimination of pollutants can be captured privately. Such practices can also save a company from national and international regulatory enforcement agencies, thereby avoiding fines and forced re-tooling.[36] An appropriate model might be a global version of the U.S. Environmental Protection Agency Pollution Prevention Information Clearinghouse.

International regimes can also provide information on the best available environmental practices and technologies. One of the main purposes of the Global Environmental Facility is to encourage technology transfer, but the focus remains on inter-governmental transfers and not on contributions from business. During the Montreal Negotiations over ozone depletion, the technical negotiating panel included industry representatives who were recognized as contributing to generating new knowledge and commercial opportunities in CFC reduction.[37] This international forum provided an arena for identifying possibilities in technology development without necessarily infringing on proprietary rights. The World Environment Center, sponsored by USAID and industry groups, provides U.S. private sector technical skills to governments and industries in the developing world.[38]

Reputation and branding are also important elements in changing business perceptions. *Fortune* magazine recently published a "Corporate Reputations" issue which highlighted the importance of reputation to success. Some chief executives whose firms were ranked at the bottom reportedly directed their staff that they never wanted the company to be listed at the bottom again.[39] Corporations which implement sustainable management practices may be rewarded by national, regional, and international agencies with public acknowledgment of their good reputations. For instance, European Union efforts to develop standards for labelling green products ("eco-labelling") can be seen as a step towards institutionalizing a process of reputation-building on a regional basis. An international organization can monitor behavior and provide information on the comparative performance of different industries and firms.

Negotiation and coordination of activities within a regime may also provide an opportunity for governments, businesses, and the environmental community to educate each other about their preferences. The very process itself may be seen as an informational activity that can generate a consensus about appropriate policies and behaviors, and act as a consciousness raising exercise.[40] Therefore, participation by all relevant groups in negotiating environmental policies can contribute directly to their success. Business is in fact a participant in regulatory development at the national and international levels although it often is viewed with suspicion. Scott Barrett points out that participation in developing regulatory standards can give a business a competitive advantage, leading to strategic competition among governments and competitors.[41]

Harmonize National Regulatory Systems

Harmonization, or bringing different regulatory systems into approximately similar shape, is one of the most contentious issues in international environmental management. The fear is that harmonization would lead to the lowest common denominator regulatory standards, i.e. setting a ceiling rather than a floor on national environmental regulations. The debate is most fierce when put in the context of international trade negotiations. This parallels to a degree the debate over capital mobility and the search for regulatory "havens." In this case, the perception is that environmental regulation increases costs for some producers, putting their products at a cost-disadvantage compared to products made in less regulated societies.

There is no doubt that recent international trade negotiations in the Uruguay Round of the GATT negotiations placed free trade and free flow of capital above any concern for maintaining high standards. However, the recent completion of the NAFTA accords, with their environmental side agreements, reflects an increasing sensitivity in negotiations to the impact of trade on non-economic policy goals. Furthermore, as argued above, environmental regulation is not always an onerous cost to producers. As Peter Haas has pointed out, international negotiations can be conducted as a means of ensuring that each government's industries remain competitive relative to those of other countries.[42]

From the standpoint of multinational business interests, harmonization of regulations at whatever level would be preferable to the patchwork of systems in existence today. Unilaterally imposed domestic rules may conflict with those of another country, requiring different products and processes for different markets. The United Nations Centre on Transnational Corporations survey of corporate environmental practices found that most respondents wanted the United Nations to negotiate a reduction in differences in environmental rules and regulations.[43] The International Standards Organization has already begun work on standardized approaches to environmental auditing and life-cycle analysis.

Paarlberg's analysis of negotiations over pesticide dumping details how international agrochemical corporations felt threatened by the spread of competing national regulatory restrictions. The relevant international institutions, the FAO and WHO, moved towards promoting international harmonization in response. Industry representatives participated as part of the national delegations sent to the Codex Alimentarius Commission on food safety standards, and industry representatives were a part of FAO institutions and weakened attempts at controlling pesticide use. However, over time, the corporations began to shift towards a more accommodating stance, and eventually cooperated in establishing limits on pesticides.[44]

Complete harmonization ignores too many local conditions to be effective in every area. As Pearson argues, harmonization of environmental standards makes sense only for internationally traded goods and transboundary and global environmental problems.[45] Harmonization need not equal uniformity, but an international framework for environmental regulations could provide the political predictability that makes long-term corporate planning possible.

Mitigate Risk

Both information and harmonization by international regimes can reduce the commercial risks inherent in corporate adoption of new "green" technologies, products, and processes. Both cost and regulatory uncertainty inhibit the development of new environmental technologies, leading to potentially significant market failures.[46] Environmentally sustainable practices are often both complex and initially expensive to implement. Therefore, widely available information on relevant research and practice combined with a stable regulatory framework would reduce the risk of pursuing what may turn out to be a fruitless path.

Businesses also face political risks because they often operate in multiple jurisdictions, confronting a changing landscape of laws, rules, and regulations. Harmonization — provided it is enforced equally among all member states — by means of international environmental rules would contribute to reducing some of the instability and uncertainty associated with global business transactions. Evidence so far indicates that international regimes are important precisely because they provide a more hospitable contractual climate for negotiation and cooperation among states. Similarly, international environmental regimes may also provide a more hospitable contractual climate for corporate investment, technology transfer, and implementation of sustainable management practices. From the standpoint of business managers, one of the most important encouragements to investment is the establishment of stable enforceable property rights for foreign investment, most recently evidenced in the effort to negotiate protection for intellectual property rights in the Uruguay Round.[47]

There are also more direct means of effecting reductions in risk. For instance, most governments provide credit and investment guarantees, which could be adapted to international environmental projects. International agencies can pursue co-production agreements and joint ventures with corporations and national governments to develop new products and processes. Investment by international organizations, as envisioned under the Global Environment Facility, may also transfer some of the risk of change.

IMPLICATIONS

Inevitably, the distribution of both costs and benefits of environmentally sound practices will not be perfectly equitable, among states or among industries, potentially leading to asymmetries in power and barriers to cooperation. Successful environmental management cannot rely on self-interested cooperation alone. Corporations have been labelled the "enemy" of nature for good reason. Traditional industrial mass production wastes and destroys natural resources at a rapid rate, and historically has been hostile to many if not all environmental goals. As community concern about ecological issues has increased, business interests have often mobilized against environmental regulation and environmental activists, stopping or slowing down the development of strong and effective resource management systems. Traditional corporate culture militates against what is often perceived by businessmen as the sacrifice of profit for dubious social goals.

Clearly, international environmental regimes must provide mechanisms for both monitoring and enforcement. The argument for strengthening the capacity of international institutions to provide incentives to encourage industrial change takes the current structure of the system for granted.[48] It assumes that business managers decide where most investment capital is allocated. It further assumes a somewhat benign view of the policies of international organizations. Finally, it rests on the idea that the processes of change can be managed. All of these can be (and have been) challenged.

The preliminary evidence presented here reflects a genuine shift in corporate culture, providing an avenue by which international organizations can seek to shape corporate activity through both regulation and persuasion. Government policymakers are concerned about how to increase national growth and development, but may perceive themselves as constrained by the transnationalization of production and finance. Multinational corporations are concerned about the competing regulatory frameworks under which they operate in different nations. Environmentally concerned citizens often remain confused over whether or not there are trade-offs between economic development versus environmental management, and whether sustainable development is possible.

International regimes can provide a means to negotiate among these competing views. In global environmental policy-making, international agreements and organizations mediate among states. The ultimate target of national regulation, however, is national and international business. The possibility presented here is that we can design regimes that go beyond coercive regulation of industry. Instead, they can be transformative.

NOTES

1. See The Case Against Free Trade: GATT, NAFTA, and the Globalization of Corporate Power. Earth Island Press, San Francisco. 1993.

2. Peter Haas in this volume discusses "epistemic communities" as they apply to scientists and policymakers, but this approach also might be applied fruitfully to a fuller understanding of corporate norms and practices.

3. World Commission on Environment and Development. 1987. Our Common Future. Oxford University Press, Oxford. For a critical survey of the concept of sustainable development see Sharachchandra Lele. 1991. Sustainable Development: A Critical Review. World Development 19(6):607-621.

4. See chapters by Stephen Kellert, and Mark Sagoff, this volume; see also Mark Sagoff. 1992. Settling America, or the Concept of Place in Environmental Ethics. Journal of Energy, Natural Resources and Environmental Law 12(2):351-418.

5. Anthony Whitworth. 1992. Questions and Answers on the Global Environment Facility. Biodiversity Information Network List.

6. John B. Goodman. 1992. Monetary Sovereignty: The Politics of Central Banking in Western Europe. Cornell University Press, Ithaca, p. 18.

7. De Anne Julius. 1990. Global Companies and Public Policy: The Growing Challenge of Foreign Direct Investment. Council on Foreign Relations, New York.

8. Worldwide Fund for Nature. August 1993. Sustainable Use of Natural Resources: Concepts, Issues, and Criteria. Position Paper. Worldwide Fund for Nature, Gland, Switzerland.

9. Kenny Bruno. 1992. The Corporate Capture of the Earth Summit. Multinational Monitor 13(7):15.

10. Charles Lindblom identified the problem as the "privileged position of business," since it is businessmen who can decide whether and where to invest their capital in the economy. See Lindblom. 1977. Politics and Markets: The World's Political and Economic Systems. Basic Books, New York.

11. See Susan Strange. 1986. Casino Capitalism. Basil Blackwell, New York; John B. Goodman and Louis W. Pauly. October 1993. The Obsolescence of Capital Controls? Economic Management in an Age of Global Markets. World Politics 46:50-82.

12. Ellen Shapiro. 1993. Three Case Studies. EPA Journal 19(3):14.

13. International regimes are more than international organizations, although they are generally implemented through one or more international agencies or associations. They consist of principles and norms, rules and decision-making procedures which guide the expectations and therefore the behavior of participants in a specific issue area. See Stephen Krasner (ed.). 1984. International Regimes. Cornell University Press, Ithaca.

14. Bruno, op. cit.

15. Ibid.

16. Charles Pearson. 1987. Environmental Standards, Industrial Relocation, and Pollution Havens. In Pearson (ed.). Multinational Corporations, Environment, and the Third World. Duke University Press, Durham.

17. The OECD sponsored research which concluded government incentives to attract foreign investment had little or no impact. See OECD. 1989. Investment Incentives and Disincentives. OECD, Paris.

18. Stephen Schmidheiny and the Business Council for Sustainable Development. 1992. MIT Press, Cambridge and London. A few years ago, the mere idea of a business council for sustainable development would have seemed like Orwellian double-speak. See also Paul Hawken. 1993. The Ecology of Commerce: A Declaration of Sustainability. Harper Collins, New York; Michael Silverstein. 1993. The Environmental Economics Revolution. St. Martin's Press, New York; and Joel Makower. March 1993. The E-Factor: The Bottom Line Approach to Environmentally Responsible Business. Times Books/Tilden Press, New York.

19. The companies include Johnson Wax, 3M, Dow Chemical, Proctor and Gamble, Chevron, DuPont and others. Bruce Smart, ed. Beyond Compliance. World Resources Institute, April 1992, p.1.

20. Gene Pokorny. 1993. Going Green. Coal Voice 16(1):12. It has been reported that 42 percent of Britons claimed they consciously shopped for green products, twice as many as in the previous year. The Economist. October 20, 1990, p. 88.

21. National Public Radio, Morning Edition. November 3, 1993.

22. There have been accusations of "greenwashing" the corporate image through public relations expenditures. Steve Sawyer, et al. 1992. How Green is Green? Communication World 9(5):22-27. See also DuPont: Friends of the Earth Assails TV Campaign, which reports the accusation of "green fraud." Greenwire August 28, 1991.

23. Robert L. Paarlberg. Managing pesticide use in developing countries. In Peter M. Haas, Robert O. Keohane, and Marc A. Levy, eds. 1993. Institutions for the Earth: Sources of Effective International Environmental Protection. MIT Press, Cambridge Massachusetts.

24. Morning Edition. National Public Radio, November 1, 1993.

25. European Information Service/Multinational Service. January 1992. United Nations Corporate Environmental Survey, Part 3, p. 11.

26. See Alan Miller. 1993. Corporations as agents for a sustainable society. Conference paper, Footsteps to Sustainable Development, The Harrison Program on the Future Global Agenda. College Park, Maryland and Washington, D.C. October 28-30, 1993.

27. The CFC-free process may also improve the products themselves. David Suzuki. 1992. Finally, A firm that puts earth first! The Gazette. Montreal (January) 25: 18. A recent analysis of 27 organic chemical manufacturing plants found that preventing waste achieves both environmental and economic gains at low cost. Lois R. Ember. 1992. Pollution prevention at chemical plants benefits the environment at low cost. Chemical and Engineering News 70(25):18-19.

28. Krasner, op. cit.; see also Volker Rittberger (ed.). 1993. Regime Theory and International Relations. Oxford University Press, Oxford.

29. Robert Keohane. 1986. After Hegemony. Princeton University Press, Princeton.

30. One very interesting development is the increasing influence of non-governmental organizations in monitoring activities. Mark Sagoff has pointed to the importance of international rules in delegitimating certain behavior, which then provides activist groups with an opportunity to publicize and essentially shame the government or corporation into changing behavior. Sagoff, op. cit.

31. Since the 1960s, oil pollution of the seas has come under stricter inter-state regulation. See Ronald Mitchell. International Oil Pollution of the Oceans. In Haas, Keohane, and Levy, op. cit.

32. Barbara Crane. International population institutions: adaptation to a changing world order. In Haas, Keohane, and Levy, op. cit.

33. The New World Dialogue on Environment and Development in the Western Hemisphere. October 1991. Compact for a New World.

34. Thomas N. Gladwin provides a list of fourteen examples of international environmental cooperation that affect multinational cor-

porations. For purposes of this chapter, I have condensed the relevant types into three. See Gladwin. Environment, Development, and Multinational Enterprise. In Pearson, op. cit.

35. Mitchell, op. cit.

36. Bretigne Shaffer. 1993. Asian Business. April: 40-42.

37. Edward A. Parson, Protecting the ozone layer. In Haas, Keohane, and Levy, op. cit.

38. Gladwin, op. cit., p. 24.

39. Corporate Reputations. Fortune. 1993. At a recent conference on sustainable development, many of the participants emphasized the importance of reputation and "shaming" in promoting and enforcing environmental policies. Footsteps to Sustainability. The Harrison Program on the Future Global Agenda, November 1993, College Park, Maryland and Washington, D.C., p. 53.

40. Thomas N. Gladwin highlights the consciousness raising impact of world conferences on food and population. Gladwin, op. cit. See also the chapters by Peter Haas and Ronnie Lipschutz.

41. Harmonization of regulations may reduce the extent of these kinds of strategic interactions. Barrett. Fall/Winter 1992. Strategy and the Environment. Columbia Journal of World Business 27(3/4):202-208.

42. Peter Haas. Protecting the Baltic and North Seas. In Haas, Keohane, and Levy, op. cit.

43. European Information Service/Multinational Service, op. cit., p. 10.

44. Paarlberg, op. cit.

45. Pearson, op. cit., p. 116.

46. Miller, op. cit.

47. For an excellent overview of the weakness of the capital protection regime, see Charles Lipson. 1985. Standing Guard: Protecting Foreign Capital in the Nineteenth and Twentieth Centuries. University of California Press, Berkeley and Los Angeles.

48. See Ronnie Lipschutz in this volume for the argument that incentive regimes retain the status quo.

14

Enlarged Citizen Skills and Enclosed Coastal Seas

JAMES N. ROSENAU

As processes of nature provide contextual limits and opportunities for the conduct of social, economic, and political life, human situations serve as context for the natural environment. More than that, the two are so profoundly interactive that often both nature and humankind blend together into a single causal stream. People consume resources, thereby transforming nature; in turn, nature's transformations alter the conduct of community and world affairs, leading to changed patterns of consumption, and a continuing cycle of interaction. Late in the twentieth century this cycle is distinguished by its fast pace. The causal stream has become a rushing river, swollen by the melting snows and bursting dams of endlessly dynamic technologies. As the pace of interactive change accelerates, so do the tasks of governance become ever more delicate and the processes of nature ever more complex. As a result, people and communities are faced with the tough question of whether the complexities can be brought into sufficient focus to facilitate management of the delicacies of governance.

These issues pose the difficult analytic question of what research strategy would best clarify the dynamics of the causal stream.

Should the interactive process be broken down in order to examine its component parts separately? That is, should the natural environment be treated as a constant while the responses and changes of human systems are probed? Should the conduct of individuals and communities then be held constant while the responses and changes of nature are investigated? If both components thus yield more fully to comprehension, is it possible to recombine them in such a way as to chart their interaction more reliably? Or is such a procedure bound to underplay, if not overlook, the dynamism of the interaction? Would it be preferable to focus on human and natural affairs as a single, integrated system, treating the changes in each as merely an input for the other? Whichever of these strategies may be adopted, what variables of natural and human systems are most consequential and should thus be the subject of intense and systematic inquiry?

These questions are controversial, important and not easily answered. They are controversial because a widely shared understanding of the dynamics of both physical and human nature has still to evolve and, instead, competing interpretations exist regarding the central variables and how they operate. They are important because different research strategies can yield vastly different results. And they are not easily answered because few, if any, among us have the skills and training to synthesize the diverse kinds of knowledge into which the questions tap. In short, the questions involve nothing less than our seeking, as is often said, "to make an exact science out of an inexact nature."

Reflecting as they do our underlying premises about the nature of knowledge and our capacity to comprehend the human condition, the foregoing questions are surely worthy of extended analysis. What follows, however, is confined to the identification of only a few key variables in both natural and human systems that appear relevant to the causal stream and an exploration of how they might be expected to interact in the context of enclosed coastal seas (ECS). More specifically, this chapter identifies four types of citizens and four types of environmental issues and then assesses how the various types of citizens might respond to the several different types of issues. The central conclusions concern the ways in which problems associated with ECS condition the conduct of each type of citizen and the appeal of each type of issue.

Natural and human systems are sources of change for each other, but both are also responsive to other transformations in the world which may serve as boundary conditions within which links between the two evolve. One obvious condition, for example, is the state of the global economy. As it fluctuates back and forth from booms to busts, so do the resources available for addressing nature's challenges.

Two overall and interrelated perspectives can usefully serve as the basis for briefly clarifying the larger setting in which human and natural systems interact. One derives from a model of global turbulence which traces the huge transformations of our time to basic shifts in three parameters that bound the conduct of world affairs. The turbulence model locates both the dramatic and the underlying changes of the present era in the bifurcation of global structures (the macro parameter), the onset of worldwide authority crises (the macro-micro parameter), and a skill revolution in which the analytic capabilities of people everywhere have undergone significant expansion (the micro parameter).[1] Each of these fundamental transformations has had important consequences for the way in which people and their political institutions cope with environmental challenges.

The bifurcation of global structures into a multi-centric world of diverse actors capable of rivaling the state-centric world has greatly increased the opportunities and access through which nongovernmental organizations (NGOs) can influence the response of governments and publics to changes in the environment. Likewise, the advent of authority crises and the intensification of the skill revolution have contributed both to a greater readiness on the part of publics to question the handling of environmental challenges by politicians and to a significantly expanded ability of citizens to fathom such issues, ponder alternative courses of action, and construct scenarios which project the future development of issues. Never before have pressure groups and individuals been better equipped to concentrate their resources on issues involving nature and its transformation.

The other perspective derives from a focus on a particular set of tensions that are both sources and consequences of the bifurcation of world politics into state-centric and multi-centric systems marked by increasingly competent citizens challenging traditional loci of authority: namely, the tensions that arise out of the simultaneity of centralizing and integrating tendencies toward globalization on the one hand and decentralizing and fragmenting tendencies toward localization on the other hand. To some extent these tendencies operate independently of each other, but in important ways they are also interactive, forming a dialectic process that links the tendencies toward integration and fragmentation and that is succinctly captured by the label "fragmegration."[2] To anticipate a major theme set forth below, the links between human and natural systems in the present era can be viewed as profoundly fragmegrative and may even be the most dynamic of all the dimensions that sustain the dialectics of fragmegration.

Among the many agents of change that reflect and shape this larger context of turbulent fragmegration, two are particularly relevant. More accurately, two general typologies offer useful points of departure for probing both the underlying structures and the dynamics of change that sustain the convergence between natural and governance systems. One typology consists of the "Self-Environment" orientations of people — those aspects of human systems which "push" individuals into patterned relationships with the world around them. The other is a typology of issues — those dimensions of the natural world which "pull" people into the specific pattern of responses they maintain with nature. The convergence of these pushes and pulls is conceived to be susceptible to transformation when changes occur in human systems that alter the Self-Environment orientations of people and when changes occur in nature that alter the salience of the issues it poses.

SELF-ENVIRONMENT ORIENTATIONS

The significance of the Self-Environment typology derives from the premise that the orientations and activities of individuals matter in world politics, that the growing readiness of people to engage in collective action has sensitized leaders to the power of the skill revolution and made them increasingly responsive to the micro sources of their macro responsibilities. Perhaps in earlier eras people complied dutifully with the directives of higher authorities, thus making it possible to ascribe causal power fully to the conduct of states; but in this turbulent era of globalized economies, weakened national governments, fragmented subgroups, and enhanced analytic skills, the responses of individuals have become increasingly problematic.[3] Today the reactions of publics are variable and far from given. As conditions change and issues get reconfigured, people may redefine the relationships to both their immediate and remote worlds. Thus, given the premise that what individuals at the micro level think and do has consequences for the course of world affairs, any major shift in Self-Environment orientations on the part of sizable numbers of people is bound to affect the coherence and policies of macro collectivities.

Irrespective of their level of analytic skill or whether they are conscious of the Self-Environment orientation that shapes their conduct in the public arena, all individuals are presumed to have Self-Environment orientations. Everyone, that is, proceeds from a comparative estimate of the relative worth of themselves and their most salient macro collectivity. The latter may be a social movement, a society, an ethnic group, a transnational organization, or any one of many other collectivities presently vying for support on the world stage; but whatever its identity, the most salient collectivity is assessed by people in terms of the priority they attach to its well being in relation to their own. Self-Environment orientations are thus an indicator of the loyalty citizens extend to their society or the macro collectivity of greatest relevance to them.

By dichotomizing between high and low estimates of both self and society (or whatever may be their most salient collectivity), several distinct types of citizens can be identified (see Figure 14.1). Those inclined to treat their own needs as far more important than those of society practice what can be called *self-centered* citizenship. Persons who have the opposite tendency and place society's needs well ahead of their own practice one of two forms of citizenship: those who have an incremental approach to societal problems practice *altruistic* citizenship, whereas those who proceed from an inflexible image of what societal life ought to be practice *ideological* citizenship. People who are skeptical about the responsiveness of macro politics to micro inputs or for other reasons attach little political significance either to their own or society's needs and are thus disinclined to enter the public arena practice what can be regarded as *apathetic* citizenship. Finally, individuals who are deeply invested in the realization of both their own and society's needs are likely to practice a *democratic* form of citizenship. This balanced form approaches the democratic ideal in the sense that citizens are not unmindful of their own interests even as they recognize the necessity of also accommodating to the processes and goals of the larger collectivities to which they belong.

It must be stressed that the Self-Environment orientations of people are more fundamental than their opinions about particular issues. The former serve as the context within which the latter may vary. Hence, while people are capable of undergoing alteration in their Self-Environment orientations, normally their conception of

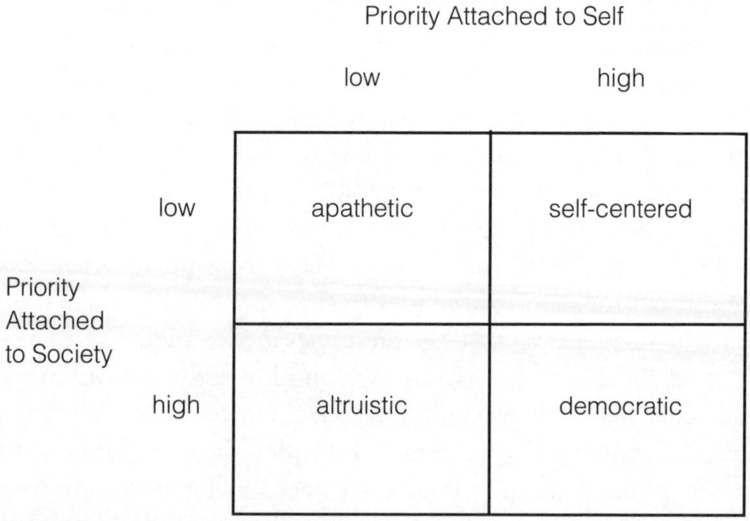

Priority Attached to Self

		low	high
		low	apathetic	self-centered
Priority Attached to Society	high	altruistic	democratic

Figure 14.1. Four types of citizenship.

themselves in relation to their Environment remains stable and re-
sistant to change. Their opinions about items on the political
agenda, the intensity with which they hold their opinions, and
their readiness to act on behalf of them may also vary as issues become more or less salient; but their basic orientations toward the
public arena, its hierarchy, and its susceptibility to improvement,
tend not to shift with the course of events. So habitual and deep-
seated are their Self-Environment orientations, moreover, that they
tend to be constant across issue areas. Whether the challenge is
posed by nature, a foreign adversary, or inflation, people are unlikely to waver in their Self-Environment orientations. Only as
major developments occur in either their personal lives or in public affairs do they experience incentives to revise the bases of their
underlying relationship to their worlds. As will be seen, in the present turbulent era such incentives do exist and some of them involve changes in the natural world.

NATURE AS AN ISSUE AREA

Although self-centered, altruistic, ideological, apathetic, and democratic citizens are likely to respond differently to environmental
challenges, the variability of their responses and the fragmegrative
processes thereby established are not simply a matter of how people are "pushed" by their self-assessments. Much may also depend
on the environment itself, on the kinds of challenges it poses, on
the "pull" that its different dimensions exert with respect to the
readiness of people to translate their Self-Environment orientations into action. In other words, the environment is also variable.
It is not so much an integrated whole as it is a congeries of diverse
issues that, among other things, differ in the degree to which they
are subject to human control and the extent to which they can
serve to advance or set back the human condition.

Again we proceed by dichotomizing the two dimensions and
constructing a typology that identifies four basic types of issues.[4]
As indicated in Table 14.1, one dimension distinguishes environmental issues in terms of the quality of their consequences
("goods" versus "bads") and the other differentiates among them

in terms of their allocative foundations ("distributive" versus "redistributive" issues). The measure of whether the consequences of an issue are "good" or "bad" is to be found in the number of people who are either positively or negatively affected by it. The distinction among allocative foundations is drawn by viewing distributive issues as non zero-sum in character — as allowing for a shifting of resources without prejudice to any potential recipients. Redistributive issues, on the other hand, are zero-sum in nature, that is, the gains achieved by some in the redistributive process are offset by those who incurred losses.[5] These are not the only dimensions along which nature as an issue area can be analyzed, but they are two key dimensions that enable us to differentiate how the course of events may unfold as people and communities seek to exploit, manage, or otherwise cope with the physical world.

In order to facilitate the ensuing discussion of how the several types of issues might evoke varying responses on the part of different types of citizens, it is useful to draw additional distinctions among the issues by comparing them in terms of the time scale, clarity, and evidential bases through which they are experienced as well as by the extent to which they are likely to be the focus of elites, publics, and organizations. These comparisons are presented

Table 14.1. Four types of environmental issues.

	Distributive	Redistributive
Goods	I newly discovered resources (in outer space, the oceans, etc.)	II technolgical breakthroughs (in genetics, agriculture, etc.)
Bads	III newly identified environmental problems (global warming, ozone depletion, etc.)	IV worsening of long-standing pollutants (disposal of toxic wastes, etc.)

in Table 14.2, where it can be seen that the different types of issues are likely to give rise to very different political processes. Other things being equal, for example, the processing of most environmental issues is confined to the elite and specialist levels of politics. Only when the redistribution of "bads" (issue type IV) gets on the political agenda are publics likely to become involved and receptive to mobilization. Otherwise, with other things being equal, the politics of the environment is shouldered by scientists and specialists, many of whom frequently cross each other's paths and form an elite network within which the technical and policy questions

Table 14.2. Four types of environmental issues.

	I	II	III	IV
Type of issue	distributive goods	redistributive goods	distributive bads	redistributive bads
Time frame[a]	long-term	long-term	long-term	short-term
Horizon of observability[b]	obscure	vague	direct	direct
Form of Proof[c]	tenuous	technical, controversial	technical, controversial	reinforced by experience
Elite concerns	a few specialists	relevant specialists	relevant specialists, bureaucrats	widespread among elites & politicians
Predispositions of citizens	unconcerned	limited interest	uneasiness	intense involvement
Mobilizability of subgroups	extremely difficult	difficult	somewhat difficult	easy
Organizational activity	low	low	moderate	high

[a] Refers to the "time frame" for the appreciation of goods and bads.

[b] Refers to the clarity of stages through which opportunities or problems will loom as relevant to daily routines.

[c] Refers to the nature of the evidence available to demonstrate the viability of the opportunities or problems.

get addressed, argued, and/or resolved.[6] Type IV issues are much more highly politicized than any of the other three, largely because they point to the possibility of immediate danger to physical well being as well as questions of equity as to how onerous burdens should be redistributed in the near term. The fact that such threats are clearly discernible and part of personal experience renders Type IV issues susceptible to intense involvement and activity on the part of publics and a broad spectrum of elites.

While Type IV issues are thus profoundly fragmegrative — in the sense that as the threat of an environmental danger becomes increasingly imminent, governments may become more cooperative even as publics become more self-interested and divisive — so are they likely to get onto the political agenda only under extreme circumstances. Other things being equal, most groups and politicians active at every level of organization are likely to resist treating a challenge posed by nature as a Type IV issue. The politics of redistribution is difficult at best, but it becomes positively noxious when it involves redistributing bads. Accordingly, most environmental challenges and opportunities are likely to be defined as falling in the other three categories, all of which are long-term. The time lag between the transformation of newly identified goods — whether they be newly discovered resources or newly developed technologies — into immediately available opportunities that people are willing to seize has been fifty years or more.[7] The data on when (and whether) newly identified bads — such as the greenhouse effect — will materialize as tangible threats to life and property seem insufficiently clear at present for Type III issues to undergo a transformation into the politics of Type IV issues.

Specialists and concerned elites may see dark clouds on the horizon, broad gaps in the ozone layer, and signs of a global warming, but the likelihood of most people — again assuming other things are equal — taking warnings of such long-run trends seriously seems to be very small indeed. If near-term success in reversing or halting these trends is to be recorded, it would appear that concerned elites will have to develop convincing proof in order for decisive actions by governments to occur. Otherwise most environmental issues are fated to be locked into that stalemated form of politics whereby the urgings of experts and a few organizations of attentive citizens are no match for the reluctance of politicians to make financial commitments in the face of ambiguous evidence and circuitous horizons of observability. Leaders and attentive citizens may be uneasy that circumstances are so dire as to suggest the possible presence of a Type IV issue, but not until the consequences of the long-term threats are immediately experienced is the politics of crisis likely to become pervasive.

THREE CONTEXTS: SCIENCE, TIME, AND DISASTER

Three other characteristics of nature as an issue area, its scientific and temporal dimensions and its vulnerability to disaster, are implicit in the foregoing analysis and can usefully be explicated before attempting to probe how different types of citizens might respond to different types of issues associated with enclosed and coastal seas.[8] Irrespective of whether they are Type I, II, III, or IV, environmental issues are inescapably embedded in a scientific context. Unlike other conventional foci of controversy, the outcomes of environmental issues are located in the vagaries of nonhuman processes and human behavior. What people do or fail to do shapes environmental processes, but ultimately the latter adhere to their own laws and not to those of organized society. Consequently they give rise to objective outcomes in the sense that what happens is not vulnerable to the vagaries of motivation, chance encounters, institutional lapses, or any of the other uncertainties that attach to social dynamics. One can specify varying human inputs and hypothesize about the corresponding environmental outputs, but the accuracy of the hypotheses will depend on one's grasp of how nature operates; that is, on how the objective circumstances whereby the nonhuman components embraced by the hypotheses interact. In short, such issues may be rife with uncertainties, but these derive as much from the mysteries of nature as from the variability of human affairs.

Thus the outcomes of environmental controversies turn centrally on the scientific method and its applications. Politicians cannot exercise control over outcomes involving the environment without recourse to scientific findings. They may claim that the

findings are not clear-cut or remain subject to contradictory interpretations, but they are nonetheless dependent on what the practices of science uncover about nature.[9] It follows that criteria of
proof are at the heart of the politics of ECS, that the outcomes of
such issues depend as much on the persuasiveness of evidence as
on the various criteria of power — superior resources, greater mass
support, skill at coalition formation — that sustain or resolve other types of issues. To be sure, the exercise of power is not irrelevant
to the politics of ECS, and it is surely the case that deft politicians
can manipulate support in favor of one or another policy, but ultimately the outcomes will be shaped by scientific proof.[10] Develop-
ment-minded groups can argue for the exploitation of the environment for only so long if that exploitation continues to lead to
discernible and measurable deterioration; at some point the data
become too telling to ignore and interest-group politics is compelled to yield ground to the politics of science. How long it takes
for nature to unfold in these ways and for the findings to force
change in the conduct of politics is, of course, an open question.
Indeed, it is itself a noteworthy political question that serves as another contextual factor.

The changes and threats posed by the uses and abuses of environmental resources normally evolve slowly. Leaving aside for the
moment large-scale disasters, a preponderance of natural threats
involve cumulative processes that, in the absence of corrective
measures, are likely to be increasingly detrimental over the long
run. As a result, the politics of such issues tends to be organized
around a continuous struggle between the few experts who recognize the need for corrective measures to offset the long-term dangers and the many producers, consumers, and citizens who are
concerned with maximizing short-term gains and minimizing
short-term losses. In other words, the political processes of communities and nations are loaded against the long run. People and
politicians often reason that long-term outcomes are too uncertain
and too distant to worry about when the current scene is so per-
vaded with immediate needs and difficulties. So the impulse to
avoid hard choices and postpone action is deeply embedded in the

structure of issues involving the environment. People seeking to preserve or improve their welfare today give scant concern to future generations.

The politics of nature is temporally different from the politics of the economy, governance, or agriculture. The collapse of a stock market, the ouster of a regime, or the failure of a crop are, so to speak, instantaneous events with enormous and obvious immediate consequences that cannot be ignored, that require unqualified responses, and that quickly come to dominate the concerns, headlines, and agenda of the day. Developments in the natural world, on the other hand, are easily relegated to peripheral status. Except when they connote disaster (see below), such developments do not pose a need for instant reactions, altered policies, or restless preoccupations. Usually they are developments in the sense that a government agency has issued a report or an NGO has called attention to an ominous trend, events which neither capture headlines nor evoke efforts to place them high on the relevant agenda. Only as interest groups keep environmental issues alive, therefore, do they come before the public. Otherwise their long-term horizons consign them to short-term oblivion.

Politicians and publics anxious to protect or enhance the quality of the environment are thus destined to be mired in an uphill struggle. Using tentative findings, they face the difficult task of delivering disturbing and onerous messages that are neither immediately relevant nor easily rejected. They have to press policy options that require altered processes of production, revised modes of consumption, and a host of other sacrifices to which the body politic is not accustomed.[11] Perhaps most difficult of all, they cannot promise early and satisfying benefits in exchange for the sacrifices. Other things being equal, therefore, support for sound policies is likely to be fragile and reluctant, ever susceptible to erosion and distortion.

There is a third condition under which this reluctance is overcome and replaced with a restless urgency that swiftly moves such issues from the periphery to the center of the political stage: namely, when forecast threats involving nature collapse into a single, dramatic, unexpected, and devastating disaster. Each marginal increment in a detrimental trend can be easily rationalized as just a temporary blip in an otherwise benign or murky pattern. But even the most adroit politician committed to dodging the taint of untoward events cannot evade the repercussions of a disaster. Chernobyl, Three Mile Island, Bhopal, and other such disasters thus become turning points in politics.[12] They are profoundly transformative. They arouse those who survive but are contaminated by the fall-out into making demands and undertaking actions that are shrill, insistent, and durable. Nor are the fears engendered by disasters confined to those immediately exposed to them. Such events can be readily imagined by people everywhere as occurring at comparable facilities near their homes. Major disasters become globalized and thereafter deeply embedded in collective memories on which future officials and publics draw for guidance in conducting their affairs.

To be sure, some individuals in communities far from disaster sites may remain oblivious to them, others may soon act as if they never occurred and still others may reason that such lightning never strikes twice. Memories can be short in politics as immediate needs press for attention. From a systemic perspective, however, things are never quite the same again. The consequences of the disaster pervade the speeches of politicians, legal precedents get adopted by courts, parties pledge "never again" in their platforms, editorial pages take note of the disaster's anniversary, interest groups remind followers and adversaries alike of its portents, and so on through all the channels whereby societies adapt to systemic shocks.

The consciousness-raising effects of disasters, however, are not necessarily salutary. The very real repercussions they initiate can lead to changes in the political process. The knowledge that disasters can quickly convert long-run uneasiness into short-run urgency can tempt pro-environment activist groups to over-interpret available data to indicate that ominous circumstances are imminent or, worse, to manipulate the data so that the likelihood of such circumstances developing seems beyond question. The more activists yield to these temptations, the more are publics likely to become apathetic, much like the reactions to the boy who cried wolf. Given this potential, it is tempting to become dispirited and hope that a major calamity will befall a region and permanently elevate environmental issues to the top of the political agenda.

ENCLOSED COASTAL SEAS AS AN ISSUE AREA

Some modification of the foregoing is in order. As implied throughout by the phrase, "other things being equal," the notion of a larger context in which natural and human systems converge is not universally applicable. Other things are not always equal and thus exceptions may have to be made when the analysis turns to a particular set of environmental issues. Much of the preceding discussion can be readily applied to issues associated with ECS, but at the same time such issues have special characteristics that do not obtain at a more general level. One of these is that these areas tend to have high population densities. For a wide variety of reasons mentioned elsewhere in this volume, people are impelled to live near coastal waters. Some 70 percent of the U.S. population, for example, lives within 50 miles of a coast and this proportion is expected to continue to rise in the future. Indeed, it has been estimated that in the foreseeable future half the world's population will live in coastal zones, regions that amount to about 5 percent of the land.[13] The political consequences of high population density are numerous. Most notably, large populations embrace diverse and conflicting interests that are not easily mobilized in support of comprehensive, long-term policies intended to achieve sustainable development in harmony with environmental processes and limits. Accordingly, assuming that the tasks of governance are all the more delicate the greater the number and diversity of people that fall within a specifiable jurisdiction, it is clear that to manage the environmental problems of ECS effectively is to address enormous complexity.

ECS are also distinguished by specified boundaries, thus according them a reality that is more readily envisioned than is the case for the many environmental issues that are global in scope and thus somewhat more difficult to frame in concrete terms. That is, ECS are confined spaces and, as such, territorial in their appeal and closer to home for those who live near them. This means that despite the diversity of their interests, the populations of ECS are likely to identify more easily with the problems, threats, and policies that involve their geographic area than they do with the less immediate issues of the global environment. Given the combination of the skill revolution and a sense of place, it also suggests that governmental and NGOs will be more capable of mobilizing support than those which seek to generate grassroots actions on behalf of challenges and policies associated with the global environment as a whole.[14]

The boundaries of ECS, being intersubjectively recognized only recently as confining a meaningful space, may not have the specificity or appeal of, say, a local community, a nation state, an ethnic minority, or any historic entity that has long commanded the loyalties of its people. But as NGOs and local governments become increasingly concerned about the well being of ECS, so does this concern get increasingly translated into a wider intersubjective recognition on the part of publics that the status of their ECS is a bounded space worthy of protection. Perhaps few if any ECS command the kind of loyalties enjoyed by historic polities, but as environmental issues become ever more salient in the public conscience and as they are increasingly defined in terms of whole ecosystems rather than as particularistic problems, so are ECS likely to come ever more into focus as of the kind of citizen preoccupation that can lead to a reshaping of Self-Environment orientations. In the words of one inquiry,

> Our study suggests that a sound and effective decisionmaking process for a particular system depends on recognizing and understanding the 'system as a whole.' The Chesapeake Bay system is more than the aquatic ecosystem we often identify. It is more than the geography of its drainage basin. The system includes its people, its economics, its history, its politics, and its culture. Failure to recognize this system in its entirety can reduce significantly the effectiveness of any decisionmaking process.[15]

Conceivably, given the closer political distance between ECS challenges and those who live within their space, Type I, II, and III issues are likely to evoke more public interest than is implied in the discussion of Table 14.2.

Not only do ECS confine space with specifiable boundaries and large populations, but normally their boundaries also encompass more than one political jurisdiction. Accordingly, even if they have the full support of their legislatures, the chief executives of governments cannot alone address the challenge of ECS issues. Rather, they must cooperate with their counterparts in other political units if they are to develop effective means for coping with such problems. Successful coastal management is thus bound to involve the building and maintenance of cross-unit coalitions. These coalitional tasks are especially challenging in the case of the Chesapeake Bay because it not only consists of a five-state watershed, but it also extends across more than 100 counties, each fearful that its independent decision-making authority might be undermined by joining an ecosystem-wide coalition.[16]

Given the dispersed authority structures of ECS, the necessity of coalition-building is equally applicable to environmental NGOs. They too must reach out to counterparts in other jurisdictions of their coastal sea to generate the pressures needed to bring about policies appropriate to meet the environmental challenges perceived as threatening their welfare. Since ECS normally encompass a wide variety of environmental problems, the coalescing processes they evoke usually involve large numbers of diverse NGOs and government agencies whose concerns may differ but who share an appreciation that their political clout is enhanced by joining together and framing their particular goals in the context of ECS-wide programs.[17] For the small stretch of the Massachusetts coast north of Boston, for example, business, government, local citizens groups, and environmental organizations from 49 communities formed a coalition supporting the Massachusetts Bays Program.[18] Similarly, an even smaller coastal stretch of 18 miles in central California, the Guadalupe-Nipomo Dunes Preserve, served as the focus of unlikely allies joining a coalition of government bodies, oil companies, farmers, and artists. As one leader of the coalition put it, "We realize we're in this together. We're stuck with each other."[19]

Consistent with the ever greater interdependence of global life the processes of ECS-coalition formation have become global in scope. As each coalition records success in generating public awareness and the adoption of new environmentally sound policies, so does word of the changes spread and lead to emulation by comparable groups in other ECS. In the United States, for instance, the coalitions formed for the Chesapeake Bay and New Jersey shoreline have served as models for similar developments elsewhere in the country. Comparisons of various problems of the Baltic Sea and the Great Lakes have also served as stimuli to new policy initiatives.[20]

The delicacies of governing ECS, in short, are profoundly transboundary in character and, as such, they are also exceedingly vulnerable to fragmegrative tensions as nongovernmental groups waver in their readiness to participate in coalitions across borders. Momentum toward greater consciousness of ECS problems is not uncontested, however. Political movement in this direction has generated opposition from groups that either oppose coalitions ready to accommodate the realities of development or that stand to be thwarted by environmentally-sound programs. As ECS increasingly become the focus of organizational activity, in other words, so do the dynamics of fragmegration become ever more pervasive.

The shifting strategy of a leading conservation organization, the Nature Conservancy (TNC), is illustrative in this regard. For some 40 years TNC sought to preserve the environment by purchasing and managing more than five million acres in all 50 states, a strategy labeled a "museum-fortress" approach of fencing in pristine acres, such as a single mountaintop for a single species; but recently the organization has expanded its conception of environmental challenges. Now entire watersheds and migratory corridors — in effect, whole ecosystems — are considered the appropriate foci of concern, entities that are too large to purchase and have thus led TNC to widen "[its] vision a little bit and [realize] there were human activities from oil drilling to housing developing that could be designed and carried out compatibly with land preservation."[21] But as NGOs and governmental agencies enlarge their horizons to the level of whole ecosystems, so can they evoke resistance on the part of single-issue groups who are fearful that their concerns may be neglected or even negated by policies designed to enhance the well-being of the whole system.[22] When this happens, when whole-system policies evoke single-issue opposition, the dynamics of fragmegration ensue.

There are good reasons to anticipate that ECS will continue to experience fragmegrative dynamics well into the future. This expectation derives from a conception in which pressures for whole-system consciousness exerted by environmental groups will be resisted by counterpressures on the part of citizens and groups who are unable to expand their horizons and are thereby self-centered in their Self-Environment orientations. The following observation offers a benign way of viewing the long-term course of fragmegration, allowing as it does for the possibility of self-centered orientations giving way to more encompassing perspectives: "It's a good deal harder to sell an ecosystem than it is to sell an [individual] animal or species, because people tend to relate to individuals rather than habitats. But it's the next major step in environmental awareness. An animal or a given species does not survive, let alone thrive, in the absence of its ecosystem and its habitat."[23] A much harsher conception of the long-run future of fragmegrative dynamics is embedded in the following passage:

> ...what can be termed the juggernaut theory of human nature, which holds that people are programmed by their genetic heritage to be so selfish that a sense of global responsibility will come too late. Individuals place themselves first, family second, tribe third and the *rest of the world a distant fourth.* Their genes also predispose them to plan ahead for one or two generations at most. They fret over the petty problems and conflicts of their daily lives and respond swiftly and often ferociously to slight challenges to their status and tribal security. But...people also

tend to underestimate both the likelihood and impact of such natural disasters as major earthquakes and great storms. [For most of human history] Life was precarious and short. A premium was placed on close attention to the near future and early reproduction, and little else. Disasters of a magnitude that occur only once every few centuries were forgotten or transmuted into myth. So today the mind still works comfortably backward and forward for only a few years, spanning a period not exceeding one or two generations.[24]

Before comparing this juggernaut theory with the more optimistic approach that allows for the evolution of widespread whole-system awareness, it is useful to note the pervasiveness of the fragmegrative dynamics that sustain the tensions between integrative and fragmenting tendencies in the unfolding of environmental and ECS issues. Once the analyst becomes conscious of the dynamism of these tensions, they appear to be everywhere. They are even manifest in the ways in which scientific knowledge is evaluated and used in the conduct of environmental politics. In the United States, for example, a backlash against science has mushroomed as the costs of environmental protection have mounted. Increasingly environmental programs are disparaged "as grossly flawed, grounded in bad science and worse economics. The critics say that the nation has wasted vast sums to fix trivial risks and that sweeping reform is needed."[25]

More specifically, there has been "a drum roll of criticism [that characterizes] the thesis of global warming as a 'flash in the pan,' 'hysteria,' 'scare talk,' and a ploy by socialists to justify controls on the economy."[26] Acknowledging that "the demands of environmental policy makers and natural-resource managers for information have rapidly outpaced the ability of science to deliver relevant data," scientists sustain the fragmegrative dynamics by responding to the criticisms with calls for those in their profession to become politically active and champion as well as better explain "their organizing concepts and research to the public," especially the concept of an ecosystem, which is "not well understood by the general public and thus creates confusion and distrust when new policies based upon the concept are discussed."[27]

An even more direct expression of the fragmegrative dynamic is the frustration experienced by people whose lives are immediately dependent on the applicability of scientific knowledge to problems of their ECS. In the case of native Alaskans whose livelihood is organized around the Bering Sea and its tributaries, for example, a dramatic decline in the number of sea lions, a sharp thinning of seal pelts, and a worrisome weakening of seabird chicks has led them to severely criticize the inability of scientists to explain the changes and to call for more attention to be paid to their store of "traditional knowledge." As a result, in 1991 representatives of coastal villages formed a statewide Native marine mammals coalition, with the aim of promoting traditional knowledge as a complement to scientific methods.

As one participant put it, "Native people live right there; they know about the fish and the animals through traditional knowledge. We want to integrate that into the management system."[28] In response, the scientists on the scene acknowledge that the insights of native experience are valuable, but emphasize that nonetheless, "native knowledge tends to be local, going deep but not ranging far beyond a particular village's hunting grounds, while sea lions may spend only a small part of their year in that area."[29] Indeed, even as the scientists accept the need for a marriage of science and traditional knowledge, they argue that the Bering Sea ecosystem is "so varied and complex that even such a marriage is unlikely to explain the fluctuations."[30] A synthesis of scientific and traditional knowledge, in short, is unlikely to bring an end to the dynamics of fragmegration in the Bering Sea.

While it is feasible to interpret the pervasiveness of fragmegrative dynamics in the environmental realm as leading to ever more extensive conflict and an eventual affirmation of the aforementioned juggernaut theory that posits ultimate failure for any efforts to effectively manage ECS, such a conclusion is here viewed as unlikely.[31] It ignores the skill revolution and the capacity of people everywhere to learn, adapt, and change their ways in the face of compelling circumstances. The sources of the skill revolution are numerous. They include trends toward increased education for every country in the world, a similar pattern for access to television, mushrooming international travel, widespread use of computers and other technologies that facilitate people's ability to locate themselves in the course of events, and perhaps most important, a continuing exposure to the tasks of coping with the complexities of an ever more interdependent world.[32]

Hence the juggernaut theory premise that people "place...the rest of the world a distant fourth" seems unduly pessimistic.[33] The movement of people away from self-centered orientations and toward democratic or altruistic orientations may still be relatively small, but all the dynamics are in place for people to appreciate how their interests may be served by whole ecosystems.[34] Moreover, even the advocates of the juggernaut theory are ready to concede that "the rules have recently changed.... Global crises are rising within the life span of the generation now coming of age, a foreshortening that may explain why young people express more concern about the environment than do their elders."[35]

In conclusion, let us turn briefly to possible ways in which the four types of citizens might differ in their responses to the different types of environmental issues. We have already noted that, other things being equal, only the redistribution of "bads" (Type IV issues) is likely to evoke the involvement of large numbers of citizens. In the present era, however, with analytic skills expanding, with nongovernmental groups and other actors in the multicentric world ever more coherent and active, and with fragmegrative tensions increasingly acute, the standard assumptions about public quiescence may not hold. To repeat, other things may not be nearly so equal as they have long seemed. Most notably, assuming no let up in the technologies that generate environmental "goods" and "bads," the increased pressures of environmental challenges in general, and ECS issues in particular, appear capable of contributing to a reconfiguration of Self-Environment orientations. More accurately, in combination with the many other dynamics presently transforming the course of events, Type III issues (the wider distribution of "bads") that surface in ECS have the potential to induce change on the part of all but apathetic citizens.

The three other citizen types may be inclined to upgrade their conception of the "Environment" relative to themselves. They can do this in one of two ways: first, by maintaining their "Self-Environment" orientations unchanged even as their responses to Type III issues begin to conform to those generated by Type IV issues (see Table 14.2); or, second, by revising the balance they have established between themselves and their Environments. Thus discernible numbers of self-centered and democratic citizens might become sufficiently distressed by newly identified "bads" that they are induced to downgrade themselves and upgrade their Environment to the extent that they take on the characteristics of altruistic or ideological citizens. Conversely, the same issue stimuli might generate movement in the opposite direction as some altruistic and democratic citizens find reasons to upgrade the priority they attach to themselves and begin to manifest the orientations of self-centered citizens. Such a transformation is especially likely when persons who see no reasons to maintain their altruism or democratic predispositions on the grounds that so many of their fellow citizens are hoarding, polluting, consuming, or otherwise avoiding environmentally sound behavior that they might as well be self-centered too. Citizenship transformations, in short, are subject to bandwagon effects.

There is substantial evidence that the constructive sense of community that underlies democratic citizenship is heightened when disasters occur. The history of oil spills, pervasive floods, and devastating hurricanes is one of volunteered support from both within and outside the affected areas. An appreciation that "it could have happened to me" can lead impressive numbers of people to upgrade their Environment relevant to themselves and then to invest time, energy, and/or resources on behalf of unknown others who have suffered. Under conditions of duress, moreover, the readiness of groups to enter cross-border coalitions would appear to increase. Since such coalitions are crucial to the management of ECS, the incentives to cast ECS developments as ominous and headed toward disaster are likely to be considerable.

In sum, it is possible to hypothesize that the transformation of Self-Environment orientations can move in contradictory directions. Whether the result in a particular society will be a groundswell favoring one of the citizenship types, or whether it will produce a set of self-cancelling changes that leaves the distribution among the four types unchanged, will probably depend on the intensity of the fragmegrative dynamics, the quality of the proof that severe environmental "bads" loom on the horizon, and the proximity in time of the environmental degradation that lies ahead.

ACKNOWLEDGMENT

I am grateful to Michael Fagen and Hongying Wang for their assistance.

NOTES

1. See James N. Rosenau. 1990. Turbulence in World Politics: A Theory of Change and Continuity. Princeton University Press, Princeton.

2. Inquiries into the dialectics of fragmegration are developed in James N. Rosenau. 1993. Distant proximities: The dynamics and dialectics of globalization. Delivered as the Morgan Lecture, October 27, Dickinson College and James N. Rosenau. 1993. The elusiveness of security in a turbulent world: Notes on the interaction of globalizing and localizing dynamics. Presented at the Symposium on Collective Responses to Common Threats, June 22-23 sponsored by the Commission on Global Governance and the Norwegian Ministry of Foreign Affairs, Oslo.

3. For a lengthy analysis of the premise that the orientations and activities of individuals matter in world politics, see Rosenau 1990, op. cit., chapters 7 and 8.

4. This typology originally appeared in James N. Rosenau. 1993. Environmental challenges in a turbulent world. In Ronnie D. Lipschutz and Ken Conca (eds.). The State and Social Power in Global Environmental Politics. Columbia University Press, New York, pp. 71-93.

5. For an extensive discussion of this distinction, see Theodore J. Lowi. July 1964. American business, public policy, case-studies, and political theory. World Politics XVI:677-715.

6. See chapter by Peter Haas in this volume.

7. See Ortwin Renn. 1983. High technology and social change. High Tech Newsletter 1:15.

8. James N. Rosenau. 1993. Environmental challenges in a global context. In Sheldon Kamieniecki (ed.). Environmental Politics in the International Arena: Movements, Party, Organizations, and Policy. SUNY Press, Albany, pp. 257-274.

9. See Ann Florini, Juliann Emmons and Laura Strohm (eds.). 1992. How Does Social Science Help Solve Environmental Problems? Working Paper No. 1 (New Series), Center for International Relations, University of California, Los Angeles.

10. See Rosenau 1990, op. cit., pp. 198-209 and 425-29.

11. For a good example of an effort to cope with this dilemma, see Sam Fulwood, III. 12 January 1992. Study urges 'revolution' dedicated to global cleanup. Los Angeles Times.

12. "Disaster" is a value-laden term. A more moderate term might be an "event," a circumstance that varies greatly from normal patterns. For a comparative study indicating that "some kind of event was needed to stimulate the policy-making process and that the nature of the event can be quite variable, ranging from actual disasters to the publication of Rachel Carson's *Silent Spring*," see Ian Morris and Wayne H. Bell. 1988. Coastal seas governance: an international project for management policy on threatened coastal seas. Maryland Law Review 47:487.

13. Oceans. 1986. International Group Studies Problems of "Coastal Seas." Oceans, March-April: 6.

14. See cases outlined in Lynton K. Caldwell, Lynton R. Hayes and Isabel M. MacWherter. 1976. Citizens and the Environment: Case Studies in Popular Action. Indiana University Press, Bloomington, Indiana.

15. Morris and Bell, op. cit., p. 490.

16. Tom Horton. 1988. Restoration of the Chesapeake Bay: a multistate institutional challenge. Maryland Law Review 47:422.

17. Presumably this is why "The presence of NGOs at official negotiations of international environmental agreements has become routine." Cited in Edith Brown Weiss. 1993. International environmental law: contemporary issues and the emergence of a new world order. Georgetown Law Journal 81:693. For a cogent analysis of the incentives toward coalition among NGOs, see John McCormick. 1993. International nongovernmental organizations:

prospects for a global environmental movement. In Kamieniecki, op. cit., pp. 135-140.

18. Alexander Reid. 1993. Coastal report to set long-range goals. Boston Globe, February 2, pp. North 1 and 3.

19. Connie Koenenn. 1992. Paradise preserved. Los Angeles Times, June 24, pp. B10-B11.

20. This is discussed in Morris and Bell op. cit., p. 482. Also see chapters in this volume by Rafal Serafin and M. Ronald Shimizu et al.

21. Koenenn, op. cit., p. B11.

22. Ibid.

23. Art Jeffers. March 1989. Quoted in Mark Hoy. Researching the Slough. Audubon, p. 105.

24. Edward O. Wilson. 1993. Is humanity suicidal? New York Times Magazine, May 30, p. 26 (emphasis added).

25. Frederica Perera. 1993. Green-bashing: A health hazard. New York Times, June 29, p. A23.

26. William K. Stevens. 1993. Scientists confront backlash on global warming. New York Times, September 14, p. C1.

27. John C. Ogden. 1993. The scientists studying environmental issues must become activists. The Chronicle of Higher Education., September 15, p. B1.

28. Ibid.

29. Ibid.

30. Julia Rubin. 1992. Frustrated Alaskan natives seek voice in the environment. Washington Post, January 5, p. A6.

31. See Thomas F. Homer-Dixon, Jeffrey H. Boutwell and George W. Rathjens. 1993. Environmental change and violent conflict. Scientific American. Febraury: 38-45; Patrick E. Tyler. 1993. Pollution in China sets off a battle fatal to two. New York Times, September 28, p. A15.

32. See Rosenau 1990, op. cit., Chapter 13.

33. Wilson, op. cit., p. 26.

34. For a discussion of the movement of people among the various types of Self-Environment orientations, see James N. Rosenau.

1992. Citizenship without moorings: individual responses to a turbulent world. Paper presented at the Annual Meeting of the American Sociological Association, August 23, Pittsburgh.

35. Wilson, op. cit., p. 26.

Part IV

Approaching Ecosystem Governance

15

Government Organizations and Great Lakes Rehabilitation

M. Ronald Shimizu, Henry A. Regier, James J. Kay, and Robert E. Ulanowicz

In the mid-1960s Lake Erie was often referred to in the press as "dead" and pollution was seen as a human health issue. Since that time public opinion has galvanized in support of restoring and conserving not only the physical water quality of the Great Lakes, but their watersheds, flora, and fauna as well. This chapter examines political events in the Great Lakes Basin focusing attention on the evolving role of governmental organizations. The chapter views the Basin as an open, self-organizing cultural and natural ecosystem. The "ecosystem approach" to problem solving and governance is fundamentally concerned with managing economic development in ways which retain or enhance natural ecosystem processes even as they are utilized by the people who are part of the system. This approach requires a clear understanding of the functions and dynamics of the natural ecosystem and the organizational dynamics of affected stakeholders. The realization that ecosystems cannot be managed to remain in a static state and simultaneously remain natural is a major challenge for environmental managers. This chapter employs several notions from theoretical ecology which contribute to our understanding of dynamic, hierarchical systems and how to best manage them within a range which is both useful for stakeholders and consistent with major natural ecosystem functions and processes.

When Europeans migrated to the Great Lakes Basin in large numbers early in the nineteenth century they generally made lasting commitments to "progress." They progressively commercialized trade, industrialized work, monetized values, homogenized products, urbanized and marginalized the natives. They internalized or privatized many of the benefits and externalized or socialized many of the costs that accompanied this progress. By the middle of the nineteenth century there was reason for environmental concern about such progress; for example, the Atlantic salmon native to Lake Ontario were notably less abundant than in earlier times. By the turn of the century, following new understandings of cause and effect relationships, widespread political concern helped to initiate a North American conservation movement.[1] This movement had special emphasis in the Great Lakes area. The preponderant emphasis was on reactive mitigation of degradation rather than on proactive precaution. In retrospect, "too little, too late" might be a fair judgement of the early conservation movement. But some early initiatives provided bases in governance for a gradual evolution of effective ways to change human activities that harm desirable natural features.

Canada and the United States negotiated a Boundary Waters Treaty (BWT) in 1909 to set out principles and establish mechanisms by which the two nations could manage uses of the boundary waters flowing along the longest unguarded border in the world. The treaty provided a framework by which to resolve the inevitable conflicts over certain uses and misuses of shared waters.[2] The water-related issues addressed explicitly in the 1909 BWT were those of highest priority at the time, i.e., domestic water supply and a number of industrial uses. Water as habitat for waterfowl and fish was not addressed and parallel international agreements were subsequently completed for these creatures and their habitats. The binational International Joint Commission (IJC) was formed to administer the BWT provisions. Parties could refer matters to the IJC to study and report back recommendations for solution of the referred problem. This device has been used quite regularly since 1912 as a fact-finding and cooling-out mechanism on controversial issues; it has established science as a necessary basis for bilateral management.[3]

In the Great Lakes Basin a political furor erupted in the early 1960s concerning the degradation of numerous parts of the Great Lakes. Sections of Lake Erie had been transformed into a decomposer system, resembling large sewage lagoons. Some took this condition to be analogous to a decomposing corpse, hence Lake Erie was diagnosed as "dying" or "dead." The initial reaction was to intensify the activities of the reactive conservation movement, in part by constructing relatively primitive sewage treatment plants. In response to the continuing public anger about offensive environmental conditions in areas of the lakes near large cities, Canada and the United States requested the IJC to investigate the conditions of these lakes, identify the problems, and recommend remedial measures. Consequently the Commission established a multi-disciplinary bilateral study team which conducted an investigation from 1964 to 1968. The study concluded that Lake Erie and parts of Lake Ontario were suffering from accelerated eutrophication due to excessive loads of nutrients, and that phosphorus inputs should be drastically reduced, using advanced methods of sewage treatment.

In accepting the reference team's recommendations IJC went further and recommended that Canada and the United States develop a formal agreement in which they:

- adopt common water quality objectives for the lakes and connecting rivers

- implement a range of programs to achieve and maintain the objectives

- charge the Commission to monitor the parties' progress publicly[4]

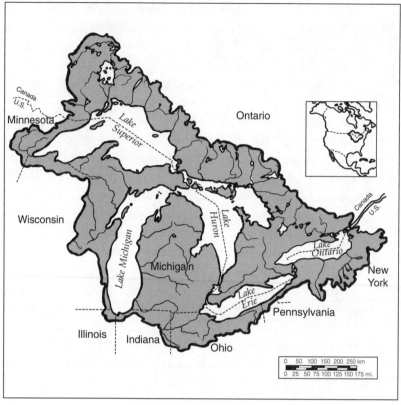

Figure 15.1. The Great Lakes watershed.

By advocating joint governance of pollution issues in each lake by various jurisdictions, the recommendations implied an important feature of an ecosystem approach. The Parties adopted these recommendations and in 1972 signed the first Canada-United States Great Lakes Water Quality Agreement (GLWQA), born of the earlier scientific study.[5] Since 1972 the Agreement has been expanded several times, notably in 1978 and in 1987.

THE ECOSYSTEM APPROACH AND ITS ROLE FOR SCIENCE

By the late 1960s numerous opinion leaders perceived that thorough reform was needed, towards a so-called "ecosystem approach."[6] The political, programmatic, and practical implications of the ecosystem approach were addressed with some vigor by networks of innovators. This approach was legitimated in the late 1970s, through concurrent initiatives under the auspices of several interjurisdictional commissions in the Great Lakes, with IJC leadership.[7] Great Lakes governance has evolved beyond reactive regulatory "control" of pollution, overfishing, water diversions, and exotic pests such as the sea lamprey. Key factors responsible for this change are: the particular roles of science; the development of a different type of regulatory framework; the development of a Great Lakes Basin constituency; evolving economic relationships; and the gradual societal acceptance of the concepts of ecosystem integrity, sustainable development, and a version of the precautionary principle.

Science has played three roles as a significant factor in shaping Great Lakes governance. It has:

- been formally institutionalized in the policy making and management process, for example in the form of "references" in which the jurisdictional setting of a scientist did not affect the scientist's status within the process

- continually generated new environmental knowledge as an informal impetus for new policies, programs, and measures

- been part of the shared activity of a "formal" Great Lakes stakeholder network which serves both as an advocate and protector of the role of science in the governance process, especially with respect to free and open discourse and disinterested peer review

These roles of science are illustrated here by the remediation experiences of various environmental pollutants. Science, which also evolved over time, played similar roles in the rehabilitation of debased fisheries, conflict resolution with respect to lake water levels and river flows, and the preservation of pristine areas.[8] In recent years these different fields of science, each interdisciplinary with respect to its political and practical focus, have become more integrated by the more comprehensive challenge of achieving ecosystem integrity.

In formal interjurisdictional treaties, conventions, and agreements regarding the Great Lakes, the kind of "science" mandated has progressively expanded over the decades. Early in the century science was mobilized as follows: physical and chemical science related to aquatic transport of pollutants across jurisdictional boundaries; ecological studies related to transboundary movements of fish stocks; and physical studies related to meteorological and hydrological causes of lake level effects. The almost exclusive emphasis on natural sciences within the formal mandate of the Agreement continues. Much of the social science as well as the interdisciplinary science relevant to Great Lakes ecosystemic issues was, until recently, done in parallel to the formally mandated natural science. Relatively little of the social and interdisciplinary science has been directly funded by government; rather it has generally come from governmental-funded granting agencies for social sciences or private foundations.

The annexes of the 1972 GLWQA address specific sources of pollution and are structured in a scientific way with research, monitoring, assessment, and development of some forms of remediation and mitigation. In the 1978 Agreement, Article VII is in effect a standing reference to permit IJC to undertake appropriate scientific studies as a transjurisdictional initiative;[9] but the parties have not provided funding to IJC for such activity. In addition, a full annex is devoted specifically to research needs. This emphasizes the importance of science to the management of lake usage.[10]

The constant generation and flow of knowledge about the conditions of the lakes and new threats to its environmental quality serve as a basis from which to assess and evaluate the adequacy of existing policies, programs and measures. In the 1972 Agreement the scientists identified phosphorus as the key nutrient to be controlled in order to reverse eutrophication. In the 1978 and 1987 Agreements scientists defined the massive contamination of the Great Lakes ecosystem by persistent toxic substances. In the face of extensive evidence of widespread contamination and given the number of chemicals in use, part of the scientific community has called for a total ban on the use of chlorine as an industrial feed stock to achieve the formal commitment by the parties to zero discharge and virtual elimination of certain organochlorines. This has been endorsed by the IJC and recommended to the parties. Other scientists argue this measure would deny the manufacture of many valuable organochlorines and that the dangerous organochlorines can be identified and eliminated by less draconian means; this latter advice has been endorsed, at least tentatively, by the parties.

These debates raise fundamental questions which go to the heart of governance. These include "cause and effect" versus "weight of evidence" criteria for scientific inference in legal conventions re garding the burden of proof necessary to prove substance safety, as opposed to the conventional approach wherein the danger of the substance had to be established. For example, some might urge that all chlorine compounds should be placed on a general manufacturing prohibition list and an exception then be granted to an appellant based on evidence supplied by the latter that would satisfy some formally specified set of rational criteria, such as the "weight of evidence" scientific criteria. Major scientific studies carried out in the Great Lakes have often generated new policies, programs, and management processes to strengthen Great Lakes management (see Table 15.1).[11]

Science in the Great Lakes Basin flourishes within a network of university departments and institutes, government research units, and nongovernmental public service organizations. Some formal institutions such as the International Association of Great Lakes Research, the IJC's Science Advisory Board and Council of Research Managers, the Great Lakes Fishery Commission's Board of Technical Experts and the Great Lakes Commission's Secretariat provide effective channels to the scientific community for interjurisdictional governance purposes. The science community serves as an advocate and protector of science in the management process. As a constituency it is constantly assessing the adequacy of existing institutional arrangements to address the environmental imperatives defined by its research. Through its communication with the public, members of the community are accorded status and thus a basis from which to exercise influence over policy.

REGULATORY FRAMEWORKS AND THE EMERGENCE OF A CONSTITUENCY

The particular evolution of regulatory frameworks in both Canada and the United States reflects a growing orientation towards ecosystem integrity.[12] Before the 1960s national and regional water pollution controls were weak and inconsistent. By the 1970s more consistent end-of-the-pipe controls were instituted, leading

Table 15.1. Major scientific studies and their impacts on Great Lakes management.

Year	Study	Result
1964-68	IJC Lower Lakes Reference	1972 Great Lakes Water Quality Agreement
1973-78	IJC Pollution from Land Use Activities References	1978 Great Lakes Water Quality Agreement
	IJC Upper Lakes Reference on Pollution from Land-Use Reference	
1981-85	Intergovernmental Niagara River Toxics Study	1987 Niagara River Toxics Management Plan
1986	National Academy of Science/Royal Society of Canada Great Lakes Study of Science in the Great Lakes Water Quality Agreement	1987 Protocol to Great Lakes Water Quality Agreement
	Great Lakes United Review of progress under Great Lakes Water Quality Agreement	
1986-89	Intergovernmental Upper Lakes Connecting Channels Study	Connecting Channels Remedial Action Plans
1989	IJC Science Advisory Board Report on Heritage Area Security Plans	Lake Superior Binational Initiative
1990	IJC Virtual Elimination Report	

to the emergence, in the 1980s, of a trend to multimedia controls. In the 1990s, a pollution prevention combined approach is being advocated and applied (see Table 15.2). The sequence of regulatory steps demonstrates progress in the depth and breadth of consideration of pollution sources. The end-of-the-pipe control can be characterized as "pollution control as an afterthought." Integrated multimedia control, while an improvement, was still trying to deal with pollution at the end of a process. With pollution prevention, however, the consideration of pollution potential moves deeper into the design of production processes and widens the scope to encompass all relevant operations. With the currency of pollution prevention, sustainable development, and a commitment to precautions, all of which are consistent with ecosystemic thinking, the range of policy options to effect ecosystem integrity increases. Over-reliance on a prescriptive and punitive regulatory process is not consistent with the ecosystem approach. A combination of instruments ranging from government incentives, to codes of practice, to legal prosecution is now favored.

A Great Lakes Basin constituency also emerged in stages.[13] In the 1960s and 1970s, there were relatively few citizen groups and most of these focused on specific local problems such as protesting a specific unwanted development. In the 1980s groupings emerged

Table 15.2. Evolution of regulatory frameworks in North America.

Time Pd.	Focus	Orientation
1960s	Rudimentary water quality standards	Public health
1970s	End of pipe, separate water and air quality standards	Separate pollution controls for different media
1980s	Multi-media, combined air and water loading standards	Integrated pollution controls
1990s	Pollution prevention, zero discharge, virtual elimination	Ecosystem integrity and public health

with broader systemic perspectives, sustaining memberships, and their own expertise. They engaged society in a continuing discussion of pollution and other degrading activities as a social issue covered by dedicated media which served to educate as well as to inform.[14] In the 1990s the media, environmental NGOs, and experts are informally working together to educate themselves and the public. This effort comes from a realization that a change in the behavior of individual citizens to act in an environmentally compatible manner is a necessary complement to changes in societal institutions. Such change in behavior follows greater public awareness and education in environmental matters (see Table 15.3). In addition, until very recently, native people did not enjoy the necessary empowered and equitable status or respect to be parties to any interjurisdictional agreement such as the IJC on the Great Lakes.

A CONFLUENCE OF ECONOMY, ECOSYSTEM INTEGRITY, AND SUSTAINABLE DEVELOPMENT?

Within large continental trade blocs, such as the North American Free Trade Area (NAFTA), regional economies exist and often flourish. A significant and self-organizing regional economy is emerging in the Great Lakes/St. Lawrence River Basin with an annual gross domestic product, at 1994 values, approximating one

Table. 15.3. Establishment of a Great Lakes public constituency.

Time Pd.	Organization	Media/Communications	Orientation
1970s	Local non-governmental organizations, NGOs	Local degrading incident	Protest
1980s	Federation of NGOs	Continuing issue of a degrading influence	Social dialogue, empowerment
1990s	Partnerships with governments and corporations	Balance of rehabilitative success and degrading influence	Public education, participatory action

trillion US dollars. One half of all Canada-United States trade begins or ends in the Great Lakes Basin. The area's vast assets include an educated work force, great educational and training institutions, a restructuring manufacturing base, excellent communications and transportation networks, and a strong agricultural sector.[15] In addition, cooperation within the Basin may help it to become more competitive in the global economy. In specific fields, such as tourism, the Province of Ontario and the eight Great Lakes states are participating in a joint marketing campaign, advertising the region as a major tourist destination for Europeans.

Expansion of Great Lakes economic relationships parallels expansion of social, cultural, and political interactions. In these relationships the necessity of achieving and then maintaining "ecosystem integrity" is a major theme emerging at all levels of governance.[16] In the Great Lakes Basin this trend is due in part to concern about the implications for human health of the contaminated ecosystem. Many citizens also realize that a healthy natural ecosystem is critical to a healthy human population and economy. As science clarifies the relationships between widespread ecosystemic degradation and its impact on human health and the economy, the increasingly informed public will infer relationships without waiting for experts to reveal their full extent.[17]

Nowhere is the need for greater institutional effectiveness made more pointedly than at the biennial meetings of the IJC concerning the GLWQA. At these meetings the IJC publicly receives the findings of its experts on various aspects of Great Lakes water quality and reviews the progress of the parties in implementing the Agreement. As part of the meeting, the IJC takes testimony from members of the public on a wide range of aspects of Great Lakes environmental quality. Citizens voice concern about lake and river pollution because they feel they are not being heard by their local, state, provincial, or federal governments. The common theme running through the presentations is this need to be heard, manifested in pleas for effective institutional responses which existing arrangements cannot seem to provide. Thus, the challenge is to find relevant and more responsive governance arrangements.

TOWARD NEW INSTITUTIONAL ARRANGEMENTS: CRITERIA AND CONSIDERATIONS

Since the late 1980s new management mechanisms with an ecosystemic orientation have emerged. One, the Remedial Action Plan (RAP), has been specifically designed to mobilize action by all stakeholders (including government agencies, industries, citizen activists, and academics) in cleaning up each of 43 severely degraded inshore areas around the Great Lakes.[18] These areas have been designated "areas of concern" by the IJC because they persistently failed to meet water quality objectives of the GLWQA and state or provincial water quality standards, with continuing impairment of one or more of 14 specified beneficial uses of such waters.

Another recent mechanism, the Lakewide Management Plan, is designed to reduce loadings of specific persistent toxins into a particular lake. Like RAPs, the process is designed to mobilize public support around a base of scientific information in which effects of pollutants are related to those of other degrading influences. The idea is to consider the total load of a particular substance going into a lake from all its sources, both within and from outside its basin, and then derive a target load reduction which will assist in restoring lost beneficial uses. The relative contributions among a variety of sources are estimated through the use of mass balance and transport models. This permits one to ascertain priority substances for control.[19] Again a public, multistakeholder committee in a highly interactive process focuses on reviewing scientific information generated by experts, and builds trust, understanding, and support for the required actions. Thus, the change from regulatory control to stakeholder participation in the management of Great Lakes uses can be partially explained by the key roles of science, the evolution of the regulatory framework, the establishment of a constituency, the increasing global importance of the regional economies, and the growing acceptance of the need to protect and enhance ecosystem integrity and move toward a state of sustainable development.

ECOSYSTEM INTEGRITY

The Great Lakes Basin ecosystem was defined, quite properly, to include humans; thus an ecosystem is a natural/cultural system in which the boundaries between nature and culture are not the preeminent concern. The term "integrity" was not defined explicitly in the GLWQA, but at least part of its meaning can be inferred from the commitments in the numerous programmatic and practical annexes to that Agreement. The commitment to integrity of the chemical, physical, and biological aspects of the water implies a commitment to the integrity of the entire ecosystem. Thus it has been inferred that integrity refers to desirable, healthy self-organizing capabilities, within both natural and cultural features and as the two interact to constitute the Basin ecosystem.[20]

In the Great Lakes Basin the shores and coastal waters bear strong ecological resemblance to the shores of medium to large rivers. A lake-shore is like a one-sided river.[21] Structures and processes at the interface between land and water strongly affect the self-organizational processes within the biota.[22] Where currents and waves are quite strong, at least periodically, the biotic organization will be relatively sparse and tough. Where currents and waves are of low to moderate strength, more complex biotic associations emerge and evolve. In benign settings with a solid substrate quite intricate persistent communities of organisms develop.[23] This benthic community tends to be dominant ecologically over a complementary pelagic community. Thus the benthic community "selectively harvests" organic substances that wash in from the land and pelagic organisms that thrive in the open waters.[24]

In their pristine state the offshore open waters of the deeper Great Lakes were rather infertile, in part because they tended to lose organisms and chemical nutrients to the bottom substrate and the benthic association. Water clarity was high and abundance of waterfowl and fish was low in offshore open waters, especially in summer and winter. As industrial progress intervened early in the nineteenth century, many different kinds of cultural stresses came into play. Sometimes these stresses acted independently of the natural stresses, sometimes synergistically with them, but seldom antagonistically so as to counteract other harmful natural stresses.

The ways in which the biotic association responded to different stresses, when one or more of them had become quite intense, often showed similarities. Thus stresses alter the fish association from one that is dominated by large riverine or benthic fish to one characterized by small pelagic species. This "general adaptive syndrome" can be interpreted with respect to the distinction made earlier between the benthic and the pelagic biotic associations.[25] The brunt of human stresses generally fell directly on the benthic association. The benthic association was less well pre-adapted to some of these kinds of industrial stresses than was the pelagic association. Thus the dominance of the benthic over the pelagic association was gradually weakened as the cultural stresses intensified locally and expanded regionally.

During the nineteenth century the benthic association provided valued products such as fish, waterfowl, furs, and gravel. By about 1960 much of the shoreline of the southerly one-third of the Great Lakes had been stressed and much of the original benthic association was degraded with many of the native species eliminated in the most degraded locales. This provided a relative opportunity for a pelagic association to become more abundant, especially in the nearshore waters.[26] Measures to correct this trend were well underway by the early 1970s. Loadings of harmful substances were curtailed, loadings of plant nutrients were reduced, overfishing was stopped (in part by closing some commercial fishing operations), and abundances of some exotic species were reduced. Twenty years later these measures can all claim notable, although far from complete, success.[27]

None of the various rehabilitation or remediation programs now underway has as yet come close to completion. The question of how much further each of them should be extended is currently debated. Best available chemical technology for treating sewage for phosphate removal may not be necessary if the coastal benthic association could be rehabilitated to perform this function — through "green technology." However some fishermen targeting an exotic salmon might welcome loading of active phosphates into offshore surface waters if it led to more abundant large salmon, as was once the case. Lakewide Management Plans now being formulated for water quality and fish associations reflect some awareness of ecosystem macro-transformations.

ECOSYSTEMS AS SELF-ORGANIZING PHENOMENA

A new understanding of ecosystems is emerging from the perspective of complex systems theory.[28] Complex systems theory provides a radically different idea of an ecosystem from the traditional Newtonian mechanistic one. From this new perspective an ecosystem is dynamic and constantly evolving; it is not deterministic, but rather is somewhat unpredictable.[29] Change in such a system can be smooth or, just as likely, sudden and surprising. Such systems can exhibit phases of rapid change, and even catastrophic behavior is not abnormal. Left alone, ecosystems are self-organizing. However, because a system is inherently not predictable does not necessarily make it unpredictable. The predictions of weather forecasters are an example. The key to such forecasting is to be able to state in a quantitative manner in which direction the system as a whole, if left to its own internal workings, is most likely to drift.

One example of how to quantify the natural direction for ecosystem development falls under the rubric of "ascendancy theory."[30] Ascendancy theory is the application of information theory to ecological networks in order to quantify the extent and internal organization of the range of ecosystem processes. The direction of system "growth and development" appears to be towards increasing higher levels, as a broad empirical generalization. With this approach one can infer which species and processes are critical to further system development. In the end, this allows one to predict, at least in terms of relative probabilities, which elements of the ecosystem should be most vulnerable to change when the system is subjected to perturbations.[31]

In a complex system a combination of seemingly random interactions are constrained by the system's physical laws and by system memory. The challenge is to understand the potential states an ecosystem may occupy and under what conditions it will do so. For example, one of the Great Lakes may exist in one of two states: either the ecosystem is dominated by the natural benthic association or by the "unnatural" pelagic association. A mechanistic cause and effect approach is useful but not nearly sufficient to explain complex systems. Some changes in ecosystems cannot be attributed to any one cause-effect link, but rather involve synergisms and emergence. To understand these behaviors a holarchic (hierarchical) perspective provides a framework for careful attention to scale and extent.[32] The spatial, temporal, thermodynamic, and information dynamics of ecosystems are all relevant.

The challenge of the ecosystem approach — with the ecosystem as an open, self-organizing entity — for management and governance may be explored further. The key issue is how to manage human activities so as to enhance desirable natural ecosystemic processes while using them for human purposes. This is a positive challenge. It is not ecosystems that need management in the first instance, but rather their use by people. By managing human activities to enhance ecosystem self-organization, ecosystems may provide additional free benefits. It is a question of understanding desirable self-organizing processes in ecosystems and then managing human actions so they interact synergistically with these self-organizational processes.

The single most important change to be made in management is to stop trying to manage ecosystems for some fixed end-state. Ecosystems are not static; they are dynamic entities made up of self-organizing processes. The only static equilibrium state is death. At any point in time an ecosystem may tend toward an optimal point of balance but the point itself is tending toward a balance in the context of an encompassing system. Disruptions can occur anywhere in such a nested system. Appropriate management focuses on facilitating and directing change, not on attaining and maintaining some fixed state for all time. The primary focus should be on managing human behavior so that it enhances the organization of that manifestation of an ecosystem which satisfactorily provides the desired benefits.

It is of paramount importance that the information needed for the ongoing ecosystem regeneration process not be destroyed. The ability of an ecosystem to regenerate is a function of the types of species available to participate in the regeneration process. This is related to biodiversity of the larger landscape of which the ecosystem is a part. Thus preservation of biodiversity is important because it preserves the library or information code used for regeneration of ecosystems.[33]

When management refocuses on facilitating and directing change, it faces issues about the desirable directions of that change. In this context, decision makers may have to change how they perceive their role vis-á-vis scientists. One of the insights of complex systems thinking, particularly of chaos theory, is that the scientific opportunity to forecast and predict is always limited, regardless of how sophisticated the concepts and computers and how great the information stores are.[34] People decide what they want the future to look like and seek expert advice to move in that direction all the while aware that there will be unexpected consequences and changes in direction. There are no simple definitive rules.

Hierarchy theory is helpful in relating to ecosystems as complex systems, since it concerns extent, scale, hierarchy, and boundaries.[35] Its premise is that one can only look at one piece of the world at a time and at only one level of detail. Having picked a systemic entity at a particular level of detail, that system's behavior is understood in the context of the constraints imposed on the system by higher systemic levels, and in terms of the processes among lower level systemic components. This may seem obvious, but the traditional linear approach is to attempt to explain everything in terms of the components, to ignore the environmental constraints and to assume there are no synergistic effects due to non-linear interactions among components or constraints.

Hierarchy theory suggests that, in practice, one first decides which systemic entity is to be examined, its hierarchical context, and the scale and extent of the study. When attempted in the past, this approach has been seriously hampered by institutional structures which are focused on one combination of level, scale, and extent to the exclusion of other combinations. There are two problems here. How may stakeholders be assembled with experts in a decision process to define the proper focus (be it scale, extent, or hierarchy) of a study? How may institutional and governance processes be reoriented in this way, instead of being limited largely to a specific discipline focused on phenomena of a specific scale and extent and serving primarily one group of stakeholders? A "soft systems approach," that is, an interactive process between stakeholders and experts to achieve a mutually agreed upon definition of relevant issues in an hierarchical context, is appropriate and consistent with complex theory and hierarchy theory as applied within an ecosystem approach. Early efforts to interrelate these in the Great Lakes Basin are now underway.[36]

The emphasis has been on rehabilitation of the degraded southerly parts of the Basin ecosystem to a state of integrity. Severely degraded areas cannot be restored to a pristine state, at least not until after the next ice age wipes away much of what we have done in the Basin. Therefore the residents of the Basin are deciding what kind of cultural/natural ecosystems they intend to foster. Large northerly parts of the Great Lakes Basin are still closer to the pristine. How the ecosystem approach relates to the challenge of preserving such ecosystems is addressed in the following chapter by Francis and Lerner. Many stakeholders are currently drafting an "ecosystem charter" for the Great Lakes/St. Lawrence River Basin Ecosystem. This activity builds on earlier efforts to specify a shared vision of ecosystemic features and a set of shared principles that will be helpful in practical efforts to realize it.[37] People collaborating to formulate the ecosystem charter know that the general agreement on shared principles does not imply prior consent on how more detailed difficulties will be resolved, but the stakeholders expect that general political agreement on these principles will help to frame practical efforts to resolve conflicts.

ACKNOWLEDGMENT

In addition to colleagues cited in the footnotes, we wish to thank all those who collaborated with us. The Donner Canadian Foundation provided financial support, and we thank in particular Claire Fortier, Leah McGinnis and Don Rickerd of the Foundation. The views expressed in this paper are the personal views of the authors and are not attributable to Environment Canada.

NOTES

1. Charles R. Van Hise. 1911. The Conservation of Natural Resources in the United States. MacMillan Co., New York.

2. Robert Spencer, John Kirton, Kim Nossals (eds.). 1981. The International Joint Commission Seventy Years On. University of Toronto, Centre for International Studies, Toronto; John E. Carroll. 1983. Environmental Diplomacy: an Examination and a Prospective of Canadian-U.S. Transboundary Environmental Relations. The University of Michigan Press, Ann Arbor, Michigan.; David J. Allee. 1993. Subnational governance and the International Joint Commission: local management of the United States and Canadian boundary waters. Natural Resources Journal 33(1): 133-151. University of New Mexico School of Law, Albuquerque; and David Lemarquand. 1993. The International Joint Commission and changing Canada-United States boundary relations. Natural Resources Journal 33(1):59-91. University of New Mexico School of Law, Albuquerque.

3. Donald Munton. 1981. Paradoxes and Prospects. In Spencer et al., op. cit., pp. 64-81.

4. IJC. 1970. Report on the Pollution of Lake Erie, Lake Ontario and the International St. Lawrence River. International Joint Commission, Washington, D.C. and Ottawa.

5. IJC. 1972. The 1972 Great Lakes Water Quality Agreement between Canada and the United States. International Joint Commission, Washington, D.C. and Ottawa.

6. Lynton K. Caldwell. 1970. The ecosystem as a criterion for public land policy. Natural Resources Journal 10:203-221; W. Jack Christie, Mimi Becker, James W. Cowden and Jack R. Vallentyne. 1986. Managing the Great Lakes Basin as a home. Journal of Great Lakes Research 12:3-17; Richard L. Thomas, Jack R. Vallentyne, Kenneth Ogilvie and James D. Kingham. 1988. The ecosystems approach: a strategy for the management of renewable re-

sources in the Great Lakes Basin. In Lynton K. Caldwell (ed.), Perspectives on Ecosystem Management for the Great Lakes. State University of New York Press, Albany, pp. 31-57; and Clayton J. Edwards and Henry A. Regier (eds.) 1990. An Ecosystem Approach to the Integrity of the Great Lakes in Turbulent Times. Great Lakes Fishery Commission, Ann Arbor. Special Publication 90-4.

7.   Henry A. Regier. 1992. Ecosystem integrity in the Great Lakes Basin: an historical sketch of ideas and actions. Journal of Aquatic Ecosystem Health 1:25-37.

8.   See Francis and Lerner, this volume.

9.   IJC. 1978. Great Lakes Water Quality Agreement of 1978. International Joint Commission, Washington, D.C. and Ottawa.

10. Ibid.

11. M. Ronald Shimizu. 1991. Great Lakes ecosystem management: a living experiment. Paper presented to the Seminar on Ecosystem Approach to Water Management by the Economic Commission for Europe, 26 May - 1 June, 1992, Oslo, Norway.

12. M. Ronald Shimizu and David Rodda. 1992. Recent trends in environmental legislation in North America and Europe. Paper presented to the Annual Conference of the Institute of Water and Environmental Management, April 28, 1992, Birmingham, England.

13. See Francis and Lerner, this volume.

14. Phil Weller. 1990. Fresh Water Seas: Saving the Great Lakes. Between the Lines, Toronto.

15. Federal Reserve Bank of Chicago. 1990. The Great Lakes Economy. Center for the Great Lakes, Chicago.

16. Regier 1992, op. cit.

17. Theodore E. Colborn, Alex Davidson, Sharon N. Green, R. Anthony Hodge, C. Ian Jackson and Richard A. Liroff. 1990. Great Lakes, Great Legacy? Conservation Foundation, Washington, D.C. and Institute for Research on Public Policy, Ottawa.

18. See the chapter by Francis and Lerner in this volume for more details about RAPs.

19. Donald Mackay. 1991. Multimedia Environmental Models: The Fugacity Approach. Lewis Publishers, Chelsea, Michigan.

20. Edwards and Regier, op cit. and Stephen Woodley, James J. Kay and George Francis (eds.). 1993. Ecological Integrity and the Management of Ecosystems. St. Lucie Press, Delray Beach, Florida.

21. Robert J. Steedman and Henry A. Regier. 1987. Ecosystem science for the Great Lakes: perspectives on degradative transformations. Canadian Journal of Fisheries and Aquatic Science 44 (Supplement 2):95-103.

22. James R. Sedell, Robert J. Steedman, Henry A. Regier and Stanley V. Gregory. 1991. Restoration of human impacted land-water ecotones. In Mary M. Holland, Paul G. Risser and Robert J. Naiman (eds.) Ecotones: The Role of Landscape Boundaries in the Management and Restoration of Changing Environments. Chapman and Hall, New York, pp. 110-129.

23. Hallett J. Harris, Victoria A. Harris, Henry A. Regier and Donald J. Rapport. 1988. Importance of the nearshore area for sustainable redevelopment: the Baltic Sea and Great Lakes. Ambio 17: 112-120.

24. Robert E. Ulanowicz and Jon H. Tuttle. 1992. The trophic consequences of oyster stock rehabilitation in Chesapeake Bay. Estuaries 15(3):298-306.

25. David J. Rapport, Henry A. Regier and Thomas C. Hutchinson. 1985. Ecosystem behavior under stress. American Naturalist 125: 617-640.

26. Henry A. Regier, Pekka Tuunainen, Zbyniew Russek and Lars-Eric Persson. 1988. Rehabilitative redevelopment of fish and fisheries of the Great Lakes and the Baltic Sea. Ambio 17:121-130.

27. Colburn et al., op. cit. and John H. Hartig and Michail A. Zarull (eds.). 1992. Under RAPs, Towards Grassroots Ecological Democracy in the Great Lakes Basin. The University of Michigan Press, Ann Arbor.

28. Erwin Schrödinger. 1951. What is Life? The Physical Aspect of the Living Cell. Cambridge University Press, Cambridge, U.K.; Arthur Koestler. 1978. Janus, a Summing Up. Hutchinsons, London; Ludwig von Bertalanffy. 1968. General System Theory: Foundations, Development, Applications. Braziller, New York; James J. Kay. 1993. On the nature of ecological integrity: some closing comments. In Woodley et al., op. cit., pp. 201-212; James

J. Kay. 1994. The challenge of the ecosystem approach. In Press Alternatives; and Timothy F. H. Allen, Bruce L. Bandurski, Anthony W. King. 1993. The ecosystem approach: theory and ecosystem integrity. Report to the Great Lakes Science Advisory Board. International Joint Commission, Washington, D.C. and Ottawa.

29. Here we agree with Thompson and Trisoglio, in this volume.

30. Robert E. Ulanowicz. 1986. Growth and Development: Ecosystems Phenomenology. Springer-Verlag, New York.

31. See Daniel Baird, Robert E. Ulanowicz and W.R. Boynton. 1995. Seasonal nitrogen dynamics in the Chesapeake Bay: a network approach. Estuarine, Coastal and Shelf Science 41:137-162; and Robert E. Ulanowicz and Daniel Baird. (Under revision.) Nutrient controls on ecosystem dynamics: The Chesapeake mesohaline community.

32. Timothy F. H. Allen and Thomas W. Hoekstra. 1992. Toward a Unified Ecology. Columbia University Press, New York.

33. Nina-Marie Lister. 1995. Biodiversity: a conceptual discussion of the sociocultural and scientific implications for decision-making in the Great Lakes Basin. Institute for Environmental Studies, University of Toronto (unpublished).

34. For a further discussion of management and complexity see Thompson and Trisoglio, this volume.

35. Allen et al. 1993, op. cit.

36. Peter Checkland and Jim Scholes. 1990. Soft Systems Methodology in Action. Wiley, New York.

37. Christie et al. op. cit.; The Rawson Academy of Aquatic Science. 1989. Towards an Ecosystem Charter for the Great Lakes-St. Lawrence. Rawson Occasional Paper No. 1. Ottawa. See Serafin and Zaleski, this volume, for a discussion of similar efforts around the Baltic Sea.

16

NGOs and Great Lakes Biodiversity Conservation

GEORGE FRANCIS AND SALLY LERNER

As demonstrated in the preceding chapter, the International Joint Commission (IJC) and the Great Lakes Water Quality Agreement (GLWQA) have been successful in many areas. As biodiversity conservation became an issue in the Great Lakes Basin, local, regional, national, and international environmental NGOs have continued the success of IJC and GLWQA initiatives. In this chapter we examine the role of several influential NGOs and NGO-sponsored initiatives in the conservation of Great Lakes biodiversity. In particular, we focus on the Nature Conservancy (TNC) and the Nature Conservancy of Canada (NCC) in establishing Heritage Areas and the role of the Center for the Great Lakes and numerous local stewardship groups in identifying and lobbying for an ecosystem-wide approach to conservation (known as the "Ecosystem Charter"). In addition, we examine the likelihood of creating four proposed biosphere reserves under UNESCO/MAB auspices and the impact of the 1987 Great Lakes United report on the state of the Lakes, written by members of its 200 or more NGO constituents. These successful collaborations demonstrate that biodiversity conservation can be achieved with broad participation by citizen groups and governments working together for clearly identified policy objectives. These examples also clarify several key elements of such a strategy. Not only have NGO activities aided a conservation agenda, they have inadvertently transformed environmental politics.

Under the GLWQA between Canada and the United States, some 43 designated "areas of concern" have been identified. These consist of nearshore sites in harbors, at river mouths, or along the rivers which join the lakes together to form this largest of freshwater resources. By 1985 these sites had degraded to the point that routine pollution control measures, applied under the terms of the Agreement since at least 1978, had failed to restore the beneficial uses of the waters as defined by water quality objectives under the Agreement, or by jurisdictional water quality standards. Special, collaborative measures are required for these areas of concern; the specifications for preparing and implementing "remedial action plans" (RAPs) for them were agreed upon by the IJC, the binational treaty body which oversees the implementation of the GLWQA. Preparation of these plans required cooperation among a variety of governmental, industrial, non-governmental, and local organizations.[1]

By the mid-1980s interest was developing, mainly in academic circles, about what should be done for the nearshore and coastal sites with high ecological value due to their biodiversity or their critical habitats for fish and waterfowl. Many such sites had been given different forms of protection over the years by different agencies in the eleven federal, state and provincial jurisdictions of the Great Lakes Basin. However, there had been no basin-wide compilations, nor overall assessments of the extent to which the conservation of biodiversity along the nearshore, coastal zone, and archipelagos of the lakes had been secured.

PROTECTED AREAS AROUND THE GREAT LAKES

A compilation of the protected sites was prepared for the Canadian side of the lakes from many diffuse sources of information.[2] An informal binational meeting of people interested in these conservation issues was convened under the auspices of the IJC Science

Advisory Board in March 1988 to review relevant issues. It recommended that the Board help with a compilation of similar information for the United States side of the lakes, which was subsequently done by Weller.[3] It was also recommended that TNC and NCC be approached to work together to provide a basin-wide database modelled after TNC's State Natural Heritage Programs. The TNC and NCC had already considered how the former's approach could be adopted to form the basis of proposed Conservation Data Centres in the Canadian provinces. Work to establish the first of these, in Quebec, began in 1989 and a pilot project to demonstrate the use of this approach was initiated for the Carolinian Canada bioregion of southwestern Ontario. This region of highly fragmented remnant areas which support species of plants and animals at the northern edge of their ranges was chosen in 1987 for a joint government and NGO collaborative program to secure the highest priority remnants found.[4]

Arrangements were made to develop The Great Lakes Biodiversity Data System (GLBDS) to assist further development of a Conservation Data Centre for Ontario and link it electronically to centers in each of the eight Great Lakes states and Quebec. The work entailed development of a suitable community-habitat classification system in Ontario which would be comparable to similar classifications elsewhere in the basin, and the identification of coastal wetlands which could serve as "high quality biomonitoring sites" to help assess the ecosystem health of the lakes.[5] The intention was to promote some linkage between the protection of sites which had important biodiversity values and the need for reference areas or monitoring sites to assess the overall environmental improvements which were being sought through binational cooperation. Cooperation developed over the years under the GLWQA, which included a commitment to protect significant coastal wetlands, as well as under other complementary agreements between the two countries, such as those for fisheries, migratory birds, and the reduction of toxic contaminants.

It was reasoned that such linkages, if forged, would strengthen support for site protection because of the oft used rationale that protected areas are necessary for baseline studies and monitoring. At the same time, they could broaden public support for Great Lakes programs by engaging a wider spectrum of interests than can be drawn to issues of toxic contaminants and polluted harbors. This was subsequently recognized and endorsed by the Scientific Advisory Board in a recommendation to the IJC that "Heritage Area Security Plans…to conserve pristine locales in the coastal zone" be drawn up, and made part of the commitments under the GLWQA.[6] The IJC in turn advised governments of the need for ecosystem reference areas and biological monitoring, the latter to include monitoring at all important trophic levels within the ecosystem.[7] By 1993, the GLBDS included available information from throughout the Great Lakes Basin. Ontario had successfully established a multistakeholder Ontario Natural Heritage Information Centre to maintain data on critical elements of biodiversity. This helped fill a major jurisdictional gap in the GLBDS. Preliminary review of information from this system noted that over one hundred types of natural communities or species of plants and animals of global significance existed in the basin. Of these, 55 are found nowhere else, occur predominantly within the basin, or have their best examples there.[8]

INITIATIVES FROM OTHER NGOS

The administration of the information system was established in Chicago in 1992, largely because an initiative had been launched by the Chicago-based Center for the Great Lakes to help mobilize support for the conservation of critical areas in the basin. The Center itself was established in 1983 to undertake policy studies and pilot projects relating to Great Lakes concerns under the direction of a prominent board of directors, including former Governors and premiers of Great Lakes states and provinces, and high profile businessmen. Seeking resources for the so called "The Great Legacy Project," staff from the Center mobilized support among governmental bodies and NGOs in the different jurisdictions, and in consultation with them, determined how best to facilitate collaboration among stakeholders associated with particular sites to help provide the security deemed appropriate for each site. This project came to a sudden halt with the closing of the Center in April 1993. However, securement of critical natural heritage areas continues through individual initiatives of TNC, NCC and other conservation organizations.

Many local environmental stewardship groups are active in the Great Lakes Basin, many of which are focused on site protection issues. While there has been little systematic research, a study of 200 such groups in Ontario provides some information about their activities.[9] Casual observation suggests that the activities and mix of local groups are similar throughout the basin. Community-based environmental groups are particularly aware of the vulnerability of natural systems and their need for stewardship. Typically, these groups formed or were mobilized in response to threatened destruction or degradation of a valued natural area in what they considered to be their "home place."

More than half of the 200 Ontario groups engage in stewardship through education (60 percent of the groups), monitoring (58 percent) and advocacy (54 percent). Other activities include restoration (45 percent), conservation (28 percent) and preservation (25 percent). The educational activities are designed to foster public awareness, appreciation and understanding of nature, particularly of local natural areas. Protection and wise use are popular themes. Groups use displays, field trips, and workshops to deliver their message to students and the general public.

The most common form of monitoring is systematic collection of information by means of sampling or inventories. Other less systematic "watchdogging" is done by groups for purposes such as keeping track of development proposals and decisions in their area, surveillance of wetlands and other environmentally-sensitive areas, and recording government decisions about environmental concerns. Just as householders often pledge to keep a neighborhood watch over children in the immediate area, many stewardship groups see themselves as guardians of local environmental quality.

Advocacy activities are seen by many groups as a politicized extension of education and monitoring. They understand that protecting natural areas requires them to function effectively in a multistakeholder struggle for the support of both the public and politicians. Preparation and presentations of briefs, letter writing, telephone calls, raising money for legal fees, and appearing before government bodies are typical advocacy activities mentioned. More revealing, perhaps, are the terms used by the groups to describe their actions: lobby, advocate, influence, oppose, pressure, protest, intervene, litigate, petition, negotiate, campaign, promote, mobilize support, and fight.

Hands-on activities such as stream clean-ups, tree planting, and reintroduction of fauna or flora into an area are typical of restoration activities reported. Sports-related groups such as hunters and anglers are more likely than others to be involved in this work, which is largely rehabilitative rather than protective. The term "conservation" was sometimes used by groups to describe their major purpose and their general activities. "Preservation" was how some groups described their activities directed toward protecting and preserving a specific place (such as Alfred Bog, Hawk Cliff or Oak Ridges Moraine), a type of natural area (wetland, wildlife habitat, beach, forested area, or wilderness), or simply natural heritage in general.

The locations of the 200 Ontario groups were mapped in relation to the 123 protected and 204 unprotected Natural Heritage Areas along the shore and nearshore zones of the Canadian side of the lakes identified previously.[10] For each group, a zone was established in which nearby Natural Heritage Areas were surveyed. This radius of activity was standardized on a lake-by-lake basis at 30 km for Lake Ontario; 50 km for Lakes Erie, Huron, and St. Clair; and 100 km for Lake Superior. These conventions were based on the population density for each basin and on presumed 'reasonable' distances for travel in each area. More than three-quarters (78 percent) of the 200 Ontario groups had proximate Natural Heritage Areas and virtually all of those identified for Lakes Ontario, Erie, Huron, and St. Clair are accessible to one or more groups. With renewed interest in protecting Lake Superior sites, there may be more groups within travel distance to them. Using this mapping approach, it is possible that stewardship group activities, which could include private landowner contact programs, can be an effective component in strategies to protect natural heritage areas.

There are parallel challenges to completing RAPs for degraded sites, and providing sufficient degrees of protection for high quality biodiversity sites in the Great Lakes Basin. At the local level much can be learned from the experiences of stakeholder groups and the processes through which they do or do not succeed in agreeing upon shared goals and cooperative means to achieve them.[11] But action at local levels, while necessary, is seldom sufficient. Remedial plans will not be effective if polluting and other influences from upstream areas or transboundary atmospheric fallout cannot also be addressed. Similarly, protection for individual biodiversity sites, in isolation from their surroundings, is known to have a number of weaknesses because of the fragmentation effects in the landscape and the inappropriate sizes of such sites for the maintenance of viable species population levels.[12] Environmental NGOs, particularly in strong coalitions, can serve as an effective constituency to demand that responsible parties implement a comprehensive ecosystem approach in the basin.

ELEMENTS OF AN "ECOSYSTEM APPROACH"

The challenge is basically one of scale. In the Great Lakes the need to take an ecosystem approach has been recognized and discussed since 1978.[13] This reasoning, adapted from a systems perspective, recognizes the crucial importance of space and time scales in the phenomena being addressed. In contrast, administrative agencies, for example, often have a fixed place in an hierarchical scale and cannot step outside to see the "big picture." From an ecological perspective, there are "macro-frameworks" within which issues can be addressed using an ecosystem approach. Landscape ecology, supported in part by new technologies for remote-sensing, image analyses, and geographic information systems, has considerable potential for guiding practical biodiversity conservation programs in terrestrial components of the ecosystem.[14] For the aquatic components, the concept of the land-stream-river-bay-lake continuum and centers of biological organization (especially in nearshore areas) provide the context for understanding aquatic ecosystems and two major subsystems, the riparian-littoral-benthic zone and the pelagic zone.[15]

The concept of "ecosystem integrity" has been given considerable academic attention in the Great Lakes Basin over the past decade, motivated in part by the stated goals of the GLWQA: "to restore and maintain the chemical, physical, and biological integrity of the waters of the Great Lakes Basin Ecosystem."[16] Work has been done to explore the concept's origins and applications, implications for ecological monitoring, possible use for lake status reports and to develop ecological theories.[17] One important conclusion from this work is that there are a number of possible ecosystems which could occur in a given geographic region, each of which would have its own integrity within certain environmental constraints. This means there is an element of human choice involved, especially in the human-dominated ecosystems which occur throughout much of the basin: we must decide what kinds of ecosystem gardens we wish to grow, and what differences of opinion on this question exist for a given geographic locale. At present there are no effective organizational arrangements for addressing these questions in the participatory manner necessary to stimulate follow-up on possible answers. Useful experience may come from the RAPs in which "visioning exercises" encourage stakeholders to achieve some consensus about the kinds of futures they would like for areas to be rehabilitated. This can come indirectly through addressing pseudo-technical questions of "how clean is clean?" At the basin-wide level, some effort has been given to the development of an Ecosystem Charter which would serve to raise the same kinds of issues.[18]

EXPLORING UNESCO/MAB AND "BIOSPHERE RESERVES"

For over 20 years UNESCO has been promoting greater international cooperation to develop the collective capabilities necessary to address environmental and sustainable natural resource issues. The Man and the Biosphere Program (MAB) emphasizes developing effective collaboration for interdisciplinary research and monitoring on issues of conservation and sustainability policy and management, along with associated information and education activities. This capability requires effective ways to bring together scientific and technical specialists, people with ownership or management interests in resources, and residents with local knowledge, to develop a common ground for their collaborative effort. In practice this remains difficult to accomplish.[19]

Countries opt into MAB by establishing a coordinating group to foster program-related activities within their country, participate in various international sessions to help develop the overall program, and to exchange experience and ideas arising from work being done. Over one hundred countries participate in the UNESCO/MAB program and Canada and the United States have done so from the start. Although the latter is not currently a member of UNESCO, it maintains close cooperation with the organization and other countries for the MAB program. Soon after the MAB program was initiated, UNESCO officials realized that recognition should be given to places in the world where MAB ideals for collaborative work were being accomplished. These designated "biosphere reserves" serve conservation, baseline research and monitoring functions and offer practical examples from which others can learn.

A biosphere reserve is now described in terms of a spatial configuration of lands representing three generic zonations (in their actual zoning or use) and three major functions. The zonations include a core area of protected, relatively undisturbed lands; buffer zones in which some human uses go on provided they are not intrusive upon the core; and a larger, often vaguely defined, transition area or zone of cooperation in which the full range of human activities continues to occur. Collectively, this configuration of lands can serve the functions of conserving ecosystems (and biodiversity); providing demonstration areas for sustainable resource use and/or management practices (including the restoration of degraded sites); and developing a logistical function to support research, monitoring, education, and information about issues of conservation and sustainability in the region. Appropriate organizational arrangements are requirements to carry out these functions along the collaborative lines suggested by the MAB ideals.

As of 1993, some 325 biosphere reserves had been designated in 86 countries. Many are not yet fully operative, largely because of difficulties encountered in developing effective local organizational arrangements to foster all of the functions. The United States has the most biosphere reserves. In recent years it has been organizing them into multiple site regional groupings with cooperative agreements among appropriate management agencies and other organizations. Thus, not every site has all three functions fully developed, but collectively the multiple sites do. There are four biosphere reserves in the Great Lakes Basin: Isle Royal in Lake Superior, the Niagara Escarpment including the Bruce Peninsula, Fathom Five National Parks in Georgian Bay, and Long Point on the north shore of Lake Erie.

In fact, much of the cooperative work fostered under binational agreements for the Great Lakes represents the types of cooperation which MAB tries to encourage. There could be mutual benefits if the MAB program were brought into closer association with Great Lakes programs. This would give greater international recognition to the latter. Given the strong ecological framework and orientation of MAB, it could also strengthen the ecosystem approach which helps to orient Great Lakes work.

After initial discussions of this idea with both the Canadian and American national committees for the UNESCO/MAB program, it was decided to explore what could be done in the Lake Superior Basin.[20] The idea was endorsed by the Congressional-Parliamentary Dialogue on Great Lakes Water Quality at its meeting in Quebec City in May 1991, and it was further encouraged by the IJC in 1992.[21] Lake Superior was chosen for several reasons: it is the headwater lake, at the time it was the only lake for which binational agreement had been reached on management objectives to be sought through both the GLWQA and the Strategic Great Lakes Fishery Management Plan, and in 1989 the IJC had called upon governments, under the general provisions of the GLWQA, to make it a demonstration area for the zero discharge of toxic contaminants.

In September 1991, the two federal governments, along with Michigan, Wisconsin, Minnesota, and Ontario, agreed to a "Binational Program" for Lake Superior to address these and other concerns on a basin-wide rather than strictly lake-wide basis.[22] The jurisdictions created a Task Force of senior administrators from lead agencies, an inter-agency Working Group to help develop and coordinate program responses, and a Stakeholders Group (or "Forum") of about 30 people who were broadly representative of major constituencies in the Lake Superior Basin. By 1993, the Working Group and Forum were working together on several initiatives, including: development of a vision statement to help guide a first stage lake-wide management plan to control and eliminate toxic discharges; creation of an outreach program to keep the public informed and involved; and exploration of possible special designations that are available under federal or international auspices. The biosphere reserve designation was the only one that could in principle apply, on a multiple site basis, to the entire basin.

All of the "pieces" and some of the organizational arrangements needed for a biosphere reserve are in place within the basin. There is a magnificent set of core protected areas in the form of national parks and lakeshores, provincial and state parks, and lake trout sanctuaries; the buffers are provided in part by management plans for these individual areas and the possibilities for special designations for other important features; the transition zone by definition includes the rest of the basin. The conservation function is provided partially by the protected areas, with possibilities for augmentation through appropriate biodiversity conservation strategies currently under exploration. The demonstration function is provided through seven RAPs under preparation and by several watershed and forest management projects. In addition, the logistical support for research, monitoring, and education activities could draw upon university, college and governmental research programs and facilities, interpretive centers at certain parks, and several initiatives to develop waterway trails, hiking trails, and cooperation with groups from Lake Baikal (to celebrate the two largest lakes in the world). Existing binational organizational arrangements include the tripartite structure set up under the Binational Program, along with a Lake Superior Committee convened regularly by the Great Lakes Fisheries Commission; a resource management consortium of federal, state, and provincial government agencies and universities/colleges; and a grass-roots Lake Superior Alliance.

Introduction of the biosphere reserve concept is being done informally through meetings with agency representatives, whose support is essential, and with members of the Forum. Preliminary results suggest that, despite the connotations of the word "reserve," the idea of an international designation of recognition has been greeted positively, sometimes enthusiastically, but with caution regarding how to proceed. As an idea originating outside the basin, it could receive a negative response from people who object to top-down decisions made without their knowledge. Furthermore, despite the emphasis often placed by UNESCO/MAB on core area conservation functions of biosphere reserves, in the Lake Superior Basin it is advisable to promote the demonstration function, focusing instead on issues of sustainable resource use, a shared concern among resource industries and small resource-based communities alike.

The Lake Superior situation is not unique. As noted in debates about sustainability, environmental issues must be dealt with in the context of economic security and social equity — and in some situations the latter are a priority. Macro-ecological analytic frameworks are helpful for purposes of understanding the ecological factors associated with the restoration of major aquatic or marine ecosystems, or for preventing initial degradation. However, actual restoration or prevention programs require land-based measures affecting human economic activities. Any framework not only must acknowledge this, but also suggest consultative decision-making arrangements needed to deal with these issues. Without this, science will merely document the symptoms of degradation which management agencies cannot address. More importantly, the declaration of "greater ecosystems" to achieve ecological objectives without dealing with organizational issues could exacerbate conflict situations, as the experience from the Greater Yellowstone Ecosystem seems to suggest.[23] The diversity of interests associated with coastal zones easily rivals those associated with mountain ecosystems.

The Great Lakes Basin may have a model for such a broad consultative decision-making framework. In 1979 a group of Great Lakes researchers offered these guidelines for developing "the collaborative inter-organizational processes required to work towards achieving some ecosystem rehabilitation goal" or, indeed, any shared social goal:

- Articulate a clear social policy goal from which to judge collective accountability

- View the whole process as one of mutual learning

- Keep it open to new perceptions, new information, and new participants

- Change reward systems to reinforce a cooperative approach and reduce dominance of individual organization objectives and careerism as ends in themselves

- Open up the decision processes to public inspection and involvement[24]

This advice was addressed primarily to government agencies in various basin jurisdictions that badly needed to coordinate their efforts. As it turned out, it was heeded primarily by basin environmental groups whose concern about Great Lakes pollution had been steadily growing since the early 1960s.[25] For example, an innovative five-year public consultation exercise, associated with the Pollution from Land-Use Activities Reference Group of the IJC, drew basin residents further into pollution issues and produced information that permitted the 1978 GLWQA to recognize the lakes as an ecosystem, and to recognize the need for zero discharge of persistent toxic chemicals into that system.[26]

In 1981 formal moves began toward a binational coalition of diverse environmental interest groups that included hunters and anglers as well as conservationists and naturalists. In 1983, the coalition Great Lakes United (GLU) held its first meeting in Windsor, Ontario. By 1986 GLU had a membership of over 200 groups and hundreds of individuals in the United States and Canada. Concern about the scheduled 1987 review of the GLWQA provided the impetus for a 1986 basin-wide GLU tour. At nineteen "Citizen Hearings on Great Lakes Water Pollution" in cities across the basin, concerns about toxic pollutants and support for the Agreement were expressed. GLU's subsequent report carried weight and, according to Ron Shimizu who was responsible for Environment Canada's implementation of the GLWQA, GLU's emphasis on the positive features of the Agreement which should not be changed, "set the tone, the public parameters of acceptability around which the governments could conduct a review."[27]

There is no longer any question about the value of volunteer environmental organizations, as local stewards or as politically-effective coalitions. Of the latter, the IJC had this to say in 1989:

> The emergence of strong, sophisticated and effective non-governmental organizations over the past decade has been a positive development. Composed of many thousands of Great Lake basin residents and others from both sides of the international boundary, these organizations are important in focusing political attention on the integration of [Great Lakes Water Quality] Agreement objectives into domestic priorities and programs. They are instrumental in encouraging governments to provide the resources necessary to implement the Agreement and actively promoting environmentally-conscious behaviour among their own membership and the public at large. As such, these organizations fill a distinct niche in the Great Lakes organizational framework...[28]

One possible path for the protection of natural areas, and thus of biodiversity, is to be found in widening and overlapping circles of government, non-government and private sector dialogue, cooperation, and contention, modelled on the GLU approach. An increasingly informed and able public, concerned about the economic and social future of its region, yet motivated to protect the environment and provided with the training and resources to do so, may be the best foundation for successful participatory decision making. In instituting such a decision-making framework, it should be clearly understood that ecological issues are closely linked to residents' concerns about economic security and social justice. Lasting environmental protection will occur only in the context of meaningful attention to the attainment of these other goals.

ACKNOWLEDGMENT

The Donner Canadian Foundation and the Great Lakes Laboratory for Fisheries and Aquatic Science provided funding support for the work on which this is based. Special thanks to Sue Crispin, The Nature Conservancy, Chicago, for her leadership in developing the GLBDS, and to the Nature Conservancy of Canada, Toronto. Thanks also to Robert Brander, Great Lakes Coordinator, U.S. National Park Service, and Gail Jackson, Lake Superior Binational Program, Environment Canada, who, as co-chairs of the Designations Committee of the Lake Superior Binational Program, are assisting with the exploration of the biosphere reserve concept for Lake Superior.

NOTES

1. John H. Hartig and Jack R. Vallentyne. 1989. Use of an ecosystem approach to restore degraded areas of the Great Lakes. Ambio 18: 423-428 and John H. Hartig and Michael A. Zarull (eds.). 1992. Under RAPs: Towards Grassroots Ecological Democracy in the Great Lakes Basin. University of Michigan Press, Ann Arbor.

2. Paul G. R. Smith. 1987. Towards the Protection of Great Lakes Natural Heritage Areas. Technical Paper No. 2. University of Waterloo, Heritage Resources Centre, Waterloo, Ontario.

3. Phil Weller. 1989. Natural Heritage Areas and Programs in the U.S. Great Lakes States. Report to the Science Advisory Board of IJC. Great Lakes Office, International Joint Commission, Windsor, Ontario.

4. Gary M. Allen, Paul F. G. Eagles and Steven D. Price. 1990. Conserving Carolinian Canada. University of Waterloo Press, Waterloo.

5. Sue Crispin. 1991. Using natural heritage data to monitor Great Lakes ecosystem health. Endangered Species Update 8(5/6):1-4.

6. IJC/SAB. 1989. 1989 Report. Great Lakes Scientific Advisory Board, International Joint Commission, Great Lakes Office, Windsor, Ontario.

7. IJC. 1989. Fifth Biennial Report on Great Lakes Water Quality. International Joint Commission, Washington, D.C. and Ottawa.

8. David Rankin. 1993. Personal communication. The Nature Conservancy, Great Lakes Office, Chicago.

9. Sally Lerner and Susanna Reid. 1993. A study of Ontario environmental stewardship groups. In Sally Lerner (ed.). Environmental Stewardship. Geography Publications Series No. 39. University of Waterloo, Waterloo, Ontario.

10. Smith, op. cit.

11. Kenneth A. Gould. 1991. The sweet smell of money: economic dependency and local environmental political mobilization. Society and Natural Resources 4:133-150; Susan H. Mackenzie. 1993. Ecosystem management in the Great Lakes: some observations from three RAP sites. Journal of Great Lakes Research 19: 136-144; and Betsy K. Landre and Barbara A. Knuth. (1993) Success of citizen advisory committees in consensus-based water resource planning in the Great Lakes basin. Society and Natural Resources 6:229-257.

12. See for example, Wendy E. Hudson (ed.). 1991. Landscape Linkages and Biodiversity. Island Press, Washington, D.C.

13. IJC/RAB. 1978. The Ecosystem Approach: Scope and Implications of an Ecosystem Approach to Transboundary Problems in the Great Lakes Basin. Special Report of the Great Lakes Research Advisory Board to the IJC. International Joint Commission, Great Lakes Office, Windsor, Ontario and Allen et al., op. cit.

14. Zev Naveh. 1991. Some remarks on recent developments in landscape ecology as a transdisciplinary ecological and geographical science. Landscape Ecology 5:63-75 and NWF. 1993. Saving all

the Pieces: Protecting Biodiversity in the Lake Superior Region. National Wildlife Federation, Great Lakes Natural Resource Center, Ann Arbor.

15. George Francis, A.P. Grima, Henry A. Regier, and T.H. Whillans. 1985. A Prospectus for the Management of the Long Point Ecosystem. Technical Report No. 43. Great Lakes Fishery Commission, Ann Arbor and Shimizu et al. in this volume.

16. Revised Great Lakes Water Quality Agreement as amended by Protocol signed 18 November 1987. Consolidated by the International Joint Commission, United States and Canada. Article II.

17. Clayton J. Edwards and Henry A. Regier (eds.). 1990. An Ecosystem Approach to the Integrity of the Great Lakes in Turbulent Times. Special Publication 90-4. Great Lakes Fishery Commission, Ann Arbor; For example IJC/CGLRM. 1991. A Proposed Framework for Developing Indicators of Ecosystem Health for the Great Lakes Region. Council of Great Lakes Managers Report to the IJC. International Joint Commission, Washington D.C. and Ottawa; IJC Task Force. 1991. Towards a State of the Great Lakes Basin Ecosystem Report. Discussion Draft, Report of a Task Force. International Joint Commission, Great Lakes Office, Windsor, Ontario; James Kay. 1991. A non-equilibrium thermodynamic framework for discussing ecosystem integrity. Environmental Management 15(4):483-495; and Stephen Woodley, James Kay and George Francis (eds.). 1993. Ecological Integrity and the Management of Ecosystems. St. Lucie Press, Delray Beach, FL.

18. RAAS. 1989. Towards an Ecosystem Charter for the Great Lakes-St. Lawrence. Occasional Paper No. 1. The Rawson Academy of Aquatic Science, Ottawa; GLC. 1993. Draft Elements of an Ecosystem Charter for the Great Lakes St. Lawrence Basin. Public Review Document. Great Lakes Commission, Ann Arbor.

19. Francesco DiCastri, Malcolm Hadley, and Jeanne Damlanian. 1981. MAB: the Man and Biosphere Programme as an evolving system. Ambio 10(2-3):52-57; UNESCO/MAB. 1988. Man Belongs to Earth: International Cooperation for Environmental Research. UNESCO, Paris.

20. George Francis. 1990. MAB and the Great Lakes: Towards a Binational MAB Programme for a Biogeographic Province. Discussion Draft, MAB, Ottawa.

21. IJC. 1992. Sixth Biennial Report on Great Lakes Water Quality. International Joint Commission, Washington, D.C. and Ottawa.

22. LSTF. 1991. A Binational Program to Restore and Protect Lake Superior. Lake Superior Task Force. U.S. Environmental Protection Agency, Chicago and Environment Canada, Toronto.

23. Edward Grumbine. 1990. Protecting biological diversity through the Greater Ecosystem concept. Natural Areas Journal 10(3): 114-117 and Tim W. Clark, Elizabeth D. Amato, Donald G. Whittemore, and Ann H. Harvey. 1991. Policy and programs for ecosystem management in the Greater Yellowstone Ecosystem: an analysis. Conservation Biology 5(3):412-422.

24. George Francis, John J. Magnuson, Henry A. Regier and Daniel R. Talhelm. 1979. Rehabilitating Great Lakes Ecosystems. Technical Report No. 37. Great Lakes Fisheries Commission, Ann Arbor, p. 72.

25. William Ashworth. 1986. The Late, Great Lakes: An Environmental History. Collins, Toronto and Wayne State University Press, Detroit and Phil Weller. 1990. Fresh Water Seas. Between the Lines Press, Toronto.

26. Jack Manno. 1993. Advocacy and diplomacy in the Great Lakes: a case history of non-governmental-organization participation in negotiating the Great Lakes Water Quality Agreement. Buffalo Environmental Law Journal 1:2-61.

27. GLU. 1987. Unfulfilled Promises: A Citizens' Review of the International Great Lakes Water Quality Agreement. Great Lakes United, Buffalo; Manno, op. cit., p. 39. Ron Shimizu and USEPA's Kent Fuller took the lead in drafting the 1987 Protocol of the GLWQA.

28. IJC. 1989. Fifth Biennial Report on Great Lakes Water Quality. International Joint Commission, Washington, D.C. and Ottawa.

17

Baltic Europe: Environmental Management in Context

RAFAL SERAFIN AND JERZY ZALESKI

The Baltic Sea has been the focus of multinational environmental management for over twenty years.[1] The Gdansk Convention on the Use of Living Resources of the Baltic Sea (1973) and the Helsinki Convention on Environmental Protection of the Baltic Sea (1974) have been portrayed frequently as the forerunners of comprehensive environmental planning for enclosed coastal seas in other parts of the world.[2] The United Nations Regional Seas Programme has long pointed to Baltic Sea management arrangements as a model for others to follow.[3]

There is little question that these arrangements have had great symbolic and practical value as a basis for international negotiation on resource management and environmental planning. Since the Baltic region was the main theater of the Cold War, the significance of any environmental cooperation should not be underestimated. Yet, after over twenty years of concerted environmental management and planning under the auspices of the two Conventions, official reports suggest that "environmental pollution of the Baltic Sea has reached proportions that may cause irreversible damage to a sea which some 80 million people use in their economic activities and for recreation."[4] Thus Baltic management arrangements represent only the initial steps in a necessary long-term evolution. To identify the direction of the next steps, it is worth reflecting on links between environmental management and the broad political and economic context within which they must take place.

Thinking about Baltic environmental management in such broad terms is timely since the major environmental investment program of the next quarter century, the Baltic Sea Joint Comprehensive Programme, is being launched with funding from the World Bank, the European Bank for Reconstruction and Development, the Nordic Bank and the European Union (EU), and national governments of the nine nations that surround the Baltic. The Programme aims to reverse environmental degradation of the Baltic Sea by investing an estimated 18 billion European Currency Units (ECU) over the period 1993-2012 in correcting the worst point sources of pollution and controlling non-point sources in agriculture and industry.[5]

With over 20 years of Baltic environmental management experience and a Programme planning horizon of 25 years, it is fruitful to examine the prospects for the Baltic ecosystem in relation to its political and economic context. This is particularly important given the growing tendency internationally to link the complex of coastal issues, such as the use of biological and mineral resources, coastal management, marine safety, pollution control, and so on to the jurisdiction of coastal nations. The Baltic Sea, perhaps more than any other sea, does not fit well into this formula. Due to its size and shape the Baltic must be an exception to the general rules. Indeed, the insensitivity to local political and economic circumstances appears to be one of the reasons why many nations refuse to ratify the Law of the Sea.

Following the identification of alarming trends in the environmental degradation of the world's coastal seas, numerous programs are being launched to reverse these trends.[6] A focus for these activities is the United Nations Agenda 21 program, and the development of the Environmental Management of Enclosed Coastal Seas (EMECS) initiative begun in Hyogo Prefecture, Japan.[7] As many coastal seas are set in multijurisdictional settings, often in complex economic and political contexts, learning from Baltic experience is of considerable interest.

The Baltic Sea has a 1.5 million square km drainage basin that now includes nine Baltic nations: Denmark, Estonia, Finland, Germany, Latvia, Lithuania, Poland, Russia, and Sweden (see Figure 17.1). The Sea itself is relatively small, shallow, and similar to freshwater in its characteristics. Indeed, it is reminiscent more of an estuary constituting the outflow of the drainage areas of central and northern Europe to the North Sea. Its coasts are densely populated: nearly 75 percent of the Baltic Europe population lives within 100 km of the sea coast. Many great cities, including massive port-industrial conurbations such as St. Petersburg (with its five million inhabitants) and five capitals lie directly on the coast. There is a growing need to coordinate efforts to improve coastal management to limit the disorderly expansion of coastal conurbations. Many of the major rivers flowing into the Sea are now almost completely urbanized at their mouths, concentrating industrial and municipal pollution. The Gdansk and Finish Bays are now heavily degraded, beaches are deteriorating, recreation values are plummeting and natural landscapes are fast disappearing.[8]

The Gdansk Convention (1973) and the Helsinki Convention (1974) contain the basic formula for Baltic Sea management. Both are now being renegotiated in response to the abrupt changes in the political and economic map of Central Europe following the collapse of the communist system in the late 1980s and the reassertion of sovereignty by the southern Baltic nations. When first signed, the Conventions did not meet all expectations, but they have formed a basis for working together on new legal and administrative formulas for enclosed coastal sea management. Indeed, the Conventions could be the antecedents of a broader Baltic agreement regulating the use of the Sea in ways consistent with sustainability principles. The Helsinki Convention was redrafted in 1992 to extend the Baltic environmental management arrangements to coastal waters and inland areas and to heighten the emphasis on biological components.[9]

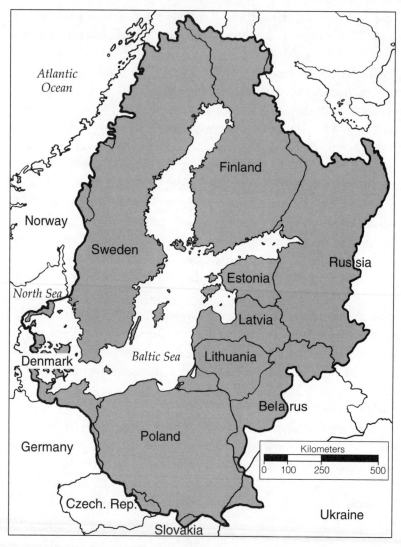

Figure 17.1. The watershed and political divisions of Baltic Europe.

With many decades of research on the Baltic Sea and over twenty years of multinational environmental management, one might well ask about the prospects of reversing trends of environmental degradation in the Baltic Sea. Giving an answer is not easy. Although the Baltic is one of the more intensively studied seas of the world, understanding of its ecological functioning remains incomplete. A great deal is known about various physical, chemical, and biological phenomena that occur in the Baltic Sea basin.[10] However, this amounts to appreciating symptoms rather than improving understanding of the causes or processes that drive degradative changes. Studying symptoms is important because it helps in preparing a diagnosis, but the aim of any treatment must be directed to eliminating causes. This means explicitly addressing economic and political matters in environmental management.

The broader economic and political implications of redesigning the Baltic environmental management regime are only slowly coming to be explored seriously.[11] Opportunity exists for using an integration between ecology and economics to add new impetus to redesigning political and economic alliances across the Baltic for a new Baltic environmental management regime. In the context of the 1992 United Nations Earth Summit and new international environmental conventions on biodiversity and climate change, it appears that an unprecedented platform exists for redefining international relations across the Baltic Sea.[12]

THE BALTIC SEA JOINT COMPREHENSIVE ENVIRONMENTAL ACTION PROGRAMME

The Baltic Programme now being implemented assumes that, given a more comprehensive focus, data gathering efforts in the Baltic states will be more effectively integrated and extended to coastal and inland areas. The intended result, a more reliable and comprehensive assessment of environmental degradation, could provide the basis for policy and planning to achieve significant environmental improvements within two decades. In this pragmatic spirit, a series of studies identified 132 hot spots, associated mainly with industry, throughout the drainage basin.[13] Almost 100 of these are in former communist states. Half are in Poland which is thus due to receive a significant amount of funding support. Approximately 4 billion ECU of a total of 8.5 billion is earmarked for the southern Baltic. The Programme earmarks an additional 14 billion ECU for monitoring and emergency response systems, reducing municipal and industrial pollution (particularly with regard to effluent into municipal sewage and waste water systems), controlling effluent and emissions from industrial sources such as the pulp and paper industry, improving waste management and reducing associated environmental risks and air pollution. Much of this is to be spent in southern Baltic countries. In all, about 5 billion ECU is earmarked for the 1993-97 period with a further 13 billion for 1998-2012.[14]

In the complex international management situation that persists around the Baltic, however, there is considerable pressure to define or diagnose the Baltic pollution problem as narrowly as possible — preferably in engineering terms. This is expedient for both research and policy communities which must account for resources committed to their respective constituencies. When outcomes are not easily attributable to specific policies or programs, as with environmental quality where improvements may take a generation or more to attain, such expediency is hard to resist. For example Poland constructed approximately 1200 sewage plants between 1989 and 1994. This effort constitutes a significant contribution to environmental improvement in the context of past neglect, but is increasingly seen as too little and too late when compared to the task of restoring and maintaining the life-support capability of the Baltic Sea ecosystem and the challenge of restructuring polluting industries across the Baltic drainage basin. Indeed, the Programme is meeting with little enthusiasm at the national government level, which is cause for concern since the greater part of the funding is to be spent in Poland.[15]

Environmental management activities are inevitably shaped by a wide range of human activities that prevail in specific areas, including political imperatives, contextual and resource limitations, as well as difficulties in problem definition for strategic policy-making. The broad context within which environmental management must take place is typically taken for granted and is seldom considered an opportunity or a constraint for securing environmental improvement.[16] More than ever before, the broad context must be explicitly included in Baltic environmental management if necessary public support and required funding are to be mobilized. Only widespread political support will assure that the Programme is implemented and sustained for the decades necessary to achieve significant benefits because the funding, largely from international lending institutions in the form of low-interest loans, must be paid back, requiring contributions from national funds. Without long-term public support and given the wide array of problems arising from the economic and political reform process, political pressures may reallocate the funds, thus assigning different priorities in national policy and planning. In Poland, for example, the Baltic Sea may simply not become a priority for the miners and their families in southern Poland unless they come to see themselves as part of a Baltic Sea ecosystem.

ADDRESSING THE POLISH CONTEXT

Poland is the key to the environmental future of the Baltic Sea: it lies almost entirely within the Baltic's drainage basin and its 40 million people make up half the basin's population. Moreover, of all the Baltic countries, Poland has the most extensive agricultural area and the most concentrated industrial complexes discharging wastes into the air and water of the Baltic Sea. Thus, reforms in Polish agriculture and industry will inevitably impact the Baltic Sea. The challenge is to relate Baltic environmental management concerns to the mainstream of Polish economic and political reforms: in short, how to see them as opportunities not problems. Thus far the Baltic Programme has failed, at least in its initial stages, to achieve this. Appeals of organizations, such as the Coalition Clean Baltic, for policy and planning in agriculture, forestry, aquaculture, mineral resource extraction, transportation, military activity, energy generation, and industrial activities to take Baltic Sea protection into account appear to have provoked little Polish response, or have been met with, "yes, but who will pay?"[17]

The Baltic Programme appears necessary to improve the environmental status of the Baltic Sea, but it is not sufficient to restore and maintain environmental values over the long run. Proponents may argue that the Programme was not intended to be the basis of a new kind of environmental management, but only a contribution to the extension and coordination of existing national programs and policies. This reasoning may be applicable to Denmark or Sweden with their stable governments and a history of Baltic Sea policy and planning, but the situation is quite different on the southern Baltic where governments are unstable and there is little in the way of established and well defined national institutions active in the environmental management of the Baltic Sea.

One reason for the seemingly dismal prospects for the Baltic Programme is its basis on a continuation of past research and management arrangements which, at least on the southern side of the Baltic, have all but collapsed. The assumption is that past policy failed due to political expediency and lack of resources, rather than because the environmental problem was defined too narrowly or misdiagnosed altogether. As a result, there is little motivation to seek a new diagnosis and vision — something desperately needed in the southern Baltic where a constituency must be built to keep environmental management of the Baltic Sea at the heart of ongoing economic and political reforms.[18]

The lukewarm Polish response to the Baltic Programme is perfectly rational and justified, when seen in terms of the economic and political upheaval within the reform process. To develop a constituency of support in Polish society the Programme must become more sensitive and responsive to broader political and economic issues concerning the nature and direction of reform. If this cannot be achieved marine environmental research and management, at least in Poland, appears destined for, at best, secondary consideration in national policy and planning. The contemporary Polish context, however, does offer an opportunity for casting the Baltic Programme in a broader framework that could potentially mobilize widespread support. Indeed, the Baltic Programme may yet be the impetus for seizing the opportunity offered by political and economic reform in the southern Baltic to redefine environmental management of the Baltic Sea. But to seize the opportunity, the Programme must move the nine Baltic nations away from a narrowly defined environmental focus toward the economic and political concerns shaping the region's future.

Early Polish economic and political reforms intended to meet the criteria for EU membership have prompted neglect of Baltic Sea environmental issues.[19] Attention has been focused on environmental restoration and effluent control. There has also been growing interest in designating new parks and protected areas along Poland's coast, including marine reserves. To date, however, there has been little central government interest in seizing the opportunities for trade and industrial restructuring offered through closer ties with other Baltic countries. Polish diplomatic efforts have also neglected Scandinavia in favor of EU countries and others further afield.[20]

Conversely, in their efforts to renew their links with the nations of the southern Baltic, the northern Baltic countries have tended to focus on environmental matters to the neglect of broader economic, political, and security issues. They have been preoccupied with reducing environmental impacts of the southern Baltic countries, rather than seeing these as linked to longer-term economic opportunities. In addition, there is a lack of experience in dealing with these countries. During the Cold War years, for example, Sweden focused its international environmental work in other parts of the world to the neglect of the Baltic. Furthermore, as communism collapsed, the Scandinavian countries were renewing their efforts to join the EC and so saw similar aspirations among the southern Baltic countries as obstacles to achieving this.

There are signs of growing interest in Poland in redefining environmental relationships across the Baltic Sea in economic terms, perhaps through the construction of a common vision for environmental, economic, and political repositioning of the Baltic region in the context of an integrated Europe. The reasons for this interest are the following:

1. To date, economic reform has focused on privatization and markets as ends and not means. A vision of a desirable future is timely because privatization has become widely

questioned and opposed as inadequate as an end in itself. The ex-communist government elected in October 1993 decelerated many reforms and reviewed the privatization program.

2. Administrative reform currently underway will re-organize Poland's 49 administrative regions (województwa) into smaller, self-governing administrative units. There is concern in coastal areas that this will prompt further decline of marine and coastal issues in national policy and planning.

3. Restructuring of marine-based industry is producing unemployment and economic recession in coastal areas, and demonstrating the need for explicit strategies to invigorate failing coastal economies.

4. Land development for residential use and second homes is increasing the stress on valuable coastal habitats and ecosystems and there is growing recognition that coastal land use planning and management is needed to avoid cumulative destruction of valuable coastal areas.

5. Offshore oil and mineral prospecting is threatening coastal habitats and is not well coordinated with environmental protection measures.

6. Despite political declarations and environmental investments, beaches and coastal waters continue to be too polluted for swimming in many areas, leading to public conviction that existing efforts at environmental management have not been sufficient.

7. Poland's prospects for membership in the EU, and its associated economic benefits, appears more remote than they did in 1989 and 1990. Moreover, in other Baltic countries (Denmark and Sweden) there was disagreement about the benefits of EU membership. With the emergence of a stronger Russia, geopolitical alternatives are being sought more actively than ever. Indeed, such activities may serve to strengthen negotiations over EU membership for all the Baltic Sea nations.

BALTIC EUROPE IN EUROPEAN INTEGRATION

Groel Thurdin, Swedish Minister of Environment, stated the following at a 1992 meeting of Baltic Environment Ministers: "We are united by the Baltic Sea but from most other aspects we are separated. This must change. But this change cannot come if we don't invent a common strategy. And for that we need a daring and far-seeing vision." The call for greater integration is tantamount to an appeal not to stop halfway in relations between the Baltic Sea countries; that is, to move beyond what Witold Andruszkiewicz, from Gdansk Technical University called "ecological courtship and cultural flirtation" to a more serious and harmonious "economic marriage."[21] Thus, practical steps to build a new Baltic Europe and give a new quality to international relations in the region are sorely needed.

Debate over the merits of a Baltic Europe could initiate a wider constituency from respective Ministries of Finance, Foreign Affairs, Industry and Trade, and others, as well as leaders in industry and agriculture to respond more explicitly to the challenge of environmental management of the Baltic Sea Basin. At the very least, such a debate might raise awareness among those in the southern industrial heartland of Poland that they too are part of the Baltic region, or that the reform of Polish agriculture will directly influence the environmental future of the Baltic Sea. A vision of the Baltic within its strategic and geopolitical context is needed to ensure Baltic environmental matters are kept within mainstream economic and political reform. Baltic issues must be moved into a public domain where the focus of concern and interest is not just water quality and effluent, but the everyday issues of economic and political life.[22]

Baltic Europe refers to an idea, born over 15 years ago, that there exists an identifiable economic region closely tied to the Baltic Sea ecosystem. The region contains a multitude of administrative and political jurisdictions associated with existing and potential economic interdependence that has an historical integrity and continuity.[23] The notion of a Baltic Europe — now coming to be taken seriously in Poland — is one response to the challenge of placing environmental management in the context of integrating social, diplomatic, cultural, political, and economic ties across the Baltic Sea. Since 1989, the number of Baltic nations has increased to nine and despite neglect at the diplomatic level a Baltic identity appears discernible.[24] There are numerous attempts to reactivate old ties and to initiate new ones. Recently, there have also been initiatives on the diplomatic front, and more beckon in the future. The Ministers' meeting in Karlskrona, Sweden in August, 1992 appears to have opened a new chapter of partnership among the countries surrounding the Baltic Sea. One of the key elements of this new era is the growing realization, still to be nurtured, of working together on a common vision or strategy.

The 1957 Treaty of Rome opened a new and ambitious era of economic partnership. The preamble of the Treaty declared that the EC was to provide member countries with conditions for rapid economic growth and sustainable development, eliminate regional disparities and promote balanced trade. In short, by establishing a common cause — a common internal market — the Treaty was to introduce a new quality to social and economic development in member countries.[25] Those who signed the Treaty of Rome openly declared that "this was a deliberate historic step into the future to build a common and united Europe" as the Belgian premier Paul Spaak put it.[26] There was much truth in these words, but the signatories may not all have had the same thing in mind. Many saw the Community as something of an extension of their own historical interests. "National Egotism" as Bismarck put it, has deep historical roots which are not easy to dismiss.[27] The Germans were interested in expanding markets for their products and calming the fears of their neighbors. The French saw the Community as a way to tie down their old German enemy, and subsidize French farmers. The Italians saw the possibility of seeking better administration and anchoring their democracy, whereas Greece, Spain, and Portugal saw the Community as a fast track to development. Indeed, the fundamentally pluralist character of the EU has proven able to accommodate widely ranging national interests that have sometimes been openly antagonistic. This pluralist character, coupled with a step-by-step approach to greater integration, has provided for robust institutional arrangements.

The impact of European integration on the Baltic region began in the autumn of 1959. The British forced passage of the European Free Trade Agreement (EFTA) which initially included the United Kingdom, Denmark, Norway, Sweden, Austria, Switzerland, Portugal, and later Finland. For these countries, it was unacceptable that the "Eurocrats" in Brussels could decide the future directions of European integration, granting preference to the initial six EC members. The same motivation led the Nordic countries in 1962 to revitalize the Nordic Council, which was created in 1952 by Denmark, Sweden, Norway, Finland, and Iceland to promote economic, social, cultural, and legal ties. The German Democratic Republic and Poland, as well as Lithuania, Latvia, and Estonia occupied by the Soviet Union, having all been forced to become part of the Soviet controlled Council of Mutual Economic Assistance, created in 1949, were simply left out of the EC orbit.

In early 1994, the EC was transformed into the twelve member EU, with only Denmark represented from among the Scandinavian countries. In 1972 and 1994 Norway rejected an offer to join the EU. Finland and Sweden, after holding referendums on EU membership in 1994, became members on January 1, 1995. The remaining Baltic countries, Estonia, Latvia, Lithuania, and Poland, have all applied to join the EU, perhaps through the mechanism of associate membership. In 1992 Poland signed an Association Treaty and on 1 February 1994 it became an Associate Member. This arrangement foresees a decade-long period of harmonization of institutions and regulations — de facto postponing membership far into the future. This will likely true for the three post-communist Baltic countries as well.

Of the Baltic countries, Germany has been a member since 1957 and Denmark since 1973. Denmark is symptomatic of the current European attitudes to integration via the EU model. It was in Denmark that significant cracks appeared in the march towards European unity. A referendum in 1992 on accepting the Maastricht Treaty on European Union was rejected and led to pan-European confusion, even debate, over the merits of Denmark leaving the Community. A second referendum was hurriedly organized in 1993 after intense pro-European campaigning leading to the negotiation of a variety of special treatment and opting out clauses to the Maastricht Treaty, subsequently adopted at an European Summit in Edinburgh. Pressure for further opting out arrangements proposed by other countries, especially regarding the proposed single European currency, may yet shake the edifice of European integration to the core.

The Danish situation showed the self-serving nature of national interest in the western countries, despite nearly thirty years of integration. Indeed, the campaign of opponents to a "Europe without Borders" is based on populist warnings that giving up national sovereignty to cosmopolitan bureaucrats will also lead to a loss of control over policy toward East and Central Europe. Poland is typically put forward as an example: "Brussels can invite new members whenever it wants, but we must keep them with our taxes" is the logic of the Eurosceptics. The argument strikes a chord of credibility with many and there appears to be an anti-EU tide rising across Europe.[28]

To counteract this trend, proponents of European Union have taken to promising benefits measurable at the household level. Pro-Europe campaigners in Denmark sought to show how the new Europe without Borders, without duties, currency exchange, or citizenship differences would benefit average families and how much would be lost should Denmark turn away. Despite the success of the second referendum, opinion polls showed that only two or three people in every 100 are aware of the opting out conditions negotiated in the Maastricht Treaty that allowed Danish ratification. This suggests that the Union has become too amorphous and remote from the day-to-day affairs of many Europeans. A smaller regional scale such as Baltic Europe appears to be at the geographical limits of a vision which can inspire a sense of identity and place. Perhaps the visions of a Baltic Europe can stem the loss of a sense of belonging that appears to be slipping away in the rush towards pan-European unity. Baltic Europe may be a timely initiative for revitalizing European Union.

Currently, each of the countries making up Baltic Europe is trying to cope with problems unanticipated even a few years ago.

No region in Europe has experienced such far reaching changes over the past fifty years as the Baltic region. The drama being played there has been the focus not only of European attention, but of the Cold War confrontation between the military super-powers. The important thing to remember is that during this period, the Baltic Sea separated its neighbors, rather than united them. Today, the nations of Baltic Europe have been left to find their own way and define their needs and strategy for the future — all in the context of the search for a new role amidst the disintegration of the "old" Europe on the one hand, and the struggle to cement an integration of a "new" Europe on the other. The current period is simultaneously one of upheaval, despair, and tragedy as in the case of former Yugoslavia, and one of great promise of a better future.

The lands surrounding the Baltic Sea contain an emerging plurality of ideas about the region's future that contrast with "business-as-usual" scenarios. In short, there appear to be the elements or pieces of a new common strategy that must yet be put together. Those involved inevitably seek to maximize their own national interest. In each case, economic and political options must be reviewed from this point of view. But in the context of a common coastal sea, it is necessary to avoid destructive competition by adopting a formula in international relations that is not prejudicial to the *common interests* of the Baltic Sea. All are convinced that close cooperation is necessary, but the means of achieving cooperation remains an open question after over fifty years of divisiveness. Solutions have to be sought on a common basis. Anyone left isolated from this search will simply have little influence on the resolution and compromises achieved. Thus a platform for communication must be sought at the international level. But just how to create this platform remains unclear. Indeed, the Baltic Environmental Programme will prove effective over the next quarter century to the extent that it can provide a foundation for broader political and economic cooperation across the region.

From the point of view of international law and arrangements, the situation around the Baltic has lost its past accent of confrontation encapsulated in the phrase *dominum maris Baltici*. Declining global imperialistic ambitions are reflected in international relations among the Baltic nations. At one time, the ambition of each nation was to act within larger alliances with limited interaction with one another. The Polish-Lithuanian Union (1385), after all, was forged to meet the threat of the Teutonic Knight, and the Kalmar Treaty (1397) was similarly motivated among Scandinavians to repel domination by the Hanseatic League. War was the instrument for resolving disputes and military domination of the region was the goal.

Today, there is little threat of armed conflict for supremacy of the Baltic. However, this does not mean there is a decline in national ambitions to dominate the region. What was once resolved through armed conflict is now being fought out in the domain of economic competition in bitter battles for contracts, licenses, patents, documentation, and "know-how." When military force no longer dominates, having your own vision or notion of economic development and marine strategy becomes all important. Those who do not possess and actively pursue such goals in contact with others are destined to lose out. But the vision of a common Baltic future must be rooted in a common point of departure; isolationism is a losing strategy. Thus there is a need to move towards a greater sense of identity for the nine Baltic states in order to search more effectively for a common policy or strategy for a Baltic contribution to building a new order in Europe.

The notion of a Baltic Europe was born out of a conviction that the region — more than the Mediterranean or Atlantic Europe — is an integrated region, precisely because the countries around the Baltic Sea are so intimately tied to this enclosed sea. However, aside from traditional ties among the Scandinavian countries, the Baltic countries are generally disinterested in one another. It is as if an invisible force directed policy and planning in economics and politics away from the Baltic. With the geopolitical changes now under way, this situation is now an artifact of the past, and the Baltic states must chart their common future.

Regional efforts to safeguard the environmental sustainability of the Baltic Sea are indispensable to the environmental and economic future of the Baltic region. Issues such as the economic use of the waters and sea bottom, coastal management and environmental protection can no longer be treated as local issues. However, what is now recognized as important is that such safeguards are essential to economic development and political stability. Moreover there is a growing realization that restoration and maintenance of life support capacity efforts must be paid for — the question is by whom. Since those living along the southern Baltic are no longer willing to pay with worsening food quality, higher incidence of illness, unemployment and declining quality of life, ecosystem health must be linked more directly and explicitly to the regeneration of economic activities in the transition process to more market-oriented economies and more democratically open societies.

ENVIRONMENT: THE KEY TO ECONOMIC INTEGRATION AND POLITICAL PLURALISM

A Baltic identity must be recreated out of something more than improved coordination of Baltic Sea resource use. A broader economic and even political integration appears warranted, with environmental quality as a point of departure. Most importantly, there may be an opportunity to improve coordination between coastal management and planning and long term investment policy, as well as macro-economic policies relating to the promotion of trade. Any common strategy will show its effectiveness in solving problems for mutual benefit. No single nation will give anything without clear self-interest, however persuasive the arguments over common benefits might appear. For the wealthy Scandinavian countries trying to overcome difficulties in penetrating industrialized country markets and having to compete against the EU, the U.S. and Japan for third world markets, it is not immediately obvious why integrating with the poor countries of the southern Baltic is likely to prove beneficial. These are countries burdened with debt, desperately trying to protect their trade balance and so striving to limit imports and force a more mercantile formula in trade.

The arithmetic of competitive advantage would show that partnership based even on conventional formulas of trade could be much improved across the Baltic. In any case, many of the interactions of past decades no longer apply. Invoking solidarity, goodwill, and altruism has little sense. This was demonstrated at an IUCN/WWF meeting on Baltic Nature held in the summer of 1993 in Nykoping, Sweden at which new marine and coastal reserves were proposed around the Baltic Sea. As the arguments for active protection were largely altruistically based or appealed to inherent rights or values of nature, there was little or no interest expressed on the Polish side, in spite of a large and diverse delegation.[29] Indeed, the argument for conservation is only now being put forward in terms of the economics of life support in international fora around the Baltic.[30]

Prospective partners are increasingly seeing the enterprise of restoring and maintaining the environmental quality of the Baltic Sea ecosystem in terms of practical economic benefits. Debates over nature protection that neglect economics appear increasingly insular. In fact, the basis for economic partnership across the Baltic Sea is already under construction through Scandinavian and German investments in the southern and eastern parts of the Baltic. The way forward lies in forging more systematic agreements that create attractive fiscal climates, tax credits, and simplification of legal requirements, duties, and other barriers; ones that recognize and account for the economic life-support value of the Baltic Sea ecosystem. The context of a Baltic Europe could serve as a rationale to break down administrative and other barriers to such initiatives giving them a regional scale, while also linking them to long term Baltic environmental quality concerns. Such investments would develop capital markets, thus overcoming one of the reasons for current economic paralysis and lack of interest in programs such as the Baltic Programme which may be seen in terms of generating more debt, rather than more wealth.

Social instability, growing unemployment, and fragile economic mechanisms threaten not only post-communist Baltic Europe, but the economic and political interests of all the Baltic nations.

The brain drain affecting the intellectual potential of Poland is also now affecting the Scandinavians. The threat of mass migrations across the Baltic to the wealthy countries may, if economic and political circumstances do not stabilize following the disintegration of the Soviet Union, create millions of refugees over the next decade, which would be tantamount to a social and economic catastrophe. As a result, there is growing interest on all sides to take action around the Baltic beyond a narrowly defined environmental field. For example, new possibilities appear to be opening up in the Southern and Eastern parts of the Baltic where new markets are being created. The Swedish, Danish, or Finnish markets are not closed to manufactured and consumer products from the south nor is the import of raw materials from the north unreasonable. The time when Sweden imported coal from the U.S. and Poland bought iron ore from Brazil must surely be over forever. If economies can become greener and sustain wealthier societies, then there is no better place to demonstrate this than the Baltic region.

BUILDING BALTIC EUROPE

Building Baltic Europe means somehow integrating a host of partial initiatives into a strategic whole based on a broad and pluralistic partnership between a wide range of interests. Indeed, the challenge is to make those interests more alike, without of course prejudicing their respective goals and integrity. One thing is clear, meeting such a challenge will require time, perhaps as much as two or three decades. The task requires impetus from a new vision, even one that may seem distant or difficult to realize. But such a vision is necessary for any development doctrine for rebuilding a nation, as in the southern Baltic, so that it can grow and compete successfully in the contemporary world. The Baltic Europe vision is inherently value-laden and must allow for changing needs and circumstances while providing a sound basis for long range planning. Intensifying economic and political ties, perhaps modestly at first, between the Baltic countries could help overcome the present system's inertia by injecting new life and making better use of a multitude of economic and other initiatives in the region.

In the late 1970s most of the Baltic countries created standing committees concerning the Baltic Sea to oversee implementation of the Gdansk and Helsinki Conventions. The environment has long provided a common platform or point of departure. Indeed, following the revolutions of 1989, it was environmental crises that initially brought together a series of high level meetings.[31] Each of these meetings resulted in a declaration stating that periodic meetings should continue and be expanded. Other initiatives include a Baltic Council formed in 1991 by Lithuania, Latvia and Estonia, and broader pro-Baltic activities include non-governmental, municipal, public, regional, and private initiatives. Some worthy of note include the Baltic Conference of Chambers of Commerce (1972), the Baltic Tourism Conference (1984), and the North Europe Club created by the government of Schleswig-Holstein (1989). There is also a Club of Baltic Nations at the International Maritime Organization and a Union of Baltic Cities has existed since 1991 and now includes 36 members and maintains a secretariat in Gdansk. Other interesting initiatives include the location of a Baltic Academy in Travemunde, Germany and there have even been suggestions to hold a Baltic Olympiad.

In 1988, a Conference of Rectors of Baltic Universities was created and there have been attempts to develop a Baltic-wide education programme called the Copernicus programme. Other more established initiatives include the Baltic University based in Uppsala and the Baltic Institute founded in Karlskrona in 1991. In addition, the Polish Baltic Institute in Gdansk is striving to return to its pre-war research tradition, and environmental groups in Lithuania, Latvia, and Estonia have been active in promoting basin-wide coastal research and planning. Also WWF publishes a *Baltic Bulletin* which is widely distributed in the region and coming to be an important vehicle for information exchange in the field of conservation.

Many local initiatives have blossomed in recent years in spite of the neglect of Baltic issues in broad economic and political strategy. A vision such as that offered by Baltic Europe may be a timely way to harness enthusiasm for common work toward restoring and maintaining the Baltic Sea ecosystem by linking them with the larger scale economic and political restructuring. A shared positive vision, however vague and distant, can help isolated initiatives to complement one another and integrate, thereby building on each others' strengths and adding impetus to securing common benefits.

One way to nurture a non-authoritarian vision of Baltic Europe in a more concerted fashion might be through an Ecosystem Charter for Baltic Europe. A Charter could help define a common institutional context and provide a vision for integrating a multitude of interests and initiatives, thus making the interconnections between the Baltic Sea ecosystem and the daily challenges of economic and political life more apparent and sensitive to local needs and circumstances.[32] An Ecosystem Charter for Baltic Europe could be little more than a short statement affirming citizens' rights and obligations in the Baltic region related to existing constitutions, legislation, and administrative practices of the Baltic nations. In effect, various ministerial meetings are already engaged in a process of Charter development. A draft version of such a Charter, based on applying relevant North American experience to the Baltic situation, is proposed here in Table 17.1.

The Charter could consolidate and add impetus to the integrative activities already underway in the region. The idea is, in effect, to restate a set of principles already accepted by governments, industry, non-government organizations, and polities with a "stake" in restoring and maintaining the Baltic Sea ecosystem.[33] In recent years, charters have been used to good effect to precipitate and nurture positive change in complex ecological, political, and economic situations, notably around the Great Lakes of North America. There are many different types of charters, but a common feature is their attempt to transcend short-term opportunities, constraints, and controversies in order to look normatively into what is desired in the long run.

Those intent on building a Baltic Europe might attempt to use an Ecosystem Charter to engage Baltic nations in a long-term enterprise of applying international norms explicitly to Baltic Sea ecosystem management.[34] These might include, for example, legal

Table. 17.1. An Ecosystem Charter for Baltic Europe.

Baltic Europe is where millions of Danish, Estonian, Finnish, German, Latvian, Lithuanian, Polish, Russian, and Swedish citizens share a portion of the global biosphere — the fundamental life-support system people share with all other living things. The Baltic Sea Ecosystem, which consists of the life, waters, air, and soils of the Baltic Sea and its drainage basin, is the basis of the life-support and natural capital of Baltic Europe. It is no more environmental than it is economic, social, cultural, and spiritual. It is all these things. It compels us forward, insisting that we seize our fundamental rights to human existence and challenges us to accept responsibility for our actions within a much larger order of things. It commits us to an ethic by which we measure progress based on quality, well-being, integrity, and dignity in the natural, social, and economic systems which we share and on which we depend for life-support.

As Baltic Europeans, we must have regard for the maintenance of the Baltic Sea ecosystem of which we are an integral part, and so we pledge:

- To promote all measures and behaviors necessary to achieve and maintain local, basin-wide, and global environments free from toxic and other degradations to the health, well-being, and enjoyment of all people and other living things now and in the future.

- To use and conserve the environment and natural resources of the Baltic Sea ecosystem in ways that meet our various needs individually, collectively, and corporately without compromising the ability of future generations to meet their needs.

- To accelerate the healing of damaged ecosystem components by restoring, rehabilitating, and protecting: (i) the ecological processes of the Baltic Europe ecosystem; (ii) its natural communities; and (iii) its populations of indigenous species of plants, animals and other forms of life.

- To accept responsibility for (i) maintaining the ecological processes and components of the Baltic Europe ecosystem; (ii) preserving biological diversity; (iii) following the principle of sustainable use of ecosystem resources.

- To promote the right to be informed and the responsibility to learn in a timely manner about (i) current conditions in the Baltic Europe ecosystem; (ii) any planned activity that might significantly affect the environment (including policy, enacting legislation and implementation); and (iii) equal access and due process in administrative and judicial proceedings.

- To cooperate in good faith with others living within the Baltic Europe ecosystem in implementing these obligations, and to cooperate with other people in other biogeographic regions to achieve mutual objectives consistent with the above.

principles for environmental protection and sustainable development formulated by the World Commission on Environment and Development, the UNEP World Charter for Nature, or the Helsinki Rules on the Use of Waters of International Rivers.[35] Other documents and experiences can be examined for their relevance in the Baltic, thereby enriching the Baltic Europe constituency building process. The "users" of the Charter would be the numerous citizen-oriented organizations and initiatives now emerging around the Baltic, all of whom share the implicit goal of integration across narrowly-defined boundaries of environmental management. In this way a Charter could serve to nurture integration processes already underway concerning political stability and economic restructuring in a way that assures restoration and maintenance of the Baltic Sea ecosystem.

ACKNOWLEDGMENT

Financial support from the EMECS '93 Secretariat and the Canadian Social Sciences and Humanities Research Council Grant are gratefully acknowledged.

NOTES

1. For an historical and comparative perspective, see Peter M. Haas. 1993. Protecting the Baltic and North Seas. In Peter M. Haas, Robert O. Keohane and Marc Levy (eds.). Institutions for the Earth. MIT Press, Cambridge, pp. 132-181.

2. For a review of the Baltic Sea Conventions and their related institutional context, see J. T. Koheonen. 1991. Protection of the marine environment of the Baltic Sea. Marine Pollution Bulletin 23: 543; George Francis. 1988. Institutions and ecosystem redevelopment in Great Lakes America with reference to Baltic Europe. Ambio 17(2):106-111; and OECD Environment Directorate. 1990. Review of the Effectiveness of the Helsinki Convention as a Tool for Integrated Coastal Resources Management. OECD, Paris.

3. GESAMP. 1990. The State of the Marine Environment. UNEP Regional Seas Report. No. 115. Blackwell, Oxford; UNEP. 1991. Status of Regional Agreements Negotiated in the Framework of the Regional Seas Programme. Rev. 3. UNEP, Nairobi.

4. HELCOM. 1991. The Baltic Sea Joint Comprehensive Programme. Interim Report of the Helcom Ad-Hoc High Level Task Force. Baltic Sea Environment Conference, Helsinki; see also U. Ehlin. 1993. The Environmental Situation in the Baltic Sea Region. Mimeo.

5. HELCOM. 1992. The Baltic Sea Joint Comprehensive Programme and Janusz Kindler 1992. Program ochrony Morza Baltyckiego i nowa Konwencja Helsinska (Baltic Sea Protection Programme and the New Helsinki Convention). Aura 9:4-7.

6. For an overview of environmental degradation in coastal seas see Mostafa Tolba, Osama A. El-Kholy, E. El-Hinnawi, Martin W. Holdgate, D. F. McMichael and Robert E. Munn. 1992. Coastal and Marine Degradation. In Mostafa Tolba et al. The World Environment 1972-1992: Two Decades of Challenge. Chapman & Hall, London, pp. 105-130.

7. A chapter of Agenda 21 is devoted to coastal seas initiatives. See UNCED. 1992. Protection of the oceans, all kinds of seas, including enclosed and semi-enclosed seas, and coastal areas and the protection, rational use and development of their living resources. In Agenda 21. UNCED, Conches, Switzerland.

8. For descriptions of the Baltic Sea and its regional situation see K. Lomniewski, W. Mankowski and Jerzy Zaleski. 1975. Morze Baltyckie (The Baltic Sea). Ossolineum, Wroclaw; Aarno Voipio (ed.). 1981. The Baltic Sea. Elsevier, Amsterdam, Oxford and New York; U. Varjo and W. Tietze. 1987. Norden: Man and Environment. Gebruder Borntraeger, Berlin and Stuttgart; and Aarno Rosemarin (ed.). 1988. Ecosystem Redevelopment. Ambio Special Issue. 17(2).

9. In the Polish context, see Narada Komisji na Szczeblu Ministrow Ochrony Srodowiska (Meeting of the Committee of Environment Ministers). 1994. Decyzje podjete przez Ministrow podczas konferencji ministerialnej 8 marca 1994 (Decisions taken by Ministers during the Ministers' conference in Helsinki on 8 March 1994), Warsaw; Bogumila Blaszkowska and Krzysztof Skora 1994. Obszary Morskie proponowane do wlaczenia w system obszarow chronionych Morza Baltyckiego (Marine areas proposed for inclusion in the protected area system of the Baltic Sea), Institute of Environmental Protection, Gdynia.

10. For one of the more definitive reviews of Baltic Sea science see Voipio, op. cit. or Fred Wulff (ed.). 1990. Large scale Environmental Effects and Ecological Processes in the Baltic Sea. Swedish Environmental Protection Agency, Stockholm.

11. Important work in this regard is underway under the auspices of the Beijer Institute of Ecological Economics at the Swedish Academy of Sciences in Stockholm. See, for example, Monica Hammer, Ann-Marie Jansson and Bengt Owe Jansson. 1993. Diversity, change and sustainability: implications for fisheries. Ambio 2-3: 97-105.

12. See Jerzy Zaleski. 1991. Long term socio-economic processes and marine ecosystem changes within Baltic Europe. Pp. 29-37 In Jerzy Jaskowski. (ed.). Baltyckie Forum Ekologiczne (Baltic Ecological Forum). Wydawnictwo Gdanskie, Sopot; B. Jalowiecki (ed.). 1992. Europa Baltycka (Baltic Europe). Studia Regionalne i Lokalne. Uniwersytet Warszawski Instytut Rozwoju Regionalnego i Lokalnego, Warsaw; Janusz Kreft. 12 January 1993. Pomruki Tygrysa (A tiger growls). Dziennik Baltycki.

13. See HELCOM. 1991. Interim Report on the State of the Coastal Waters of the Baltic Sea. Baltic Sea Environmental Commission, Helsinki; HELCOM. 1993. Second Baltic Sea Pollution Load Compilation. Baltic Sea Environment Commission, Helsinki and HELCOM. 1993. High Level Conference on Resource Mobilization. Gdansk, Poland, 24-25 March 1993. Baltic Sea Environment Commission, Helsinki; HELCOM. 1993. Summaries of the Prefeasibility Studies. Baltic Sea Environment Commission, Helsinki.

14. Kindler, op. cit.

15. Krystyna Forowicz. 1994. Wspolne Morze: 20 lat Konwencji Helsinskiej (A common sea: 20 years of the Helsinki Convention). Rzeczpospolita, March 18.

16. Rafal Serafin and Jerzy Zaleski. 1988. Baltic Europe, Great Lakes America and Ecosystem Redevelopment. Ambio 17(2):90-98.

17. World Wide Fund for Nature and Coalition Clean Baltic. 1992. NGO Statement on the Protection of the Environment of the Baltic Sea region, April 5-6. Helsinki; Coalition Clean Baltic. 1992. Baltic Sea Action Plan. Swedish Society for Nature Conservation, Stockholm.

18. The Baltic Sea has been recognized as a priority area for environmental investments in Poland and is one of four such areas in the debt-for-environment facility or Eco-Fund that has been created as part of Poland's debt renegotiation. However, to date the Fund and the Ministry of Environment have confined their efforts to engineering investments, notably in sewage and waste-water treatment. See, for example, Krystyna Forowicz. 1993. Ekofundusz wspiera 9 nowych projektow (Eco-Fund supports nine new projects). Rzeczpospolita, October 9-10.

19. There is a discernible trend in Polish reforms to pay less attention to the environmental dimension of economic reforms. A recent special survey of reform in Poland by The Economist failed to mention environmental considerations. See The Economist. 1994. Against the grain: a survey of Poland. The Economist, April 16. See also Rafal Serafin and Maciej Zebrowski. 1993. Environmental Management in Polish Economic and Political Reforms. Paper prepared for the international seminar on Environmental Management in a Transition to Market Economy: a Challenge to Business and Government, January 6-8. University of Geneva, Geneva.

20. Jerzy Zaleski. 1993. Ku wspolnocie Europy Baltyckiej (Towards a Baltic Europe community). Komunikaty Instytutu Baltyckiego 30(42):141-157 and Jerzy Zaleski. 1991. Polska lezy nad Baltykiem (Poland lies on the Baltic). Gazeta Gdanska, June 18.

21. Eugeniusz Pudlis. 1992. The Baltic factor. Warsaw Voice, January 19.

22. Jerzy Zaleski. 1993. Razem czy osobno? Przyczynek do koncepcji baltyckiej wspolnoty regionalnej (Together or separately? Steps to a Baltic Regional Community). Vision & Strategy 2010 around the Baltic. National Planning Bureau, Office of Regional Planning in Gdansk, Sopot and Marek Dutkowski, Tomasz Parteka, Witold Toczyski and Marian Turek. 1992. Makroregion Polnocny w Europie Baltyckiej (The Northern Macro Planning Region in the context of Baltic Europe). National Planning Bureau, Office of Regional Planning in Gdansk, Sopot.

23. Jerzy Zaleski and Czeslaw Wojewodka. 1977. Europa Baltycka (Baltic Europe). Ossolineum, Wroclaw and Gdansk; see also Serafin and Zaleski, op. cit.

24. Zaleski 1993, op. cit.; Zaleski and Wojewodka, op. cit.

25. For reviews of the EC integration experience see 1991. The European Revolution. The Economist pp. 56-60; and Rosemary P. Piper and Alan Reynolds. 1991. Lessons from the European experience. In Continental Accord: North American Economic Integration. The Fraser Institute, Vancouver, pp. 125-149.

26. Remarks on the occasion of the Treaty of Rome signing cited in Zalesky 1993, op. cit.

27. Cited in Zaleski 1993, op. cit.

28. George Soros has devoted much attention to the prospects of integration and disintegration in Europe and has tried to influence positive trends towards an open society through a network of foundations. For some of his ideas and motivations see George Soros. 1993. Nationalist Dictatorships Versus Open Society. Expanded version of a lecture delivered at the Harvard Club of New York on November 18, 1993. Soros Foundations, New York; George Soros. 1993. Prospect for European Disintegration. Speech delivered to the Aspen Institute, Berlin, September 29, 1993. Soros Foundations, New York; and George Soros. 1994. The Soros Foundations Network. Soros Foundations, New York.

29. The background documents for the conference are contained in: Britt Hagerhall Aniansson (ed.). 1993. Coastal and Marine Protected Areas in the Baltic Sea Region. Background Report to the Seminar on the Establishment, Protection and Effective Management of Coastal and Marine Protected Areas in the Baltic Sea Region, Nykoping, Sweden, 7-11 July 1993. World Wide Fund for Nature, Stockholm.

30. Carl Folke, Monica Hammer and Ann-Marie Jansson. 1991. Life support value of ecosystems: a case study of the Baltic Sea region. Ecological Economics 3:123-137.

31. Such meetings took place between Prime Ministers (Ronneby, 1990), Ministers of Foreign Affairs (Copenhagen, 1991; Helsinki, 1992) and Ministers of Transport, Planning and Environment (Karlskrona, 1992), and were followed up by a high-level conference on resource mobilization with international lending institutions (Gdansk, 1993).

32. For a review of the Charter approach see Rafal Serafin. 1988. On Designing an Ecosystem Charter for the Great Lakes Basin. Notes for a workshop held on May 16, 1988. University of Waterloo, Waterloo. See also the Rawson Academy. 1989. Towards an Ecosystem Charter for the Great Lakes-St. Lawrence. The Rawson Academy of Aquatic Science, Ottawa.

33. Ibid.

34. See VanDeveer in this volume for a discussion of the influence of transnational norms.

35. WCED. Our Common Future. 1987. Oxford University Press, Oxford; William A. Irwin. (ed.). 1988. The World Charter for Nature: Legislative History and Commentary. Schimdt-Verlag, West Berlin and International Law Association. 1966. Helsinki Rules on the Uses of the Waters of International Rivers. International Law Association, London

18

Networks of Knowledge and Practice: Global Civil Society and Protection of the Global Environment

Ronnie D. Lipschutz

The Earth's environment is under stress. Of this, there is little question. Who degrades the environment? Why do they do it? The answers to these questions may seem obvious, but are they? What is to be done? Who is to do it? Who *can* do it? Here the questions are much more problematic. What, after all, do we mean by "global environment?" For that matter, what do we mean by "global?" Thinking about these questions — let alone finding answers — requires a reconsideration of their framing and meaning. Not only do we need to better understand the physics and biology of environmental degradation, we must also come to comprehend its sociology and politics, for, although we might bemoan the crudities and imprecision of the global circulation models that warn us of the possibilities of climate change, our understandings of human social behavior and change are far cruder. Still, it is social change that will be needed if the Earth's environment is to be protected and sustained. The degree of change required may be small or large; that remains to be seen. The *process* of change, however, is happening and it can be observed.

Describing and analyzing such social change, and its policy implications, is the goal of this chapter. There are three parts. First, I examine the question: what do we mean by "global environment?" What are the implications of our meanings for the policy process, especially when we "globalize" them? I will suggest that, although holism is essential to our analysis, so is particularism, especially with respect to those parts that we experience firsthand, rather than vicariously or intellectually. In other words, the particularism and diveristy found at the local level is essential for attempts to address "global" environmental issues and change. The central proposition is that global environmental change is a social process, rather than a physical one, and this introduces even greater complexity into policy than is ordinarily imagined. In the second part I take up the question of knowledge and practice where environmental protection is concerned, and its relationship to this *social complexity*. I argue that groups of people, working collectively in pursuit of environmental goals, are beginning to add up to a whole greater than the sum of its parts, and that this phenomenon has great potential where environmental protection is concerned. How can we explain such collective action, especially in the face of analyses that tell us it is not possible?[1] I call this form of action "global civil society," inasmuch as it is neither state-centric nor private, but conceptually and explicity transnational.[2] Finally, in the third part of this chapter, I offer brief case studies of efforts by civil society in Hungary to protect the Danube and other rivers and tributaries, and similar efforts in the United States directed toward the Chesapeake Bay and its associated rivers, and discuss how these civil societies have become linked into global civil society.

GLOBAL ENVIRONMENTAL CHANGE AND SOCIAL COMPLEXITY

According to the National Academy of Sciences:

> Global environmental changes are alterations in natural (e.g., physical or biological) systems whose impacts are not and cannot be localized. Sometimes the changes in question involve small but dramatic alterations in systems that operate at the level of the

whole earth, such as shifts in the mix of gases in the stratosphere or in levels of carbon dioxide and other greenhouse gases throughout the atmosphere. We speak of global change of this sort as *systemic* in nature because change initiated by actions any-where on earth can directly affect events anywhere else on earth. Other times, the changes in question result from an accretion of localized changes in natural systems, such as loss of biological di-versity through habitat destruction and changes in the bound-aries of ecosystems resulting from deforestation, desertification or soil drying, and shifting patterns of human settlement. Global changes of this sort we describe as *cumulative* in nature; we can consider them global because their effects are worldwide, even if the causes can be localized…The boundary between systemic and cumulative change is not sharp; it depends on how rapidly an environmental change spreads in space.[3]

This description contains a set of phenomena whose origins are obscured by a focus on the *physical* mediation of the changes in question; the human element is almost entirely absent, except for two brief references to "events" and "shifting patterns of human settlement." This does not mean that the study itself ignores the human element but, rather, that this, a most concise description of "global environmental change," does.

This is not a minor error of omission, inasmuch as global envi-ronmental change is better understood as a *social* phenomenon, rather than a "natural" one. As a social phenomenon, it results from specific human activities, embedded in institutional practices that, in many cases, have become second nature by virtue of long years of habit.[4] These practices are not discrete, uncoupled ones; in many instances, they are embedded in a whole range of "nested" institutions and linked to a variety of other similar practices, each of which appears, at least at first glance, essential to the more-or-less continued functioning, and reproduction, of society.

In other words, as a social process, global environmental change is the result of human agency operating within long-lived social structures. Thus practices are often automatic but changes are possible, if not absolutely demanded, where those practices lead to environmental degradation.[5] The ordinary focus on physical changes rests on the fact that, however complex they may be, they are infinitely simpler and easier to measure or analyze than are social interactions. Given sufficient memory and time, super-computers can produce fairly credible, albeit crude, approximations of how climate might change under certain specified conditions. There are no computers that can do the same for human societies.

Thus most analyses of global environmental change end up meaning global climate change, ozone depletion, tropical deforestation, and loss of biodiversity, phenomena thought to have global import. As a social process, however, global environmental change is a much more complex phenomenon, in terms of both its causes and consequences. Indeed, the term "global environmental change" itself conceals as much as it reveals, since it seems to relegate "local" environmental problems to another realm of behavior and politics, and presumes that "global" problems can be handled through a top-down process of centralized management.[6]

In part, the separation between "global" and "local" phenomena is the result of boundary-drawing exercises with roots in history and political economy. What, after all, makes powerplant pollution in one part of North America a "transnational" problem even as, in another part of the same continent, it is a domestic one? Why is soil erosion the "fault" of farmers, if they are all exposed to similar global market conditions? And why, if toxic wastes are generated by an electronics firm whose products are sold around the world, is their disposal a strictly local matter? From this perspective, use of the term "global" in "global climate change" confuses rather than clarifies. First, global climate change will be a secondary consequence of a broad range of localized human activities that are also implicated in other forms of environmental degradation.[7] Second, while global climate change is, indeed, mediated via a physical system of planetary dimensions, its effects are likely to be highly localized, in both physical and social terms. Third, the term makes no distinction between so-called subsistence- and luxury-based causes. Finally, add to this differences in social capacities within even very small regions, and it becomes clear that impacts could well have very different consequences on dimensions as small as one city block.

The way in which we conceptualize environmental problems thus has a great deal of influence on how we try to address them; more than this, some conceptualizations reinforce structural biases already present.[8] Global perspectives allow us to see the big picture, but they wipe out the micro-level details where agency meets structure, so to speak, and where people live.[9] I use the term *social complexity* — intended to capture the intricate webs of social and productive relations within human societies and among them — as one way of thinking about these micro-macro linkages and their social consequences.[10] This framework is relevant because many of the relationships between local causes and global effects arc the result of coupling between particular economic and political arrangements at the local, national, and global levels, with so-called local ecosystems tied to them and vice versa, through complex, transnational networks of exploitation (of people and nature), transaction, and exchange. For example, deforestation, even in temperate regions of the world, not only results in net emissions of carbon dioxide into the atmosphere (so long as replanting does not take place), it can also contribute to soil erosion, water pollution, and loss of habitat and biodiversity; each of these has different social consequences that depend on the histories, political economies, and social structures of the groups involved in causation.[11]

Globally-linked biogeophysical systems can, of course, aggregate the effects of local sources of pollutants, such that the consequences of an increase in atmospheric carbon dioxide, coming from a multitude of fossil fuel-burning systems, may be redistributed in ways that vary dramatically with locale as, for example, changes in regional climate regimes alter precipitation rates or coastal flooding due to sea level rise. When viewed in narrowly physical terms, soil erosion can be seen as a local phenomenon occurring simultaneously in many places across the planet. But such local physical changes may be linked to each other through various global connections, both in terms of causes (e.g., global market pressures) and consequences (e.g., global food productivity and distribution).[12] Species extinction is, in part, a side-effect of the destruction of ecosystems, many of which are exploited under pressure from global systems as well as national and local ones.[13]

This does not mean, however, that environmental problems are unbounded; lines can and should be drawn. Although the consequences of certain activities may be manifested or mediated via physical and social systems of global extent, the actual activities contributing to these effects tend to be bounded both in social, economic, and physical terms. As Ronald Herring points out: "[A]ll local arrangements for dealing with natural systems are embedded in a larger common interest defined by the reach of eco-systems beyond localities."[14] Thus local systems of production and consumption are nested within larger ones, together comprising networks of resource users and polluters, rather than being either discrete or totally-aggregated systems. These networks, moreover, are embedded in overlapping but not necessarily coterminous social, political, economic, and physical spaces.[15] Thus, environmental change is, somehow, integral to social processes, and not exogenous. Indeed, as anthropologists, ecologists, and rural sociologists are increasingly coming to recognize, even "Nature" is rarely natural; where human beings have lived, they have, inevitably, engaged in a continuous pattern of transforming what they have found there.[16] Environmental change itself is, consequently, not a new phenomenon; if we regard the demographic consequences of the European expansion as a form of environmental "change," even global scope is not new.[17]

The articulation of global environmental change in these terms implies an approach to understanding and dealing with various types of environmental degradation not as international problems, as they are often treated, but as the outcome of operation of myriads of "resource regimes" at different levels of analysis.[18] These regimes are interlinked, moreover, in the sense that the inputs of some are outputs of others. Richard Norgaard notes the implications of such structural relations:

> While institutions [for sustainability] will have to be locally tai-
> lored to support ecosystem-specific technologies, local institu-
> tions, nonetheless, will still have to mesh with regional and glob-
> al institutions designed to capture the gains of ecosystem
> management on a larger scale and to prevent untoward broader
> consequences of local decisions.[19]

How, then, might the foregoing observations play out in terms
of addressing environmental degradation? Or, to restate questions
posed at the beginning of this chapter: What is to be done? Who is
to do it? Who *can* do it?

There is a growing body of functional evidence suggesting that
environmental protection and conservation of resources might be
accomplished more efficiently and effectively through efforts at the
local level (international coordination problems notwithstanding).
There is also an analytical justification for this approach, based on
the structure and nature of resource-using "regimes" or social institutions. If we regard a social institution as, first, an embodiment of
power relations within a society and, second, having as one of its
primary goals production and its own "reproduction" over time,
the possibilities of significant, large-scale reform, in the absence of
major crisis, would appear to be severely circumscribed. At the international level, environmental regimes are hardly likely to impose on states the obligation to seriously alter domestic social institutions; indeed, this is why so much attention is paid to economic
"incentives" as a means of changing consumer behavior on a large
scale.[20] Such incentives leave untouched fundamental structures of
and relationships in society and, in many instances, impose costs
on those who are in no position to challenge these social relations
and relations of production.[21]

Moreover, incentives legislated at a distance may produce behavior or outcomes quite different from those intended.[22] In trying to modify behavior within social institutions through legislative and fiscal mechanisms, one is, in essence, recreating the relationships that caused the environmental degradation in the first
place. In other words, if we regard resource regimes and social in-

stitutions as arrangements intended to maintain and reproduce structural relations of power within societies, in addition to facilitating collective action and cooperation (as is more commonly assumed), we need to ask what might be the appropriate level and scale of efforts intended to reconstruct collective behavior and social relations not only instrumentally but also structurally.

This, then, is the analytical basis for a focus on local action and, as we shall see, there is a growing number of cases in which resource regimes are being reconstructed at a local level, and which bear a striking resemblance to common property resource regimes.[23] The functional argument for focusing locally rests on five points related to the foregoing analysis: (1) scale of ecosystems and resource-using institutions; (2) assignment of property rights; (3) location of knowledge; (4) participation of stakeholders; and (5) sensitivity to feedback.[24]

System Scale

Since practices contributing to global environmental change tend to be bounded in social, economic, and natural terms, local systems of production and action can be seen as nested within larger ones, comprising networks of resource users or abusers. These networks, embedded in social, political, and economic "space" are not identical, although they may be interconnected in many ways. Thus, we are confronted with problems of, on the one hand, collective action to modify practices on a limited spatial scale and, on the other, coordination among social-political units at larger scales. For example, consider U.S. carbon dioxide emissions from automobiles. One could view the "automobile" as a unified and highly-integrated system, amenable to regulation and restrictions imposed at the national level, or one could view it as the aggregation of many spatially-limited metropolitan regions, coupled together via physical (highways) and economic linkages, and traffic and trade flows, among other things. With this approach, however, it is important to recognize the contribution of other sources, within the demarcated area, to carbon and other emissions. Efforts to regulate air quality by air basin pollution control agencies might be such an

arrangement. Thus the term "local" needs to take into consideration not only ecosystems, but economic and other systems as well.

Property Rights

Standard neo-classical economic analysis argues that environmental degradation results from the inappropriate "assignment" of
property rights and, absent such rights, resources will remain open
access and subject to overuse and destruction.[25] Only if a user has
firm expectations about the future availability of a resource, it is
argued, can she make a rational decision about both the pattern of
resource use over time and the rate of use that will maximize return and efficiency.[26] But the assignment of appropriate property
rights to resources is not simply a matter of auctioning them to the
highest bidder, in the expectation that this leads to sustainable or
maximally-efficient exploitation. The condition of an ecosystem
can change across time periods and may be variable across a large
number of such cycles and/or as a function of a large number of
biogeophysical variables. Indeed, it seems likely that, without basic
information about the nature of a resource, including but not limited to its spatial extent and micro-geography, its reproduction or
regeneration cycle, its relationship to other resource systems, and
so on — information that often cannot be acquired easily or
quickly — any strictly economic assignment of property rights
could well lead to degradation of the resource because it does not
incorporate other forms of knowledge.[27]

Knowledge

The information required for "sustainable" use of a resource is often available only as "local knowledge," embedded, for example, in
long-standing usage practices of communities and groups who
have utilized the resource in ways that incorporate this information.[28] Local knowledge is not, however, restricted to antediluvian
societies. A corporation's understanding of localized social relations can make a big difference in its being accepted by a community; "old-timers" and "stakeholders" may know things that new
arrivals cannot.[29] Local knowledge may also reflect non-economic

values held by residents, such as historical experiences and memories, aesthetics, and emotional bonds to land and water, none of which can be known with any great certainty by those who do not reside in the area. In any case, localized systems of property rights, and associated rules of access, can be more closely tailored to the temporal, spatial, social, and cultural variations in a system of resource use.

These property rights systems can be regarded as localized "resource management regimes," in the sense that they provide a "conjunction of convergent expectations and patterns of behavior or practice." The result of this conjunction is "conventionalized behavior or behavior based on recognizable social conventions...[that] are guides to action or behavioral standards which actors treat as operative without making detailed calculations on a case-by-case basis."[30] Documented arrangements of this type include various types of social, economic, and moral constraints, as well as intimate knowledge about the character of a resource; some of these systems, moreover, are found in industrialized societies.[31]

Stakeholders

Stakeholders are actors such as individuals, groups, corporations, and agencies with an interest, economic or otherwise, in a resource regime. Inclusion of all stakeholders in a resource management regime is essential, because failure to do so can lead to free-riding or defection. Stakeholders, as suggested above, often possess important local, relevant knowledge. They may also possess strong social and obligatory bonds to each other that can help to modify individual behavior.[32] Local participation is currently a buzzword in the sustainable development literature, but there is a logic in this notion that extends beyond the strictly economic self-interest of local users.[33] Knowledge may be distributed among the users of a resource, and successful management may therefore come to depend upon its pooling. Finally, to the extent that collective action is based on non-economic factors, political solidarity among users would seem to be essential, and this also argues for broad participation.

The process of forming or changing a localized resource management regime is fundamentally political and, therefore, messy. Simple access to technical information about the condition of a resource is rarely sufficient to generate a consensus on solutions within a community of stakeholders.[34] Moreover, technical information can be problematic because it is often uncertain. Consequently, not only is there disagreement about technical information, there is little consensus about what constitutes proper social relations within resource-using communities. Only via an extended discursive process can this knowledge be pooled and put to good use.[35] Because some resources, water collection and distribution systems, for example, have many and varied users, the definition of a problem is likely to be a process of social reconstruction, rather than simply a matter of identifying shortfalls in supply or damage to wildlife or habitat.[36] Legislation originating from "above" is rarely able to take into account the valid concerns of all stakeholders in a resource because of a lack of information about institutional history and path dependency of a resource management system, which are of critical importance to its revision.[37]

A community of resource users acting through a resource regime is not simply an economic construct, it is an entity constituted through history and political economy, linking individuals together through implicit and explicit bonds of social obligation, whose access to the resource is based upon patterns of access and distribution devised in the past.[38] While these patterns may not be distributionally just, they do have the weight of history behind them.[39] Moreover, the costs of altering this pattern can be significant; sunk costs are high and institutionalized paths are difficult to renegotiate.[40] The process of social reconstruction is, obviously, not as simple as the foregoing paragraphs might suggest. Stakeholders are often at odds with each other because they bring differing, and often contradictory, values into a situation of reconstruction. Changing a resource regime can also change the distribution of costs and benefits to particular stakeholders, and changes must be rationalized and accepted. Thus the process is complicated, drawn-out and messy. Nonetheless, only through such discussions and debates can new rules, roles, and practices be developed.[41]

Feedback

Successful resource management regimes are very dependent on feedback, that is, a constant flow of information regarding the state of an ecosystem and the state of social relations within the regime. Some information about the former can be obtained from scientific instrumentation, via air pollution monitors for example, but additional data are often only available from stakeholders, who are in a better, day-to-day position to observe the condition of the resource and their relationships with other stakeholders.[42] To the extent that such data are observable only on a spatially-limited scale, this also argues for a more localized focus where resource management regimes are concerned.[43]

Given these functional arguments for a local focus, what political or social forms are available to (re)construct resource regimes, and how might such forms be relevant to global environmental change? In the second part of this chapter, I have more to say about the process of (re)negotiating meanings and practices; here I will only suggest four ways in which such "localization" may be emerging. First, there are a variety of groups and organizations involved in local restoration and development projects. By themselves, they are not very significant; taken even in aggregate, they still do not amount to very much. But each, by itself, stands as a form of social organization that can be studied and reproduced elsewhere. For example, individuals working on a small-scale watershed restoration project in the Sierra Nevada foothills may not think of themselves as being linked into global networks. But, they often receive visitors from other parts of the United States and the world, who come to study the project as a model for restoring other watersheds.[44] Those projects, in turn, inform others, and so on.

A second approach depends on locally-based activists (local to specific resource regimes). These are the people who undertake education, demonstrations, and proselytizing on behalf of specific resources or habitats. Some of these are groups engaged in an effort to revise the constitutive basis for relationships between human society and nature; others are less ambitious in their goals.[45] Traditionally urban, such groups are appearing in increasing numbers in rural areas where many resources are actually found. Moreover, there is a growing convergence in strategies between the more and less radical groups.

The third element of this process is based on networks of communication and practice. In the realm of environmental activities, global networks of actors linked together by common strategies and goals are emerging.[46] These networks exist under the overarching rubric of a general environmental ethic — what might be called an "operating system" — although the specific form of relations through the network and the structure of the actors at the ends and nodes of the network vary a great deal.[47] Some of these networks are consciously anti-state, others are oriented toward state reform and some simply ignore the state altogether. Greenpeace, for example, constitutes a global network in itself, with both anti-state and state-reforming tendencies.[48] The Asian Pacific People's Environmental Network, based in Penang, includes both urban and rural organizations, and operates at the international and regional levels; even so-called indigenous peoples are creating such networks.[49] Large numbers of these networks have been organized around concepts of place, nationality, culture, species, and other issues.[50]

In the Third World, there are burgeoning numbers of small-scale organizations engaged in providing a vast range of services to marginal and neglected populations, in a manner that is largely autonomous of the overarching state.[51] Often, these organizations are coupled into the global political system through transnational alliances established with other organizations in both the North and South. For example, non-governmental organization (NGO) activities associated with the June 1992 UN Conference on Environment and Development were coordinated through extensive transnational alliances and networks of communication. Indeed, according to some participants, NGOs were instrumental in formulating the language for various agreements and charters under negotiation for presentation at the conference.[52]

Finally, the number of efforts underway to renegotiate resource management regimes is impressive; one need look only at the anthropological or sociological literature on virtually any developing or developed country to find stories of struggles over common property resources that reflect a variety of violent and nonviolent approaches. The key question is: Can these efforts, taken together, substitute for international agreements on environmental protection? The answer is no, but it is possible that they can form the basis for systems of implementation of those agreements.

Once it has been more generally recognized that environmental protection and resource management regimes must be individually tailored to meet local conditions, it will also become evident that implementation cannot be achieved through unilateral management or control by state bureaucracies, military or other forms of coercion.[53] Instead, bureaucracies will have to become participants in a complex network of resource regimes, helping to coordinate among them, and fostering the creation of large numbers of "mediating organizations" whose purpose is to act as a buffer and filter between local contexts and these bureaucracies.[54] In a sense, the model of environmental protection and restoration suggested here consists of a consciously-developed system of multiple layers and actors.

These four forms of activity also suggest, in one form or another, movement toward common property or common pool resource systems (CPR). A CPR is one managed and exploited by a limited group of qualified users. Each user, by virtue of his or her membership in this group, is entitled to use or exploit the resource up to an amount determined by the group as a whole. Any member that repeatedly exceeds this quota can lose the right of access. The CPR is a "self-enforcing" system, in that each member has an interest in seeing that quotas are observed since repeated violations could lead to premature depletion. Moreover, since the users presumably interact in a variety of different contexts, the desire to maintain good social relations also contributes to observation. A CPR approach to environmental protection works best with a spatially-limited resource like an enclosed coastal sea. If the extent of the resource becomes too great, or the number of users too large, the self-enforcement mechanisms become difficult to maintain, if not completely ineffective.[55] A central problem with any system of legally-constituted property rights is that they generally provide an unlimited individual right to use property, as opposed to providing a limited right to use it in a fashion that protects the common interest. In other words, access to resources in private property systems is framed simply as a right, rather than as a combination of rights and responsibilities. As a result, efforts to foster a common interest among users within a Western legal system take the form of restrictions that must be legislated in the face of opposing interests and conflicting values. In other words, if we choose to limit the harvesting of trees or mandate certain standards to be achieved by automobiles in the interest of controlling the production of greenhouse gases, we must do so by passing laws to this effect. Such laws, at first glance, would seem to undermine the interests of those served by their prior absence, so we might well expect political opposition. The rights of individuals exist in such arrangements, for the most part, prior to the interests of the community.[56] The activities described above suggest movement away from the reification of individual rights in that they indicate a transformation of relationships between human beings within communities and Nature. They involve, as suggested above, the renegotiation of the rules governing a resource management regime and the establishment of user communities, not unlike a CPR.

The ideas in the first section of this chapter are recognized by most development practitioners and an increasing number of analysts of environmental policy and practice. The policy implications of this analysis are, from the international perspective, significant: greater attention must be paid to the articulation of the local and the global, and the recognition of particularism and diversity are central to any attempts to come to grips with global environmental change, however it is understood. The section that follows looks more closely at the content of the renegotiation process, with a particular focus on the relationship between knowledge and practice and their transmission and application through global civil society.

SOCIAL LEARNING AND GLOBAL CIVIL SOCIETY

The process of learning about global environmental change, imagining new strategies, and (re)constructing resource regimes is clearly more complex than simple description, computer networking or the telling and retelling of tales, feedback cycles and equations; it is about communicating bodies of knowledge and subsequently applying them to real world circumstances. It is about social learning. More to the point, such learning is integral to renegotiation of resource regimes, and such renegotiations are about the (re)constitution of a diverse set of environmental phenomena as a linked set. While there are, of course, physical associations among many of these phenomena, it is the combination of social and physical aspects that makes them a linked set. It is, moreover, social learning about this process, and responding accordingly, that makes global environmental change more than just a policy issue to be addressed by governments; as suggested above, policy must take into account social actors other than the nation-state. It is the integration of new conceptions of these environmental phenomena into everyday worldviews and practices, and the ways this changes human-environment relationships that, ultimately, may allow us to address them.

What does the term "social learning" mean? All learning is, in some sense, social, since all learning is the result of social interactions. Here, I mean to suggest the transfer of a body of knowledge and practice from one distinct social entity or institution to another. Ernst Haas applies the notion of "learning" to what he calls "consensual knowledge" and asks: "How does knowledge about nature and society make the trip from lecture halls, think tanks, libraries, and documents to the minds of political actors?"[57] "Knowledge," he suggests, can be viewed as "a social epistemology, as a shaper of world views and notions of causation..."[58] The dissemination of knowledge takes place through the transmission of consensual knowledge, which involves "generally accepted understandings about cause-and-effect linkages about any set of phenomena considered important by society..."[59] Specifically addressing the case of international organizations, he proposes that:

[A]s members of the organization go through the learning process, it is likely that they will arrive at a common understanding of what causes the particular problems of concern. A common understanding of causes is likely to trigger a set of larger meanings about life and nature not previously held in common by the participating members.[60]

There is no a priori reason to think that this applies only to international organizations.

Emanuel Adler writes of "cognitive evolution" in a similar vein:

[W]e can find the sources of collective learning in international relations at the national level — more precisely, in processes of intellectual innovation and political selection — and that with increasing interdependence and diplomatic, political, economic, and cultural contacts, nations transmit to each other the political innovations that have been selectively retained at the national level.[61]

Finally, Peter Haas and his colleagues have pointed to "epistemic communities" as one type of agent important in this process of learning and cognitive evolution:

[M]embers [of epistemic communities]...not only hold in common a set of principled and causal beliefs but also have shared notions of validity and a shared policy enterprise. Their authoritative claim to policy-relevant knowledge in a particular domain is based on their recognized expertise within that domain.[62]

According to Ernst Haas, consensual knowledge is not fixed, since it is subject to "continuous testing and examination through adversary procedures."[63] By the same logic, the understandings held by an epistemic community may change as new information and understanding emerges from their joint enterprise. The assumption in both cases is that policy, and practice, can and will change accordingly in response to the findings of new research projects. But this view of knowledge and learning is largely focused on instrumental action; it also presumes a more-or-less uniform set of social processes to which knowledge can be applied, with an expectation of more-or-less uniform results. At one level, this is obviously a valid assumption: ignoring differences in management and maintenance, the same scrubbing technology applied to coal-fired generating plants around the world will, for the most part, work in the same fashion. But the social impacts of that technology cannot be assumed to be the same, even within a single country. Generally, this is true of social relations and modes of production everywhere.

Indeed, once we get past the level of hardware, or a mechanistic view of society and Nature, we find ourselves in a world of enormous diversity and difference.[64] While there are obviously some general rules, both scientific and social, that apply universally, one cannot take much else for granted. This point is illustrated with respect to another, apparently natural or biological phenomenon as follows:

> Health phenomena that have long been regarded as natural manifestations of universal biological processes are now understood to be — to a significant degree —*locally variable, culturally mediated, socially situated, historically contingent, politically conditioned, and differentiated by gender and age* [65]

In addition, consider ecology as a science. There are certain ecosystemic laws and relationships that are universally applicable, or are applicable to certain specified domains (fresh water, ocean, soil, atmosphere, forests, etc.). Nonetheless, ecosystemic structures may be quite different from one locale to another — even at very small spatial scales. Moreover, specification of the structures of a region or locale can only be accomplished through detailed and localized field research. Once we consider social process and Nature together, we may find that difference comes to overwhelm similarity.[66]

When thought of in this way, knowledge — here used in a general sense — becomes more than just a set of cause-and-effect relations subject to repeated testing via the scientific method. There may be good reason to believe that, within a specific social context, generalized principles can be formulated — after all, what is "tradition" but the repetition of certain practices intended to elicit identical outcomes? — but there is no basis for assuming that more specific principles apply even to neighboring social units within a larger society. Knowledge, in other words, can be, to a significant degree, "local knowledge," where it functions as something akin to a structural element in a social process, becoming embedded in everyday life as a set of beliefs (or meanings) about the operation of sets of social relations and relations of production.[67]

In industrialized societies, local "differences" manifest themselves, to a large degree, in so-called "culture": language, customs, dress, the stories told to children, television programs, modes of production, and, in rural areas, differing relationships to land and resources. Economic rationality is generally presumed to prevail in these situations and, thus, it makes sense to impose taxes on resource use or pollution as a means of adjusting individual and social behavior. The same cannot be said for much of the rest of the world. Economic rationality exists, to be sure, but it is a rationality wrapped within a "web of social relations," in Joel Migdal's words.[68] As a result, while scientific principles apply across countries and cultures, social principles do not.[69]

The implications of this point for environmental policymaking are significant: it means that centralized policy formulation at the global, or even the national, level is likely to run into serious difficulties in implementation. Thus, no matter how much is learned about global environmental change — understood as a *global* phenomenon — it will never be sufficient to "solve" the "problem(s)." Only by reconstructing our understanding of the global environment as the outcome of myriads of micro-level practices — which, consequently, requires changes in micro-level practices — can we even begin to think about problem-solving. Needless to say, there is probably no way to conceptualize the aggregation of all of these micro practices in anything remotely approaching manageable terms; thus, a focus on international or even national level action may well be doomed to failure. It may only be through social learning, and the transformations it accompanies or generates, that we can begin to deal with global environmental change as the social phenomenon it really is.

So what *is* being learned about global environmental change? I would suggest that, aside from the exercise of data collection, a significant body of technological knowledge and practice — which I call "Ecology," to differentiate it from the science of ecology — is being disseminated as part of a growing global understanding of environmental change as a social phenomenon.[70] Understood in classical terms, ecology is not much different from any other body of consensual scientific knowledge.[71] But, from a different perspective, ecology is more than just a body of consensual knowledge; rather, it is more akin to a body of *technological* knowledge and practice, one that is contingent, and not determinate. As such, it carries with it a set of beliefs and values that strongly influences how it is understood and applied.[72]

The most important mechanism for the process of social learning is so-called "global civil society;" a system that increasingly engages in a transnational politics characterized by a surprising degree of autonomy from the state system.[73] This does not mean that global civil society is independent of the state system; but neither is it a wholly dependent formation. In some sense, as in domestic settings, the state system (or, perhaps, international society) and global civil society are, to some degree, constitutive of each other.[74] Nonetheless, global civil society is increasingly influential in the politics and governance of both the local and global, and it is precisely this juxtaposition of the micro and macro that gives it its influence.[75]

In fact, it may make more sense to understand global civil society as a manifestation of the diffusion of governance away from a concentration in the state to both the global and local levels. Civil society becomes important because the institutionalized instruments of governance — international organizations, regimes, national, state, and municipal governments — suffer from deficits of both legitimacy and competence. The organizations of global civil society are, via their own specializations, able to compensate to some degree for these twin deficits. Of course the point is not to reify global civil society nor endow it with extraordinary powers but, rather, to suggest that this particular mode of transnational politics is worthy of attention.

The key element that gives global civil society its growing influence is what I call "networks of practice." The understanding of "network" is overwhelmingly influenced by the image (and realities, however limited) of electronic communication networks, through which bits and bytes flow between electron collection devices, replicating inputs on fax paper or computer screens. This model does not capture the essential qualities of the social and political networks characteristic of global civil society. The literature on social networks tends to focus on the positions of individuals relative to other individuals within social institutions, for example, villages or corporations. As one volume puts it, "network analysis…[focuses] upon communication links, rather than on isolated individuals, as the units of analysis [and] enables the researcher to explore the influence of other individuals on human behavior."[76] Strictly speaking, the focus of network theory is the relationships between social roles and, as noted, the reciprocal influences that result. Moreover, because structural roles within a network are important to this type of analysis, such networks are, inevitably, about power and hierarchy. Some of the literature on "new social movements" (NSMs) also addresses the network phenomenon, but fails to explore the dynamics of exchange through a network.[77]

Networks of practice are not simply relational, they are channels for the transfer of bodies of technological and social knowledge and associated systems of hardware, practice, and values. As such, they include much more than the "data transfer" of television, phones, computers, and faxes; they include that part of the social framework that makes practices useful and applicable in one location adaptable and transferable to another.[78] In essence, the "structures" of global civil society — if it can rightfully be called structure — are networks.[79] The term "network" is a somewhat imprecise one, but it connotes the flow of something between

points, or nodes. At each node we find an organization, and between the nodes we find flows of knowledge, practice, people,
money, and other resources.[80] This picture should not be taken to
mean that hierarchy does not exist in such a network. Some of the
larger and wealthier organizations certainly see themselves in a
vanguard position, and they control a great deal in the way of resources and access to power.[81] Still, as "local" knowledge acquires
greater cachet and credibility, vanguards will tend to fall back into
the pack, so to speak.[82]

There is also an inherent tension between these global networks
and the local organizations that are being "coupled" into them. By
their very nature, the networks of global civil society tend to be
cosmopolitan, inasmuch as the members of organizations tend to
share a global environmental ideology.[83] But, as noted above, the
world is characterized by Ecological (social) and ecological (bio-
physical) diversity. Hence, there is a continual struggle between
the global and the local, as the latter resists losing its particularistic
identity in the global. The local does have some leverage, however,
since those whose reach is "global" cannot succeed unless they
have access to the knowledge possessed by the local. Lest all of this
sound too abstract and rarified, this tension becomes quite visible
when one goes asking questions of local groups.

Finally, it would be a mistake to think that global civil society,
or even its environmental component, is constituted by a single
network. It might be more accurate to say that there are many
such networks, accessible to one another by virtue of the multiple
social and institutional roles filled by both organizations and individuals. Thus, some organizations deal with both governments
and "local" groups; some individuals go through the "revolving
door" from public to private life and vice versa. And some people
and groups wear multiple "hats," moving from one to the other as
seems appropriate.[84] All of this helps transmit knowledge and
practice more efficiently so that it can be put to more effective use.

One of the most common forms of environmental protection
and restoration found throughout the world focuses on water, via
creek and river watersheds, lakes, wetlands, and coastal waters.

Perhaps this is because, as Stephen Kellert suggests in his contribution to this volume, water, in concert with hills, valleys, and beaches, is so evocative of place, and the intimacy with place that he, and others, believe essential to human health and well-being. Perhaps it is the emergence of a bioregional paradigm focused on watershed. Whatever the reason, the numbers of groups dedicated to the protection and restoration of creek and river watersheds are myriad. Two illuminating examples are found in Hungary and around the Chesapeake Bay, although there are many more.

RIVERS RUN THROUGH IT: PROTECTING THE WATERS OF HUNGARY

The first thing to understand about Hungary is that rivers run through it. The Danube (or Duna) River, roughly bisecting the country, is the "heart" of Hungary, both physically and emotionally. The river's watershed constitutes the core of the Carpathian Basin, which encompasses, more or less, Hungary as it was prior to the Treaty of Trianon which, following World War I, reduced its size by two-thirds. Thus, the Danube also has historical resonance.[85] Lest such symbolism seem pat, the river has fulfilled a variety of mundane utilitarian functions, as well, including serving as the municipal and rural water source, commercial waterway, and sewer, for the eight countries through which it passes. It also bears some responsibility as the political catalyst for the change of regime in Hungary in 1989.

In the 1970s, the old Communist regime of Hungary signed an agreement with Czechoslovakia and a contract with Austrian firms, to construct a complex system of barrages and dams on the Danube. This system was intended to generate electricity while rendering the river passable to traffic and to have certain military applications, as well. In doing so, however, it would also have inundated large areas of valuable farmland, causing considerable damage elsewhere along the river and altering the border between the two countries. The response to this plan, first publicized by biologist turned journalist Janos Vargha, was a mass social movement, known as the "Blue Danube" or "Duna Kor" (Danube Circle).[86] The issue first was taken up by those concerned about the ecological impacts and, later, by those more interested in a political issue around which to rally in opposition to the regime. As one of Vargha's colleagues has put it, "The barrage — the monster made of concrete — was the unintended symbol of political power running rampant over everything; it signified the model of totalitarian party rule."[87]

Of course, 1989 was a watershed year for Eastern and Central Europe. For environmental civil society in Hungary, it was a year of collapse. In the transition to political pluralism, many activists in the Danube movement and other groups now saw their chance to practice "real" politics, within an institutionalized system of political parties.[88] Since 1990, the environmental component of civil society in Hungary has had to rebuild and relocate itself within the politics and society of the country. Many groups have become engaged in local conservation, restoration, and education projects. Although they do so without a larger strategy in mind, it is these groups that are, in some sense, most representative of global civil society, inasmuch as they are the most active in monitoring, restoration, and networking around the Danube, Tisza, and Drava Rivers, and their tributaries. A few examples follow.

Zold Sziv ("Greenheart"), a "youth movement for nature conservation," based in Pomaz on the Danube, just to the north of Budapest, claims more than 3,000 members in 150 Hungarian cities and towns, and seven foreign countries (including the United States, Russia, Netherlands, Germany, and the Czech Republic). It collaborates on projects with the Riverwatch Network in Vermont, the Green Rivers program in Michigan, and the National River Watch in England. It has established a project for monitoring water quality along the Danube, with 28 member groups from Germany to ex-Yugoslav republics. Members of Zold Sziv also monitor and try to maintain water quality in creeks that run through their individual towns.[89]

Goncol Alapitvany (Goncol Foundation; Goncol is the Big Dipper) is located in Vac on the Danube, also north of Budapest.[90] Goncol's riverine projects include monitoring of water quality in the Danube and restoration of Gombas Creek, which runs through Vac. The former project is operated in cooperation with the River-watch Network, in Vermont, which has provided technical training to members of Goncol. The GAIA subgroup of Goncol has also set up a "Please Adopt a Stream" project to monitor water conditions in streams elsewhere in Hungary.[91]

There are a number of groups engaged in water quality monitoring, protection, and restoration activities, and project development along the Tisza River, which rises in Slovakia and Ukraine, runs through northeastern Hungary, parallels the Danube and eventually enters what is now Serbia in the south. In Nyiregyhaza, in the northeastern part of the country, the *Felso-Tisza Alapitvany* (Upper Tisza Foundation), with support from the Regional Environmental Center for Central and Eastern Europe and some advising from the Lancastershire Wildlife Trust, has undertaken an initial survey of the upper Tisza watershed, riverside forests, and habitat, and plans to begin monitoring water quality. The organization also would like to develop environmental tourism along the upper Tisza, inasmuch as it is one of the cleanest stretches of river in the country.[92] There are 15 to 20 other groups engaged in projects along the Tisza in its run through Hungary.[93] Another project in the region, now completed, focused on the environmental health impacts of water quality in the River Maros (Mures in Romanian), which runs from the Carpathian Mountains in Transylvania and joins the Tisza River in Szeged. The *Tisza Klub*, in Szolnok, ran the project, which involved academics and activists associated with NGOs in both countries.[94]

On their face, these widely-scattered projects do not resemble anything like common property resource systems; they are only the beginnings of such arrangements. What they do accomplish, however, is to communicate to group members and the public the notion of shared resources that must be cared for rather than abused. Prior to 1989, rivers were seen largely in utilitarian terms and were, therefore, treated rather badly. Today, they are still polluted, but there is a growing recognition not only of the economic importance of water quality, but of the significance of rivers in bi-

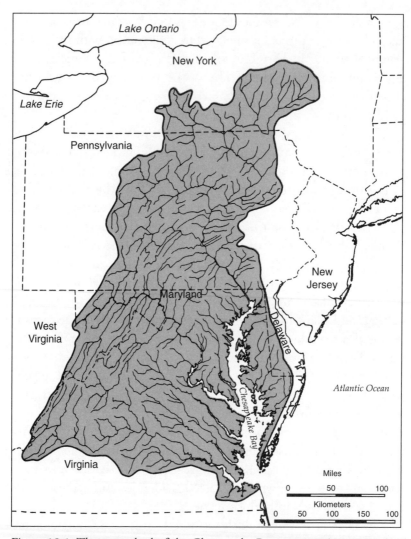

Figure 18.1. The watershed of the Chesapeake Bay covers a six-state region of some 64,000 square miles.

ological as well as cultural terms. Under current economic circumstances, with production dropping and unemployment rising, it is rather too much to expect a mass movement to coalesce around protection of creeks and rivers, as one did under rather different circumstances during the 1980s. In the future, however, we may expect to see a growing appreciation for these rivers and creeks, and a much greater sense of shared responsibility for their protection.

TREASURING THE CHESAPEAKE

The Chesapeake Bay, like the rivers running through Hungary, is more than just a body of water surrounded by 15 million people; it is, as Mark Sagoff suggests, a place that "goes to our identity more than to our interests — to who we are, not just what we want."[95] In spite of its appearance as a single, large, inland body of water, the Bay is many such places, comprised of dozens of rivers and creeks, marshes, and estuaries. Throughout these watersheds and wetlands, hundreds of groups, such as the Monocacy Watershed Conservancy and members of the Alliance for the Chesapeake Bay, have organized to "adopt" streams, clean beaches, plant trees, monitor water quality, and educate residents of the region about their environmental linkages to the Bay and each other. These projects are funded through a variety of private and public sources and are supported, as well, by numerous government agencies and educational and research institutions throughout the the Bay's watersheds. Here, as elsewhere, the environmental component of civil society is part of the regional system of governance.

More important, perhaps, is the way in which the Chesapeake Bay has been changed conceptually.[96] The Bay was once an open access commons, with few or no restrictions on exploitation or degradation. It was polluted, trashed, filled in, fished out, and generally abused. Only over the past two decades — for reasons both economic and aesthetic — has the Bay been gradually transformed into a common property resource regime, managed, and monitored by a variety of agencies and organizations. To be sure, this change was brought about, in part, through institutionalized political processes; of equal importance was the environmental sensibility created through a public process of renegotiation.

This renegotiation took place, and continues to take place, on a number of levels. The Chesapeake Bay should be seen and understood not only as a "single" ecosystem within a single social context but rather, as a place where many many small-scale ecosystems and resource management regimes lie nested within much larger ones. In many of these smaller regimes, environmental organizations have come to take a major role in protection, restoration, and governance. In doing so, and in scientific and social collaboration through networks and alliances, civil society has come to be extremely important in the revival of the Bay. Moreover, through longer-distance networking and exchange with organizations throughout the world, the restoration of the Chesapeake Bay has become a model for many similar efforts around the world.[97]

Lest all this sound too laudatory or idealistic, "saving the Bay" is not a project that can ever be completed; indeed, it should never be completed because, as Michael Thompson's "rubbish theory" suggests, it may be necessary to have some bad in order to appreciate the good.[98] Backsliding is also possible and there may arrive a time when economic and political conditions within American society make environmental protection difficult, if not impossible. Finally, while we can measure various indicators that show waters to be cleaner, healthier and so on, there are no metrics that can measure the meaning of places in our politics and culture. Nonetheless, in the long run, it is these meanings, embedded in the organizations and structures of civil society, that are most important in protecting and preserving coastal seas such as the Chesapeake Bay and the Baltic, Mediterranean, and Black Seas.

Global environmental change is a social process and a consequence of a multitude of micro-level practices within resource management regimes. These regimes are social institutions and therefore are based on rules, roles and relationships among actors and with the natural world. Dealing with global environmental change requires modification of these regimes, a task that may well be beyond the capabilities of international regimes and national governments. Change will have to be centered within these localized regimes, and it can come about only through a process of "renegotiating" the rules, roles, and relationships that constitute them. Such renegotiations are becoming increasingly common and the result is a form of common property resource in which stakeholders are invested by virtue of their participation in the renegotiation. The policy implications of this analysis differ greatly from the conventional wisdom which looks more to the national and international levels as the source of action.

In addition, even as analysts and diplomats puzzle over the intricacies of protocols, frameworks, conventions, side payments, and so on, the organization-based nodes of a growing system of networks — characterized here as "global civil society" — engage in the exchange of knowledge, practice, and actions oriented toward protection of their small piece of the global environment. To be sure, these networks do not yet command anything like the power, resources, or reach of the members of the state system or the corporate entities of the global economy; their influence lies in their command of knowledge and practice, and their ability to change the terms of public understanding of environmental problems. I do not mean to idealize global civil society, or credit it with powers that it does not have. Successful environmental protection, however one might define it, is by no means guaranteed. In the final analysis, global environmental "rescue," as Dan Deudney puts it, will depend on the concerted action not only of civil society, but states and corporations as well.[99] But, if the social changes needed for such rescue are to come from anywhere, it seems more likely than not that they will come from "below."

ACKNOWLEDGMENT

This chapter is based on a forthcoming work, Ronnie D. Lipschutz. 1996. *Global Civil Society and Environmental Governance: The Politics of Nature from Place to Planet.* SUNY Press, New York. The research on which this chapter and the related book are based was supported by the UC-Systemwide Institute on Global Conflict and Cooperation (UC-San Diego), the Center for German and European Studies (UC-Berkeley), the Academic Senate of UC-Santa Cruz, the Social Science Division of UC-Santa Cruz, and a UC Regent's grant provided through the Social Science Division of UC-Santa Cruz.

NOTES

1. See, for example, Mancur Olson. 1971. The Logic of Collective Action. Harvard University Press, Cambridge and Russell Hardin.

1982. Collective Action. Johns Hopkins University Press, Baltimore.

2. See Ronnie D. Lipschutz. 1992. Reconstructing world politics: the emergence of global civil society. Millennium 21(3): 389-420.

3. National Academy of Sciences/National Research Council Committee on the Human Dimensions of Global Change. 1992. Global Environmental Change: Understanding the Human Dimensions. National Academy Press, Washington, D.C., pp. 25-26. Emphasis in original.

4. See, for example, James N. Rosenau. 1986. Before cooperation: hegemons, regimes, and habit-driven actors in world politics. International Organization 40(4):849-94.

5. See, in particular, Joni Seager's comments on the agency-structure problem as applied to environmental problems in Joni Seager. 1993. Earth Follies: Coming to Feminist Terms with the Global Environmental Crisis. Routledge, New York, pp. 2-3.

6. For a trenchant critique of global management, see Pratap Chatterjee and Matthias Finger. 1992. The same old order. Ecocurrents 2(3). See also Seager, op. cit.

7. See William C. Clark. 1989. The human ecology of global change. International Social Science Journal 121:315-46.

8. Neil Evernden. 1993. The Natural Alien: Humankind and Environment. Second Edition. University of Toronto Press, Toronto.

9. This is not meant to imply that agency does not meet structure at the global level. For reasons that will become clear below, however, the importance of the micro-level must be recognized. See David Dessler. Summer 1989. What's at stake in the agent structure debate? International Organization 43(3): 441-74 and Leo Marx. Summer/Fall 1990. Post-modernism and the environmental crisis. Philosophy & Public Policy 10(3/4).

10. Joel S. Migdal. 1988. Strong Societies and Weak States: State-Society Relations and State Capabilities in the Third World. Princeton University Press, Princeton. pp. 33-38.

11. Robert Repetto. 1990. Deforestation in the tropics. Scientific American 262(4):36-42.

12. This point has long been recognized in anthropology, geography,

and rural sociology. See, for example, Piers Blakie. 1985. The Political Economy of Soil Erosion. Longman, London.

13. See Susanna Hecht and Alexander Cockburn. 1990. The Fate of the Forest. Harper Perennial, New York; João Pacheco de Oliveira Filho. 1990. Frontier security and the new indigenism: nature and origins of the Calha Norte project. In David Goodman and Anthony Hall. The Future of Amazonia: Destruction or Sustainable Development? St. Martin's Press, New York, pp. 155-178; and Edward O Wilson (ed.). 1988. Biodiversity. National Academy Press, Washington, D.C.

14. Ronald J. Herring. December 1990. Resurrecting the commons: collective action and ecology. Items (SSRC) 44(4):65.

15. See, for example, Chadwick F. Alger. 1990. The world relations of cities: closing the gap between social science paradigms and everyday human experience. International Studies Quarterly 34:492-518; Lipschutz 1992, op. cit.; and Knut H. Sørensen and Nora Levold. 1992. Tacit networks, heterogenous engineers, and embodied technology. Science, Technology & Human Values 17(1): 13-35.

16. See, for example Emilio F. Moran (ed.). 1990. The Ecosystem Approach in Anthropology: From Concept to Practice. University of Michigan Press, Ann Arbor.

17. See, for example, Alfred W. Crosby. 1986. Ecological Imperialism: The Biological Expansion of Europe, 900-1900. Cambridge University Press, Cambridge; E. L. Jones. 1981. The European Miracle: Environments, Economies, and Geopolitics in the History of Europe and Asia. Cambridge University Press, Cambridge.

18. See Christopher Stone. 1993. The Gnat is Older than Man: Global Environment and Human Agenda. Princeton University Press, Princeton and Oran Young. 1982. Resource Regimes: Natural Resources and Social Institutions. University of California Press, Berkeley.

19. Richard B. Norgaard. 1988. Sustainable development: a co-evolutionary view. Futures: December: 609; See also Simberloff, in this volume.

20. See Karen Litfin. 1993. Eco-regimes: playing tug of war with the nation-state, pp. 94-117 and Ken Conca. 1993. Environmental

change and the deep structure of world politics. In Ronnie D. Lipschutz and Ken Conca (eds.). The State and Social Power in Global Environmental Politics. Columbia University Press, New York, pp. 306-326.

21. See Ken Conca. 1992. Environmental Protection, International Norms, and National Sovereignty: The Case of the Brazilian Amazon. Paper prepared for the Dartmouth College/U.N. University Conference on Sovereignty and Collective Intervention, May 18-20, Dartmouth College.

22. Vandana Shiva. 1991. The Violence of the Green Revolution. Zed/Third World Network, London/Penang; Jesse C. Ribot. 1990a. Markets, States, and Environmental Policy: The Political Economy of Charcoal in Senegal. Energy & Resources Group, University of California, Berkeley. Unpublished Ph.D. dissertation.

23. See Daniel W. Bromley (ed.). 1992. Making the Commons Work — Theory, Practice, and Policy. ICS Press, San Francisco.

24. Although there are long-standing arguments for the decentralization of administrative systems and functions in development planning, the argument presented here has roots in the "sociology of knowledge." For a discussion of problems with decentralization, see M. Bazlul Karim. 1991. Decentralization of government in the third world: a fad or panacea? International Studies Notes 16(2): 50-54. For a good summary of the sociology of knowledge literature, see Peter M. Haas. 1992. Introduction: epistemic communities and international policy coordination. International Organization 46(1):20-26.

25. "Property rights" here refers to all of those arrangements, either codified as law or less-formal, that "define or delimit the range of privileges granted to individuals [or organized collectivities] to specific assets"; Gary D. Libecap. 1989. Contracting for Property Rights. Cambridge University Press, Cambridge, p. 1.

26. R. J. Smith. 1981. Resolving the tragedy of the commons by creating private property rights in wildlife. CATO Journal 1: 439-68; and Terry Anderson and Donald R. Leal. 1991. Free Market Environmentalism. Westview Press, Boulder, Colorado.

27. This is an intuitively logical conclusion discussed, albeit in a

slightly different form, by Richard B. Norgaard. 1987. Economics as mechanics and the demise of biological diversity. Ecological Modelling 38:107-21.

28. Ibid.; Richard B. Norgaard. 1981. Sociosystem and ecosystem co-evolution in the Amazon. Journal of Environmental Economics and Management 8:238-54; Nancy Peluso. 1991. Rich Forests, Poor People: Resource Control and Resistance in Java. University of California Press, Berkeley and Lori Ann Thrupp. 1989. Legitimizing local knowledge: from displacement to empowerment for third world peoples. Agriculture and Human Values 6: 13-24. See also the explicit discussion in David Orr. 1992. Ecological Literacy: Education and the Transition to a Postmodern World. SUNY Press, Albany, pp. 31-33.

29. This point was made with some emphasis in interviews with Jon Kennedy and Harley Greiman, U.S. Forest Service, Sacramento Area Office, June 11, 1992 and with Vicki Campbell, Arcata BLM, July 30, 1992. While "indigenous knowledge" is a reasonably well-understood concept, the application of this concept to industrialized society is somewhat more problematic. See Charles E. Lindblom and David K. Cohen. 1979. Usable Knowledge: Social Science and Social Problem Solving. Yale University Press, New Haven, pp. 12-13.

30. Young 1982, op. cit., p. 16.

31. I do not mean to idealize such systems; under external pressure, they often prove less than robust, and the entry of growing numbers of users may also lead to resource degradation. See Elinor Ostrom. 1990. Governing the Commons: The Evolution of Institutions for Collective Action. Cambridge University Press, Cambridge. Chapters 3 and 4; Fikret Berkes (ed.). Common Property Resources: Ecology and Community-based Sustainable Development. Belhaven Press, London, especially David L. Miller. The evolution of Mexico's spiny lobster fishery, pp. 185-98, and James M. Acheson. Where have all the exploiters gone? Co-management of the Maine lobster industry, pp. 199-217; and Bonnie J. McCay and James M. Acheson (eds.). 1987. The Question of the Commons: The Culture and Ecology of Communal Resources. University of Arizona Press, Tucson.

32. See, for example, Biology meets the dismal science. 1994. The Economist Dec. 25, 1993-Jan. 7, 1994, pp. 95.

33. See, for example, Sustainable Development: From Theory to Practice, a special issue of Development: Journal of the Society for International Development 2/3. 1989; David Korten (ed.). 1986. Community Management: Asian Experience and Perspectives. Kumarian Press, West Hartford, Connecticut and Dharam Ghai and Jessica M. Vivian. 1992. Grassroots Environmental Action: People's Participation in Sustainable Development. Routledge, London.

34. See Simberloff in this volume.

35. John S. Dryzek. 1987. Rational Ecology: Environment and Political Economy. Basil Blackwell, Oxford.

36. See, for example, Luther Gerlach. 1990. Cultural construction of the global commons. In Robert H. Winthrop (ed.). Culture and the Anthropological Tradition: Essays in Honor of Robert F. Spencer. University Press of America, Washington, D.C., pp. 319-342. See also Ann Hawkins. 1990. "Contested ground": international environmentalism and global climate change. In Lipschutz and Conca 1993, op. cit., pp. 221-245. For an overview of the social construction of reality see Walter Truett Anderson. 1990. Reality Isn't What it Used to Be. Harper & Row, San Francisco.

37. Oran Young. 1989. International Cooperation: Building Regimes for Natural Resources and the Environment. Cornell University Press, Ithaca and London; interview with Vicki Campbell, op. cit.

38. See, for example, Berkes, op. cit. and McCay and Acheson, op. cit.

39. What then, is the difference between "local" and "international" regimes if both are unjust and the reproducers of power relations? This is a valid question for which I do not have an answer; indeed, it was the U.S. federal government's use of its leverage against "states rights" that was responsible for the legislation of civil rights in the 1960s and 1970s. Localism is not always a democratic force; see the discussions in David Harvey. 1989. The Condition of Post-modernity. Basil Blackwell, London and David Pepper. 1984. The Roots of Modern Environmentalism. Croom Helm, London, Chapter 7.

40. See, for example, Libecap, op. cit.

41. Ronnie D. Lipschutz and Judith Mayer. Not seeing the forest for the trees: rules, roles, and the renegotiation of resource management regimes, In Lipschutz and Conca, op. cit., pp. 246-273; Luther Gerlach. Negotiating ecological interdependence through societal debate: the 1988 Minnesota drought. In Lipschutz and Conca op. cit., pp. 185-220; Elinor Ostrom. July 1989. Microconstitutional change in multiconstitutional political systems. Rationality & Society 1(1):11-50. See also Liebcap, op. cit., Chapter 3.

42. Ostrom 1990, op. cit., p. 79; Campbell interview, op. cit.

43. The relationship between scientific-technical and local knowledge is not one that has, to the best of my knowledge, been explored. For some thoughts on the matter, see Peter Haas (ed.). 1992. Knowledge, Power, and International Policy Coordination. Special edition of International Organization 46(1). For an analysis of the relationship between science and the "Green" movement, see Steven Yearley. 1991. The Green Case: A Sociology of Environmental Issues, Arguments, and Politics. HarperCollins Academic, London, Chapter 4. For an exploration of the role of knowledge in social movements, see Steven Breyman. Knowledge as power: ecology movements and global environmental problems., pp. 124-57 in Conca and Lipschutz, op. cit.

44. According to Kim Rodrigues, University of California Extension Forester in Eureka, California, members of the Mattole Restoration Council, from the Mattole River valley in northern California, have travelled all the way up to British Columbia acting as advisors to other watershed groups (interview, August 18, 1993). The idea of environmental restoration is documented in John J. Berger. 1990. Environmental Restoration: Science and Strategies for Restoring the Earth. Island Press, Washington, D.C. A survey of such efforts in the central Sierra Nevada uncovered approximately 200 projects (Kennedy and Greiman interview). For a more skeptical view of ecological restoration, see Ambrose in this volume.

45. Lipschutz and Mayer, op. cit. and Robert D. Benford and Scott A. Hunt. February 1992. Dramaturgy and social movements: the social construction and communication of power. Sociological Inquiry 62(1):36-55.

46. The notion of networks is briefly addressed by Sidney Tarrow. 1988. National politics and collective action: recent theory and research in Western Europe and the United States. Annual Review of Sociology 14:421-40. See especially pp. 431-33.

47. Lipschutz 1992, op. cit.

48. Some even tend to view Greenpeace as a purveyor of environmental "imperialism." See, for example, Paul Wapner. 1994. Making States Biodegradable: Ecological Activism and World Politics. SUNY Press, Albany; Joni Seager 1993, op. cit., Chapter 4.

49. John Brown Childs. 1992. Rooted Cosmopolitanism: The Transnational Character of Indigenous Particularity. Stevenson Program on Global Security Colloquium, University of California, Santa Cruz, Oct. 19, 1992; Bice Maiguashca. 1992. The Role of Ideas in a Changing World Order: The Case of the International Indigenous Movement, 1975-91. Paper prepared for the International Conference on Changing World Order and the United Nations System, Yokohama, Japan, March 24-27, 1992.

50. See Gareth Porter and Janet Welsh Brown. 1991.Global Environmental Politics. Westview, Boulder, Colorado, pp. 56-60 and Sheldon Annis. April 1992. Evolving connectedness among environmental groups and grassroots organizations in protected areas of Central America. World Development 20(4):587-95.

51. See, for example, David Korten. 1990. Getting to the 21st Century: Voluntary Action and the Global Agenda. Kumarian Press, West Hartford, Connecticut; Alan B. Durning. 1989. Action at the Grassroots: Fighting Poverty and Environmental Decline. Worldwatch Institute, Washington D.C.; Robin Broad, John Cavanagh, and Walden Bello. 1990-91. Development: the market is not enough. Foreign Policy 81:152-60; Ghai and Vivian 1992, op. cit.

52. Conversation with Frances Spivy-Weber, Director, UNCED U.S. Citizens Working Group on Forests, March 7, 1992; see also Sandra Hackman. 1992. After Rio: Our Forests, Ourselves. Technology Review 95(7):33-40; UNCED Secretariat. 1992. In Our Hands: Directory of Non-governmental Organisations Accredited to the United Nations Conference on Environment and Development; Lawrence T. Woods. 1993. Nongovernmental organizations and the

United Nations system: reflecting upon the Earth Summit experience. International Studies Notes 18(1): 9-15.

53. See, for example, Nancy Peluso. 1993. Coercing conservation: the politics of state resource control. In Lipschutz and Conca, op. cit., pp. 46-70.

54. Michael F. Maniates. 1990. Organizing for Rural Energy Development: Improved Cookstoves, Local Organizations, and the State in Gujrat, India. Energy & Resources Group, University of California, Berkeley. Unpublished Ph.D. dissertation; Thomas F. Carroll. 1992. Intermediary NGOs: The Supporting Link in Grassroots Development. Kumarian Press, West Hartford, Connecticut; and Lipschutz 1996, op. cit., especially Chapter 4.

55. See, for example, Ostrom 1990, op. cit. The process is documented in Lipschutz 1996, op. cit. especially chapter 4. See also Bromley, op. cit.

56. See Orr op. cit. and Herman E. Daly and John B. Cobb, Jr. 1989. For the Common Good: Redirecting the Economy Toward Community, the Environment, and a Sustainable Future. Beacon Press, Boston.

57. Ernst B. Haas. 1990. When Knowledge is Power: Three Models of Change in International Organizations. University of California Press, Berkeley, p. 20.

58. Ibid., p. 21.

59. Ibid., p. 22.

60. Ibid., p. 24.

61. Emanuel Adler. 1991. Cognitive evolution: a dynamic approach for the study of international relations and their progress. In Emanuel Adler and Beverly Crawford (eds.). Progress in Postwar International Relations. Columbia University Press, New York, pp. 500.

62. P. Haas. 1992, op. cit., p. 16. See also Haas and Jasanoff, this volume and Breyman. Knowledge as power. In Lipschutz and Conca op. cit.

63. E. Haas, op. cit., p. 21.

64. See Thompson and Trisoglio in this volume.

65. Frank Kessel. 1992. On culture, health, and human development. Items (SSRC) 46(4):65. Emphasis in original.

66. This is one more form of the universalism-particularism dialectic alluded to earlier. See Harvey, op. cit. and Simberloff in this volume.

67. Indeed, Ernst Haas notes that "Consensual knowledge may originate as an ideology." (E. Haas, op. cit. p. 21). I have argued elsewhere that "organizing principles," which "posit a relationship between individual action and ideal objectives," function as "soft constraints" on social action. See Ronnie Lipschutz. 1989. When Nations Clash: Raw Materials, Ideology and Foreign Policy. Ballinger/Harper & Row, New York, pp. 26, 29.

68. Migdal 1988, op. cit., pp. 33-38.

69. See, for example, Jesse Ribot 1990a, op. cit. and Jesse Ribot. 1990b. Sustainable development? The role of urbanization and market-state relations in Africa's rural decline. Paper prepared for a panel on Sustainable Development. Association of American Geographers' 1990 Annual Meeting. Toronto, 19-22 April 1990.

70. Paul Wapner uses the term "ecological sensibility," although he says little about the processes by which this sensibility becomes integrated into worldviews. See Wapner, op. cit.

71. See Max Oelschlaeger. 1991. The Idea of Wilderness: From Prehistory to the Age of Ecology. Yale University Press, New Haven. chapter 7; Wolfgang Sachs. 1992. Environment. In Wolfgang Sachs (ed.). The Development Directory. Zed Books, London, pp. 26-37. See especially pp. 30-32.

72. See Ronnie D. Lipschutz. 1993. Learn of the green world: global environmental change, global civil society and social learning. Transnational Associations 3:124-138.

73. For discussions of this term and others like it, see Lipschutz 1992, op. cit. and 1996, op. cit.; Stephen Gill. 1991. Reflections on global order and sociohistorical time. Alternatives 16; Ken Booth. July 1991. Security in anarchy: utopian realism in theory and practice. International Affairs 67(3); Paul Wapner. 1992. Ecological Activism and World Civic Politics. Paper prepared for a panel on the Role of NGOs in International Environmental Cooperation and Security, International Studies Association annual meet-

ing, Atlanta, March 31-April 4, 1992; Paul Ghils. August 1992. International civil society: international non-governmental organizations in the international system. International Social Science Journal 133:417-29; Richard Falk. 1992. Explorations at the Edge of Time: The Prospects for World Order. Temple University Press, Philadelphia; Laura Macdonald. 1993. Globalizing Civil Society: Interpreting International NGOs in Central America. Paper presented at the International Studies Association annual meeting, Acapulco, March 24-27, 1993 and Catherine J. Tinker. 1993. NGOs and Environmental Policy: Who Represents Global Civil Society? Paper presented at the International Studies Association annual meeting, Acapulco, March 24-27, 1993.

74. For a discussion of international society, see Beyond International Society. Millennium 21(3). 1992. Special issue. To fully explain the emergence of global civil society, we have to apply a version of historical materialism that incorporates the mutually-constitutive nature of culture and production. David Harvey and Robert Cox, among others, have carefully considered how the transformative project championed by the United States following World War II has, since the early 1970s, gone on to foster a major shift in economic and political organization in many parts of the world. Harvey, op. cit.; Robert Cox. 1987. Power, Production and World Order. Columbia University Press, New York; and Lipschutz 1996, op. cit.

75. It may be that the role of NGOs lies primarily in their ability to channel local knowledge upward and global knowledge back down to the local level. This is consistent with Maniates, op. cit.

76. Everett M. Rogers and D. Lawrence Kincaid. 1981. Communication Networks: Toward a New Paradigm for Research. The Free Press, New York, p. xi.

77. See Tarrow 1989, op. cit.; Alberto Melucci. 1989. Nomads of the Present: Social Movements and Individual Needs in Contemporary Society. Hutchinson Radius, London, pp. 97-98; and Kathryn Sikkink. 1993. Human rights, principled issue-networks, and sovereignty in Latin America. International Organization 47(4):411-42.

78. Thus computer networks are only a small "hardware" part of global civil society, facilitating the exchange of news; for a critique of

the power of computing, see Langdon Winner. 1986. Mythinformation. In The Whale and the Reactor: A Search for Limits in an Age of High Technology. University of Chicago Press, Chicago, pp. 98-117. I discuss the difference between "data" and "knowledge" in Lipschutz 1992, op. cit.

79. There are many of them, having to do not only with environment, but also development, human rights, indigenous peoples, health, AIDS, gender, religion, racism, and anti-abortion; networks are not, a priori, "progressive," although the tendency for right-wing movements to be nationalistic and somewhat xenophobic means that their transnational contacts are somewhat limited.

80. Networks reduce the costs of gathering information. Their relative effectiveness comes to depend on who is in the network, which is not necessarily the same as where the most information is held. See, for example, Georgi M. Derluguian. 1993. Power, Ethnicity, and the Real Economy in the Ex-Soviet Southern Tier. Paper presented to the Conference on Reconfiguring State and Society: Social and Political Consequences of Liberalization in Comparative Perspective, University of California, Berkeley, April 22-24, 1993.

81. In truth, organizations such as the World Wildlife Fund and World Resources Institute more closely resemble multinational corporations, with annual budgets in excess of $50-100 million, offices and projects around the world, executing "friendly" mergers and takeovers (WWF and the Conservation Foundation, WRI and the U.S. branch of the International Institute for Environment and Development). One could go so far as to suggest that some organizations are engaged in "cultural capitalism," as they try to sell environmental goods and services.

82. Judith Mayer points out that "vanguards" are those groups with the most intensive and transformative contacts with other organizations. (Personal communication.)

83. See, for example, Daniel Deudney. 1993. Global environmental rescue and the emergence of world domestic politics. In Lipschutz and Conca, op. cit., pp. 281-305.

84. For example, one individual in Hungary who has been instrumental in the establishment of several environmental NGOs, served an abbreviated term as a junior minister in the government of the late

Josef Antall, was on the Board of the Regional Environmental Center for Eastern and Central Europe, subsequently employed by the European Community's "embassy" in Budapest for his environmental expertise, and ran for the Hungarian Parliament in 1994 as a candidate — with environmental credentials — of the Young Democrats.

85. The potentially incendiary quality of rivers and watersheds should not be under-estimated, especially in the context of the nationalist revival in Hungary. According to an article in Budapest Week, an English-language newspaper, reporting on the activities of Istvan Csurka, a right-wing member (since expelled) of the then ruling party in Parliament, "At the Early February national meeting of the Magyar ut [Hungarian Way Foundation] circles [established by Csurka], there was a map behind the rostrum which showed Hungary's rivers but not the national borders...In the eyes of many observers, that map was yet another example for [sic] a drive to reconsider the peace treaties which had defined Hungary's borders." To this, Csurka replied, "Rather than calling it a map, I would say it was a symbolic manifestation of our desire to eliminate the borders, to make them fully penetrable...On that illustration, there were no borders. There were rivers and ways. Hungarian ways." (Tibor Szendrei. Istvan Csurka: Keeping Hungary Hungarian. Feb. 25-March 3, 1993, p. 5.)

86. See, for example, Mark Schapiro. 1990. The New Danube. Mother Jones 15(3):50-52, 72, 74-76; and Judith Vasarhelyi. 1991. Hungarian greens were blue. In Craig L. LaMay and Everette E. Dennis. Media and the Environment. Island Press, Washington, D.C., pp. 205-215; John Feffer. 1992. Shock Waves: Eastern Europe after the Revolutions. South End Press, Boston, pp. 151-56. An insightful analysis of the "pre-history" of the project and its current state is Tamas Fleischer. 1993. Jaws on the Danube: water management, regime change, and the movement against the middle Danube hydroelectric dam. International Journal of Urban and Regional Research 17(3):429-43. Quotation p. 441.

87. See Fleischer, op. cit., p. 18.

88. A detailed assessment of environmental civil society in Hungary appears in Lipschutz 1996, op. cit.; an earlier version can be found in Ronnie D. Lipschutz. 1993. Environmentalism in One Coun-

try? The Case of Hungary. Paper presented to the Conference on Reconfiguring State and Society: Social and Political Consequences of Liberalization in Comparative Perspective. University of California, Berkeley, April 22-24, 1993, and to the Spring Workshop of the European Political Relations and Institutions Research Group, Center for German and European Studies, University of California, Berkeley, April 30, 1993 (CGES Working Paper 2.15).

89. Interview with Aniko Orgovanyi, August 28, 1992; Aniko Orgovanyi and Mary Houston, March 8, 1993, Pomáz; Informational flyer, The Danube Project. 1993.

90. An *alapitvany* is a not-for-profit organization, and not a private foundation in the American sense.

91. Interview with Agoston Nagy, Vacs, March 1, 1993; Goncol literature.

92. Interview with Zoltan Belteki, Csilla Csisztu and Imre Vass. Upper Tisza Foundation, March 2, 1993; pamphlet, The Upper Tisza Foundation.

93. Interview with Istvan Bogdan. Szeged, March 4, 1993.

94. Regional Environmental Center. Annual Report 1991. Budapest, p. 30.

95. Sagoff, as quoted in the program for the International Conference on the Environmental Management of Enclosed Coastal Seas 1993 in Baltimore, Maryland, p. 17.

96. Sagoff, in this volume, discusses underlying motivations for this conceptual change, taking the Chesapeake as one of his examples.

97. For example individual researchers, academics, policy makers and active citizens from all over the world came to the EMECS '93 Conference in Baltimore, Maryland, November 10-13, 1993, at which scientific, aesthetic and governance experience from the Chesapeake basin was prominently featured.

98. See Thompson and Trisoglio, in this volume, and Michael Thompson. 1979. Rubbish Theory: The Creation and Destruction of Value. Oxford University Press, Oxford.

99. Deudney, op. cit. See also Haufler in this volume.

EMECS

In order to encourage an ongoing inquiry into issues addressed in this volume, the International Center for the Environmental Management of Enclosed Coastal Seas (EMECS) has been established in Kobe, in the Hyogo Prefecture of Japan, and a series of EMECS conferences have been launched, beginning in 1990. *Saving the Seas* consists of papers commissioned both for this volume and for the 1993 EMECS Conference, which was held in Baltimore, Maryland. It has been our hope that bringing together scholars and practitioners from around the globe to share their ideas about coastal and regional seas governance will foster the "upward percolation" of these ideas, and our expectations have been amply fulfilled. The 1997 EMECS Conference, held in Stockholm, will make further progress toward the resolution of questions raised during previous meetings and in this volume. We wish all the scholars, managers and citizens active in the EMECS effort the best of luck and ask only that they continue their good work.

About the Authors

Richard F. Ambrose is Associate Professor in the Environmental Science and Engineering Program at UCLA. He received his Ph.D. in Zoology from UCLA in 1982, and has published many articles on marine and coastal ecology. His environmental research interests currently center on techniques for mitigating resource losses in coastal environments and ecological monitoring and assessment. His mitigation research has focused on coastal wetland restoration and artificial reef construction, while his monitoring and assessment research aims at detecting both long-term and short-term changes in ecological communities. He is also developing habitat valuation methodologies for use in mitigation plans, and is currently Chair of the Scientific Advisory Panel overseeing power plant mitigation measures for the California Coastal Commission.

L. Anathea Brooks is Assistant Director of the Center for Environmental Research and Conservation, a consortium of Columbia University, the American Museum of Natural History, The New York Botanical Garden, the Wildlife Conservation Society and Wildlife Preservation Trust International. Previously she was a Conservation Policy Analyst with the Institute for Philosophy and Public Policy at the University of Maryland, College Park. She began her career at the United Nations' International Fund for Agricultural Development, and subsequently helped found two environmental organizations, Europe Conservation and Gaia Risorse in Milan, Italy. She has published articles and translations on estuarine restoration, natural history, and population and the environment, most recently in *Beyond the Numbers: Population, Consumption and the Environment.* She received her M.S. in Sustainable Development and Conservation Biology from the University of Maryland.

Lynton K. Caldwell is the Arthur F. Bently Professor Emeritus of Political Science and Professor of Public and Environmental Affairs at Indiana University where he carries on research in environmental and science policy studies. He received his Ph.D. from the University of Chicago, and the LLD from Western Michigan University. In addition to serving on the faculty of several universities, he has worked for governments including the United States Senate, Congressional Research Service, U.S. Departments of State, Commerce, Defense and Interior, the United Nations, UNESCO, and the International Joint Commission. He was the principal architect of the National Environmental Policy Act of 1969 and "inventor" of the environmental impact statement. He has published more than two hundred articles and ten books, including *Science and the National Environmental Policy Act: Redirecting Policy Through Procedure, International Environmental Policy,* and *Between Two Worlds: Science, the Environment Movement, and Policy Choice.*

Elizabeth Dowdeswell joined UNEP as its third Executive Director in January 1993. Before joining the United Nations, Ms. Dowdeswell was Assistant Deputy Minister at Environment Canada and head of the Atmospheric Environment Service, the primary weather and atmospheric agency of the national government. Ms. Dowdeswell was Canada's principal delegate to the International Panel on Climate Change and Co-Chair of the working group on mechanisms in the negotiations leading to the Framework Convention on Climate Change, which was adopted in June 1992 at the United Nations Conference on Environment and Development in Rio de Janeiro.

Jean-Paul Ducrotoy received his Doctorate in Biology from the François Rabelais University in Tours, France. After teaching in Scotland and Algeria he headed the estuarine ecology research program at the University of Picardy, France from 1981 to 1990. From 1990 to 1993 Dr. Ducrotoy played a key role in coordinating and promoting the North Sea Task Force. He is Head of Sciences at University College, Scarborough, England, where he teaches coastal marine biology and coastal management, in addition to managing the Marine Forum. His research interests include population dynamics and the eco-physiology of benthic fauna. He is also interested in the role of science in policy-making, and thus serves as an observer to the North Sea Commission's Conference of Peripheral Maritime Regions.

George Francis is Professor in the Department of Environment and Resource Studies at the University of Waterloo, Ontario, Canada. He has a longstanding interest in the policy and institutional implications of adopting "an ecosystem approach" towards issues of the Great Lakes, and has participated over the years in a number of binational advisory groups to governmental bodies and in inter-university studies on these and related matters. His interest in biodiversity conservation is associated with extensive voluntary work for organizations such as the Nature Conservancy of Canada, the Canadian Council on Ecological Areas, and the Canadian national committee for the UNESCO Man and the Biosphere Programme.

Peter Haas is Associate Professor of Political Science at the University of Massachusetts at Amherst. He received his Ph.D. in political science from the Massachusetts Institute of Technology (MIT). He has published widely on international environmental subjects, including pollution control in the Mediterranean, Baltic, and North Seas, stratospheric ozone protection, and international environmental institutions. He is the author of *Saving the Mediterranean: The Politics of International Environmental Cooperation*, editor of a special issue of *International Organization* on "Knowledge, Power, and International Policy Coordination," and co-editor of *Institutions for the Earth: Sources of Effective International Environmental Protection*. He has consulted for The Commission on Global Governance, UNEP, the U.S. Department of State, the U.S. National Academy of Sciences, the American Association for the Advancement of Science, and the World Resources Institute.

Virginia Haufler is Assistant Professor in the Department of Government and Politics at the University of Maryland, College Park. She studied at the Institute for International Studies in Geneva under a Gallatin Fellowship, and received her Ph.D. from Cornell University. Her research examines the linkages between the growing institutionalization of international affairs and changes in corporate behavior. She has just completed *Dangerous Commerce: State and Market in the International Risks Insurance Regime*, and her current research examines the creation and management of institutions for the financing and sharing of risk in the conservation of biodiversity.

Sheila Jasanoff, Professor of Science Policy and Law, is the founding chair of the Department of Science and Technology Studies at Cornell University. Her primary research interests are in the areas of risk management and environmental regulation, interactions between science, technology and the law, and the implications of social studies of science for science policy. Her publications on these topics include *Controlling Chemicals: The Politics of Regulation in Europe and the United States, Risk Management and Political Culture, The Fifth Branch: Science Advisers as Policymakers,* and *Learning from Disaster: Risk Management After Bhopal.*

James Kay is Professor of Environment and Resource Studies at the University of Waterloo, Ontario, Canada. His principal research interest is the application of non-equilibrium thermodynamics, information theory and systems theory to the problem of understanding the organization of ecosystems. He has served as an advisor to numerous international organizations and participated in many conferences on ecological integrity. He is an editor of *Ecological Integrity and the Management of Ecosystems*, and his work formed the basis of UNESCO's *Network Analysis in Marine Ecology: Methods and Applications*. He is a member of the Royal Society of Canada and the Royal Swedish Academy of Sciences.

Stephen R. Kellert is Professor in the School of Forestry and Environmental Studies at Yale. His most recent book is *The Biophilia Hypothesis*, co-edited with E.O. Wilson, which highlights his interest in conservation biology and the value of nature. One of his numerous earlier works, *Ecology, Economics, Ethics: The Broken Circle* highlights his interest in environmental ethics, and he has been a major figure in conservation biology.

Sally Lerner is Associate Professor in the Department of Environment and Resource Studies at the University of Waterloo, Ontario, Canada. The focus of her current research is the implication of the changing nature of work for income distribution, education, and environmental protection. She recently edited *Environmental Stewardship: Studies in Active Earthkeeping*.

Ronnie Lipschutz is Assistant Professor of Politics, and Director of the Stevenson Program on Global Security at the University of California, Santa Cruz. He has a degree in physics from MIT, and a Ph.D. from the Energy and Resources Group at the University of California, Berkeley. He has worked on the scientific staffs of the Union of Concerned Scientists, the Massachusetts Audubon Society, and the Lawrence Berkeley Laboratory. Professor Lipschutz is the author of *Radioactive Waste*: *Politics, Technology, and Risk*; *When Nations Clash: Raw Materials, Ideology, and Foreign Policy*; and *Global Civil Society and Environmental Governance: The Politics of Nature from Place to Planet*; as well as co-editor of *The State and Social Power in Global Environmental Politics*, and editor of *On Security*.

Craig Murphy is Professor of world politics and international political economy in the Political Science Department at Wellesley College. He has written several books, including *International Organizations and Industrial Change: Global Governance*, and has written extensively on international institutions, including the United Nations, and on Gramscian analysis.

Robert Nelson is Professor at the School of Public Affairs at the University of Maryland, College Park. From 1975 to 1993, he was a member of the economics staff of the Office of Policy Analysis of the U.S. Department of the Interior, working closely with the rangeland management, forest management and coal leasing programs of the Bureau of Land Management and with the economic and education programs of the Bureau of Indian Affairs. He has been a visiting scholar at the Woods Hole Oceanographic Institution and the Brookings Institution. He is the author of many professional and popular articles, and of three books, including *Zoning and Property Rights* and *Reaching for Heaven on Earth: The Theological Meaning of Economics*.

Henry A. Regier is Director of the Institute for Environmental Studies and Professor of Zoology at the University of Toronto. He received his Ph.D. from Cornell in 1961. Throughout his career he has participated in United Nations conferences on population and environmental issues, as well as taking an active role in fisheries biology for many international organizations. He has written extensively on the rehabilitation of degraded aquatic systems. In 1986 he was awarded the Centenary Medal by the Royal Society of Canada for leadership in a binational non-governmental review of the Great Lakes Water Quality Agreement.

James N. Rosenau is University Professor of International Affairs at The George Washington University in Washington, D.C. He formerly was the director of the School of International Relations at the University of Southern California. He is the author or editor of numerous publications, including *Global Voices: Dialogues in International Relations*, *The United Nations in a Turbulent World*, and *Turbulence in World Politics: A Theory of Change and Continuity*.

Mark Sagoff is Senior Research Scholar at the Institute for Philosophy and Public Policy, University of Maryland, College Park. He received his Ph.D. in philosophy from the University of Rochester in New York. He is the author of *The Economy of the Earth: Philosophy, Law, and the Environment*, and other articles on the boundaries between philosophy and environmental science. He is a Pew Scholar in Conservation and the Environment, and President of the International Society of Environmental Ethics.

Rafal Serafin is the Director of the Heritage Research Program at the Progress & Business Foundation in Kraków, Poland and a research associate of the Heritage Resource Centre, University of Waterloo, Ontario, Canada. He has been concerned with comparative studies of environmental management and development planning in the North American Great Lakes and the Baltic Sea basins. His current research interests include redefining the role of environmental management in economic and political transformations underway in central Europe. He holds degrees from the University of East Anglia, U.K., and the Universities of Toronto and Waterloo, Canada.

Ron Shimizu has worked with Environment Canada since 1972, and was associated with the Great Lakes Water Quality Program from 1987 to 1990. He has a Masters of Arts in Political Science and Canadian Government from McMaster University, and taught at the Institute of Environmental Studies at the University of Toronto in 1991-92. At present, he is Manager of the Environmental Citizenship, Assessment, and Economics Division of Environment Canada in the Ontario Region, and is a part-time faculty member at the Institute.

Daniel Simberloff received his Ph.D. from Harvard. He has taught at Florida State University most of his career, and is now Robert O. Lawton Distinguished Professor of Biological Science at that institution. He is currently editor-in-chief of *Biodiversity and Conservation*, and has served on the editorial board of many other journals, including *Ecology, Oecologia*, and *Biological Conservation*. He has written over 200 influential papers and book chapters on island biogeography, community ecology, the biology of extinction and the effects of introduced species, and has served on numerous government panels and on the boards of conservation and ecology NGOs.

Frieda B. Taub is a professor in the School of Fisheries and an adjunct professor in the Institute of Environmental Studies at the University of Washington, where she has taught for over twenty years. She received her Ph.D. from Rutgers University. She has played a fundamental role in eco-toxicological simulation modeling and the role of biotechnology in risk assessment and reduction. Her research focuses on the community response to environmental perturbations such as toxicants in aquatic systems, the environmental risks of bioengineered organisms, and closed ecological systems. She has contributed numerous technical reports, journal articles and book chapters on these subjects, and has received grants from numerous government agencies.

Michael Thompson is an anthropologist by training, but has strayed into the messy area of science for public policy. His particular interest is in the way different institutions define the problem under their consideration, in such a way that it matches the solutions they happen to be able to provide. After working in a number of international think-tanks including the International Academy of the Environment, he is now Director of the Musgrave Institute in London. He is the author of several important books, including *Cultural Theory, Divided We Stand: Redefining Politics, Technol-*

ogy and Social Choice, and *Rubbish Theory.* Most recently he published "Good Science for Public Policy."

Alex Trisoglio is Managing Director of Environmental Strategies, a consultancy specializing in environmental strategy and policy, especially for the business and finance sectors. Prior to this he was policy advisor at the Business Council for Sustainable Development, and Business in the Environment. He holds a first class degree in theoretical physics from Cambridge University and received a Fullbright Fellowship to Harvard Business School, and has been an advisor to UNCED, UNEP, and IIED on business and environment issues.

Robert Ulanowicz is a professor of Theoretical Ecology at the University of Maryland Center for Environmental and Estuarine Studies' Chesapeake Biological Laboratory. He received his Ph.D. from The Johns Hopkins University and began his teaching career at The Catholic University of America, where he first began applying mathematical methods to the analysis of ecosystems, still one of his active research interests. He has linked this analysis to trophic exchange networks, and also conducts research on the application of thermodynamics and information theory to ecology, and the nature of causality in living systems. He is the author of *Growth and Development: Ecosystems Phenomenology* and numerous scientific papers.

Stacy D. VanDeveer is a Ph.D. candidate in international relations and comparative politics in the Department of Government and Politics at the University of Maryland, College Park. He is an International Environmental Researcher at the Institute for Philosophy and Public Policy at the University of Maryland, and has taught classes in political ideologies, international relations, environmental politics, and technology and society at The George Washington University and the University of Maryland. His current research

interests are in the areas of international environmental cooperation and institutions, state sovereignty, and civil society.

Jerzy Zaleski is a Professor Emeritus of Economic Geography at the
University of Gdansk, Poland. He has written several books and
numerous scholarly papers on the economic geography of the sea.
Over the past fifteen years, he has campaigned widely for Baltic
Europe and its potential as a basis for sustainable redevelopment of
the Baltic economy.